Rethinking Drug Use in Sport

Drug-free sport is an unattainable aspiration. In this critical, paradigm-shifting reappraisal of contemporary drug policy in sport, Bob Stewart and Aaron Smith argue that drug use in sport is an inexorable consequence of the nature, structure and culture of sport itself. By de-mythologising and de-moralising the assumptions that prop up current drug management controls, and re-emphasising the importance of the long-term well-being and civil rights of the athlete, they offer a powerful argument for creating a legitimate space for drug use in sport.

The book offers a broad ranging overview of the social and commercial pressures impelling drug use, and maps the full historical and social extent of the problem. With policy analysis at the centre of the discussion, the book explores the complete range of social, management, policy, scientific, technological, and health issues around drugs in sport, highlighting the irresolvable tension between the zero-tolerance model as advanced by WADA and the harm-reduction approach adopted by drug education and treatment agencies. While there are no simple solutions, as long as drug use is endemic in wider society the authors argue that a more nuanced and progressive approach is required in order to safeguard and protect the health, social liberty and best interests of athletes and sports people, as well as the value of sport itself.

Bob Stewart is Associate Professor of Sport Studies at Victoria University, Melbourne, Australia. Bob has been teaching and researching the field of sport management and sport policy for 15 years, and is currently working with the University's College of Sport and Exercise Science, and Institute of Sport, Exercise and Active Living. Bob has a special interest in cartel structures, social control, and player regulation in elite sports, and the ways in which neo-liberal ideologies shape sport's governance and management practices.

Aaron C.T. Smith is Professor and Deputy Pro-Vice Chancellor in the College of Business at RMIT University, Melbourne, Australia. Aaron has research interests in the management of psychological, organisational and policy change in business, and sport and health. In recent times he has focused on the impact of commercial and global sport policy, the ways in which internal cultures shape organisational conduct, the role of social forces in managing change, and the management of social policy change such as those associated with health and drug use.

Routledge Research in Sport, Culture and Society

Rethinking Drug Use in Sport

Why the war will never be won

Bob Stewart and Aaron C.T. Smith

Routledge
Taylor & Francis Group

LONDON AND NEW YORK

First published 2014
by Routledge
2 Park Square, Milton Park, Abingdon, Oxon OX14 4RN

and by Routledge
711 Third Avenue, New York, NY 10017

Routledge is an imprint of the Taylor & Francis Group, an informa business

British Library Cataloguing in Publication Data
A catalogue record for this book is available from the British Library

Library of Congress Cataloging in Publication Data
Stewart, Bob, 1946–
Rethinking drug use in sport : why the war will never be won / Bob Stewart, Aaron Smith.
    pages cm. – (Routledge research in sport, culture and society ; 30)
    1. Doping in sports. 2. Athletes – Drug use. I. Smith, Aaron. II. Title.
    RC1230.S745 2014
    617.1′027–dc23   2013028102

ISBN: 978-0-415-65915-4 (hbk)
ISBN: 978-0-203-07514-2 (ebk)

Typeset in Times New Roman
by HWA Text and Data Management, London

MIX
Paper from
responsible sources
FSC   FSC® C013604
www.fsc.org

Printed and bound by CPI Group (UK) Ltd, Croydon, CR0 4YY

Contents

Figures

Tables

1 Revisiting the drugs in sport debate

Introduction: what this book is about

In a thought experiment with a blank social slate, and where the objective is to optimise the collective use of alcohol, nicotine/tobacco, performance enhancing substances, and recreational drugs, we could do no better than create sport. However, in the real world, thought experiments of this type are not required since sport in all of its forms and all of its accoutrements – from clubs and championships to muscles and machines – exemplifies socially driven performance. It's in the DNA. Sport stimulates fierce competition, cultivates unyielding tribal allegiance, and celebrates success with vast rewards in both material and symbolic forms. Drug use occurs in sport because it is a prototypical human endeavour and ubiquitous cultural phenomenon that reflects our unique and natural drives found at the intersection of competition and corporeality. The boundaries are there only to be tested, with the goals of faster, higher, stronger, front and centre. Yet, the idea that drugs can be eliminated from sport remains a persistent delusion.

Our position in this book begins with a triumvirate of premises. First, drug use in sport is here to stay, as athletes employ every advantage they can in order to secure success at the confluence of hyper-commercialised, spectacle-driven contemporary sport, and a broader society deeply committed to a pharmaceutical culture endorsing better health, well-being, pain relief, functional outcomes, and good times. Second, the majority of negative consequences from drug use in sport have little to do with on-field performance and more to do with the off-field experience of sport through the unhelpful combination of alcohol, nicotine/tobacco, and masculine bravado. In addition, the most dangerous and prolific usage of drugs can be found in groups primarily interested in recreational performance and image-enhancement, be it building muscle or ironing out facial wrinkles (Evans-Brown *et al.* 2012). Third, when it comes to elite sport, drug testing does not work as a deterrent, and fails to reveal the full extent of drug use.

This book focuses on drug use in sport, but unlike other publications addressing this problematic issue, we aim to demythologise the assumptions that prop up the current drug controls in sport, and argue for a legitimate space for their use. In taking this position we will not only explain the flaws and contradictions in the current anti-doping policies, but also reveal their adverse consequences for the long-term well-being of athletes, including how they damage athletes' reputations and civil rights. In short, we want to provide workable policy options that 1) safeguard sport participation, 2) ensure the ongoing value of sport brands, and 3) protect the physical health and social liberty of athletes and players.

In this book we examine the drugs in sport debate, and interrogate the factors that make drug control in sport such a vexing problem. We suggest that no simple solution to the problem exists, and note that what seems appropriate drug use in a work, social or health and medical setting may not be apposite to a sport-related situation. At the same time, we cannot bring ourselves to conclude that while there are good reasons to allow drug use in the wider society, there is no space for it in the world of sport. The fact of the matter remains that drug use has always been part of the sporting scene, with tobacco, alcohol, caffeine, and analgesics prominent.

To our way of thinking the drug use in sport problem cannot be resolved with more heavily targeted investigations, more frequent testing, and more punitive fines and bans. Players and athletes, especially at the professional level, already wield significant knowledge about the ways in which different substances and compounds impact upon bodily functions. They appreciate the risks and benefits of using drugs in order to secure a competitive edge, but also understand how anti-doping rules can be circumvented by taking cocktails of so-called 'natural' supplements that deliver noticeable, if less dramatic results.

We also note the absence of evidence demonstrating that drug-free sport will make the playing field any more level, where everyone has a better chance of succeeding. Demands for drug-free sport assume that anyone who takes banned substances will, like cream, rise to the top. However, it does not happen as neatly or quickly as this. The evidence shows that superior sporting performance results from an advantageous genetic inheritance, thousands of hours of training and practice, quality coaching, extensive sport-science support, high levels of skill, tactical know-how, significant amounts of mental toughness, a sound base of sports nutrition, and abnormal quantities of psychological resilience.

In this book we suggest that the drugs in sport debate has been clouded by shifting views about the relative merits of different drugs and related substances. Not all drugs receive equal treatment under the current arrangements. Some are demonised, while others are tolerated, and even romanticised, despite similar health risks and performance advantages. From our perspective such inconsistencies confuse drugs in sport policy, and do little to assist the development of fair and consistent rules.

We also propose that drug controls incur serious costs, increasing exponentially with year-round testing for both performance-enhancing and illicit drugs. Little discussion has transpired about the costs of establishing and operating anti-doping programs. For example, costs increase when authorities receive the power and resources to not only test for drug use in periods of competition, but also test out of competition, extend the drug use reach to include all illicit drugs, organise a 'whereabouts' process where athletes must advise on their day-to-day movements, administer a biological passport regime, and investigate allegations of drug use. As a significant management load, these responsibilities can only be properly delivered if sufficient resources underpin their implementation. In addition, we should keep in mind that players and athletes – like any of us – take drugs to feel happier, reduce discomfort or pain, relieve stress, and enhance recreational experiences. These benefits, which most of us take for granted, are denied to sport's participants under their drug control arrangements.

This book is intended to be a scholarly piece of multidisciplinary analysis that examines the politics, economics and sociology of drug use in sport. We initially thought we could deliver a neatly compartmentalised and self-contained book that navigates readers through the technical and policy issues embedded in the current drug control rules. However, we concluded that this approach would constrain a critical analysis of the topic, and provide a one-dimensional and mechanistic treatment of what rarely appear as straightforward issues. While our critical, multidisciplinary approach has produced an occasional rag-bag of cases, commentary and analysis, we were also able to deliver a stronger narrative that provides a context for both locating and explaining the issues being discussed.

We begin our analysis of the drugs in sport problem by asserting that drug use is both endemic in modern society and a feature of contemporary sport. We also suggest that drug use in sport has few 'black and white' features, as its critics tend to suggest. Rather, the contextual complexities associated with drug use in sport make its management problematic. As a result, the rationale for and mechanisms of, drug control remain subjects of heated debate. On the one hand, powerful global sport authorities like the International Olympic Committee (IOC), the World Anti-Doping Agency (WADA), and international sport federations claim that drug use is cheating and should be eliminated through the imposition of severe punishments. On the other hand, we propose an alternative approach which focuses on the protection of athlete health, the retention of their civil rights, and the reduction of drugs' negative social impacts. In short, we spend considerable time examining the ongoing tension between 1) the benefits of a deterrence-only, zero-tolerance model of drug control as enacted by WADA, and 2) a multi-level approach of harm reduction as adopted by many drug education and treatment support agencies.

Our approach in this book prioritises a multidisciplinary exposure of the drugs in sport issue, with policy analysis at the forefront. We 1) examine how drug use in sport has come about through the social and commercial pressures impelling drug usage; 2) map the extent of the problem, its history and current policies; 3) establish the impact of the drugs in sport problem from the sport, health, social, and scientific perspectives; and 4) provide tools for policy analysis and formulation in order to combat the problem. The book consequently aims to supply a comprehensive and open-minded account of the drugs in sport issue, and guide sport policymakers through the maze of legitimate and illegitimate use, cheating and ethics, regulation and control options, health and welfare, resource implications, player and athlete rights, and the desire to protect the integrity, good standing, and brand equity of sport.

A central premise of this book is that the drugs in sport problem remains an inexorable corollary of the nature, structure, and culture of sport itself. As a result, we regularly point out that policy solutions must address these dimensions of sport or risk exacerbating the problem and further marginalising the well-being of athletes. Few other books targeting the drugs in sport issue have ventured beyond a cursory comment on the relationship between sport's unique features, the often rigid expectations sport has of its participants, and the immorality of doping practices. Other works either vilify doping as unredeemable behaviour, or condemn hyper-commercialised elite sport as hopelessly corrupt and devoid of social value. Our approach accepts that elite and professional sport reflect the demands of a textured social reality where insatiable appetites for extreme physical performance and heightened drama loom large. Equally, we acknowledge the prodigious impact that unfettered drug use can have on athletes and players. However, and unlike most commentators on drug use in sport, we argue that punishing athletes to within an inch of their sporting careers for taking substances will not resolve the drug use problem. Nor will it safeguard the health and welfare of athletes, or, for that matter, ensure the integrity and longevity of sport as an important cultural and economic institution.

Structure and themes

Our analysis gets under way in the following chapter with the observation that we all live in a society where drug use is widespread and taken for granted. We stake a claim for the pharmaceutical industry by suggesting that despite the occasional scandals arising from drugs that come with damaging side effects, and despite the many marketing campaigns that normalise drug use (and especially prescription drugs), they have, over the long term, made a significant contribution to the health and well-being of communities around the world. We next examine in Chapter 3 the history of drug use in sport by signposting the key international cases, explaining how they have shaped the drug-use narrative, and describing what controls were put in place to curb drug use. While many of the cases have an Australian flavour – which reflects the biases of the authors – special attention is given to critical international incidents, including detailed analyses of cases from cycling, snow-skiing, swimming, and track and field. Irrespective of the case locations, our choices depict incidents and policies of universal relevance. In Chapter 4 we also contextualise drug use in society. Our brief here is to take a holistic look at drug use in society by discussing not only illicit drug use, but also prescription drugs, over-the-counter drugs, and socially embedded drugs like alcohol and tobacco. In Chapter 5 we examine those factors, attitudes and beliefs that lead people to take drugs, and how they view the relationship between drug use and the body's capacity to perform at a higher level, look more attractive to others, feel better, or get through the day more productively. These four chapters – from 2 to 5 – provide the foundations for our analysis, or what we have called 'setting the scene'.

From 'setting the scene', we turn to 'framing the debate' in Chapters 6 to 9. Chapter 6 begins with an overview of the key historical policy periods that cumulatively shaped the current system's emergence. As part of this debate framing we explore how the pivotal trend towards neo-liberal policy, along with the simultaneous expansion of consumer individualism, created the high-tension mix of moralism and liberalism we now experience. With the historical, social and economic parameters firmly established, and some of the more recent empirical works unravelled, in Chapters 7 to 9 we explore theories and models that can be used to explain the drug-use motivations, choices, and behaviours of players and athletes. A number of critical theories of social behaviour receive attention. They are 1) the social ecology model (Chapter 7), 2) the capital building model (Chapter 8), and 3) the life course model (Chapter 9). This theoretical analysis enables us to more sharply interrogate the policies and regulations that currently exist. Special attention is directed to the WADA regulations and policies, and the ways in which they have filtered through to international sports organisations, national governments, and national sports bodies.

With the scene set and the debate framed, our attention moves to 'the WADA revolution' in the book's third section. This penultimate section of the book takes a broader look at policy issues and options, beginning in Chapter 10 with how WADA came about, lingering on sport league responses in Chapter 11, and culminating in a critical appraisal in Chapter 12. 'The WADA revolution' section contrasts zero-tolerance policies with harm-reduction policies, and assesses their social impacts. A special focus is reserved for the ideologies and belief systems that underpin each of the policy options, including commentary on a specific bundle of cases and policy problems.

The final section of the book considers the way forward under the theme 'rethinking drug control'. Chapter 13 discusses the application of a regulatory framework, Chapter 14 brings the options together into a cohesive form, and Chapter 15 delivers a set of recommendations for a policy alternative. Collectively, the section critiques a range of policy possibilities and develops the best policy option in view of 1) sport's special features, 2) what drives athletes and players to do whatever it takes to achieve their highest performance, and 3) the probability that drugs can never be eliminated from sport.

Making the case for a 'another way'

In this book we argue that drug use will never be eliminated from sport. Of course, this position begs a seriously important question: just what policy alternative exists to the current approach exemplified by the mission and operational goals of WADA? WADA holds adamant that its current policy is the only workable one, and believes that any weaknesses in its arrangements can be supplemented with more comprehensive analysis technologies, more rigorous and frequent testing, an expanded investigative role, more punitive sanctions, and more severe suspensions. WADA's position seems consistent with perceptions amongst the general public, where no softening in attitudes can be seen.

At the same time, rumblings of another vision for controlling drug use in sport may be heard in the distance. While this 'other vision' enjoys the support of drug policy analysts in the broader field of drug dependency, it has not yet captured the imagination of sport officials or politicians. The alternative model, which flies under the banner of harm reduction, begins with the premise that so long as drugs exist and so long as their use in sport remains culturally and socially embedded, then their elimination remains implausible. With this proposition as the policy backdrop, harm reductionists argue that the punitive codes currently in place are not only ineffective, but also a waste of scarce resources. Taking the logic a step further – as we do in the forthcoming chapters – drug-use policy in sport becomes effective only if it reduces harm at either the individual or community level.

To foreshadow our defence of a harm-reduction position, we note that drug use in sport can take a multitude of forms. For example, it begins with sport clubs providing space for the consumption of alcohol and other social drugs like nicotine and caffeine. Building a network of acquaintances drives sport club membership, and drugs allow this to happen with less friction and greater intimacy. We also know that sport clubs provide the space for the use of illicit recreational drugs. But socially enhancing drugs are only the tip of the sport club drug-use iceberg. No matter what their performance level, clubs want their players back in the game as soon as possible after injury, so over-the-counter and prescription painkillers are widely used to relieve discomfort and enable mobility. Since sport rewards winners, drugs conferring a competitive edge also command attention. Even though many such drugs, especially the stimulants, can be secured on prescription, many are banned under anti-doping rules.

Another noteworthy issue we raise relates to the diverse perspectives around which drug-use problems in sport can be viewed. The first perspective sees drug abuse as a moral problem where drug taking reflects unworthy behaviour. In this case little distinction is made between the performance enhancement and recreational use of the drug. Neither is stakeholder discussion required, since any transgression of a moral code demands immediate punishment. The second perspective views drug use as an ethical problem of cheating, giving the user an unfair advantage. The cheating argument seems incontestable. Who would suggest that sporting contests should allow one participant an artificial advantage before it even begins? The third perspective perceives drug use as an equity problem. In this instance the problem is less about ethics or cheating, and more about other athletes being disadvantaged by not taking performance-enhancing drugs. The final perspective considers drug use a health problem in which unregulated behaviours can create serious illnesses and chronic health problems for athletes.

This book's central proposition holds that the perspective that mostly allows for an impartial analysis is the health and well-being impact, which forms the foundation stone of the harm-reduction model. In taking this position we do not anguish over the morality of drug use, or struggle over which of the stakeholder groups might be the most offended. We do not attempt to formulate what type of moral re-education will be required, or outline the most appropriate bundle of threats, sanctions, punishments, and suspensions that should be dealt out to transgressors. No decision needs to be made about the drug's legality or illegality. Finally, we spend no time assessing the performance impact of a substance, and whether or not it actually improves an athlete's ability to run quicker for longer, or lift a heavier weight. Rather, the question we ask is, how will the use of the drug impact on the athlete's health and well-being? If it can be shown that the risk of illness or loss of health is high then athletes should be warned off, counselled, and treated by professional health care workers.

The harm-reduction approach weighs up the consequences of drug use rather than punishing the act of drug use. By using the harm-reduction model, the health costs associated with drug use can be broadened to not only cover the risk of death and serious illness, but also social stigmatism, the loss of personal dignity, the invasion of privacy, and the loss of individual rights that might come from being 'outed'. While harm reduction does not necessarily marginalise the effect that drug use might have on the reputation and good standing of the sport, it aims to bring the rights and well-being of athletes to the front and centre. It also forces sport bureaucrats to consider the broader social impacts of coercive models of drug control, and in particular the unwanted collateral damage that accompanies naming, shaming, and delivering punitive suspensions. Whilst harm-reduction policies may incorporate strategies to promote the reduction of drug use, they do so in a harm-sensitive manner so as to avoid the social fallout and high-ground moralising often associated with the punitive zero-tolerance approach.

We also believe that draconian rules and sanctions will not eliminate the use of drugs in sport; an axiom we address through the historical record. Instead, punitive models only send drug use further underground as players search for more exotic and less detectable options from physicians or dealers with sometimes dubious credentials and crime syndicate connections. Moreover, evidence which indicates an improvement in the health and well-being of players resulting from the current anti-doping policies is difficult to obtain. In addition, the moralistic values that underpin the current arrangements do little to secure a level playing field, to balance up competitions, or to protect the health and welfare of players and athletes.

We understand that a harm-reduction approach may be offensive to those wanting some sense of moral certitude in their sport worlds. However, it constitutes the only policy model enabling players and athletes to manage drug use in all its guises within a safe environment that 1) is free from ill-informed advice and contaminated supply, 2) restricts the possibility of a traumatic invasion of privacy, 3) lessens the threat of severe shame and punishment, and 4) provides a secure environment in which to seek professional guidance and support.

We also understand that harm reduction 'stakes out' controversial ground in a sporting context since it appears to condone illegal and apparently unfair practices while accepting the fact that drugs will always be part of a risky and tilted playing field full of moral ambiguity. However, in the forthcoming chapters we argue that harm reduction also allows for a stronger platform of education and social marketing, and the provision of personnel and facilities that ensure a safe and protective sport environment where player welfare holds priority. We propose that a socially responsible philosophy that focuses on the reduction of collateral damage, and seeks out a sound evidence base, should be sovereign in determining all future drugs in sport policies. Our immediate attention in the following chapter, however, shifts to a contextualisation of drug use in society in order to lay the groundwork for our subsequent analysis. Chapter 2 opens our 'setting the scene' section by sketching out the drug problem and highlighting its historical drivers.

Part I

Setting the scene

2 Drug use in contemporary society

Introduction: a short history of drug use in society

Despite the antagonism many people hold towards drug consumption, and the personal and social damage inflicted through addiction and abuse (Babor *et al.* 2010), they provide staple substances for helping people do more, and feel better (Kramer 1993). Drugs offer the potential to make people less inhibited, less overwhelmed, more socially aware, happier, calmer, less traumatised, more energetic, and generally more functional and productive (Jay 2010; Young & Feeney 2002). This means that drugs strongly appeal to people who want to make their lives more exciting, successful, meaningful, comfortable, or just be 'cheered up on a bad day' (Courtwright 2001: 194). In other words, just about all of us use substances of one kind or another to get through our daily lives.

Some drugs suffer from a poor reputation in that they generate associations with social problems such as apathy, prostitution, mental illness, violent crime, and most sadly of all, a miserable death. To some, drugs are best left alone, even where they have a history of being useful in medical conditions, or if they have been part of a society's popular culture and religious practices. The negative reputations connected to drugs are accentuated by their illegality, their propensity to send heavy users into psychotic states, and their association with an underground economy governed by criminal gangs (Marcy 2010). Opium – and its derivatives, morphine and heroin – provides a powerful case in point. It possesses a rich history as a calmative and painkiller, beginning with the cultivation of white poppies, the source of all opium, in the Nile and Mesopotamian valleys around 4500 BC (Dormandy 2012). By the late 1700s, opium's pain-relieving powers had become legendary, but so too had its capacity to build addiction. Over the last 200 years the poppy has been demonised despite delivering one of humanity's most effective means of alleviating physical and mental pain, thereby justifying the claim as 'God's own medicine' (Dormandy 2012: 1).

Cocaine, derived from coca leaves, also has a chequered history. Having been isolated in 1859 it quickly became the stimulant of choice on the back of claims that it provided 'nourishment for the nerves', and was a 'harmless way to cure sadness' (Escohotado 1999: 71). With the endorsement of the founder of psychoanalysis, Sigmund Freud, by the 1890s there were 'more than 100 beverages' (including the soon to become internationally recognised Coca Cola) containing 'concentrated extracts of coca or pure cocaine' (Escohotado 1999: 71). Marijuana – otherwise known as Indian hemp, hashish, and cannabis – similarly gained prominence around this time. This time it was the German philosopher Frederick Nietzsche who claimed that it had allowed him to 'get close to the prodigious velocity of mental processes'. Cannabis gained further credibility in 1894 when the British Government's Indian Hemp Drugs Commission concluded that 'moderate use does ... not result in any harmful effect', that the 'disturbance created by excessive use is generally limited to the consumer himself', and that there is 'rarely any appreciable [adverse] effect on society at large' (Escohotado 1999: 72).

War has encouraged drug use, especially when serving to calm the nerves, diminish fear, or increase physical alertness. Rum and alcoholic beverages were used to sedate front-line soldiers in World War I, while bromide became the sedative of choice during the 1920s. Drug use as a means of handling the terrors of war has continued unabated. For example, most recently, cocaine, cannabis, amphetamines, and tranquilisers have been used by soldiers in the Iraqi and Afghanistan conflicts (McCanna 2007).

At the same time as the popularity of drugs spread, attempts were made during the early part of the 20th century to regulate drug use on the grounds that the harms frequently outweigh the benefits. In addition, the moral harm, the likely descent into 'cultural decadence', and risk of addiction arising from drug use became a major talking point (Jay 2010: 36). In response to intensive lobbying from the clergy and temperance groups, the United States (US) government passed the Harrison Act in 1914 prohibiting the supply of opium and cocaine. The Hague Convention was signed in the same year, which required all signature nations to control the preparation and distribution of opium, morphine, and cocaine (Boyum & Reuter 2005). This 'reforming zeal' culminated in two punitive initiatives. First, in 1915, 12 American states declared it illegal to smoke tobacco. Second, towards the end of World War I the US Government decided to ban the production and sale of alcohol. Its prohibition continued until 1933, at which time the costs of enforcement were deemed to outweigh any fall in consumption and decline in public drunkenness (Hart & Ksir 2011).

Public attitudes to drug use shifted in the 1930s as drugs were legitimised as a means of better coping with the strains and tensions of living in fast-moving and rapidly changing industrial societies. Barbiturates became popular amongst the sleepless with Veronal – a popular brand – being available over the counter until the late 1930s. All sorts of stimulants also entered the market, and in the early part of the 20th century, adrenaline appeared as a remedy for asthma. Ephedrine was formulated in the early 1930s, and soon became a favourite drug for relaxing the bronchial passages. In the mid-1930s the amphetamine Benzedrine found popularity as a decongestant before its discovery by military personnel who wanted to beat fatigue, truckers who wanted to drive through the night, and students who wanted mental concentration and energy boosts (Rasmussen 2008).

Amphetamine use exploded during World War II and continued to grow during the post-war period. Its use increased rapidly in the 1960s, mainly due to its success as a diet drug. During the 1990s, amphetamine consumption multiplied as it became the drug of choice for an epidemic of Attention Deficit Disorder (ADD) conditions supported by major brands such as Adderall and Ritalin (Hart & Ksir 2011). This coincided with its rediscovery as a recreational drug, with MDMA – or Ecstasy as it is now more widely known – being the most popular variety.

Miltown, the first mass-consumption tranquiliser, crashed onto the US drug use scene in the 1950s. Penicillin research in the 1940s had inadvertently discovered compounds that had relaxant effects, but without the heavy sedation that accompanied the first generation of barbiturates (Tone 2009). After many trials and some occasional setbacks, Miltown 'debuted' in 1955, and by the end of the following year had become a 'runaway bestseller' (Tone 2009: 84).

Calmatives like Valium, and anti-depressants like Prozac, soon became stock consumer products. During the 1980s and 1990s a range of new barbiturates also built lucrative markets for their increasingly market-driven suppliers. Prozac's proponents maintained that it not only eliminated many forms of depression, but also allowed 'fairly healthy' people to better manage their anxieties and obsessions, and, in so doing, transform their lives for the better (Kramer 1993). One common claim held that people, who before taking Prozac were agitated, introverted and socially inept, became calm, confident, and socially capable after its use (Kramer 1993).

Today drug use is visible at every turn, occupying a part of nearly every domestic and social space. The global market for pharmaceuticals is estimated to be around US$900 billion, with an expected growth rate of 3–5 per cent per annum, having achieved a remarkable 10 per cent average annual growth rate during the buoyant 1990s. On average, 30 new drugs appear on the market every year, while at least 100 drugs exist in a development phase at any one time (Floyd 2008). Many drugs have achieved blockbuster status as consumable products with annual sales exceeding US$1 billion, the largest being Atorvastatin (US$13 billion), which lowers cholesterol, Fluticasone (US$9 billion), an asthma treatment compound, Quetiapine (US$7 billion), for depression and schizophrenia, and Etanercept (US$7 billion), for relieving rheumatoid arthritis (Haakonsson 2009).

A 'black market' for drugs must be considered here as well. The global market in illicit drug use is immense, mainly comprising heroin, cocaine, cannabis, and amphetamines. While freely available in the early part of the 20th century, their use is now prohibited in most parts of the world. The most recent report of the United Nations Office on Drugs and Crime (UNODC) estimated that up to 300 million people around the world had used some form of illicit drug at least once over the previous 12 months, which accounts for around 6 per cent of the planet's population (UNODC 2012). Cannabis accounted for 4 per cent of all users, heroin accounted for 1.5 per cent, cocaine for 0.4 per cent and amphetamine-type substances including Ecstasy, for just under 2 per cent. When these patterns of use are monetised, it accounts for US$330 billion of annual turnover, or approximately one third of the total annual sales of legal pharmaceuticals worldwide (Rolles *et al.* 2012).

Another massive consumer market exists for common, legal drugs. These include alcohol, tobacco, and caffeine. According to the World Health

Organization (WHO), the worldwide per capita consumption of alcohol exceeds six litres per person per year aged 15 years and over (WHO 2011). Just under 29 per cent of this alcohol is homemade or sold outside normal government controls. Consumption also varies enormously between countries. For example, where Estonia and Demark have per capita consumption levels of around 15 and 13 litres respectively, Syria has a per capita figure of just over one litre. Russia's per capita consumption reaches 16 litres, but China manages around 4 litres (WHO 2011). Overall, around 50 per cent of the world's adult population of 4.2 billion consume alcohol (Anderson 2006).

Tobacco use has fallen significantly in western industrialised nations over the last 30 years, but per capita figures have increased in developing nations. Taken as a whole, just under 30 per cent of the world's adults smoke cigarettes in one form or another (Anderson 2006). Like alcohol, consumption rates vary from region to region. Whereas 63 per cent of all adult males in East Asia and the Pacific smoke cigarettes, it falls to 32 per cent in South Asia (Anderson 2006). Heavy tobacco consumption can also be lethal. For example, the WHO estimates that around five million people worldwide die prematurely from regular tobacco use (WHO 2009).

The figures for caffeine are rubbery, but most estimates suggest that around 80 per cent of the world's adults regularly use caffeine through the consumption of coffee, tea, and 'energy' drinks. Estimated global consumption reaches more than 120,000 tonnes per annum. This is the equivalent of one caffeinated beverage per day for each of the planet's seven billion inhabitants (ABC 1997). Caffeine therefore holds the title of the most widely consumed psycho-active substance in the world.

Finally, we should take into account the dietary supplement industry. These products are not drugs in the strict sense although they tend to be consumed with similar motives in mind: to feel better, relieve stress, deliver more energy, lessen discomfort, lose weight, recover faster, and build additional muscle. Dietary and nutritional supplement (DNS) use has become a taken-for-granted practice in modern society. They occupy a pivotal place in the health-product sector, and stimulate significant levels of consumer spending. Over the past two decades especially, 'health' supplement use has exploded. In the US for example, consumption of supplements more than doubled between 1990 and 1997, increasing from US$6.5 billion to just under US$13 billion (Baylis *et al.* 2001). By 2010 total DNS sales in the US alone exceeded US$20 billion (Skolnik & Chernus 2010).

DNS use encompasses a wide variety of products, ranging from concentrated mineral capsules, vitamin tablets, and carbohydrate bars, to fatty acid compounds, protein drinks, and plant extracts. Little regulation oversees their sale. As a result, the claims supporting DNS health and fitness-giving properties are frequently extravagant, and often short on scientific evidence. Despite the problematic status of many DNS, their use continues to escalate with increasing numbers of consumers testifying to their efficacy to heal, reduce pain, increase energy levels, improve physical appearance, speed up recovery, and, more generally, increase longevity. One study of the American population between 2003 and 2006 found that 49 per cent had used some form of DNS, with female use (53 per cent) slightly higher than male use (44 per cent). Multivitamins and multi-minerals were used most frequently (33 per cent), followed by botanical supplements (14 per cent), and amino acids (4 per cent). For adults the use level was 54 per cent, while for people over 70 years of age the use level was an age-cohort high of 70 per cent (Bailey *et al.* 2011). Recent studies of German and New Zealand adult residents show a daily usage rate of 35–45 per cent (Reinert *et al.* 2007; Smith *et al.* 2005).

The role of the pharmaceutical industry

At the centrepiece of the drug and substance use jigsaw resides an immense multinational pharmaceutical industry. It not only supplies – with the support of heavily resourced promotional strategies – a massive array of products to the market, but also researchs, develops, and trials them (Braithwaite & Drahos 2000; Goldacre 2012). The industry's research and development budget outstrips nearly every other business on the planet (Haakonsson 2009). And, like any commercialised industry with profit-centred shareholders, it naturally holds a vested interest in both broadening and deepening the markets for its products (Weyzig 2004). It does this through two channels: first, through sophisticated and costly public relations, advertising, and sales strategies, and second, through direct marketing to medical practitioners, who prescribe the drugs to patients and end-users.

The pharmaceutical industry has enormous global reach (Weyzig 2004). It includes many of the world's best-known corporate brands, the nine most prominent being Johnson and Johnson, Pfizer, Roche, Glaxo Smith Kline, Novartis, Sanofi-Aventis, AstraZeneca, Abbott Laboratories, and Merck. Operating on a prodigious scale their combined annual revenues exceed US$350 billion. Of course, rarely do we see the big pharmaceutical companies joining up to the 'war on drugs' army, since they have a vested interest in growing their markets and broadening their customer bases.

Starting at the source, the drugs and related substances 'value-chain' begins with pharmaceutical companies and the multipronged distribution networks they employ to provide a convenient array of delivery outlets to substance customers (Haakonnson 2009). While legitimate market arrangements like doctors' surgeries and pharmacies exist in abundance, so too do less regulated outlets such as dietary supplement stores and internet sites. Finally, the shadowy world of gymnasium dealers, street-sellers, and nightclub suppliers offer a suite of illicit methods of obtaining drugs.

The complexity of sales arrangements confirm that the drugs and related substances sector is built on a multipronged structure that channels its products through a variety of distribution networks. While some of these networks undergo tight regulation and receive intensive monitoring, others proceed relatively unrestricted. The situation becomes even more complicated when taking into account the black market for those substances banned outright, but for which strong demand still exists. As the US prohibition experiments revealed, a ban on drugs may dampen demand, but never fully eliminate it (Benavie 2009). As

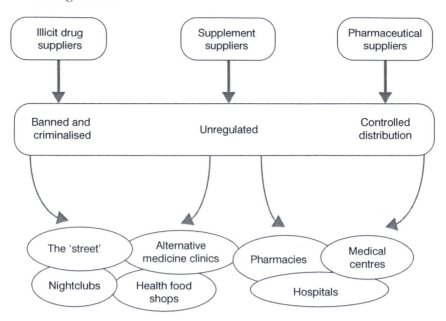

Figure 2.1 Mapping the supply chain of supplements and drugs

a result, the black market in heroin, cocaine and cannabis – the three main illicit drugs – remains as large as it has ever been, and in middle and South America it has spawned a vast, wealthy criminal class that will do all that it takes to secure a profit (Marcy 2010). Figure 2.1 provides a broad illustration of the organisation of drug distribution networks.

In summary, the drugs and related substances industry is both massive and growing. At every turn new products arrive purporting to offer a better life with solutions for every conceivable personal and social problem. Such problems represent new marketplaces constructed around behaviours and conditions that were once thought to be nothing more than endearing idiosyncrasies and minor, but manageable irritations (Conrad & Schneider 1992). And, for every additional problem created, a drug and related substance solution appears on the market to resolve the issue or alleviate its symptoms. According to Conrad (2007), society is becoming more 'medicalised' by the day, driven by an intense 'problematisation' of common experiences like insecurity, baldness, erectile dysfunction, hyperactivity in children, introversion, laziness, and apathy. As a result, 'a whole range of life's problems have … received medical diagnosis and are subject to medical treatment, despite dubious evidence of their medical nature' (Conrad 2007: 3). However you look at it, the use of drugs and related substances to resolve problems has become a taken-for-granted part of everyday life.

Why a war on drugs?

At the same time as drug and related substance use around the world has accelerated, a concurrent drive to regulate and even eliminate their use has emerged. Many reasons have been used to explain why drugs – especially cocaine, cannabis, and heroin – must be either eradicated from society at best, or tightly regulated at worst. While the call to eliminate drugs has a long history, the battle escalated with the election of Richard Nixon to the US Presidency in 1968. Nixon's election campaign featured striking rhetoric about restoring stability to America, to corral the 'lawless wreckers' of the 'quiet lives' of middle Americans, and then punish all those 'bra-less women' ... 'treasonous priests'... 'homicidal Negroes', 'stoned hippies', and 'larcenous junkies' who had seduced so many impressionable young people into drug use (Baum 1996: 11). Nixon subsequently declared a 'war on drugs', and in 1971 announced a new 'all-out offensive... against... America's public enemy number one' (Robinson & Scherlen 2007: 27). From then on, drugs – but in reality a few targeted drugs – were seen to have no social utility whatsoever, since they would inevitably undermine people's physical health, destroy their mental states, increase the crime rate, lead to rampant immorality, and precipitate an irreversible breakdown in social order.

A war on which drugs?

As it turned out, the war on drugs was essentially a war on illicit drugs; those drugs that governments have decreed to be a serious social and moral hazard. In short, we would all be better off without them, at least according to official statements. Targets for bans include the turbocharged stimulant cocaine, heroin, a narcotic that produces a warm, but often 'comatosed' inner glow, and the hallucinogenic relaxant, cannabis. As already noted, alcohol was targeted in the 1920s in the US, but now forms an intractable part of the recreational furniture for most communities around the world (Hart & Ksir 2011). In addition, the drug we know as caffeine stimulates the central nervous system, but, like alcohol, is considered a substance that nearly anyone can use. Analgesics and other assorted pain relief medicines are sold in supermarkets, and chemists dispense a raft of drugs that radically affect body physiology, brain chemistry, and mood. Add to this list a bundle of prescription drugs sold by the millions to lower blood pressure, reduce blood cholesterol levels, decongest the bronchial system, and manage severe pain. Most of these drugs are judged as socially beneficial so long as their use is supervised by experts, which means medical doctors and pharmacists. Drugs which fall outside this field of supervision and distribution control are deemed to be dangerous. So, the logic of this policy arrangement holds that dangerous drugs must be banned, and while it might be tempting to extend this logic by claiming that drugs not banned are by definition not dangerous, this is clearly not the case. The heavy use of alcohol, nicotine, and anti-depressants represent powerful cases in point. A small twisting of the same policy logic also suggests that as soon as a drug is banned it becomes dangerous. Hence the war on illicit drugs!

Table 2.1 Drug use in society: a performance-based typology

Ease of access	Contribution to performance enhancement			
	Performance reduction	*Performance neutral*	*Performance maintenance*	*Performance enhancement*
Illicit	Heroin	Marijuana	MDMAs (Ecstasy)	Amphetamines Cocaine
Prescription	Barbiturates	Selective serotonin reuptake inhibitors (SSRIs) (anti-depressants)	Analgesics	Beta-blockers Androgenic anabolic steroids (AAS) Erythropoietin
Over-counter	Alcohol	Nicotine	Medicines	Caffeine

From whatever angle you look at it, banned drugs create their own social toxicity, while drugs that are not banned secure social approval, or at least ambivalence. Prescription drugs and medicines register social approval when dispensed by a chemist under supervision, but not when taken without a prescription. Interestingly, an exponential growth in the use of prescription drugs for non-medical conditions means that their use comprises 'more than the total number of people who abuse … cocaine, heroin, hallucinogens, MDMA and inhalants combined' (DuPont 2010: 128). The main substances used 'off label', so to speak, are narcotic analgesics – especially Vicodin and Oxycontin – sedatives, tranquilisers, and prescription stimulants, particularly those used to treat attention deficit and hyperactivity disorders (ADHD). In order to better navigate this minefield of licit, controlled, and illicit substance supply, we have devised a system for classifying and categorising drugs, which is presented in Table 2.1.

Table 2.1 shows the many legitimate purposes and distribution outlets for substances. It also highlights the confusion that surrounds drug use. While on the one hand drugs like beta-blockers offer important prescription medicine for people with heart conditions, they constitute a prohibited substance in the world of elite sport. Caffeine delivers a known performance boost for athletes, but no longer appears on the list of banned substances. In fact, its removal has stimulated a new generation of users (Del Coso *et al.* 2011). Even these few anomalies lead to the question as to how drug control agencies can manage drug use in sport effectively within a society where their use is so common, and where stakeholders have many competing interests.

Sport and drug use

Sport has always experienced high levels of drug use, which should not be surprising given many drugs' capacities to build confidence, eliminate pain, ease discomfort, increase awareness, and enhance energy levels. In fact, the use of drugs and other medicinal concoctions to enhance physical performance go back to the beginnings of recorded history. Dried figs were used to secure a winning edge in the Ancient Olympic Games, while the Ancient Egyptians used potions containing ground asses' hooves to improve performance. In the 19th century caffeine, cocaine, and strychnine were used by European endurance cyclists, swimmers, and runners (Verroken 2003). Alcohol was also occasionally used to augment performance around this time, but its use to bolster physical outcomes waxed and waned mainly because it actually reduced performance. However, the use of alcohol as a social lubricant has become an embedded part of the western sport experience for centuries, and evidence suggests that currently alcohol consumption in sport clubs and associations exceeds its use in the broader community.

There was also an occasional use of stimulants during the 1920s, with one of the most illuminating being a match between Arsenal FC and West Ham FC during the 1924–1925 English football season. Some matter of fact newspaper reporting records that the Arsenal players had resorted to 'pep pills' in order to 'provide [some] extra punch and stamina' (Waddington 2000b: 98–99). Most likely, players were either using adrenaline, which was developed as a remedy for asthma around this time, or ephedrine, which had just become available through new methods of extraction from the ephedra plant. The broadsheets did not mention cheating or the moral inadequacies of the Arsenal footballers.

A major catalyst for the increase in drug use in sport came with the production of amphetamines and related stimulants in the 1940s. Initially used to help soldiers stay awake during battle, in the post-war years they became drugs of choice for truck drivers, shift workers, and sportspeople who wanted to increase their endurance. The other significant pharmacological advance occurred in the 1950s with the development of synthetic testosterone, or anabolic steroids as they came to be called. They were first synthesised by German medical scientists during World War II. This initiative, together with evidence that Russian athletes had used testosterone at the 1956 World Games, led prominent American sport physician, John Zeigler, to assist the CIBA pharmaceutical company to produce Dianabol, which soon became a favourite steroid amongst strength athletes and weightlifting communities (Taylor 1991). By the 1960s drug companies had developed numerous synthetic growth hormones and anabolic steroids. Although primarily for use in hospitals and medical clinics, these powerful new drugs quickly found their way into locker rooms and sport training centres around the world. At the same time, mood altering drugs like marijuana became a feature of the counter-culture that swamped most industrial nations in the 1960s, although there was never any claim that they could enhance sporting performance. Drug taking became common, and many of the social and moral barriers to their consumption were removed.

Athletes and coaches were quick to seize the performance benefits of steroids, none more so that the Soviet Union and East Germany, which provided pharmaceutical support to their elite Olympic athletes during the 1970s. The East German team's phenomenal success at the 1976 Montreal Olympic Games came largely as a result of chemistry skill (Parisotto 2006). Steroid use spread inexorably to commercialised, professional sports where strength was important, and the rewards for achieving on-field success were high. At the same time, the IOC and its Medical Commission, which first compiled a list of banned substances in 1967, became aware of these developments and ramped up their drug-testing program (Boyes 2000).

By the end of the 1970s the conditions facilitating the rapid diffusion of drug use in sport were solidly in place. On one side, the pharmaceutical industry had developed a product line of steroid-based drugs that could be applied to sport by improving athlete rehabilitation and muscle development, making them faster, stronger, and capable of training longer and harder. On another side, sport's expanding revenue streams enabled teams and clubs to secure the services of physicians, chemists, dieticians, physiotherapists, and trainers as a means of improving athlete performance. Sport had not only become politicised and commercialised, it has also become medicalised (Waddington 2000a). With the 1988 Ben Johnson affair, in which Johnson was stripped of his Olympic Games 100 metres track gold medal because of a positive test for steroids, the drugs in sport problem snapped into sharp relief. Since then, a raft of anti-doping polices have been implemented under the guiding hand of the IOC and WADA.

In recent times an increasing variety of drugs have captured the attention of players and athletes. While a few drugs such as alcohol, nicotine, and caffeine have always been stalwart 'players' on the sport scene, we now find a cocktail of over-the-counter painkillers and stimulants, prescription painkillers, stimulants, anti-depressants, sedatives, muscle-building compounds – including amino acids and peptide hormones – and illicit stimulants being offered to players and athletes. From an outsider's perspective, some professional sports seem to provide in-house pharmacy services.

We must also note that for 40 years after World War II, tobacco companies were major sponsors of sport events, and even provided funding to support nationwide coaching and instructional programs in a wide variety of sports. Smoking was a taken-for-granted part of the sport experience, and most sport organisations jumped at the opportunity to build relationships with tobacco companies (Taylor 1984). Sporting club cultures also became heavily masculinised during this period, and delivered welcoming spaces for the consumption of alcohol and other social drugs since they provided the opportunity to build networks of friends and acquaintances. At the core of sporting culture lies the potent triumvirate of alcohol, nicotine, and caffeine, which facilitate social connections with less friction and greater intimacy. Paradoxically, sporting cultures rarely excel at delivering consistent health messages, with heavy alcohol use, regular smoking, and poor diets providing a recipe for untimely ill health.

Sport clubs also provide space for the use of illicit substances. But recreational drugs merely cover the tip of the sporting club drug-use iceberg. Sport clubs, no matter what their performance levels, like to see their athletes back on the field of play as soon as possible after injury. Over-the-counter painkillers relieve discomfort and enable an increased range of physical movement. Moreover, given that sport rewards winners, it should also come as no surprise that drugs offering a competitive, performance-enhancing edge receive serious attention from serious athletes. Even though many performance-enhancing drugs, especially the stimulants, can be secured on prescription, for the most part they are banned under anti-doping rules. Nevertheless, a considerable amount of ambiguity exists around what substances may and may not be utilised. For example, a grey area surrounds the use of banned substances for medical conditions such as asthma, as athletes must seek 'therapeutic exemptions' to compete without being sanctioned.

In light of sport's structural demand for substances that enhance the player experience, re-engineering a guaranteed drug-free sporting environment seems a distant and implausible prospect. Sport, at the leisure and elite levels, remains fertile ground for the propagation of both licit and illicit drug use. Drug use is inexorable because sport often attracts 'obsessive compulsives', it rewards risky behaviour, it produces stress (which requires release and relief), its social dimension works best when pharmaceutical lubricants and mood altering substances are freely available, it demands quick recovery from injury, and, finally, it encourages players and athletes to do all it takes to secure a competitive edge.

The battle to defeat sport's drug cheats

With the omnipresent use of drugs in most societies around the world, and given their capacity to make a difference to both psychological moods and bodily functions, it should come as no surprise to find that drug use in sport has become so problematic that a global law enforcement body was established to regulate their use. The formation of the World Anti-Doping Agency (WADA) in 1999, and its inaugural anti-doping policy in 2003, not only strengthened the view that drugs in general had few redeeming features, but also assumed that uncontrolled drug use would threaten sport's social utility, and undermine its long-term viability. WADA was established on the basis that drug use provides an unfair advantage. Accordingly it constitutes blatant cheating, threatens the health and playing longevity of players and athletes, tarnishes the reputation and good standing of sport, and, as WADA likes to remind us, devalues the 'spirit of sport'. In short, taking drugs erodes all those good character-building and social development properties that accompany sport (WADA 2011b).

The argument for mounting a campaign against drug use involves protecting sport's status as an important social institution that confers character improvements upon its participants through discipline, hard work, and fair play. According to WADA and the IOC, drugs do the opposite; they provide a soft and seductive pathway to short-term pleasures and easy wins. Drug use in sport to bolster social connectedness is one thing, but drug use for performance enhancement is another altogether.

Despite aggressive interventions by the IOC and WADA, drug use in sport persists. United Kingdom (UK) surveys of elite athletes suggest that 30–50 per cent believe fellow athletes take drugs (UK Sport 2005). In the US, surveys of college athletes suggest that their drug-use levels are higher than for non-athletes: 40–70 per cent binge drink, 24–30 per cent use cannabis, and 10–20 per cent engage in illicit drug use (Ford 2007). In Sweden a study revealed that athlete use of asthma inhalants is six to ten times higher than in broader society, while in Hungary 32 per cent of competitive athletes reported using recreational drugs, and 15 per cent used performance-enhancing drugs, which is well above average usage levels in the broader community (Uvacsek *et al.* 2009).

A messy problem?

To summarise so far, consumer and market forces conspire in building the demand for sport drugs. On the demand side of the market, players and athletes will scratch around for the next big substance. On the supply side, drug and supplement manufacturers assiduously extol the benefits of their products. With the pressures on both sides, drug usage levels are sustained and unlikely to fall. When added to the use made of drugs in the broader community, it is difficult to deny that we live in a drug dependent society.

Part of the problem is that drug use offers many benefits including pain relief, better mood, a calming effect, improved temperament, more confidence, better decision making, cognitive clarity, more energy, better concentration, more endurance, more strength, more muscle, more creativity, more pleasure, and, finally, a longer lifespan. In short, drugs successfully treat a range of illnesses as well as reduce pain, enhance mental capacities, and improve athletic performance. Furthermore, people often 'crave for psychoactive substances' to provide moments of fleeting pleasure, heightened arousal, and less anxiety (Benavie 2009: 113). While there are many 'natural' ways of achieving these outcomes, they can be time absorbing and resource intensive. A few weeks on Prozac is likely to be a more time-efficient way of settling the nerves than a 12-month course of Gregorian chanting and meditation.

At the same time, the whole drugs in sport issue is far more obtuse than first meets the eye. Few regulatory initiatives are underpinned by evidence, with decisions mostly emerging from an uncompromising moral stance as to what is right or wrong while assuming that drugs in sport induce more costs than benefits. Many policy regulators are fearful that the sight of players securing good results or having a good time without putting in the appropriate effort, or making sufficient sacrifices, will induce impressionable youth to do the same. Sport officials and commentators believe that the use of drugs is wrong, and therefore immoral, and sometimes 'evil' (Benavie 2009: 4). In the American tradition, they often advocate crusades to eliminate one more temptation from a smorgasbord of immoral excesses, and to save people from their own incapacity to save themselves.

Policy implications

What does the previous discussion tell us about drug-use policy, the forces that have shaped its development, and how drug-use problems might be best managed? First, it illustrates the convoluted nature of sport policymaking processes, where competing stakeholders are having to balance their ideologies against the evidence (Althaus *et al.* 2007; Bessant *et al.* 2006; Stewart *et al.* 2008a). On one side of the debating table sit the proponents of strict controls and hefty sanctions. They argue that players who take drugs have not only done a disservice to themselves, their sport, and their communities, but have also let down the millions of fans who idolise them, and mimic their behaviour. On the other side are those stakeholders, typically overrepresented by professional health workers, who argue for a more player-centred model which privileges counselling and rehabilitation over heavy sanctions and severe punishment.

Second, these competing pressures create a messy policymaking environment where 'policy communities' (Nutley & Webb 2000: 31–32) bring their political weight to the policy analysis table, and use 'political opportunism', 'partisan values' and passionately held belief systems to shape the arguments presented (Edwards 2001: 9; Guess & Farnham 2000: 8). In the case of drug use in sport, a sharp divide can be seen between punitive, zero-tolerance policy supporters, and player-welfare, harm-reduction policy supporters; a battle between those stakeholders who want both performance-enhancing and illicit drug use eliminated from sport, and those who see the need to manage it from the perspective of player health and welfare. In each case, the values, beliefs, and ideologies of the two stakeholder groups within their respective policy communities take centre stage.

Third, the moral certitude that underpins punitive controls seems seductive for those stakeholders who want to see sport grow and prosper through an authoritarian guiding hand that positions players in the best possible light. However, little research evidence confirms that role-modelling assumptions apply to sport, where the behaviour of elite sport players shapes the behaviour of children and adolescents (Payne *et al.* 2003). While many professional footballers, golfers, tennis players and cricketers receive mass adulation, it has not been shown that their off-field illicit drug use is duplicated by impressionable teenagers and children (Hogan & Norton 2000; Keresztes *et al.* 2008; Lines 2001). Assertions about athlete role-modelling raise more problems than they solve, leaving us with policy options based on moral certitude. For us, this is not an ideal foundation for 'achieving social progress' (Sanderson 2002: 19). Conversely, evidence from the broader community indicates that polices providing education, private support and rehabilitation to drug users can lower the social costs and cultural 'damage' associated with their use (Eldredge 2000; Gray 2001).

Fourth, we find that the punitive drug policy proponents – comprising senior government ministers and media commentators – have captured the moral high ground by denouncing 1) the evils of drug use in general, 2) the cheating that underpins performance-enhancing drug use, and 3) the criminality involved whenever illicit drugs are involved. In contrast, player-welfare and harm-reduction proponents including drug workers and policy analysts, whose arguments centre on player support, counselling, and treatment, have failed to gain policy traction, despite their reliance on international research studies and the advice of drug treatment experts (Caulkins *et al.* 2005; Kayser & Smith 2008). Harm-reduction advocates are regularly accused of being soft, failing to understand the culture of sport, and not realising how easily its positive values and good standing can be contaminated by drug-use incidents and allegations.

Fifth, not only do policy initiatives come at a cost to the community, but these costs are not shared equitably. For example, estimates suggest that it costs a minimum of US$1,000 to conduct and process a single sport-related drug test in industrialised nations. As a result, most sporting bodies cannot support this level of spending for thousands of players and athletes. Alternatively, in market-driven sports such as the major professional sport leagues, participants could conceivably be invited to fund their own testing in order to secure drug-free certification. Either way, a program that aims to test for all types of drug use all year round comes with a huge price tag, and will be quickly mirrored in higher operating costs and increased admission prices for sporting competitions.

Finally, the moral panic that frequently surrounds the 'drugs in sport debate' has marginalised the real and endemic health-related problem facing sport, which is heavy alcohol use. While performance-enhancing and illicit drug use are important policy concerns for sport officials and administrators, it is widely acknowledged that alcohol abuse is still the single largest drug problem for players and athletes, not to mention fans (Ford 2007; Hildebrand *et al.* 2001). For the most part alcohol dependency and abuse occurs at the periphery of the main drugs in sport policy game, and are not part of drug testing regimes for out-of-competition testing periods. While there has been a concerted effort to re-educate sport club officials about the problems of excessive alcohol consumption, heavy alcohol use remains an integral feature of sport practice, both at the elite and community level. On the other hand, a policy that regulates alcohol use might not only upset some of sport's major sponsors, but also deprive many sport clubs of a major source of revenue. There is little in the drug control policies of industrialised nations to suggest that governments hold a strong interest in advancing the overall health and well-being of players, since, if they did, then the policies would take a much greater interest in the abuse of not only alcohol, but also painkillers, barbiturates, antidepressants, tobacco, and perhaps even caffeine.

Conclusion

As we demonstrated in the early part of this chapter, drugs have become an indispensable part of daily life for people around the world. First and foremost, they enhance quality of life and enable some additional pleasures to be extracted from what can often be a banal and routine existence. Second, the social utility that comes from drug use has provided the catalyst for drug companies to do further drug research, and in doing so, deliver even better quality drugs-use outcomes. Equally, it has to be conceded that drugs represent a source of misery, trauma, and ill health (UNODC 2012). Drug use can cause immense damage when people become dependent upon their use and even worse when they become addicted. We are therefore faced with a problem of how to control the harms associated with drug use, while at the same time securing its health and pleasurable-experience benefits.

From a policy viewpoint, the intuitive reaction aims for zero tolerance to eliminate problematic drug use across the board. Here the policy goal is abstinence, which works in the same way that sexual abstinence does when aiming to control transmittable diseases and unwanted pregnancies: if you do not want the negative side effects of use, then do not use. This slogan has been taken up on the illicit drug front, where a war on drugs has been raging since Richard Nixon's campaigning of the 1970s. An alternative policy option leads to regulated use with a view to reducing the harms to people who decide to use. This harm-reduction model concedes that drug use is part of the life experience, but also claims that the smarter approach is to make drugs safer to use while allowing the pleasures and benefits from their use to continue. In the following chapters, we examine these issues in more detail, beginning with the emergence of drugs in sport, and then examining the prevalence of socially driven drug cultures.

3 Critical drug use incidents and cases in sport

Introduction: myths and realities

In the previous chapter we pointed out two fundamental realities of contemporary society. First, drug use is embedded in the commerce and culture of most nations around the world. This drug use can take many forms, be it the illicit use of cocaine and cannabis, the regulated use of narcotic analgesics and beta-blockers, or the legitimised – that is, over the counter – use of alcohol and pain tablets. Second, players and athletes in every sport run their daily lives in this wider world where drug use is entrenched in community culture and practice. Consequently, drug use cannot be dismissed as an aberrant behaviour confined to a problematic subculture of deviants and misfits. Rather, it presents a common leisure practice undertaken by ordinary citizens living prosaic lives in mundane circumstances within run-of-the-mill suburbs. In short, drugs help people cope with the pressures and tensions of their daily lives, make them feel psychologically confident, and assist them to become physically better. In this chapter we consider the patterns of drug use and the dominant perspectives held about drugs in sport. To assist our exposition, we highlight a number of significant cases in drug use in sport. To illustrate the patterns of drug use at a deeper level, we also delve into some drugs in sport cases from Australia, which reveal the nature and extent of the problem, and expose the ways in which the economic, social, and cultural context can shape patterns of use.

Despite the drug culture that characterises affluent western nations and the social benefits that come from responsible drug use, especially in health and medicine, the general perception holds that apart from alcohol, nicotine, caffeine, and a few mild painkillers, sport and drugs should not mix. Rather, sport is supposed to present a special case where the use of illicit and performance-enhancing drugs can undermine its standing, good name, and overall credibility. According to those who want see a drug-free sports world, eradicating drugs should happen for three reasons.

First, if performance-enhancing drugs were permitted in sport, they would 'tilt the playing field', giving users a massively unfair advantage over clean athletes. Under these conditions not only is the use of performance-enhancing drugs considered unfair, it also threatens the entire rationale for sport, which stands for open access, parity, and an equal opportunity of winning.

Second, if illicit drug use were condoned, it woul
utility of sport by linking it with illegal and criminal b
as illicit drug users will not only disappoint their fans,
but also fail the test as positive role models. Worse st
might be copied by highly impressionable young fan
severe social problems.

Finally, drug use in sport undermines the health
and athletes. While many drugs used to enhance spo
important medical benefit in the wider community, the
dose levels in sport increase the risk of serious illnes
with the claim that a ban on drug use preserves the good health of sporting
communities.

Notwithstanding the moral certitude that underpins the above claims, the drugs
in sport issue becomes increasingly ambiguous when we work through the mixed
messages circulating within our communities about when it may be appropriate
or inappropriate to use drugs. The most confusing one suggests that, on the one
hand, athletes will be punished for taking drugs that help them cope with the
pressures of their sporting careers, while on the other hand, it is taken for granted
that non-athletes can take drugs because it will improve the quality of their lives,
their working performances, or just help them get through the day.

The confusion escalates with prescription and illicit drugs. For example, a
behind-the-counter drug with significant side effects is acceptable while the use
of an illicit drug with no greater side effect indicates a serious moral failing. The
message can be further mangled when officials, journalists and fans not only
demand players perform at their best, but remind them that the only thing more
despicable than drug use to enhance performance is a soft defeat. So, in the minds
of athletes, it is heinous to play both too well and not well enough.

The other mixed message suggests that while anything that undermines the
quality of job performance in the workplace (like coming to work drunk) should
be regulated, players and athletes may not use a substance (like an anabolic
steroid, or indeed a strong anti-asthma inhalant) that might actually improve or
sustain their on-field (i.e. workplace) performance.

To add another layer of confusion, drugs like cannabis and Ecstasy are treated
as social poisons, but other drugs like alcohol and tobacco are treated as benign,
even though alcohol and tobacco cause far more individual and community
hardship. Keep in mind that in most industrialised nations these two substances
account for around 80 per cent of the total social and economic costs associated
with the accumulated use of licit and illicit drugs (Ministerial Council on Drug
Strategy 2004).

In the following sections we illuminate these ambiguities and contradictions
by exploring the patterns of drug use in sport, beginning with international cases
and working towards a deeper analysis of Australian sport's war on drugs in sport.
Australia is an especially interesting case to consider since there has always been
an underlying belief that 'real' Aussie athletes do not use drugs because they do
not need to, and possess higher moral principles any way. Superior performance

come from natural talent, external discipline, hard work, and self-confidence. This was the enduring myth that underpinned the of Australian sport around 50 years ago, but it has not withstood the test me. The latter part of this chapter returns to evidence around the different pes of drug use that persist in sport generally, with Australia front and centre. Next, however, we examine some high profile international incidents and cases that have shaped attitudes and policies associated with drug use in sport.

An international spotlight on drugs in sport

When international sport falls under the spotlight it becomes clear that drug use occupies a multitude of darkened nooks and crannies. Substance use has a long history in sport, and numerous examples showcase highly talented athletes using performance-enhancing substances to secure a competitive edge. In 2003, CBC Sports Online recorded 10 critical cases that changed the face of international sport. Collectively, these cases demonstrated that some drugs secure athletes a decisive competitive edge, while also revealing that drug use was widespread, occupying the minds and bodies of some of the best athletes the world has ever seen.

According to the CBC report, the drug use 'flood gates' opened with the amazing successes of East Germany's Olympic teams during the 1970s and early 1980s. Despite its economic fragility, this tightly regulated Communist state of around 18 million people suddenly became an Olympic sports powerhouse, for a short time occupying the third highest medal winner position behind the much vaunted United States of America and Soviet Union. East Germany's global successes were initially explained through superior coaching and the sophisticated use of biomechanical and physiological principles. However, as it turned out, thousands of East German athletes – especially the women – were routinely given performance-enhancing steroids, often under the guise that they were merely taking a variety of dietary supplements (Ungerleider 2001). The swim teams did especially well under the supplementary regime, with Kornelia Ender, Barbara Krause, and Carola Nitschke standing out as world-beating athletes (Pampel 2007). Ender, who won eight medals at the 1972 and 1976 Olympics, reported that she started receiving injections of performance-enhancing substances at the age of 13, while Krause, a three-time Olympic gold medallist, was unable to compete at the 1976 Olympics because team doctors had miscalculated her drug dose, and were concerned that she might test positive at the Games. Nitschke was also 13 when she was placed on a testosterone program, but in 1998, after serious misgivings about her swim-career treatment became the first East German athlete to return her medals and ask that her name be removed from the record books. A German court later found the East German sports official Manfred Ewald and his medical director, Manfred Hoeppner, culpable for what it called systematic doping in (East German) competitive sports (Ungerleider 2001).

The second drug-use milestone occurred at the 1983 Pan American Games in Caracas, Venezuela. A team of drug testers led by Manfred Donike, a German sport scientist, developed a new method for steroid testing. As it turned out, Canadian weightlifter Guy Greavette along with teammate Michel Viau were stripped of their medals and handed a two-year suspension after testing positive for anabolic steroid use. At least nine American athletes in various events also suddenly withdrew from the competition and returned to the US. Another 10 athletes from other nations left the Games without explanation. In all, 19 athletes tested positive to banned compounds (Pampel 2007).

The third significant incident involved a 12-year drug-use cover-up of elite level US track and field athletes. A report compiled by Wade Exum, a prominent Olympic sports physician, found that 19 American athletes were allowed to compete at various Olympic Games from 1988 to 2000 despite having failed earlier drug tests. This came as a horrifying surprise to the American sporting community since its athletes had, for many years, passionately condemned the systemic doping practices of sporting regimes such as East Germany and China. Track star, Carl Lewis, a multiple Olympic Games Gold medallist offered a case in point. In 2000 he commented that 'people know the sport is dirty … the sport is so driven by records', but at the same time was named by Exum for using banned performance-enhancing substances at different times during his career. According to Exum's report, more than 100 athletes from different sports tested positive for banned stimulants between 1988 and 2000, but were cleared by internal appeals processes. Exum's evidence suggested that Lewis was one of three eventual Olympic gold medallists who tested positive for banned stimulants in the lead up to the 1988 Seoul Games (Hunt 2011).

The fourth incident involved Ben Johnson, the Canadian track sprinter, who won the 100-metre sprint title at the 1988 Seoul Olympic Games in a world-record time of 9.79 seconds. Ironically, he defeated his arch-rival Carl Lewis, who entered the race as the favourite. However, Johnson's euphoria shattered when it was announced that he had tested positive for stanozolol, an anabolic steroid. Johnson claimed that the positive test stemmed from a spiked herbal drink the night before the race, but officials viewed his excuse as a complete fabrication. As a result, Johnson was stripped of his gold medal, had his world record deleted, was banned from competition for two years, and watched his gold medal be awarded to his rival Lewis. As it turned out, at least three of the race competitors had tested positive for drugs just prior to the Games, with Lewis being one of them (Cooper 2012).

The fifth incident involved Irish swimmer Michelle Smith, who won three swimming gold medals as a 26 year old at the 1996 Atlanta Olympic Games. Smith's successes came as a great surprise to officials and fans alike, since at the previous Olympic Games, she could not even secure a top 15 ranking. In 1993, Smith was ranked only 90th in the world in the 400 individual medley race, but after training under the watchful eye of her husband Erik de Bruin – a former Dutch discus thrower who was under a four-year suspension for failing a drug test – won several European swim titles. Subsequent to the 1996 Games, Fédération Internationale de Natation (FINA), swimming's international governing body, expressed concern that Smith was often unavailable for out-of-competition drug tests. Finally, in 1998 drug testers showed up at Smith and de Bruin's home, and not only gained entry, but also administered a drug test. Smith delivered what was supposed to be a 'real time' urine sample, but the tests showed an alcohol reading that would normally make the drinker comatose. FINA concluded that the sample had been manipulated, and that whiskey had been added as a masking agent. Smith received a suspension from competitive swimming for four years (Todd & Todd 2001: 105).

The sixth case revolved around a number of Chinese swimmers during the 1990s. Going into the 1992 Barcelona Olympics, the Chinese swim team had done little of international significance, but by the end of the Games had won four gold medals. Their results at the 1994 world championships were even more staggering when they secured 12 of 16 women's titles. However, the explanation for their phenomenal swim successes was in part revealed at the 1994 Asian Games when 11 athletes tested positive for ihydrotestosterone, a powerful anabolic steroid (Todd & Todd 2001). Additionally, four positive tests occurred before the 1998 world championships in Perth, Australia, while a bundle of vials of human growth hormone was found in breaststroker Yuan Yuan's luggage upon her entry to Australia. Moreover, just before the 2000 Sydney Olympics, China removed four swimmers from its team due to 'suspicious' drug test results. Overall, more than 40 Chinese swimmers failed drug tests during the 1990s, a number three times that of any other nation over this period.

The seventh case involved the Tour de France between 1998 and 2004. Most sport commentators agree that the Tour de France is the one of the most brutal endurance races on the planet, with many competitors prepared to do whatever it takes to either secure a competitive edge, or just stay in the event. Drugs, especially stimulants, have been a long-time substance of choice, with amphetamines a favourite (Mignon 2003a). Things came to a head in 1998 when race officials, accompanied by police, caught an employee of the Festina cycling team with a carload of performance-enhancing drugs, including erythropoietin (EPO), a hormone that helps the blood deliver more oxygen to athletes' muscles, thereby allowing them to ride harder for longer periods of time. Following a series of arrests, six of Festina's nine riders conceded they had used performance-enhancing drugs (Hoberman 2001; Voet 2001; Walsh 2007c). Additionally, Credit Agricole team leader Christophe Moreau later tested positive for anabolic steroids. This major scandal did not act as a deterrent to subsequent drug use, since, in early 2002, Italy's Stefano Garzelli, leader of the Caldirola team, tested positive for traces of probenecid, a diuretic that masks the use of other drugs. Also, Spanish cyclist Igor Gonzalez de Galdeano was banned from the 2003 Tour de France after a test during the 2002 event found excessive levels of an anti-asthma drug. In early 2004, French police seized testosterone, EPO, and amphetamines, and arrested two cyclists in the anti-doping investigation involving Cofidis, one of France's top teams (Walsh 2007c).

The eighth critical incident nominated by CBC Sports Online involved America's Major League Baseball (MLB). One of the earliest transgressions involved Mark McGwire, who, according to the CBC report, had transformed himself from the 'svelte American League rookie of the year in 1987' to the 'heavy-hitting home run king who broke Roger Maris' single-season home run record' in 1998. McGwire candidly commented that the transformation resulted from a combination of not only hard work, but also from the use of an over-the-counter testosterone-producing pill called androstenedione, or 'andro', as it was colloquially known (Bryant 2005). The interesting thing about 'andro' is that while it had been designated as a banned substance by the IOC, the American National Football League (NFL), the National Basketball Association (NBA), and the National Hockey League (NHL), its use was initially permitted in MLB. As it turned out, a cocktail of drugs were used by elite baseballers to improve their on-field performance. In 2002, *Sports Illustrated* published an investigative report describing professional baseball as 'a pharmacological trade show'. In the article, former National League MVP Ken Caminiti commented that 'at least half the guys … were using steroids'. Additionally, in 2003, MLB announced that around 6 per cent of nearly 1,500 anonymous tests on players came back positive. San Francisco Giants left fielder Barry Bonds was also linked to the use a designer steroid, Tetrahydrogestrinone (THG), which had the nickname of 'clear' because of its ability to fly under the drug-testing radar (Fainaru-Wada & Williams 2006). Bonds, who became MLB's home-run record holder, was subsequently indicted for perjury and obstructing justice by telling a federal grand jury he did not knowingly use performance-enhancing drugs, when in fact he had (Carroll 2005: 129–132).

The ninth incident was linked to the Austrian cross-country skiing team at the 2002 Salt Lake City Olympic Games. The IOC began an investigation after cleaners found blood-transfusion materials in a residence used by the Austrians during the Games. The Austrians claimed that the equipment was used for the ultraviolet radiation treatment of athletes' blood in order to manage and prevent colds and flu. However, this implausible explanation was dismissed after an intensive investigation whereupon two athletes were disqualified and two team officials were banned from the next two Winter Olympics. In addition, three skiers tested positive to the drug darbepoetin, which is used to treat severe anaemia by boosting the production of red blood cells. This was just the tip of the iceberg, so to speak, since doping had been rampant in cross-country skiing for many years. According to the CBC Sports Online report, EPO use was 'as common as ski wax' while blood doping had 'become an art-form'. For example, six Finnish skiers tested positive for HES – a banned plasma volume expander – at the 2001 world championships in Finland, and implicated some of Finland's finest skiers including Jari Isometsa, Mika Myllyla, Janne Immonen and Harri Kirvesniemi.

The tenth incident cited by CBC involved the use of nandrolone, a banned steroid, and the concomitant use of nutritional supplements. During the last half of the 1990s especially, a 'rash' of positive tests for nandrolone occurred, giving it the unofficial title of the most common drug used by elite athletes. Nandrolone had in fact been implicated in hundreds of doping cases across a range of sports. In nearly every instance the offending athletes claimed that it must have been the result of using contaminated nutritional supplements. In 2004 Canadian-born British tennis star Greg Rusedski, along with fellow professional, Peter Korda, joined a long list of athletes who tested positive for nandrolone. Rusedski, like many others caught using the steroid, claimed it was inadvertent, and could only explain its use by applying the 'supplement contamination' defence. According to the CBC report, nearly 50 tennis players on the WTA tour had tested positive for the banned steroid during the early 2000s.

The CBC Sports Online drug use survey offers an exemplar in sports reporting since it not only indicated how drugs and related substances have been used to deliver incredible sporting performances, but also showed how pervasive drug use had been over a long period of time. However, this report was compiled in 2003, and as a result it did not capture the explosive revelations about the drug use of Marion Jones, one of the greatest female track sprinters of all time. In October 2005, Jones, an American who won five medals at the 2000 Sydney Olympic Games, pleaded guilty to lying to federal investigators about using anabolic steroids. While Jones had initially pleaded her innocence, her fate was sealed when she became ensnared in the Bay Area Laboratory Co-operative (BALCO) scandal, which involved the supply of performance-enhancing substances to an array of elite players and athletes. BALCO founder Victor Conte maintained he had seen Jones inject herself with steroids, as did her ex-husband, C. J. Hunter. In addition, Hunter admitted he used steroids, and told a Grand Jury that Jones did too (Assael 2007; Pampel 2007).

Neither was the 2003 CBC report able to document the doping farce associated with the women's 1,500 metre track race at the 2005 Athletics World Championships in Helsinki. According to Cooper (2012: 6–8) this event could easily lay claim to being the 'most corrupt race ever'. The winner, Russia's Tatyana Tomasova, was banned for two years in 2008 for tampering with her urine samples, as was the second place-getter, Yuliya Chizhenko-Fomenko, who was also from Russia. Olga Yegorova, the third place-getter, and another Russian, had not only previously tested positive to EPO, but was also suspended from competition in 2008 for providing false urine during a test procedure. Bouchra Ghezielle, from France, who finished fourth, was found guilty of doping with EPO in 2008, and was suspended for four years. Finally, Yelena Soboleva, who finished fifth was found to have tampered with her urine and was likewise suspended.

As the above discussion demonstrates, exposés and scandals involving the illegal use of drugs in sport have been regular affairs. However, none can compare with the scathing indictment of Lance Armstrong – arguably the world's greatest ever road racing cyclist – made by the United States Anti-Doping Agency (USADA) in October 2012. For many years Armstrong had fervently denied he had ever taken performance-enhancing substances despite the constants claims made by his cycling counterparts that he had a long record of use (Coyle 2005). Armstrong also has a compelling personal and professional history. It is worth reflecting on some of the events and incidents that led up to the 2012 events which tarnished his larger-than-life image, the serious denting of his reputation, and the stripping of so much value from what, in the commercial arena, could be best called 'brand Armstrong'.

Armstrong was born in the American state of Texas in 1971, and by mid-adolescence discovered that he had the ability to become an elite endurance athlete (Armstrong 2000). In 1988 he became a professional triathlete, and a year later the US Olympic development team invited him to train as a road cyclist. He established his elite racing credentials very quickly, and in 1992 represented the US at the Barcelona Olympic Games. Although he was unable to secure a top-ten place, he turned professional soon after the Olympics and joined the US-based Motorola cycling team, where he quickly made his mark by finishing second in a World Cup race in Switzerland (Armstrong 2000). He competed in his first Tour de France in 1993, but, having slid to a languid 62nd place, withdrew from the event. However, Armstrong rebounded sharply, and in late 1993 won the World Road Race Championship in Norway.

By 1996, however, Armstrong's cycling career had stalled. Having secured a lucrative contract with Cofidis, a well-credentialed French team, he was again unable to complete the Tour de France and failed to achieve much of any significance at the 1996 Atlanta Olympic Games. In late 1996 Armstrong was diagnosed with testicular cancer. To add to this tragic news, shortly later his doctors discovered brain tumours. Armstrong was given a 40 per cent chance of surviving, but after many rounds of chemotherapy received the now famous declaration of being cancer-free in early 1997 (Armstrong 2003).

Two years later in 1999, Armstrong won the first of seven consecutive Tour de France races as a member of the United States Postal Service team (Armstrong 2000). He went on to win another six tours, making him the one of the best, and probably the most famous road cyclist of all time. Having achieved this extraordinary level of success, Armstrong retired in 2005, only to announce three years later that he planned to race once again in the Tour de France in 2009. In his own amazing way, Armstrong placed third in the race, beaten only by his teammate, Alberto Contador, who had his own drug-use problems to face in the 2010 Tour de France, and Saxo Bank team member Andy Schleck, whose brother Frank was alleged to have taken banned substances at various times during his career. After the race, Armstrong told reporters that he intended to compete again in 2010, with a new team sponsored by Radio Shack.

During the 1990s, Armstrong also became a world-renowned philanthropist and a sporting celebrity. He established the Lance Armstrong Foundation for Cancer, now called *LiveStrong*, in 1996, and supported the Lance Armstrong Junior Race Series to help promote cycling and racing among America's youth. In 1998 he married Kristin Richard, a public relations executive he met through his cancer foundation, and they had a son using sperm frozen before Armstrong began chemotherapy treatment for his illness. Twin daughters were born in 2001. Lance and Kristin divorced in 2003. Since then Armstrong became, for various lengths of time, romantically attached to singer Sheryl Crow, fashion designer Tory Burch, actress Kate Hudson, and television personality Ashley Olsen. In 2008, Armstrong became a father again when his partner at the time, Anna Hansen, delivered a baby boy. Adding to his remarkable accomplishments, Armstrong found the time to become the author of two best-selling autobiographies. The first was *It's Not about the Bike: My Journey Back to Life* (2000), and the second was *Every Second Counts* (2003).

Despite the amazing success achieved by Armstrong, his celebrity status, his incredible physical resilience, and his demonstrable mental toughness, there were signs that his professional and personal worlds were beginning to crash down around him after his 2009 cycling successes. In 2010 Floyd Landis, a former teammate, alleged that Armstrong had used banned drugs throughout his career, which included at least three Tour de France events (USADA 2012). Landis also alleged that Armstrong had raised funds for his team's doping program by selling-off expensive racing bikes supplied by a major sponsor, the Trek Bicycle Corporation. Landis, by the way, had his 2008 Tour de France title stripped after testing positive to a banned substance.

In 2011 a second 'massive attack' was made on Armstrong by Tyler Hamilton, another former teammate of Armstrong's and a former world road time-trial champion. In a television interview with CBS's *60 Minutes* current affairs show, Hamilton claimed that Armstrong had injected EPO on numerous occasions during his cycling career. Hamilton also conceded that, like Landis, he too had used synthetic testosterone and blood transfusion practices to maintain a competitive edge, a practice which Armstrong regularly encouraged.(Hamilton & Coyle 2012). Armstrong retorted that Hamilton was nothing more than a 'confessed liar in search of a book deal', and like Landis, was a 'washed-up cyclist talking trash for cash' (O'Connell & Albergotti 2011).

Events began to unravel uncontrollably for Armstrong in 2012. USADA brought formal charges against him, and threatened to strip the famous cyclist of his Tour titles. For years Armstrong had vehemently denied using illegal drugs to boost his performance, and the 2012 USADA charges received the same dismissive response. Armstrong disparaged the new allegations, labelling them 'baseless'. The case heated up in the middle of 2012, when some media outlets reported that four of Armstrong's former teammates, George Hincapie, Levi Leipheimer, David Zabriskie and Christian Vande Velde – all of whom had competed at the 2012 Tour de France – were planning to testify against him (USADA 2012).

In August 2012 Armstrong announced that he was giving up his fight against USADA's charges, advising that he would attempt to reach an arbitrated outcome because he was tired of dealing with the case and wanted to end the stress. He went on to say that 'there comes a point in every man's life when he has to say, "enough is enough" ... for me ... that time is now' (Moore 2012). Armstrong also said that

> I have been dealing with claims that I cheated and had an unfair advantage in winning my seven Tours since 1999 ... the toll this has taken on my family and my work for our foundation and on me leads me to where I am today... finished with this nonsense.

USADA dismissed Armstrong's claim to the moral high ground. It firmly announced that Armstrong would be stripped of his seven Tour titles as well as other so-called 'honours' he received from 1999 to 2005. In short, he would be banned from cycling for life because there was incontrovertible evidence to show that Armstrong had used illegal performance-enhancing substances throughout most of his career.

In October 2012 USADA released a 1,000 page report delivering damning evidence against Armstrong. It included laboratory test results, emails, and monetary payments which, according to USADA, showed that 'beyond any doubt ... the US Postal Service Pro Cycling Team ran the most sophisticated, professionalised and successful doping program that the sport had ever seen'. USADA evidence contained testimony from 26 people, including several former members of Armstrong's cycling team who claimed that not only had Armstrong used performance-enhancing drugs, but he had also served as a 'ringleader' for the team's doping efforts (USADA 2012).

Armstrong vehemently disputed the USADA findings. His chief legal representative, Tim Herman, called the USADA's case against Armstrong 'a one-sided hatchet job' featuring 'old, disproved, unreliable allegations based largely on axe-grinders, serial perjurers, coerced testimony, sweetheart deals and threat-induced stories' (Cutler 2012). However, all the evidence pointed to Armstrong's heavy involvement in organised doping over a long period of time, and the media had a field day in pointing to Armstrong's overwhelming hypocrisy and chronic lying about the real situation in international road cycling. Relatively speaking, the Armstrong affair made the Ben Johnson doping scandal at the 1988 Seoul Olympic Games look like a trivial indiscretion.

Patterns of drug use in sport: Australian cases

Drug use in Australian sport reflects some quite different cases to the ones provided above, but they tell similar stories, typically beginning with strong initial denials followed by ugly confrontation, and in some cases highly emotional, if perhaps manufactured, contrition.

Sporting drug use and abuse in Australia has attracted significant media commentary and debate over recent years. One of the most widely reported but bizarre cases involved Sylvester Stallone, the American film star and part-time bodybuilder, who in a visit to Sydney in 2007 imported 48 vials of human growth hormone. According to a court report, he needed the substance to 'give him a boost', and make him look and feel good (King 2007: 3). Stallone additionally claimed that he was taking the growth hormone for a medical condition, although the nature of the condition remained unclear. Stallone wrote an apology to the court in which he stated that 'a truly unfortunate occurrence happened when arriving in your country' and that he had made a 'terrible mistake' (King 2007: 3). Stallone was found guilty of importing a prohibited substance, and given the maximum penalty of AUS$22,000.

The Stallone case provided the impetus for Peter Faris, a leading Melbourne legal advocate and former chair of the National Crime Authority, to claim a widespread illicit drug-use problem amongst the law fraternity. He suggested that it represented 'quite a problem, with high-flyers in Victoria and New South Wales using cocaine for a number of years'. Faris further suggested that there 'should be random testing of lawyers like those already in place for AFL footballers' (AAP 2007).

Another drug scare emerged in early 2008 when the National Centre on Drug Addiction claimed that binge drinking had escalated to alarming levels. The Centre cited studies indicating that 20 per cent of all 16–17 year olds were regularly drinking to harmful levels (Noonan 2008). Moreover, the Centre claimed that illicit drug use had become endemic amongst school children, and demanded strong action to remedy the situation in the form of a compulsory drug testing program in all Australian schools. However, the proposal was challenged as being overzealous and an unsustainable financial drain on the health system. A study by the Australian National Council on Drugs estimated that it would cost AUS$335 million to conduct a single saliva test for all students in one year, while at least AUS$2 billion was needed to test students regularly throughout the year (Tomazin & Smith 2008: 4). A testing program for schoolchildren was abandoned as a poor use of scarce resources where the net benefit appeared to be marginal.

These illustrative events reflect a drug-taking culture. According to a 2007 survey undertaken by the Australian Institute of Health and Welfare (AIHW), the following patterns of drug use prevailed (AIHW 2008: xi–xii):

- Just under 83% of people over 14 years of age consumed at least one serve of alcohol in the previous 12 months. Just over 39% drank at least once a week, while 8% drank at least once a day.
- Around 17% of people over 14 years of age were daily smokers.
- Nearly 39% of people over 14 years of age had used an illicit drug of one sort or another at least once, while 13% had used an illicit drug over the last 12 months.
- Cannabis was the most commonly used illicit drug, with 29% of people having used it at least once, and 9% having used it over the last 12 months.
- Ecstasy and related drugs (like methamphetamines) had been used by 6% of people over the last 12 months, with the usage rate increasing to 12% for the 20-24 year old age group.

Although these figures seem startlingly high, the most dramatic drug use occurred with prescribed pharmaceuticals. Just over 220 million prescription medicines were dispensed in 2003, but this had risen to 234 million by 2007, an increase of 6 per cent (AIHW 2008). On average, each person over 14 years of age uses 15 prescriptions per year. When the total number of over-the-counter medicines was included as well, it became clear that most Australians were taking drugs on a regular basis. While many drugs were probably misused, producing significant personal and social costs, they also provided the Australian community with respite from chronic pain, allowed for the superior administration of disabilities, and generally made lives more manageable and pleasurable.

At the same time, these figures are not excessive by western standards. A 2007 study of drug use in the US found that 6 per cent of the adult population used cannabis in the previous 12 months, while 1.5 per cent used stimulants. Around 51 per cent of the adult population used alcohol regularly, while 29 per cent used tobacco products at least once a month (SAMHSA 2008). In countries such as

Australia, drug use is embedded deeply not only in wider society, but also within the cultural fabric of sport. Despite the evidence demonstrating widespread personal use, Australian sport followers have been reluctant to accept that their athletes could possibly be drug users. In the following section we examine the place of drugs in Australian sport through several critical incident case studies.

Creating the conditions for a drugs in sport culture

Australia has an enviable sporting history. Not only have Australians played organised sport in significant numbers since the 1840s, but they have also achieved many international successes along the way. Australian identity rests upon the nation's sporting achievements, exemplified by a raft of sporting heroes, legends, and halls of fame. Cricket possesses a special capacity to produce sport heroes such as Donald Bradman and Shane Warne. In track and field Betty Cuthbert and Cathy Freeman have also become household names. Swimming has Dawn Fraser and Ian Thorpe, while competitive cycling produced Phil Anderson, Robbie McEwen and Cadel Evans. Embedded deeply in the Australian popular and political cultures, social planners view sport as a way of building character, enhancing self-confidence, controlling juvenile crime, and building better communities (Cashman 1995).

Sport in Australia also houses many confronting social problems. It has received accusations of violence, sexism, homophobia, and racism while preserving many long-standing class divisions (Booth & Tatz 2000; Kell 2000). Sport supporters are frequently seen as philistines, officials perceived as self-interested bordering on corrupt, and bookmakers are vilified as match fixers. A recent critique of sport claimed that it is 'infested' with drugs, leaving athletes no option but to take illegal substances in order to maintain their place in the team and on the winners' podium (Wright 2005: 17). No matter what we think of players and athletes who take drugs, and despite detailed anti-doping rules and regulations accompanied by heavy fines and suspensions, drug use in sport has been a common occurrence in Australia since the 1980s, when anabolic steroids became a popular substance for building muscle. A number of high profile drug-related incidents in sport over the last few decades have exposed an unpalatable reality.

By the end of the 1970s the conditions for the rapid diffusion of drug use in sport were in place. The pharmaceutical industry had created an innovative and powerful product line featuring anabolic androgenic steroids at the same time as the sporting world itself had become more sophisticated in several pivotal ways. First, governments were increasing funding sport in order to bolster national identity in a Cold War-fuelled frenzy. Second, amateur competitions were making way for professional sport leagues and events where players could gain materially from improving their athletic performances. As a result the amateur ideals of sport as an end in itself, and sport as a bastion of self-reliance and fair play, had been overwhelmed by instrumental reasoning and win at all costs attitudes (Cashman 1995). Finally, sport's expanding revenue streams enabled teams and clubs to secure the services of physicians, chemists, dieticians, physiotherapists and trainers as a means of improving athlete performance. Sport had already succumbed to politicisation and commercialisation, and was now racing towards medicalisation as well, with drug use being an inevitable outcome (Ferguson 2006).

The response from Australian sport governance was soft at first, partly because its community assumed a smug distance from the drug problems of Eastern Europe. Additionally, the endemic use of alcohol and tobacco did not count as cases of problematic drug use. Australian athletes were believed to be clean, their moral incorruptibility used to explain poor performances at the Olympic Games during the 1970s (Bloomfield 2003). However, the myth that Australian athletes relied solely on clean living and hard work to achieve sporting success exploded in the 1980s, coinciding with the establishment of the Australian Institute of Sport (AIS). While the AIS sought to enhance the country's international performance in sport through science and technology, it also provided fertile soil for a drug culture to emerge. Ironically, the catalyst for the AIS emanated from the superior athletic performances of communist Europe, many of which were primed with drugs (Hoberman 1992).

Malcolm Fraser, Australia's Prime Minister, officially opened the AIS in 1981, proclaiming that it 'would bring together Australia's most talented youngsters guided by the best coaches that can be found' (Bloomfield 2003: 57). In addition, to hiring well-credentialed coaches, the Commonwealth Government established the Australian Sports Commission (ASC) in 1984 (Stewart *et al.* 2004). The ASC funded programs and developed policies to help athletes improve their levels of performance. It additionally introduced anti-drugs programs to complement the IOC's regime of testing, sanctions and education.

The 1987 AIS scandal

The first major drugs in sport scandal emerged in late 1987 when the Australian Broadcasting Commission's (ABC) *Four Corners* program examined the use of anabolic steroids in sport. While most of the program focused on bodybuilding, it talked to weightlifters and track and field athletes as well. In each sport, allegations were made charging coaches with supplying anabolic steroids to athletes on AIS scholarships. In the following year the steroids and sport performance debate exploded when the Seoul 100 metres gold medallist, Ben Johnson, was stripped of his medal (Pampel 2007; Todd & Todd 2001). In 1988, under enormous public pressure, the Commonwealth Government, with the backing of the Australian Olympic Committee (AOC), instructed the Senate Standing Committee on Environment, Recreation and the Arts (SSCERA) to undertake an inquiry into the drugs in sport problem.

The Standing Committee's *Interim Report* (1989) found that a number of athletes had taken steroids regularly during the 1980s, citing as examples discus thrower and shot-putter Gael Martin and javelin thrower Sue Howland. Both athletes had tested positive for an anabolic steroid. Martin, who won a bronze medal in the discus at the 1984 Los Angeles Olympic Games, estimated that 30 per cent of the AIS track and field team were using steroids (SSCERA 1988). In addition, five weightlifters from the AIS admitted to steroid use. They claimed that every weightlifter on an AIS scholarship was 'using steroids at peak training times' (SSCERA 1988: 188). Coaches came under scrutiny too. Howland and Martin alleged that field event coach Merv Kemp had given athletes suspicious tablets and injected them with steroids at a training camp in Italy in 1984. Martin identified the substances as steroids because it 'was the same stuff I was getting' (SSCERA 1988: 343). Kemp denied the allegation. The *Interim Report* concluded that the Commonwealth Government should immediately establish an authority to carry out sports drug testing, and Graham Richardson, the Minister for Sport, foreshadowed the establishment of the Australian Sports Drug Agency (ASDA).

The Standing Committee's *Second Report* confirmed the scope of the drugs in sport problem, giving special attention to weightlifting and its culture of steroid use. Again, both coaches and athletes were implicated. Lyn Jones, the head weightlifting coach at the AIS, admitted that a number of young weightlifters at the Institute had taken drugs (SSCERA 1988). The Standing Committee found that Jones had supplied AIS athletes with imported steroids (SSCERA 1989). In fact, steroid use in weightlifting was endemic. Former weightlifter-turned-coach Nigel Martin claimed that at least one club provided young weightlifters with an envelope full of pills to assist their training programs (SSCERA, 1988). Notwithstanding protests from AIS officials that the whole drug abuse problem was exaggerated, the Commonwealth Government legislated for the establishment of ASDA, giving it the power to expand the testing regime, undertake research into improved testing for banned substances, and educate athletes about ethics, health problems, and sanctions associated with drug use in sport (Bloomfield 2003).

Cycling

Even ASDA failed to deter some of Australia's best international athletes from experimenting with banned substances. At the 1991 World Cycling Championships, Carey Hall and Stephen Pate – who finished first and second in the sprint event – tested positive to anabolic steroid use, receiving suspensions from competitive cycling for two years (Buti & Fridman 2001). In the same year, leading time-trial cyclist Martin Vinnicombe tested positive to a steroid compound whilst competing in an event in the US. Vinnicombe incurred a two-year suspension, although he appealed the penalty to the Federal Court of Australia on the grounds that the tests did not comply with ASDA procedures, the penalty was excessive, and that cancelling his licence was a restraint of trade because it prevented him from continuing his career as a professional cyclist (Buti & Fridman 2001). The appeal led to a suspension reduction. The Vinnicombe case, like others that followed, revealed some legal loopholes in the anti-doping rules.

Track and field

Stanazolol, a popular anabolic steroid at the time, proved to be a problem for sprinter Dean Capobianco. Capobianco was Australia's leading track sprinter and had become the fifth ranked 200 metre runner in the world in 1995. However, a test undertaken at an athletics meet in the Netherlands revealed a positive sample leading an International Amateur Athletics Federation (IAAF) tribunal to ban him from competing for four years. An appeal to Athletics Australia on the grounds of faulty testing processes in Europe was upheld, however, and Capobianco competed at the 1996 Atlanta Olympics Games. Undeterred, the IAAF appealed against the Australian ruling, and after further consideration the appeals tribunal handed Capobianco a two-year ban (Buti & Fridman 2001).

The big league

During the lead up the 2000 Sydney Olympics, the Commonwealth Government, the AOC, and national sporting bodies were furiously promoting the success of their anti-doping policies. But, cracks in the shiny image were becoming more difficult to ignore. Australia's largest sporting league, the Australian Football League (AFL), was eager to be a model of drug-free sport, having implemented an anti-doping code in the early 1990s in the wake of the ASDA's establishment. However, this clean image suffered a setback in 1997 when elite player Justin Charles tested positive to boldenone, a banned steroid. Charles defended his actions by claiming that his use was purely remedial since, in order to recover from injury, he used the drug to assist the healing process. According to the AFL tribunal, injury-recovery constituted no excuse, and Charles received a 16-game suspension (AFL 1998).

Another AFL case involved Alistair Lynch. Unlike Charles, Lynch announced that he was seeking to employ a banned steroid. However, he provided a more convincing explanation by declaring that he was recovering from chronic fatigue syndrome. Lynch had approached the AFL to secure permission for the drug's use under the AFL's anti-doping code, and received advice from ASDA that given his illness, the therapeutic use of the normally banned steroid was permissible. The AFL initially claimed that Lynch had contravened the rules, and therefore should be banned from playing (Buti & Fridman 2001). An ensuing public-relations disaster accompanying the AFL's handling of the case led to a policy change accommodating drug use on legitimate medical grounds.

The net widens

The Lynch case illustrated some alarming cracks in Australia's anti-doping policies. In 1999 the Commonwealth Government, with the assistance of the ASC and the AOC, reviewed the existing programs, and subsequently initiated a nationwide drug education and enforcement program through the Tough on Drugs in Sport (TODIS) policy (Kelly 2000). The TODIS policy's formation arrived in the aftermath of the 1998 Tour de France scandal where, as noted in the early part of this chapter, several of the world's top cyclists had been supplied with a smorgasbord of drugs (Mignon 2003b). A damning IOC inquiry recommended the establishment of a centralised drugs in sport crime-fighting organisation to take the form of the WADA, later established in 1999 (Pound 2006). Around the same time, Werner Reiterer, one of Australia's best performing discus throwers, published an autobiography alleging that drug taking commonly occurred amongst the Australian athletic community. He also confessed to taking performance-enhancing drugs in the run-up to the Sydney Olympics (Reiterer 2000). Not long after the Games had finished Gennadi Touretski, the coach of world champion swimmers Alexander Popov and Michael Klim, faced charges of possessing anabolic steroids, and in early 2001 agreed to stand down from his coaching position at the AIS (Clarke 2001).

The Warne case

Not even cricketers were clean. Cricket occupies a coveted position as Australia's national game, but despite its commercial scale does not seem to be the type of sport normally associated with drug use. Notwithstanding its gentlemanly traditions and purist uniform of white trousers and collared shirt, a number of players tested positive to banned substances between 2001 and 2003, including Australia's greatest ever bowler, Shane Warne.

Cricket Australia is one of Australia's most powerful sporting bodies. Its anti-doping policy established in 1998 was the first developed by any national governing body in cricket, and has been used as a benchmark for anti-drug policy in other cricketing nations. Leading up to the Warne case, Cricket Australia condemned the use of performance-enhancing drugs, having announced that doping practices contravene proper sporting ethics and harm players' health (Cricket Australia 2003). The list of prohibited substances included masking agents, muscle-building drugs like steroids, and the increasingly popular endurance boosters such as EPO. Cricket Australia's anti-doping policy aimed to prevent drug use by first, imposing sanctions on players who commit a doping offence, second, educating its players about the drugs in sport issue, and finally, supporting the Government's drug testing programs. Under anti-doping regulations, a player has committed a doping offence if a prohibited substance is found in his or her body tissue, or if the player is found to have utilised a prohibited method to cover up their use. At the same time, Cricket Australia acknowledged that players might be permitted to take advantage of a prohibited substance if able to demonstrate a legitimate therapeutic purpose or show exceptional circumstances (Cricket Australia 2003).

Cricket Australia's anti-doping rules were activated in 2003 when Australia's highest profile player, Shane Warne, tested positive to a banned substance. At the end of the 2002 cricket season he dislocated his shoulder, had major surgery, and was expected to be absent from the game for at least three months. However, Warne made a quick recovery after intensive rehabilitation, and resumed practice in early 2003. In the light of his unexpectedly speedy recovery Warne was asked to provide urine samples as part of ASDA's testing program for Cricket Australia (McKinnon 2003). The test showed a positive reading for hydroclorothiazide and amiloride, two banned diuretics. Not only do diuretics remove fluid from the body, they also mask the use of anabolic steroids. While prohibited for use by cricketers, these diuretics remain readily available on a doctor's prescription.

In line with Cricket Australia's anti-doping policy, Warne attended a hearing of its Anti-Doping Committee. In his defence, Warne admitted he had taken Moduretic, a prescription drug, but claimed ignorance of its diuretic properties, having apparently taken it on the advice of his mother who counselled that it would get rid of excess fluid prior to a media conference. Warne noted that he took the tablet in order to remove his double chin before facing reporters (Cricket Australia 2003). Warne also claimed to be unaware that Moduretic was on the list of banned substances, and argued that his case should be treated as an exceptional circumstance. The Committee remained unconvinced by Warne's evidence. The statement that he did not know the tablet was a diuretic because the flaps of the tablet packet were missing seemed flimsy. To make matters worse, Warne had made no attempt to contact Cricket Australia's medical officers before taking it. Warne confessed that while he attended player drug education seminars, he learnt nothing about the diuretic problem, or the consequences that would arise from testing positive for banned substances. The Committee concluded that the evidence given by Warne and his mother was vague and unsatisfactory (Cricket Australia 2003).

The Committee agreed that Warne did not establish the 'exceptional circumstances' case necessary in order to receive favourable treatment. Rather, it concluded that Warne had acted recklessly, disregarding the possible consequences of his action. At the same time, the Committee acknowledged that no evidence proved that Warne had taken steroids, and agreed that taking Moduretic tablets would not enhance his sporting performance. The Committee reduced the minimum two-year ban to a one-year ban (Cricket Australia 2003), which meant that Warne would lose one year of his contract fee with Cricket Australia, as well as having his product endorsement potential diminished. While Warne's suspension sent a message that Cricket Australia took its drug code violations seriously, it simultaneously signalled that drug use was more widespread than previously believed. It once again busted the myth that Australian athletes dismiss drug use as a legitimate means of securing a competitive advantage.

Shifting the goalposts

In 2004 the Commonwealth Government broadened its anti-doping policy in the light of the WADA Anti-Doping Code of 2003 (ASC 2004; WADA 2003). They collaboratively proclaimed the use of performance-enhancing and illicit drugs to be unethical, unfair, and harmful to the health of athletes. According to this logic, athletes who take drugs to enhance their performance (or take illegal drugs even if they do not enhance performance), should be banned from participating in sporting competition. This expanded stance was defended on the grounds that all drug taking, whether performance enhancing or illicit, undermined the spirit of sport since it contradicted values like respect for the law, self, fun and joy, health, honesty, character and education, excellence in performance, and community and solidarity

(WADA 2003). The Commonwealth Government endorsed the WADA position that drug use constituted cheating, went against the spirit of sport, and damaged the health of athletes. And, if a drug met two of these criteria it qualified for prohibition.

Under the new policy arrangement, the Commonwealth Government aimed to stop doping practices in sport by instituting a series of new measures. The first measure provided financial assistance to drug-testing programs. The second measure employed educational programs to inform athletes about the consequences of performance-enhancing drugs. The final measure imposed sanctions on athletes committing anti-doping offences (ASC 2004). In support of these measures, the Commonwealth Government employed the services of the ASC to implement the policy, and restructured the ASDA by arming it with a stronger investigative role under the renamed banner of the Australian Sports Anti-Doping Agency (ASADA) (Kemp 2005a). It also acquired the support of the Australian Sport Drug Testing Laboratory (ASDTL) and the Australian Customs Service (ACS) in identifying drug cheats. In addition, the Commonwealth Government mandated that all national sporting associations receiving government funds should have a strict anti-doping policy in place, otherwise funding would be discontinued. It was expected that sporting associations would invoke sanctions of no less than two years for a first offence, and a life suspension for a second offence (ASC 2004). While the Commonwealth Government instructed sporting associations to establish processes that ensured fairness and natural justice for athletes, along with the delivery of education programs across the nation, severe punishment remained the primary weapon for ensuring compliance. The Government, like WADA, had declared that it was serious about its war on drugs and that doping would not be tolerated.

Notwithstanding these punitive measures, athletes continued to take drugs stimulating a stream of doping allegations demanding investigation. In addition to the Shane Warne case, rugby league player Andrew Walker tested positive for cocaine in 2004, and in the same year Commonwealth Games weightlifter Belinda van Tiernan faced accusations of supplying banned substances to her training partners, Camilla Fogagnola and Jenna Myers, who were in turn banned for steroid use. Around the same time, cyclist Sean Eadie, a former world champion, had a mail-order pack of human growth hormones addressed to his home intercepted by Australian Customs, while weightlifter Caroline Pileggi failed to attend a scheduled drug test while training in Fiji. Meanwhile, Sergo Chakkoy, another weightlifter, tested positive to a banned substance whilst preparing for the 2004 Commonwealth Games. In 2005, Nathan Baggaley, Australia's top kayaker and an Olympic silver medallist, tested positive to steroids, incurring a two-year ban. In early 2007, Baggaley was again found in possession of drugs, this time involving a large quantity of Ecstasy tablets. Despite the professional and personal impact of being caught using drugs, athletes seemed prepared to run the gauntlet.

The French case

Of all the drug-use cases in Australia over the last decade, the most explosive involved Mark French, an elite cyclist, and other members of the Australian men's sprint cycling team that trained out of Adelaide in 2003 in preparation for the 2004 Athens Olympic Games. In December 2003 a batch of injecting paraphernalia were located in French's room containing traces of Testicomp, an over-the-counter homeopathic compound containing a banned steroid, and eGH, a banned equine growth hormone. In addition, a range of legal vitamins and other bodybuilding supplements were discovered (Gallen 2004). An internal inquiry in early 2004 found that French had breached Cycling Australia's anti-doping code, and the matter was referred to the Court of Arbitration for Sport (CAS) for an independent hearing. The CAS determined that French had breached the code on eight occasions, despite no evidence that he had actually used eGH. Nevertheless, French was found to have possessed, but not supplied eGH, and as a result received a ban from cycling for two years. The hearing further revealed that French had claimed most of the Australian track cycling team, which included Graeme Brown, Jobie Dajka, Sean Eadie, Shane Kelly, and Brett Lancaster, had used his room for injecting substances (Anderson 2004a, 2004b). The CAS accepted French's allegations when it noted in its ruling that French was 'overcome by a culture ... where he was under the dominating influence of others' (Anderson 2004a: 75). These confidential allegations were raised in Federal Parliament when Senator John Falkner referred to a shooting-gallery incident at the Adelaide training centre (Kogoy 2004).

A second inquiry led by Justice Anderson investigated the 'shooting-gallery' allegations, but determined that insufficient evidence sustained the claim that the other cyclists had also taken banned substances. Anderson disputed the CAS conclusion that French had been pressured by his peers to use banned substances. However, Dajka's testimony appeared untruthful when responding to Anderson's questions, as he had clearly been in French's room in Adelaide when he said he had not (Anderson 2004b, 2004c). In the meantime, the AOC banned French from all international competition under the AOC and Cycling Australia banner, but noted that his punishment may be reviewed if he cooperated with Justice Anderson.

In the wash-up from the Anderson inquiry, Dajka was expelled from the Athens Olympic track cycling team. Twelve months later, French's appeal to the CAS over its original decision was upheld, and he was again free to compete in cycling competitions. According to the CAS Appeals Tribunal, Testicomp, the supposedly homeopathic drug injected by French, did not in fact contain any of the banned substance that its label signified. Moreover, even though the eGH supplies found in French's room were contaminated by his DNA, it could not be established that he had used it, or been the supplier or sole owner (Stevenson 2005). In a further series of twists to this convoluted incident, Dajka became the scapegoat. French used his victim status and a legal loophole to reclaim his reputation, and Australia achieved its best ever international track cycling results at the 2004 Athens Olympics.

The Sailor case

Another high profile anti-doping investigation involved Wendell Sailor, one of the nation's rugby icons. Sailor, who had originally played rugby league for the

Brisbane Broncos, transferred to rugby union where he became a key member of the national team and the Queensland Reds Super-14 team. During the 2006 Super-14s rugby union season, Sailor took an illegal but non-performance-enhancing recreational drug. However, under the new anti-doping policy, the performance-enhancing status of a drug does not matter if it is illegal. Sailor had gone to a nightclub and enjoyed a long evening of socialising. He subsequently failed a drug test leading to the Australian Rugby Union (ARU) finding him guilty of taking cocaine in-season. In line with the WADA and Australian Government drugs in sport code, the ARU terminated his contract and banned him from the sport for two years, which at his age, effectively meant for the remainder of his career. Moreover, under the policy, Sailor could not play any other sport signed up to the WADA and Commonwealth Government anti-doping code. ARU Chief Executive, Gary Flowers, announced that 'drugs of any sort have no place in our sport, and won't be tolerated' (Harris 2006: 3).

Other critical incidents

In an explosive admission in 2007, Andrew Johns, one of Australia's greatest ever rugby league players, revealed that he had taken illicit drugs and alcohol throughout his football career (Ritchie & Mascord 2007). His admission produced a storm of criticism amongst Australian sport officials and fans. Some commentators felt Johns had betrayed their trust in his capacity for fair play and honourable conduct, while others believed that he had brought the game into disrepute, and failed the test as a role model for impressionable children and a standard-bearer for socially responsible behaviour (Read 2007).

While Johns explained his drug-use problem, sports fans were stunned when Ian Thorpe, Australia's greatest ever competitive swimmer, faced rumours about testing positive to banned substances. A French newspaper claimed that an out-of-competition drug test undertaken in Australia in May 2006 had revealed elevated levels of testosterone and luteinising hormone, colloquially known as LH (Burke 2007). Apparently someone linked to the ASADA, which had conducted the test, had leaked the results to the newspaper. ASADA had initially resolved not to take any action because of some ambiguities in test results (Magnay 2007). In response, Thorpe declared that while he had no case to answer, he would nevertheless contemplate legal action in view of the damage the leak had done to his reputation. The allegations against Thorpe were subsequently dismissed on the grounds that the elevated levels of testosterone and LH could have occurred naturally, and therefore could not be directly linked to the use of performance-enhancing substances (Silkstone 2007).

Meanwhile, another highly publicised case involved Ben Cousins, an AFL player. Cousins, one of the most outstanding players of his generation, had acquired significant notoriety for his off-field behaviour. At different times during his career, Cousins had 1) links to underworld crime figures, 2) obstructed traffic and police to avoid a drug charge, 3) assaulted teammates, and 4) been arrested for being drunk in a public place (Walsh 2007a). However, these incidents paled into insignificance when compared to events that unfolded in 2007, when the West Coast Eagles football club suspended Cousins indefinitely just before the start of the season. At the time, the club cited two missed training sessions, but also hinted at a 'number of personal and professional issues'. Within days the club confirmed that Cousins had used a prohibited drug, suffered from a substance abuse problem, and would be seeking rehabilitation at a clinic in the US. However, at the time, the nature of Cousin's substance abuse problem remained unclear, as well as whether it involved performance-enhancing or illicit substances. It turned out to be an illicit drug issue.

Cousin's rehabilitation was on course when he resumed his playing career later in the 2007 season, but his comeback was jeopardised following an erratic driving incident, a charge of possessing a prohibited drug, and failing to comply with a police-ordered drug assessment (Fife-Yeomans & Cazzulino 2007). Both charges were dropped when the police admitted that their evidence was flawed, since the drug they cited as prohibited could in fact be purchased with a doctor's prescription. The Assistant Police Commissioner apologised, and Cousins received AUS$2,000 in court costs (Walsh 2007a). While this incident stopped the West Coast Eagles from terminating his contract, the club's patience evaporated when Cousins travelled back to the US on the premise of receiving more rehabilitation, but needed hospitalisation following a cocaine binge. Cousins faced the AFL Commission where he was found guilty of conduct unbecoming, and of bringing the game into disrepute. The 12-month suspension rendered Cousins ineligible for the 2008 season, and also required him to secure a medical clearance if he wanted to enter the 2009 national player draft. He recommenced his playing career in 2009 with the Richmond Football Club in Melbourne, and retired at the end of 2010 with some of his reputation intact, but his drug habit unresolved.

The Johns and Cousins cases appear trivial when contrasted with the fallout from a 2013 Australian Crime Commission's (ACC) report on organised crime and drug use in professional sports leagues. According to the ACC the problem stemmed from sport scientists and their product suppliers, who had initiated programs of 'high end' supplement use involving such substances as 1) 'cerebrolysin' (a pig brain extract for improving cognitive awareness), 2) 'thymic peptide' (an extract from the thymus glands of young calves that can aid recovery from heavy physical work), 3) 'colostrum' (a cow-milk extract used to increase muscle mass), 4) 'ubiquinone' (an antioxidant that sustains energy levels), and 5) peptide hormones (which comprise a complex mix of amino acids which can accelerate the production of human growth hormone). The ACC noted that while most of these products were not listed as banned substances under the WADA Code, some were.

The ACC also announced that it had identified individuals with 'extensive criminal associations' building 'business partnerships with major Australian sporting codes' (ACC 2013: 33). It not only considered this development to be demonstrably unhealthy from an organisational perspective, but also hinted that it may adversely influence the behaviours of some club officials. The ACC pointed to evidence it had acquired that some coaches, sport scientists and support staff had 'orchestrated the use of prohibited substances and/or methods of administration' (ACC 2013: 9).

The ACC report coincided with the eruption of a drug-use scandal at the Essendon Football Club (EFC), a long-standing member of the AFL. It was discovered that players had been given a mysterious cocktail of 'supplements' during the 2012 season, encompassing every one of the substances listed above. Having expressed concerns about their efficacy and legitimacy, senior EFC officials sought advice from the AFL Commission and the ASADA. Supplements are usually not a problem, since they are freely available over the counter, and are relatively benign from a health-risk perspective. In the EFC case, though, there were suspicions that the club's supplementation program had crossed the 'legitimacy' line.

First, the sport scientist in charge of supplement use asked players to sign a consent form – a waiver of sorts – transferring the risk of use from the club to the player. Second, the 'supplements' were administered by injection rather than taken orally, and were done off site, at a medical centre. Third, it appeared that players were not fully informed about the nature of the supplements, their chemical composition, and where they fell within the WADA and AFL drug control regulations. Finally, and surprisingly, neither the club's chief medical officer, nor the head coach, initially said they were aware of the fact that players were taking this cocktail of substances.

The ACC report and EFC cases deserve consideration for a number of reasons. The first is that problems will always arise when supplements are used without proper knowledge about their contents, efficacy, and legitimacy. There are many incidents which involve the inadvertent use of banned substances through supplement use, and subsequent player suspensions for doping (Amos 2007). And, as we understand, under WADA/AFL rules, a plea for leniency on the grounds that banned substances were not listed on the packet is no defence. The second is that players have the right to know what they are ingesting into their bodies, and supervisors who fail to deliver appropriate advice are derelict in their professional responsibilities. Some players remain poorly informed on technical issues, and are therefore vulnerable to the pronouncements of medical officers, coaches, trainers, and the like. The third is that if some of the supplements used by EFC players were on the banned list then the drug-testing program being used to detect doping infringements was totally ineffective. As it turned out, this did not reflect well on the reputation of ASADA.

Conclusion: what does it all mean?

The sample of cases we presented in this chapter confirms the seriousness of the drug-use problem in sport around the world. While track and field, cycling, cross-country skiing, weightlifting, and professional team sports are the most vulnerable to drug use, it would be naive to think that other sports are exempt. Some commentators claim that team sports have little time for drug use as a means of improving performance, since skill and strategy rate highly, but the spate of steroid use in MLB tells us a different story. In reality, all sports that require strength, endurance, rapid recovery, and the capacity to absorb pain and discomfort present potential sites for performance-enhancing drug use. Moreover, those sports imposing stress and anxiety on their participants will also be conducive to recreational drug use, be it licit or illicit.

These cases also suggest that the threat of naming, shaming, fines, and suspensions do not always work. Surprisingly, the players and athletes who you would, at first glance, least expect to use – the gifted, the highly trained, the experienced, and the well-resourced – are in fact the ones cited in most of the cases we discussed. It confirms the view that drug use will never convert the ordinary, the solid, and the mediocre into high level elite competitors. What drug use does is make the talented and the very good even better for even longer. It makes great players and athletes into champion players and athletes, and this is neither difficult to understand, nor an irrational thing to do. On the other hand, hard-working, earnest, but genetically disadvantaged athletes who take drugs to transform their sporting performances from ordinary to superior will always be disappointed, since their aspirations will be inevitably be thwarted by their limited capabilities. Not everyone can become an elite performer and a sporting champion, even with additional substance use. If, then, we are going to allow drug use in sport, then it makes sense to make it accessible to the talented minority who will be able to benefit the most, and deliver the greatest pleasure to fans.

4 Scale and scope of drug use in sport

Introduction

The previous chapter painted a heavily textured picture of drug and related substance use in sport by delving into a variety of incidents and cases. Our approach sought to illustrate the different forms drug use takes and the impact it can have not only on the implicated players and athletes, but also on the image and progress of the sport itself. However, when it comes to understanding the scale of the drug and substance use problem, and its coverage amongst different sports and different user segments, our previous analysis only fills in part of the canvas. It is also important to examine the data available from the systematic study of various cohorts of players and athletes. In this chapter we review the studies revealing first, the drugs and substances being used, second who takes them more or less frequently, third, with what intent, and finally, where it takes place. As a result, this chapter provides a broad feel for the scale and scope of drug use in sport, as well as what drives consumption. Included in our analysis are data from a variety of sources in order to provide an evaluation of the objective facts available. Although these studies do not deliver a complete and integrated picture, they collectively cover a great deal of territory by including a review of anecdotal reports, drug testing results, survey outcomes, and in-depth interviews.

Over the last 50 years, concern about the increasing amount of drug and substance use in sport has been steadily growing. As we noted in Chapter 1, drug use constitutes a multidimensional problem that begins with everyday drugs like alcohol and caffeine, moves into over-the-counter drugs that contain stimulants or analgesics, goes into prescription drug use that involves even heavier stimulant and analgesic effects, shifts into a range of clearly identifiable performance-enhancement drugs, and finishes up with potent recreational drugs that take users into another state of consciousness altogether.

Many of these substances deliver improvements to sporting performances. However, sporting officials judge this situation intolerable, since it creates a tilted playing field where already well-resourced players and athletes obtain an even greater advantage through access to new products as they 'come to hand'. As a form of cheating, drug use therefore constitutes a corrupt practice undermining the integrity of sporting contests analogous to the moral bankruptcy displayed in match fixing. Such was the social context within which a global anti-doping regime arose in the form of the WADA in 1999. However, 15 year later it remains unclear as to whether the WADA-driven anti-drug stance has reduced either the incidence or prevalence of drug use in sport. The cases we outlined in the previous chapter suggest that drug use in sport persists, which is not surprising in the context of the growing politicisation, commercialisation and medicalisation of sport, along with the increasing pressures for players to use whatever it takes to win.

We remain poised to question just how successful the current anti-doping policy has been, and whether a policy that widens the drug-use net by including illicit drugs offers the most effective path in a world where drug use offers a taken-for-granted tool for achieving a better quality of life. As the previous chapter shows, even supposedly squeaky clean Australian athletes have utilised pharmacological assistance to improve their sporting performances, despite the potential shaming and punishment that comes from being caught. In the following section we venture further into the prevalence of drug use in sport by compiling more hard data that might, as Yesalis *et al.* (2001) noted, better inform the debate. Over recent times too much space has been given to off-hand accounts, media inspired rumours, a few insider anecdotes, selective investigative stories, and occasional government reports. Such a compilation offers a useful beginning, but it is also important to take the next step. Here we interrogate the results of drug tests conducted by the regulatory authorities, and critically assess surveys and studies undertaken on different player samples and athlete cohorts.

Overall prevalence of drug use in sport

Anecdotal accounts of drug use

A common view amongst officials, politicians, and commentators holds that sport throughout the world faces a drug-use epidemic. Many high-profile international incidents reinforce this perspective as the previous chapter showed. Professional road cycling in particular receives significant attention, and in each of the last few Tour de France races, a number of participants were disqualified for testing positive for banned substances. In addition, track and field athletes have yielded numerous high-profile positive tests, the most explosive incident involving Marion Jones who, along with several prominent athletes became embroiled in the BALCO scandal (Assael 2007). Like the Australian cases, these incidents created enormous angst amongst sport's stakeholders. As already noted, concerns continue to mount that drug use in sport not only undermines the health and well-being of players and athletes, but also threatens the good reputation of sport by inducing cheating and extreme anti-social behaviour. Drugs therefore constitute a significant challenge to the economic and social value of sporting brands.

Of course, and as Lentillon-Kaestner and Ohl (2011) have noted, all of the above discussion places some uncertainty over the prevalence of drug use in the world of sport, exactly what type of drugs are being used, and for what performance or personal gains. The available drug-use data has its strengths and weaknesses, and while each data source – and the methods used to extract it – exposes a selective picture, when viewed collectively they produce a detailed overview of usage, motives, and the contextual forces shaping their use. In the following section we review the current state of play.

From an anecdotal viewpoint, and as reported in the media, a drug scourge in sport has not only tilted the playing field in favour of those players with close pharmaceutical connections, but has also destroyed sport's capacity to bolster the moral fibre of its participants. Media reports tend to trade on creating 'moral panic' by connecting drug use in sport with social chaos. In these instances, colourfully exaggerated stories are dredged up from the past leading to calls for restoring control through some top-down regulatory mechanism, typically involving coercion, fines, suspensions, and even jail sentences. A classic case of moral panic arose out of a US Judiciary hearing into steroid use in 1989, when Pat Connolly, a coach of the women's track and field team, claimed that 15 out of the 50-strong women's team at the 1984 Los Angeles Olympics had used steroids on a regular basis. Moreover, she noted that '… some of them were medallists' (BMA 2002: 76). Connolly elaborated that drug use escalated even further for the 1988 Seoul Olympics, estimating that 'at least 40% of the women's team … had probably used steroids at some time in their preparation for the Games' (BMA 2002: 76). In Australia, in 2003, a serious case of moral panic similarly erupted when an Australian rules footballer suggested that 80 per cent of elite footballers had some experience with recreational drugs. This created enormous consternation amongst the football community, and the only consolation the media could offer officials and fans were quotes from other players who said the figure was nearer 30 per cent (Turner & McCroy 2003). While media driven narratives always have an element of truth in them, they also revel in juicy scandals, and as a result need to be tempered by a broader base of evidence through first, athlete drug-testing data, and second, studies that have secured information about athletes' attitudes and behaviours regarding drug use. As with all research, we should lend most weight to results guided by sound protocols and legitimate methodologies.

Results of drug testing regimes

We begin by reviewing the data compiled by the IOC and WADA over recent years. These figures reveal that throughout the 1990s less than 2 per cent of all drug-test results were positive, exhibiting inappropriate levels of banned substances. Table 4.1 gives the IOC testing figures from 1996 to 2008.

The most commonly used drugs were anabolic androgenic substances or what we commonly refer to as 'steroids', which accounted for 1131 positive tests in 1996, 856 tests in 1998, 946 in 2000, 1191 in 2004, and 3259 in 2008. The 2008 figure accounted for 59 per cent of all positive tests. The next most frequently used drugs were beta-agonists, more commonly known as the active ingredients in various forms of anti-asthma and respiratory management medications. They accounted for 350 positive tests in 2008. Stimulants also seem to be substances of choice accounting for 281 positive tests in 1996, 412 in 1998, 453 in 2000, 382 in

Table 4.1 IOC/WADA drug testing figures 1996–2008

Year	No of tests	Positives tests as % of total
1996	96,000	1.6
1998	105,000	1.8
2000	117,000	1.9
2004	169.000	1.7
2008	275,000	1.8

Source: Mottram (2003, 2011b)

2004, and 472 in 2008. At the same time, peptide hormones (which includes EPO), delivered fewer positive tests, with four in 1996, 12 in 1998, 12 in 2000, 78 in 2004, and 106 in 2008. Although cannabis and its derivatives are not, technically speaking, performance-enhancing drugs, they remain banned during competition. For both 2004 and 2008 there were more positive test for so called 'cannabinoids' (518 and 496 respectively) than there were for stimulants (382 and 472).

At the 2000 Sydney Olympic Games just over 2800 tests were conducted, including 310 tests for EPO. However, these tests yielded only 12 positives results (five of which involved steroids), amounting to just 0.47 per cent of all tests. Similarly, the positive test figures for the 2002 Salt Lake City Winter Games were modest. Only five of 1960 tests were positive, not even 0.3 per cent of all tests. At Athens, in 2004, 26 athletes tested positive to banned substances, but when taken in the context of nearly 3700 tests, they accounted for only 0.7 per cent. Torino in 2006, and Beijing in 2008, delivered even lower positive test rates. Nearly 4800 drug tests were undertaken at Beijing, but only 0.42 per cent delivered a positive result, which was slightly lower than Sydney (Procon 2011).

The low positive test rates for the Olympics need to be tempered by the results of studies undertaken in the broader sporting community. Independent studies of elite athletes by sport scientists in Norway (Bahr & Tjørnhom 1998) and the UK. (Mottram 2003; 2011b) each found a banned drug usage rate of less than 2 per cent. These are slightly higher than the IOC/WADA drug test figures, but hardly suggest an epidemic of illegal drug use running rampant through the global sporting community.

By most standards the positive test rates seem pleasingly low. Equally, most sport commentators concede that the officially measured rates severely underestimate the true level of banned drug use (Lentillon-Kaestner & Ohl, 2011; Pitsch & Emrich 2011; Striegel *et al.* 2010). There are three reasons for this. First, most drug use occurs during periods of intense training rather than competition, but for many years most testing was done in periods of competition. Second, some drugs were not detectable, and therefore did not show positive in any tests. Third, athletes utilise masking agents and methods: other legal drugs, compounds, and techniques that camouflage the presence of banned substances in their systems. As a result of these three challenges to accurate testing, researchers employ surveys of athletes and players in the hopes of securing a more plausible picture of drug use in sport.

Surveys of reported drug use

Numerous surveys have sought to establish realistic levels of drug use in sport as well as the ethical attitudes players and athletes hold towards use. The surveys focus on both the broad community and sport participants, utilising a range of techniques such as questionnaires and in-depth interviews. Results indicate a complex range of reported usage levels of banned substances with varying usage levels for different drug types and sport practices.

Community surveys

During the late 1980s and 1990s a series of revealing studies examined anabolic steroid usage. According to a study of high school male adolescents in the US (Johnson *et al.* 1989), around 11 per cent were current or previous anabolic steroid users. This constituted a substantial increase over the results secured by Pope *et al.* (2004), which concluded that only 2.5 per cent of adolescent males used steroids. A later study by Tanner *et al.* (1995) found a 5 per cent usage rate amongst young men aged 18 years with a 3 per cent rate for those participating in sporting competitions. In a far more broad ranging study, Melia *et al.* (1996) reported caffeine as the drug of choice given the 27 per cent of all informants declaring that they used it regularly. Alcohol and painkillers came in at around 9 per cent, while stimulants generated a usage level of just 3 per cent.

A study of an American high school football team by Stilger and Yesalis (1997) provided a sharp insight into drug use in local community settings. The researchers initially found that just over 6 per cent of team members had used anabolic steroids. When asked to explain their use, 47 per cent said they did it to improve their athletic performance, 29 per cent did it to improve their appearance, and 14 per cent said they did it to keep up with the competition. When asked to respond to the statement, 'I would use anabolic-androgenic steroids if I knew opponents playing against me were using it', 54 per cent of the players who had used confessed that they would do it again. Those students who had previously used also said they had no difficulty securing their steroids, with 30 per cent getting them from athletes outside of school, 29 per cent getting them from teammates and friends, 25 per cent getting them from a local doctor, and 19 per cent obtaining their supplies from their school coach.

Another revealing community study of drug use was undertaken by Parkinson and Evans (2006). Having noted that just under 3 per cent of young American adults had taken steroids at least once in their lives, the researchers invited 500 anabolic steroid users to complete a web-based questionnaire. The results revealed that just under 80 per cent had used steroids for what they called 'cosmetic reasons', which meant they were mainly concerned with looking good and feeling strong (Parkinson & Evans 2006: 644). Dosage levels also varied enormously between respondents, with 40 per cent not going beyond 1,000 mg per week, with 26 per cent regularly exceeding 1,500 mg on a weekly basis. Additionally, just under 25 per cent reported that they practiced 'polypharmacy', which meant they complemented their steroid use with growth hormone and/or insulin (Parkinson

& Evans 2006: 650). While 60 per cent of respondents said they were concerned about the possible negative side effects – with acne, testicular shrinkage, insomnia, sexual dysfunction, injection site pain, fluid retention, and mood changes front and centre – only 37 per cent had discussed their steroid use with a physician (Parkinson & Evans 2006: 650). Finally, the respondents admitted to securing their steroids mainly from illegal sources, with 50 per cent obtaining their supplies from 'bootleg' operators and illicit laboratories.

A Finnish study of nearly 11,000 male conscripts with an average age of 19 years also provided some illuminating results. Matilla *et al.* (2010) invited these young men to comment on their substance use and health status. Some of the questions invited participants to record their use of anabolic steroids, and if they did initially use, to explain what provided them with the incentive to continue. It was found that only 0.9 per cent of respondents had used anabolic steroids over their lifetime, a figure well below those from other studies. According to Matilla's team, American studies had shown a usage rate of 3–11 per cent, while European studies had shown prevalence rates of 2–3 per cent. What caused such low levels of anabolic steroid usage amongst this cohort of 19-year-old Finnish conscripts remained unclear. It was noted, however, that high use levels had been previously associated with engagement in weight training programs at fitness centres, frequent drunkenness, daily smoking, and low levels of educational attainment.

The claim that gyms and fitness centres can be the catalyst for an increase in steroid use was supported by Striegel's (2006) research. This study invited around 620 members of fitness centres in Germany to complete a survey about gym practices and substance use. Just less than 14 per cent of respondents had used steroids at some point during their fitness centre activities. When asked to identify their motive for using, more than 80 per cent of respondents emphasised the importance of building a better looking and stronger body, while only 8 per cent were interested in improving their levels of fitness and sporting performances. In addition, around 30 per cent of users used complementary substances to enhance the bodily impact. Clenbuterol and middle range stimulants like ephedrine were recorded as the most popular 'add ons' (Striegel *et al.* 2006: 12). When users were asked to identify the source of their training 'products', just over half cited the 'black market'. In practice, this meant acquiring supplies from friends and informal contacts. Just under 50 per cent of users had also accessed pharmacies for some of their complementary products as well.

Player and athlete surveys

Player and athlete surveys provide a different perspective on drug and related substance use. One of the earliest but most extensive studies of players and athletes delivered the startling finding that 64 per cent of informants believed that at least one of their fellow athletes used drugs on a regular basis (Anshel 1991). Similarly, Pearson and Hansen (1990) completed a survey of US Olympic athletes around the same time, and found that many athletes had either used or knew of others who used. Just under 44 per cent of those who completed the survey believed that at least one in ten of their peers were taking some sort of performance-enhancing substance, while another 34 per cent estimated that somewhere between 1 per cent and 9 per cent of their colleagues were using. In another study, this time of endurance athletes, 41 per cent of informants thought that some of their teammates were taking performance-enhancing drugs (Laure & Bisinger 1995).

In 1998, the *Independent* newspaper in the UK surveyed 300 elite players and athletes, finding that more than 50 per cent considered sport to be contaminated with drug use. Responses varied between sport categories, with the highest response rate coming from weightlifters, where every one of them thought drug use permeated their sport (Waddington *et al.* 2005). When questioned about their own drug use, just over 40 per cent of the 300 elite players and athletes admitted to using caffeine in order to secure a competitive edge, 15 per cent admitted to using testosterone, 15 per cent admitted to using some form of stimulant, while 8 per cent admitted to using narcotic analgesics. A study of 706 English professional footballers confirmed the problematic and pervasive nature of drug use in sport (Waddington *et al.* 2005). Of all respondents surveyed, 34 per cent claimed that other players were commonly using performing-enhancing drugs, although only 6 per cent indicated a personal knowledge of performance-enhancing drug-taking players. Interestingly, only 29 per cent of informants suggested that other players were taking recreational drugs, although when questioned about personally knowing someone who took them, 45 per cent responded positively.

In a more recent study, Alaranta *et al.* (2006) found that 44 per cent of power sport participants reported that they personally knew of other athletes who used banned substances, while 37 per cent of endurance athletes harboured similar suspicions. The argument for thinking that positive drug-test ratios comprehensively underestimate 'real' drug-use levels was further supported by a study done by Uvacsek *et al.* in 2009. In this study, 82 Hungarian athletes were invited to talk about their drug-use attitudes and behaviours. The results revealed that just under 15 per cent of all respondents admitted to using performance-enhancing substances, while just under 32 per cent admitted to using recreational and/or illicit drugs (Uvacsek *et al.* 2009). Uvacsek *et al.* (2009) also found that users overestimated the drug use of others when compared to non-users. For example, whereas those who doped imagined that on average 35 per cent of others doped, non-dopers provided an average estimate of 17 per cent. In the case of recreational drug use, users anticipated that 51 per cent of all others used, while for the non-users, the figure was a much lower 39 per cent.

Another revealing study was undertaken by Dunn *et al.* (2009), which used a web-based survey of 214 exercising males who had not previously used anabolic steroids, to obtain a better understanding of what so-called 'rank and file' participants do to improve their physical appearances and general levels of well-being. It was initially found that 80 per cent of all respondents used some form of supplement or conditioning aid to assist them in their 'body improvement' projects. Illicit substance use was also common, with 52 per cent of respondents admitting to administering amphetamines, cannabis, inhalants, cocaine, off-label narcotic analgesics, or sedatives in the previous six months. There were no reports of heroin use. At the same time, when asked to comment on their views about anabolic steroids, 16 per cent said they were likely to use some form of synthetic testosterone in the future as a way of getting stronger and more muscular (Dunn *et al.* 2009).

It should come as no surprise to discover that sport participants, especially at the highly competitive level, are likely to at least think about using performance-enhancing substances. On the other hand, it is sometimes argued that sport participation can act as a shield against recreational drug use since it engrains the idea that sport can only be played properly if its participants have a clear head and a well-functioning body. On this logic, we would anticipate that people who play more sport would use fewer recreational drugs. However, the data suggest that sport participation does not necessarily discourage recreational drug use. Two research teams – Peck *et al.* (2008) and Wichstrom and Wichstrom (2009) – found that adolescent participation in team sports, especially those rewarding aggression, often led to an increase in alcohol and cannabis use in early adulthood. Peck, Vida and Eccles (2008) reported that adolescents who both played sports and were already consuming moderate levels of alcohol, were highly susceptible to heavy drinking in early adulthood. Another – albeit earlier – study of university athletes determined that 96 per cent of informants drank alcohol regularly, with just over 20 per cent smoking cannabis, and 18 per cent popping painkillers (Spence & Gauvin 1996).

When it comes to elite sport, the relationship between drugs and lifestyle becomes even more perplexing. Peretti-Watel *et al.* (2003) surveyed 460 elite student athletes in France, concluding that the overall prevalence of cigarette, alcohol, and cannabis use was less than half the rate of non-athlete students. However, girls competing at an international level were more likely to smoke cigarettes and cannabis, perhaps due to the belief that their consumption would alleviate competitive stress and anxiety. Finally, the study revealed that adolescent athletes involved in team sports were more 'prone to drink alcohol at least once a month' (Peretti-Watel *et al.* 2003: 1254).

While providing some revealing insights about drug use in sport, including the probability that it is widespread and multifaceted, the survey results we have summarised also raise some additional questions. For example, overall, do players and athletes actually use drugs more often than non-players and athletes? Surveys of university athletes point to some answers.

Surveys of students

At first glance it would seem reasonable to think that university students, and especially those who regularly play sport, would be thoughtful about drug use, whether performance enhancing or recreational. Notoriously, university students suffer from time-allocation problems at every turn and therefore cannot afford to undermine the capacities of their bodies and minds to work hard and long. In fact, the opposite appears to be the case. For example, North American college students describe alarmingly high rates of drug use. In one study, about 70 per cent of college students admitted to drinking alcohol at least once in the month before the survey, while 40 per cent reported intermittent binge drinking. In another study of US college students about 18 per cent used illicit drugs during the 12 months prior to the survey (O'Malley & Johnstone 2001).

The trends persist through further studies of college athletes, who have higher rates of substance use than college non-athletes, and generally engage in more high-risk behaviours (Wilson *et al.* 2004). Alcohol presents the case in point. For example, Ford (2007) concluded that college athletes used alcohol more freely than non-athletes. Where 49 per cent of male non-athletes engaged in binge drinking, the number increased to 54 per cent for athletes. Similarly, 29 per cent of female non-athletes claimed to binge drink while the figure for athletes climbed to 39 per cent. On the other hand, male athletes had lower cannabis and illicit drug use of 26 per cent and 12 per cent respectively, compared to 31 per cent and 16 per cent for non-athletes. The general theme of these findings was reinforced by results from Eitle *et al.* (2003: 211), who found that 'playing high school sport' was 'positively associated with alcohol use'.

Some evidence also suggests that different substance usage rates apply for different sports (Ford 2007). For example, while 75 per cent of male college ice hockey players indulged in binge drinking, the percentage decreased to around 41 per cent for track athletes and runners. Reported cannabis use also varied between sports, with a usage rate of 39 per cent for male ice hockey players, but only 19 per cent for basketballers. Differences emerged for females as well, with 47 per cent of soccer players binge drinking compared with only 27 per cent of runners. Based on the available evidence, drug usage varies considerably depending on the substance type and sporting code. Table 4.2 provides a summary of the responses for different sports.

Table 4.2 US college athletes reporting substance use by type of sport participation (% of total informants)

Type of sport team	Binge drinking by males	Binge drinking by females	Cannabis use by males	Cannabis use by females	Other illicit drug use by males	Other illicit drug use by females
Football	58		26		15	
Volleyball	48	40	24	25	15	12
Soccer	47	47	25	38	16	23
Aquatic	54	29	30	17	11	5
Basketball	50	37	19	23	9	9
Hockey	75		39		19	
Base(soft)ball	65	38	27	27	13	12
Running	41	27	16	24	10	12

Source: Ford (2007)

Australian studies of young people in a sporting context also depict an alarming level of alcohol consumption. Duff *et al.* (2004) discovered that 88 per cent of community sport club members regularly drank alcohol on club premises. Of those 88 per cent, around 23 per cent drank at their club on at least two occasions per week. Another 41 per cent said they drank alcohol at the club on average once per week. When asked to explain the cultural factors influencing the pattern of drinking at their club, just over 80 per cent of respondents agreed with the statement that 'drinking is a good way to relax after training or after playing a match', 79 per cent agreed that 'drinking is an important part of club camaraderie', while 77 per cent agreed with the statement that 'drinking is an important part of celebrating' after the game.

Although survey percentages offer important quantifications of substance use in sport, they reveal little of the deeper motivations, attitudes, and beliefs. As a result, researchers supplement their analyses with more probing qualitative methods.

In-depth qualitative research using player and athlete interviews

Although now dated, one of the more illuminating qualitative drugs in sport studies by Anshel (1991) provided a detailed analysis of 1) player attitudes to drug use, 2) the reported and perceived incidence of drug use in elite level sport, and 3) the motives for using different types of drugs. Anshel (1991) conducted a series of in-depth interviews with 126 elite American athletes, comprising 94 males and 32 females, over a three-year period beginning in 1986. His results showed that 64 per cent of all informants were aware of some type of illegal drug use in their sports. The figures were higher for male athletes (72 per cent) than for female athletes (40 per cent). When questioned about performance-enhancing drug use, 64 per cent of informants responded positively, while a marginally smaller 63 per cent indicated that some of their colleagues and teammates were taking a form of illicit recreational drug. The most commonly used drugs were perceived to be anabolic steroids, amphetamines, diuretics, painkillers and narcotic analgesics, cannabis, hallucinogens, and anti-depressants.

When informants were asked to explain what motivated them to take drugs, they referred primarily to the need to be competitive, such as becoming stronger and faster. The next frequently cited motivators included the desire to better cope with stress, the desire for fun, satisfying curiosity about the effects of different drugs, the importance of being able to better manage pain, and the need to avoid failure. The 11 most frequently mentioned motivators, together with the drugs used in association with, and linked to each motivator, are listed in Table 4.3.

Some significant gender differences were observed with these motivators. For example, where 29 per cent of male informants cited the need to increase energy and help 'psyche-up' as a prime motivator, the equivalent for females was only 1 per cent. The responses were reversed when it came to resolving personal problems as a motivator with just over 32 per cent of females citing it compared with only 1 per cent of males.

Table 4.3 Motivations for drug use

Motivating factor	Frequency of citation (%)
Need to be competitive, stronger, faster and higher	57
Need to relax and cope with stress	49
Desire to have fun and satisfy curiosity	35
Need to reduce pain	33
Fear of failure	33
Control weight	29
Overcome boredom	25
Build self confidence	25
Increase energy and arousal	23
Speed up healing process	20
Resolve personal problems	13

Source: Anshel (1991)

Despite the shortage of qualitative studies examining drug use in general amongst sporting populations, a few insightful studies have focused on steroid use in the broader community. One such study was undertaken by Petrocelli *et al.* (2008), which involved a series of semi-structured interviews with 37 steroid users who frequented gyms in various US states. The researchers began their study by noting the risky associations anabolic steroids generate. A number of earlier studies suggested that unsupervised steroid use, especially amongst teenagers, was associated with poor self-esteem, elevated rates of depression, a greater risk of attempting suicide, little knowledge of positive health issues, concerns about body weight, eating disorders, increased rates of violent behaviour, and an unhealthy obsession with being strong and building muscle (Petrocelli *et al.* 2008). The study confirmed that people who combined gym work with steroid use were doing it to build a stronger and more muscled body. It was also evident that nearly every one of the respondents felt the need to use steroids because their aspirations for a heavily muscled body were unlikely to be attained under a standard gym-work routine. These 'frustrations' led the informants to seek out substances that would enable them to 'get huge' and 'get ripped'. All respondents declared that steroid use not only helped them build muscle, but also made them feel more confident, and, surprisingly, often calmer and more rational, thus offsetting the claim that steroid use was unavoidably linked to 'roid rage'. The steroid users had, for the most part, a strong inner feeling of 'raw, primitive strength and enthusiasm' (Petrocelli *et al.* 2008: 1194–1195). Neither were the informants overly concerned about the risks steroid use posed to their long-term health. When asked to comment on side effects such as hair loss, infertility, aggression, and liver damage, they critiqued these claims as 'unbelievable … and intentionally manipulative on the part of the medical community and government' (Petrocelli *et al.* 2008: 1196). Instead, the major concerns voiced were first, the high financial costs of maintaining their training and supplementation regimes, and second, the problems they encountered with doctors when aiming to secure their supplies legally. For the older users, doctors had to be convinced that the request for synthetic testosterone and human growth hormone was important to restoring testosterone levels back to those associated with fit and active young men.

The impact of culture, values, and ethnicity

As the previous analysis confirms, drug use undeniably constitutes a problematic feature of sport around the world (Pound 2006). Of course, boosting sporting performance with drugs can hardly be considered a new issue given that a variety of stimulants have been used to increase endurance since the late 19th century. However, the range of drugs now available, and their capacity to produce demonstrable and significant improvements, reflects a new suite of problems (Dimeo 2007). The various types and choices of muscle-building compounds, stimulants, blood boosters, and beta-blockers now available would fill an entire pharmacy. But, anabolic steroids, amphetamines, and EPO reflect just the tip of the drugs in sport iceberg. We noted the evidence suggesting that an array of licit and illicit drugs also receive liberal use in sport, ranging from alcohol, nicotine, and narcotic analgesics, to cocaine, cannabis, barbiturates, and hallucinogenic cocktails (Pampel 2007). In fact, alarmed sport officials concerned about the apparent increase in drug use imposed a raft of sanctions and prohibitions culminating in the establishment of the WADA in 1999, and the publication of its inaugural Anti-Doping Code in 2003.

Numerous policy challenges, ideological issues, and unanswered questions accompany the data we highlighted earlier. The first question concerns to what extent drug use in sport occurs with more or less prevalence than in the broader community. The second question is to what extent drug use varies between different sports. The third question is whether or not there are any significant variations within sports.

To the first question, many commentators intuitively answer that drug use in sport will occur less than in general society due to its emphasis on getting the most out of the body and fine-tuning it to achieve optimum performance. Moreover, a strong groundswell of opinion proclaims that sport provides a sanctuary against drug use because of the values it inculcates into its participants. It does this by 1) demanding conformity, 2) ensuring close supervision, 3) producing bonding and cohesion, and 4) providing a structured forum for displays of masculinity. Sport thus lessens the need for young men, in particular, to build identity through anti-social and deviant behaviours (Eitle *et al.* 2003) and, as a result will build character leading to lower levels of alcohol and drug use.

Off-the-cuff answers to the second question acknowledge that different sports and games require unique structures and organisation, and revere distinctive histories and traditions. They go on to say that these variations produce practices and cultures where different skills, physical capabilities, and personalities will be required to ensure high levels of performance. For example, highly combative sports like football and boxing demand severe levels of aggression, while more aesthetic and technical sports like gymnastics and equestrian encourage precision and control. Taking a further step in the argument, aggressive and combative sports placing a premium on winning necessitate higher levels of drug use. Furthermore, sport's commercial scale affects drug use levels where performance pressure escalates in sports where player salaries are high, and extensive wagering takes place on the outcome of the game or event. It would also be reasonable to expect quite different cultures to be built around high-risk sports like ultimate fighting and motorcycle racing, on the one hand, and low-risk sports like lawn bowls and darts on the other.

A reflexive response to the third question predicts significant differences within sports. Players and athletes do not grow up in a social and cultural vacuum, but rather import attitudinal and behavioural baggage that has been accumulated through their personality development, family upbringing, adherence to ethnic expectations, the retelling and ceremonial re-enactment of cultural traditions, schooling experiences, the influence of peers, and the impact of religious education and socialisation (Bourdieu 1984). Additional influences arise as gender expectations and class distinctions play out. It would therefore be expected, for example, that players and athletes raised in strict households underpinned by strong religious and/or moral convictions would be less likely to use drugs than players and athletes bought up in libertarian households where parents exercised ambivalence about strict moral codes and organised religion (Richard *et al.* 2000).

Another interesting question considers how competing values play out in practice. Will, for instance, the values embedded in a player's ethnic identity override the customs and beliefs built into a particular sport club or sporting community? Or alternatively, does a player's core personality or sense of gender identity establish the main behavioural cues when decisions need to be made about using or not using certain drugs in a sport setting? Despite the salience of these questions, little research examines the ways in which ethnicity and religion influence drug use in sport. However, solid evidence indicates that in the wider community ethno-cultural factors mediate drug use in a number of important ways. For example, in a study of high school students in the US, respondents self-identified as African- and Mexican-American had the lowest reported levels of drug use, while those respondents who self-identified as white had the highest usage levels (Marsiglia *et al.* 2001). Miller-Day and Barnett (2004) replicated the results, reporting that nearly 51 per cent of white respondents aged 12 years and over had used alcohol in the past 12 months compared with 34 per cent of African-Americans. The study by Eitle *et al.* (2003) on college students also revealed higher levels of alcohol consumption by white respondents than by African-American respondents.

A survey of illicit drug use by McCabe *et al.* (2007) highlighted differences between various ethnic groups in a sample of US college students. Where the level of usage for cannabis amongst women was highest for white respondents at 38 per cent and Hispanics at 40 per cent, it fell to 25 per cent for African-Americans and 23 per cent for Asians. While the illicit (non-prescription) use of pain medication drugs was lower for all female groups, significant differences appeared between ethnic groups. The highest level was recorded by Hispanic respondents, who reported a 10 per cent usage level, and lowest amongst Asian respondents, who claimed a 3 per cent usage level. Illicit stimulant medication usage ranged from just over 7 per cent for white and Hispanic respondents, to a low of 1 per cent for African-Americans. Similar inter-ethnic differences appeared for college men, although the overall levels of use exceeded female rates. For example, while the usage level of cannabis was 46 per cent for Hispanics and 43 per cent for white respondents, it fell to 34 per cent for African-Americans and 28 per cent for Asians. For pain medication the highest usage level was 9 per cent for white respondents, while the lowest was 5 per cent for Asians and African-Americans. Finally, the usage level of stimulant medication varied from 9 per cent for Hispanics to 4 per cent for Asians.

An earlier study by Bachman *et al.* (1991) discovered similar differences based around ethnicity. High school students who used alcohol at least once in the previous 12 months reached a high for white males and females at around 88 per cent, with Mexican and Native-American males not far behind at just over 82 per cent. The lowest percentage usage occurred in the African-American female and Native-American female cohorts at 64 per cent and 61 per cent respectively. The variation in use was equally pronounced for cannabis. Whereas 42 per cent of Native-American males, 40 per cent of white males, and 38 per cent of Mexican-American males had used cannabis in the last 12 months, the usage rates for Asian males, African-American males and Asian males was 20 per cent, 18 per cent and 17 per cent respectively. The available data are summarised in Table 4.4.

Some severe gaps can be seen in the ethno-cultural evidence base. For example, the limited empirical data say little about sport-related correlations, and at this point it remains unclear what differences occur in sport settings. One of the few studies examining the interplay of sport affiliation and ethno-cultural identity was undertaken by Eitle *et al.* (2003), which noted a marginally greater level of drug use amongst young adult white males, as well as a significantly greater level of alcohol use. We can speculate on a number of possible explanations. First, perhaps playing high school sport for this cohort is a 'gateway to a hyper-masculine subculture' (Eitle *et al.* 2003: 210). Second, perhaps these results indicate a tradition of young white men following football, accompanied by a strong drinking culture (Bloom *et al.* 1997). Finally, perhaps the data reflect higher levels of alcohol consumption amongst white males in the wider society.

We should proceed carefully, however, since these results do not directly tackle the question of exactly how ethno-cultural identity impacts upon drug use in a sporting context, and to what extent the values and culture of sport clubs or associations will supersede the values, customs, and norms that different ethno-cultural groups bring with them to their sport practice. Many research gaps remain to be filled. We need additional research to determine just how strongly sport club cultures support, and indeed encourage, drug use activities, and whether sports participation actually increases drug and alcohol use. To phrase the research questions conversely, we

Table 4.4 Ethnic differences in average per cent drug use: USA (American) schools and colleges

	White male	White female	African male	African female	Hispanic male	Hispanic female	Asian male	Asian female	Native male	Native female
Alcohol	51	51	34	34	–	–	–	–	–	–
Cannabis	43	38	34	20	46	40	28	23	42	–
Pain killer	9	8	5	6	9	10	5	3	–	–
Prescription	43	42	36	25	48	44	29	21	–	–

Source: Bachman *et al.* (1991)

need to know to what extent the practice of sport and immersion in its culture acts as a buffer to drug and alcohol use, or whether it encourages it.

Conclusion

While the premises that sport's capacity to 1) build character, and 2) channel the energies of its participants into constructive social activities receive wide acceptance, the evidence we reviewed suggests otherwise. For the most part, the studies indicate that people who play sport, regularly hang around sport clubs, and use gyms to build their bodies, do actually use drugs, with a special emphasis on alcohol, more often that those who do other things with their spare time (Duff *et al.* 2004). Moreover, as noted previously, a longitudinal study by Peck *et al.* (2008) that followed US adolescents through to adulthood returned a similar relationship. That is to say, sport participation as an adolescent does not of itself lead to increased alcohol use. Alarmingly, however, when combined with 1) sport as a central life focus, 2) a preference for broader drug use, and 3) aggressive attitudes, sport participation actually showed a high correspondence with excessive levels of alcohol consumption.

Overall, sufficient evidence allows us to confidently claim that drug use – be it prescription, over the counter or illicit – takes place in all sorts of sport and physical recreation settings around the world (Alaranta *et al.* 2006). It occurs in school sport, although most of the data discussed here applies to American high schools where inter-school sport is highly valued, and where it contributes significantly to a school's reputation and financial viability. Substance use also seems prevalent in community gyms and fitness centres, with Europe and the US featuring prominently in the research findings (Simon *et al.* 2006). Drugs appear liberally in colleges and universities as well, where American studies show that both licit and illicit substance use is usually higher amongst athletes than non-athletes. Finally, drug use in all its guises is clearly a common practice in both elite amateur and professional sport, especially where strength and endurance constitute key success factors. Moreover, little evidence suggests that drug use in sport will fall any time soon. In fact, when substance use is expanded to cover dietary and herbal supplement consumption – including caffeine – then the usage rates increase exponentially (Bojsen-Moller & Christiansen 2010). It would be reasonable to think that more than 90 per cent of all people who play sport, irrespective of performance level, have used some form of supplement, drug, or related substance to get a competitive benefit at some time in their sporting lives.

In the next chapter we turn to the forces and factors that have shaped the current drugs in sport debate. From a regulatory perspective, we trace the evolution of participants' attitudes to drug use in sport, and see how these views are moulded by their values and previous experiences. We aim at a better understanding of key stakeholder's beliefs, and to expose the assumptions driving them. As with all policy formulation, however, we must first secure a firm intellectual grip on the underlying ideology, politics, and power structures that frame the drive to eliminate drugs from sport.

5 Player and athlete attitudes to drug use in sport

Introduction

The problematic nature of the drugs in sport issue raises questions about why some athletes and players willingly jeopardise their sporting careers by deciding to sidestep the anti-doping code and use banned substances. Despite the enormous amount of public discussion that goes on around sport's drug control programs and anti-doping policies, we have only a limited understanding of how players and athletes view policy issues, and even less about the contextual pressures that affect their decision making. While a study by Stamm *et al.* (2008) identified differences between public and athlete perceptions about drug use in sport, and revealed the seductive appeal of experimenting with banned substances, the results did not distinguish between different drug categories. Additionally, they only skirted around socioeconomic schemas that shaped perceptions, and did not ask informants to comment on specific drug policy initiatives. To assure a better understanding of the drivers of drug use in sport, the patterns of use, and who is more or less likely to use, we need to dig deeper into the drug problem, and examine the ways in which different sports and their participants are more or less responsive to the offer of specific substance use.

As we noted in the early part of Chapter 1, several kinds of drug-use problems exist in sport. First, there is the problem of performance-enhancing drugs such as steroids, stimulants, and 'blood boosters'. While these substances can increase the chances of a podium finish, they also increase the risk of sustaining negative health impacts including premature or even sudden death (Parisotto 2006; Savulescu *et al.* 2004). Prescription-based drugs may also be used to indirectly bolster performance, such as those employed to manage pain and injury, or to conceal the use of other prohibited substances. Second, there is the problem of illicit drug use by athletes for recreation and stress management. Although these drugs do not usually enhance performance, and therefore do not involve 'cheating', their prolonged use can undermine an athlete's physical and mental health (SAMHSA 2008), stimulating accusations of moral failure. Some illicit drugs are difficult to eradicate, since they link strongly to sporting culture and rituals, particularly at the elite level of sport (Washington *et al.* 2005). Third, there is the problem of the legal but entrenched use of alcohol in and around sport, mainly as a social lubricant, and typically as the principal means of celebrating victory. As a result, alcohol remains firmly embedded in the cultural fabric of sport clubs at the recreational and elite level (Burstyn 1999; Duff *et al.* 2004).

The dangers of drug use in sport are well rehearsed, but tend to fuse evidence with myth (Ingram 2004). In fact, conclusions about the effect of drugs can sometimes emanate from only a handful of studies focusing on extreme behaviour and taken out of context by media reports. For example, Parisotto (2006) reported that between 1988 and 1990 at least 18 European cyclists died from EPO. However, some of the cases were short on medical details. Overall, firm conclusions remain distant in the absence of reliable evidence documenting the adverse effects of performance-enhancing drugs and the prevalence of their use in sport (Yesalis *et al.* 2001). To complicate matters, the majority of published studies have focused on clinical populations or case studies which tend not to address the supra-therapeutic regimens and complex pharmacology employed by serious athletes (Dawson 2001). As Yesalis *et al.* (2000) counselled, the absence of evidence does not mean evidence of absence, an ongoing issue further obfuscated by the failure to separate out the impacts of different substances. The media and sport's governing bodies prefer to focus on steroids and EPO rather than alcohol and tobacco, while freakish muscles and breath-taking performances are more newsworthy than an exposé on retired and unemployable players with drinking problems and sedative dependencies.

Despite all the talk around the moral and health dangers associated with uncontrolled drug use in sport (Ingram 2004), and the hostile views that a majority of citizens have about drug use in sport (Moston *et al.* 2012) we still have only a meagre knowledge of the attitudes, values, and motivations of sportspeople who employ drugs to boost performance, relieve stress, and lighten moods. Yet understanding athlete and player attitudes should be the foundation upon which to build an effective policy (BMA 2002). At the same time, a number of conceptual papers aim to show the role that drugs play in sporting club culture, how players and athletes go about building their beliefs and attitudes about drugs, and the processes they use when deciding whether or not to use a specific drug (Donovan *et al.* 2002; Gucciardi *et al.* 2010, 2011; Strelan & Boeckmann 2003). In this chapter, we address the theory–practice gap by first, considering players' and athletes' attitudes to substances in sport, and second, by exploring their implications for policy development.

Contextual influences and athlete attitudes to drugs in sport

As we noted in the previous chapter, research has shown that young people who play competitive sport may actually engage in more drug and alcohol use than those who play little organised sport (Ford 2007; Hildebrand *et al.* 2001). Some evidence even reveals that substance use correlates to engagement in other high-risk consumption behaviours (Laure & Binsinger 2005; Wiefferink *et al.* 2008). For example, studies of college students in the US found that those involved in athletics engaged in more risky behaviours than non-athletes (Selby *et al.* 1990), with a special preference for binge drinking (Wechsler *et al.* 1997). Moreover, the focus in sport on team bonding on the one hand, and intensive competition on the other, makes it fertile ground for the growth of drug use and abuse. Brissonneau (2008: iii) remarked in a European Union (EU) discussion paper about the anti-doping policy, that 'if we take sporting events as they appear to exist in some Anglo-Saxon countries or in the United States, the rules of fair play do not seem fundamental and doping is ultimately only a means of enhancing performance, and thus improving the "spectator value" of the sport'. In other words there seems to be something about sport that makes it susceptible to various types of drug use.

Players and athletes are often reticent to revealing their views on substance use in sport (Petróczi 2007; Petróczi & Aidman 2008). As a result, it is unclear as to 1) how player and athlete attitudes to drugs in sport are initially formulated, 2) what factors have influenced those attitudes over athletes' formative years, and 3) the contextual and cultural factors that may have shaped athletes' attitudes during their playing careers. Exposing the contextual pressures and factors that influence attitudes to drugs in sport helps reveal which drug policy interventions may modify players' propensities to take drugs.

According to Backhouse *et al.* (2007), attitudinal research tends to be descriptive and not always capable of establishing the causal relationship between attitudes and behaviour. They also claimed that most research relies on under-developed theory and needs to explore the complex 'social matrix within which drug use becomes established' (p. 2). Similarly, Petróczi's (2007) predictive model seeking to connect goal orientation, win orientation, and competitiveness with doping behaviour, left a considerable proportion of behaviour unexplained. In this chapter we want to bolster the utility of attitudinal constructs by developing theory that might more effectively explain the role of sociocultural variables in shaping drug-use attitudes and drug-use behaviour. An understanding of athlete and player attitudes is central to an effective drugs in sport policy (BMA 2002).

A study by Donovan *et al.* (2002) identified six inputs that influence changes in the attitude-behaviour of athletes towards performance-enhancing drugs. These were first, threat appraisal, reflecting the deterrence factor or the cost of being caught; second, incentive appraisal, representing the benefits of drug use; third, reference group opinions, highlighting the importance of peer approval; fourth, personal morality, illustrating an athlete's views on right and wrong; fifth the perceived legitimacy of the drug authority's position; and finally, personality factors which are individualised variables linked to self-esteem and optimism. Consistent with the theory of planned behaviour (Azjen 1991; Azjen & Fishbein 1980), Donovan's team make two central assumptions. First, behaviour is basically rational and that athletes use information in a systematic manner to inform their decisions about drug use. Second, athletes consider the implications of their behaviour before they act. These twin assumptions represent a kind of rational intentionality, but they may not always be satisfied in practice, and consequently predictions about behaviour based on them will be compromised.

The importance of coercion, punishments, and the risk of getting caught were at the hub of Strelan and Boeckmann's (2003) analysis of behaviours involving performance-enhancing drugs. Using the concept of deterrence, which has its theoretical basis in criminal decision making, Strelan and Boeckmann (2003) specified four categories of salience. The first was legal sanctions, which can take the form of fines and suspensions. The second was social sanctions, which includes disapproval, ostracism by friends and colleagues, and potential material losses from sponsors who may elect to find someone else to endorse their products. The third was self-imposed sanctions that are bound up in the guilt, loss of face, and plummeting self-worth arising as a consequence of being publicly identified as a cheat. The final category was a health concern from the likely side effects associated with the chronic use of a specific drug. These costs and sanctions are then weighed against the benefits that might arise from the use of performance-enhancing drugs. Accordingly, '… deterrence theory assumes that individuals make conscious decisions that are well-informed, well-planned, rational, and designed to maximise the decision maker's best interests' (p. 178). Strelan and Broeckmann (2006) furthered the case for the salience of deterrence theory in their analysis of AFL players' moral beliefs around the use of drugs in sport.

The previous models focus on compliance with anti-doping policies rather than on actual substance use behaviours. As a result, they do not take into account the possibility that the choices made by athletes to use drugs may also be influenced by external factors including a sport culture centred on winning at almost any cost, the personal importance of fame and wealth, or the need to demonstrate masculinity. These factors can lead to decisions that may have elements of the unplanned and subjective where strong emotional energies overrun any calmly considered cost–benefit calculus. Strelan and Boeckmann (2003) conceded this weakness when they observed that a better understanding of athletes' motivations might highlight the utility of policy interventions which do not rely exclusively on threats and punishments. They acknowledged that the earlier in life an attitude towards drugs in sport is ingrained, the more likely it would endure. Equally, Stelan and Boeckmann noted that empirical work was needed on player and athlete career-path development in order to explain how values around drug use are formed. In addition, the problem has been compartmentalised into performance-enhancing drugs, illicit drugs, or alcohol and tobacco, but this divide does not withstand scrutiny given evidence from studies finding links between all three categories of use.

A more empirically based research project that addressed contextual issues was commissioned by what was then known as the ASDA, and undertaken by Mugford *et al.* (1999). Using an early version of Donovan's model as an investigative framework, Mugford's team unsurprisingly concluded that commercialisation has tempted athletes to take performance-enhancing drugs, particularly those at the elite level. The report observed that in general athletes are inwardly focused, individually motivated, professional in orientation, and driven by both financial and intrinsic rewards. Moreover, they want to achieve their personal best, are at the centre of their families and friends' lives, are not necessarily physically healthy, have changing needs over time, and believe that elite sport is not 'normal'. While the correlation between these traits and the motivation to use performance-enhancing drugs was unclear, Mugford's team concluded that most athletes view performance-enhancing drug-use as cheating. Nevertheless, some athletes will use performance-enhancing drugs in response to the pressure to win and the related perception of needing to compete in an unequal playing field. It was also noted that athletes who use drugs do so with considerable planning and forethought. Equally, those who do not take drugs are more likely to be influenced by the deterrents associated with getting caught, including the disaffection of the broader community.

While appreciating the insights embedded in these behavioural models, we propose that an athlete's decision to utilise substances is more complex and socially nuanced than the compliance-focused approaches suggest. In practice, numerous contextual factors affect an athlete's cost–benefit calculus by changing the values attributed to the central variables contained in these models. That is, many important contextual influences operate upon decisions made about sport and substance use, which create a differential impact depending on the substance and circumstance. In addition, the decisions taken by athletes are not necessarily rational or reflective of a keenly calibrated risk assessment. Our view is that a full account of substance use in sport requires the inclusion of contextual variables, some of which may inhibit use, and others which may lead to greater use. As we noted earlier, a popular view suggests that players and athletes undertake a rational cost–benefit analysis underpinned by a strong ethical framework in order to work out the balance between deterrents and incentives for the use of both licit and illicit substances. We do not support this mechanistic view of attitude formation and drug-use behaviour. Instead, we propose that players and athletes engage in morally unrelated, pragmatic assessments of what is permissible and what is not, and, as noted by Petróczi and Aidman (2008), are subject to the values, beliefs, and practices of their sporting colleagues. Their attitudes about substance use consequently form within a defined context where situational factors and the behaviour of coaches, peers, friends, and teammates represent powerful influences on their attitudes and practices.

Table 5.1 presents a taxonomy of attitudes towards substances in sport. In the table, substance performance has been divided into four levels of probable affect, from performance reduction at one extreme to performance enhancement at the other. Substance access is divided into three categories, and comprises illicit, prescription, and over-the-counter delivery.

Our own research data suggest that attitudes are contingent upon the ease of access to the substance, its performance impact, and the substance's social acceptance (Smith *et al.* 2010). In general, the use of banned performance-enhancing substances is viewed as cheating, although for different reasons between elite and non-elite athletes, with non-elite players and athletes being more moralistic. The use of 'hard' non-performance-enhancing recreational or illicit substances is viewed as foolish, but not morally reprehensible, by non-elite and elite players and athletes alike, while the use of legal non-performance-enhancing

Table 5.1 Taxonomy of athlete attitudes to substances

Substance access	Substance performance			
	Performance reduction	*Performance neutral*	*Performance maintenance*	*Performance enhancement*
Illicit	Heroin	Cannabis Ecstasy	Amphetamines Cocaine	EPO Steroids
Prescription	Tranquilisers	Anti-depressants	Analgesics	Beta-blockers
Over-counter	Alcohol	Inhalants	Vitamins	Caffeine Creatine

substances are acceptable to everyone. Legal performance-enhancing substances are viewed as essential for improving performance, especially for elite players and athletes. According to our studies (Smith *et al.* 2010), only an idealistic amateur or someone obsessively risk averse would hesitate at using controlled doses of legal substances such as caffeine or analgesics.

Contextual variables and attitudes towards substances in sport

When reflecting on our own studies of players and athletes, and studies of drug use in sport undertaken by other researchers, it appears that attitudes and use are shaped by far more than an individual calculation of the weighted costs and benefits of using and not being caught, using and being caught, not using and being caught, and not using and not being caught. The influences on player and athlete practices are both multifactorial and subjectively interpreted. They begin with the impact of micro factors that include a mix of intra- and interpersonal influences that shape personal identities and their subsequent expression. They move onto a range of so-called external forces that include people with expertise, authority, and a charismatic presence on one hand, and the rewards and benefits that come from achieving excellence on the other. Each receives attention in the following sections.

Personality and identity

While at a societal level an individual's personality and sense of identity influences behaviour (Burke & Stets 2009; Mittal 2006), the research evidence fails to highlight any specific traits and dispositions that correspond to particular attitudes about drug use in sport. The studies do not reveal any clear-cut association between a particular self-identified temperament, gender identity, life experience or moral code, and a particular position on substance use in sport. Although these factors appear to be intuitively relevant, particularly gender, it remains unclear as to how they affect attitude formation around drug use in sport. One recurring theme, however, is the self-driven nature of elite athletes and their early awareness of a single-minded desire to excel that had been evident from childhood. Recent studies have also shown that young people with high emotional intelligence ratings – which means they have a strong capacity for self-awareness, empathy, and impulse control – are likely to be low users of cannabis and alcohol (Claros & Sharma 2010), although the results were not explicitly related to sport. No studies we have encountered can corroborate the Donovan *et al.* (2002) claim that morality is a principal variable in shaping attitudes towards substance use in sport. Barkoulis *et al.* (2011) for example, found no relationship between an athlete's sportspersonship orientation – or moral sensitivities, if you like – and their past and future drug use.

People of influence

Five categories of influential people shape the ways young people make their way through the sports world, and provide space for substance use. They are: 1) family, 2) peers, 3) teachers, 4) coaches, and 5) heroes. Players and athletes are influenced by adult mentors during their sporting careers, and their attitudes to substance use are partly shaped by these relationships. Parents, and particularly fathers, loom large, playing instrumental roles in shaping their children's sport-career paths, a view consistent with previous work in sport development studies (Lenskyi 2003; White *et al.* 1998). However, parental influences are not necessarily positive. Fathers can be excessively ambitious for their children, pressuring them to become highly competitive. For elite athletes, in line with Strean and Holt (2001), the most important influencers are coaches, usually the first elite level coach. Coaches are seen as not only inspirational and knowledgeable, but also to be obeyed without question. Dunn *et al.* (2010) on the other hand, reported that a majority of the elite athletes they studied believed testing for use, together with punitive suspensions, were likely to deter drug use.

Early sporting experiences

In concert with influential people, critical early sporting experiences also shape attitudes towards substances, with the key issues including the places where athletes grew up, the sports they participated in, and the level of competition they played in. These all constitute points highlighted by Morris *et al.* (2003). The more frequently the early experiences of players and athletes emphasised serious competition, the more likely those players and athletes would hold permissive attitudes towards both licit and illicit performance-enhancing substances.

Commercial pressures

Amongst the commercial pressures impacting upon attitudes to substance use, the most prominent are professionalisation, sponsorship, rewards, and fame. These factors help explain the pressures to use performance-enhancing substances. Financial incentives tempt players and athletes to use various substances, whether available over the counter, secured by prescription, or obtained through illegal trafficking. Some empirical studies on the impact of commercial incentives on player and athlete behaviour have reflected similar issues (Bairner 2003; Belk 1996; Gems 1999; van Bottenburg 2003). The drive to secure a competitive edge is strongest where the rewards – psychic, social, or financial – are highest.

The commercial imperative highlights the common attitude amongst elite players and athletes that despite the pressure to be role models and good sporting citizens, the pressure to use performance-enhancing substances lies not with players and athletes, but with societies that created cultures of relentless competition and grand expectations, where a competitive advantage, regular record-breaking performances, and constant improvement is only possible with the use of banned performance-enhancing substances. This theme threads its way through the commentary on global and professional sport (Wenner 1998; Wilson 1990; Wright 1999). As Waddington (2000b: 4) observed: 'sport is played for higher, sometimes much higher stakes, whether these be economic, political-national, personal or a combination of all three'. Sport's consequent corporatisation has created a world where players' salaries and tenure conditionally respond to high and sustained levels of performance (Stewart 2007a). Consequently, drug use is embedded in the world of sport since the combination of pressure to perform and the availability of so many drugs that can improve athletic performance – even if only at the margin – provide the perfect conditions for regular substance use.

Sporting culture

No one single sporting culture exists, even within a single sport or competition. A sport's culture – its prevailing values and beliefs – builds around a number of features, which nearly always includes masculinity, risk taking, and aggressiveness. The prominence of these features will, in turn, influence a participant's attitudes towards substance use. Values and beliefs form in complex ways, unique to individual sports, and influenced by not only the above factors, but also by the physical performance requirements of the sport. A sport's demands can focus on 1) power and strength (e.g. weightlifting), 2) endurance and stamina (e.g. road cycling or triathlon), or 3) technical skill (e.g. sailing). It can sometimes also involve a distinctive combination of all three (e.g. gymnastics). Other features that can shape a sport's culture include the level at which it is performed (i.e. elite or non-elite), whether the sport is team or individually based, its level of medicalisation and scientisation, and the degree to which it values social engagement over success and winning.

Given the different ways in which sport activities can be structured and organised, the radical cultural differences hardly seem surprising. For example, elite cycling involves strong medical and scientific support, including a heavy reliance on physicians, support therapists, sport scientists, biomechanists, and engineers (Brissonneau 2006; Waddington & Smith 2008). For elite cyclists, licit performance-enhancing substances like caffeine, analgesics, and nutritional supplements present a way of life, essential for completing long and gruelling road races, and an accepted part of the culture of competitive cycling. Another

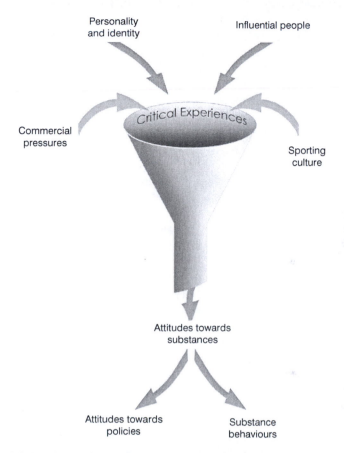

Figure 5.1 A conceptual model of contextual variables and attitudes towards substances in sport

example can be found in football codes where, at the non-elite level in particular, the social club, being the distribution point for alcoholic beverages, is a focal point for building camaraderie and ensuring social cohesion. This emphasis on social networking and social capital investment is accompanied by a heavy drinking culture that includes a few weekly beers at one end of the continuum, and regular binge drinking at the other. A model of contextual variables and attitudes towards substances in sport appears in Figure 5.1.

Attitudes to substance use in sport

Based on the findings from our own research amongst others (Smith *et al.* 2010; Stewart & Smith 2010), most serious athletes and players concede that drug use of one sort or another constitutes an ongoing feature of their chosen sports. Furthermore, we found that substances have been used in sport over a long period of time, although in recent years the varieties of substances, and their potency in improving performance, have increased significantly. Alcohol has become embedded in sport club culture because of its unique capacity not only to bring people together in a convivial atmosphere, but also to dissipate stress and anxiety, particularly after the completion of a highly competitive sporting contest. Illicit recreational drugs have secured a place in sport for the same reasons. In addition, elite players and athletes generally take a positive stance towards the use of painkillers, anti-inflammatories, and any other substances that get them back on the field of play as quickly as possible. From our perspective there was little player and athlete anguish associated with the ethics of drug use. If, for example, a performance-enhancing substance was removed from the prohibited list, most elite athletes would be immediately interested in testing its performance efficacy. It therefore becomes a question of not whether it is fair, equitable or appropriate, but whether it is legal or prohibited.

The research further indicates that non-elite athletes are far more rigid and moralistic in their views than their professional and high-performing counterparts. Non-elite athletes agree with WADA's policy platform on performance-enhancing substances, maintaining that athletes should not be allowed to utilise drugs that artificially bolster performances, harm their health, or undermine the 'spirit of sport'. While non-elite athletes seem comfortable with stronger penalties for transgressors, we found that elite athletes take a more practical approach towards performance-enhancing substances where banned equals 'wrong' and legal equals 'opportunity'. For example, strong painkillers and some narcotic analgesics are acceptable, along with caffeine because they are not banned, even though dosages might be unhealthy and potentially dangerous. For elite athletes, moral issues are not particularly relevant, which partly explains why their attitudes appear to be unconnected with their personality or identity. Elite athletes see themselves operating in a sporting culture supporting the use of medical treatments and substances to sustain performance. Furthermore, coaches and managers have a vested interest in getting injured players back on to the field of play in the shortest possible time, and will employ a cocktail of painkilling and anti-inflammatory drugs to speed up the process. Earlier studies have similarly found that athletes receive their first substances from trusted sources close to them (Laure & Binsinger 2005).

A similarly pragmatic position holds regarding illicit non-performance-enhancing substances, which are viewed as a problem only in so far as they are illegal, and that their use can incur penalties. Most athletes and players maintain a casual attitude about 'lighter', recreational drugs such as Ecstasy and alcohol. Occasional use of party drugs and bouts of binge drinking are dismissed as being essential to relieve stress or act as a social lubricant. Although elite athletes drink less frequently than their non-elite counterparts, they express a greater inclination to overindulge. Elite athletes possess obsessive natures that exacerbate a 'work hard, play hard' mentality where everything is pursued to the limit. Our position consequently supports previous studies finding that sport cannot only increase the risk of injury, but also encourage binge drinking, and undermine an athlete's long-term health prospects (Ford 2007; Loland 2002; Long & Sanderson 2001; Waddington 2000a).

Any analysis of attitudes to substances in sport begs the questions as to how these attitudes were formed in the first place, and what were the major factors that shaped them. As noted earlier, player and athlete attitude formation about drugs in sport is a complex amalgam of factors, incorporating sporting culture, its commercial scale, the influence of others, critical incidents experienced through the player and athlete life cycle, and the level at which players and athletes perform their sport.

Sporting cultures that emphasise victory and dominance above all else represent an especially powerful influence on attitude formation. This is closely linked to the drive for performance improvement, constant competition, the stress it creates, and the importance of team bonding and group cohesion. Additionally, the celebration of heroic deeds via sport encourages excessive alcohol consumption (Peretti-Watel, Beck & Legleye 2002), which further reinforces the need to damage the body in order to exude masculinity. Elite sporting pursuits demand performance at the outer limits of physical capacity where risk taking and pain tolerance become core capabilities. Our position lends support to the work of Dodge *et al.* (2008), which showed that higher outcomes on 'Muscularity Drive' and 'Muscularity-oriented Body Image' scales differentially predict performance-enhancing substance use. More ambiguous is the best way of conceptualising the role of masculinity in choosing to use substances. It is unclear, for example, whether the same cultural and contextual factors encourage different substance choices. The usual response leads to the conclusion that the use of substances in sport signals individual weakness and lack of any moral compass, and should be solved with more vigilant policies for intervention, control, and punishment. Mixed messages under which it may or may not be appropriate to use substances add further layers of complexity to the drugs in sport conundrum. It is counterproductive to declare that athletes will be punished for using substances that help them cope better with the pressures of sporting life, while encouraging everyone else in society to ease their problems with pharmaceuticals. The ambiguity becomes reinforced when the anti-doping code determines that one over-the-counter drug with significant side effects is acceptable, while another illicit drug with no greater side effect is banned and considered indicative of a serious moral failing. Meanwhile, coaches, journalists, and fans not only demand that players always perform at their best, but also remind them that underperformance is the greatest possible failure. Confusion compounds and the mixed messages escalate when off the field of play, alcohol and tobacco act as essential lubricants to the social world of the sport machine.

It is especially clear to us that sport's commercialisation functions as an important element in explaining drug use in sport, operating as a subtle and insidious force on player and athlete behaviour. As Li *et al.* (2001) concluded, sport is driven principally by the need for new revenue opportunities, and under these conditions the market becomes a powerful determinant of behaviour in which the use of performance-enhancing substances becomes a logical option for players and athletes intent on winning (Aghion & Williamson 1999).

Critical incidents and experiences also play a crucial role in forming and strengthening attitudes, which in part explains the ways in which players' and athletes' attitudes differ between different drugs types. Take, for example, the differing views found between elite and non-elite athletes on the use of substances to improve athletic performance. For the former, performance-enhancing substances were a concern only because they were banned, and this pragmatic logic led them to report that non-banned performance-enhancing substances were not a significant ethical concern. For elite level participants, substances were an essential part of training and competition, but for non-elite participants, the use of performance-enhancing substances is morally wrong because they provide an unfair advantage, compromise the good name of sport, and undermine athlete health. Such observations offer lessons for strategic interventions at pivotal moments in athletes' decision-making life cycles. In this context, we suggest a revisit to Petróczi and Aidman's (2008) model since it suggests that deterrence strategies focusing on the use of prohibited substances are less effective than those initiatives targeting contextual factors at those career stages of athletes' professional lives when they are most vulnerable to external influences.

Policy implications

As we have previously noted, the prevailing policy approach to substance use in sport rests on the proposition that stiff sanctioning will deter drug use and remove 'drug cheats' from competition (Canadian Centre for Ethics in Sport 2005; Henne 2010; Pound 2006; WADA 2004a). This policy position emanates from WADA, supported by the IOC and United Nations Educational, Scientific and Cultural Organization (UNESCO), and is dutifully followed by national and international sporting bodies all over the world. Current global drug controls aim to regulate drug use by 1) specifying a list of prohibited drugs, being careful to distinguish between those drugs that demonstrably improve on-field performance, and those drugs that are illicit and undermine the health and well-being of players and athletes as well as tarnishing the reputation of sport itself, 2) listing a raft of suspensions and fines for players and athletes who have been found to have used, possessed, supplied, or trafficked any banned substances, and 3) providing for a tribunal-style process whereby allegations are heard, judgements made, and penalties imposed where appropriate.

This highly legalistic structure rests on a particular type of behavioural understanding of the drug-use decision-making process. It starts with an underpinning view that when individual players and athletes balance the costs and benefits of substance use, they do so logically, allocating significant weight to the morality of the decision, the impact on their health, and the shaming and loss of face that comes with being caught. A similar philosophical position can be found in the analysis of Donovan *et al.* (2002) and Strelan and Boeckmann (2003), which were reviewed in the early part of this chapter. However, our position – which is more in line with the Petróczi and Aidman (2008) model – show that the decision-making calculus used by players and athletes is far more abstract and non-linear, reflecting a range of contextual variables. We suggest that substance use in sport is neither a matter of rational decision making, nor one of fundamental morality. Despite the appeal for moral certitude made by WADA in their policy statements

(Henne 2010; WADA 2003), our analysis remains consistent with recent evidence suggesting that testing is ineffective at trapping athletes who use drugs (ACC 2013: USADA 2012). In fact, the evidence shows that despite the sanctions, shaming, and health threats that players and athletes face, many continue to use because of the performance, financial, and social rewards they expect to secure (BMA 2002; Smith & Stewart 2008).

We consequently suspect that the current WADA inspired system of prohibitions and punishments does not provide an effective deterrent to drug use in sport (Caulkins & Reuter 2005; Jiggens 2005; Mosher & Yanagisako 1991; Voy 1991). Paradoxically, it is both too narrow, since it says little about alcohol, and too wide, since it tries to cover drug use that does little to improve performance. At the same time, scope remains for an overhaul of current policy, where a range of options are worthy of consideration (Backhouse *et al.* 2007; BMA 2002; Kayser *et al.* 2007; Miah 2006; Rushall & Jones 2007; Savulescu *et al.* 2004). At present, the politically safe policy approach means taking the moral high ground, and arguing that illicit and/or performance-enhancing drug use conflicts with sport's fundamental values of fair play and participating within the rules. Essentially, WADA delivers a 'judgemental' form of policy making (Parsons 1995: 371) that increasingly involves 'legalistic strategies' underpinned by discourses that fuse 'crime-control' with moral certitude (Henne 2010: 321).

Given the increasing level of research into the drugs in sport problem, it is now appropriate to give greater weight to evidence-based policymaking where current 'interventions' and policy options are 'systematically reviewed' and a range of models are evaluated (Pawson 2006: 7). An evidence-based approach to policymaking is consistent with our own research, which suggests that many player and athlete attitudes do not fit either the conservative assumptions supporting current anti-doping policy, or its rigid structure and highly punitive sanctions that signal zero tolerance. We now see a range of options emerging, which include 1) an essentially laissez-faire policy where drug use is permitted so long as the drug has no adverse side effects and users have registered it with a monitoring agency, 2) the above policy supported by social marketing campaigns to educate players and athletes about drug use in sport, with the aim of modifying their behaviour, 3) a regulatory model that aims to minimise harm to athletes by requiring counselling and support for identified problem drug users, 4) a policy based on a system of rewards for complying with an anti-doping code, 5) a policy that sanctions the use of performance-enhancing drugs only, 6) a policy that sanctions the use of both performance-enhancing and illicit drugs, and 7) a policy that sanctions all drug use in one form or another, including the most insidious and harmful of all, which is alcohol. While the tough stances built into options 6) and 7) are intuitively appealing, mainly because they take the moral high ground and leave little room for counterargument, they fail to take into account the highly competitive context in which sport takes place and the rights of players and athletes to have a life outside of sport. We suggest that the balance between the credibility and reputation of sport and community expectations on one hand, and the rights of players and athletes to pursue sporting excellence with an appropriate duty of care provided on the other, has not yet been struck. We expand on these policy options in later chapters.

Conclusion

Having reflected on our discussion of the 'whats', 'hows' and 'whys' of drug use in sport, we are concerned that current drug control policy stands on shaky conceptual ground. Fundamentally, it fails to concede that sport, by its very structure and operation, encourages and in many instances, demands drug use (Waddington 2000b). We contend that drug use in sport will remain endemic for the following reasons. First, sport operates as a highly social institution, fertile ground for the growth of substances like alcohol and illicit party drugs that bond people together and make them feel happy, if only for a brief series of hedonistic moments. Second, sport mandates fierce competition, and attracts people who need to play hard and long both on and off the field. Third, sport rewards winners leading to a powerful incentive to do whatever it takes to secure a winning edge. Substances that speed up the recovery process, allow players and athletes to participate while injured, build strength, improve endurance, and heighten arousal, all command great value. At the elite level in particular, many players and athletes have incorporated drug use into their sporting lives, and see it as a part of their sport experience, and what it means to be an elite performer. In short, it has become a matter of routine and habit. WADA driven drug use policy, being underpinned by a punitive theory of behavioural change, fails to understand this reality. Every year a clutch of internationally recognised athletes admit to some type of substance use for which they never tested positive.

In this chapter we reinforced the importance of addressing the contextual factors that shape the attitudes of players and athletes to drug use in sport. We argued that players and athletes do not run their lives in an economic, social, or cultural vacuum, and nor do they undertake systematic cost–benefit analyses where they allocate weightings to likely outcomes associated with a range of substance-use scenarios. Rather, the culture of sport lends itself to drug use through its emphasis on competition and sociability, and the use of drugs to enhance both sets of experiences. Herein lays the vexing problem for policymakers. It is one thing to impose coercive rules that punish players and athletes for wanting to secure an advantage, reduce anxiety, alter their mood, or modify their temperament. It is another thing to thwart these ambitions, which are regularly sought within a sport setting. The challenge for sport policymakers is to change the culture of sport so that it takes a more circumspect line on drug use, and persuades virile players and athletes that it is not always in their interests to engage in activities that gain them significant short-term kudos while leading to a serious disability or illness in the longer term.

Substance use in sport is neither a matter of linear and logical decision making nor one of fundamental morality. Like Bloodworth & McNamee (2010), Breivik 2009, Lambros *et al.* (2011), and Petróczi (2007), we acknowledge that doping-specific attitudes and beliefs are instrumental to doping behaviour, but we do not claim to know whether they are causes or consequences of other associated attitudes and behaviours. A better understanding of drug use in sport is only likely to emerge from more systems-based frameworks, or what Mazanov (2009) refers to as 'cosmopolitan' research, that breaches disciplinary boundaries and focuses on the economic, social, and cultural complexity and interdependency of substance use in sport.

Part II
Framing the debate

6 Neo-liberalism and the cult of individualism

Introduction

As the previous two chapters have revealed, drug use has become embedded in sport practices around the world. Consumption involves a broad spectrum of drugs and related substances, some of which are used to enhance performance and recovery, some of which are used to ease discomfort and relieve stress, some of which are used to cope with the pressures of daily life, and some of which are used to simply kill time. Usage also involves a spread of spaces and places. It begins with school and community sport, where young people first encounter drug use through licit substances like alcohol, caffeine, and tobacco. In some instances, these household substances open the door to 'soft' illicit drugs like cannabis and the off-label use of prescription medicines. As some young people advance up the sport performance ladder, they become exposed to illegal substances that seductively guarantee to build muscle, lose weight, increase bodily strength, produce an increase in energy levels, enlarge one's work capacity, dismantle frustrating endurance barriers, increase pain and discomfort thresholds, and generally provide some sort of competitive edge. The seduction heightens commensurate with sport's highly competitive ethos and its scale of rewards – both economic and symbolic – that flow from accessing its top echelon.

Sport's high-performance culture delivers many outstanding sporting achievements leaving ordinary fans not only aghast, but also filled with a deep sense of awe. For many people, and especially the sport purist, any admiration can be soured by a suspicion that remarkable achievements in sport received assistance from more than just hard work, mental toughness, flawless skill, and being extremely well prepared. At the same time, some leeway seems to be granted to players and athletes who have suffered adversity, battled on despite lesser natural talent, demonstrated monk-like discipline, or have just 'done it tough' in their personal lives.

In this environment the idea of a 'level playing field' seems uncontentious, since no one individual or team should hold so great an advantage that they will inevitably win. Equally, we accept that on any given day some players and athletes will enter the field of play with a greater capacity to achieve than others. A bit of luck is fine, access to clever technology is acceptable, a platform of sport science is permissible, coaching expertise is taken for granted, and the use of special dietary supplements is seen as essential attention to detail. However, a line in the sand is often drawn at this point, and, as a result, any assistance that arises from drug use becomes unacceptable. Simply put, where drugs get used, the 'fair play' line has been crossed, relegating the offending athletes to the level of cheats. However, this begs the question as to who decides where the line should be drawn, and who decides what constitutes real or authentically 'superior performance' on one hand, and fabricated and contrived 'superior performance' on the other. This issue has presented a thorny dilemma for sports officials to ponder.

The WADA experiment

For sport officials, the dilemma-breaking event occurred in 1999 with the establishment of the WADA. WADA became the global voice for the drugs in sport problem, identifying itself as the official anti-doping 'watch-dog' (Horvath 2006: 358–359). The 2003 anti-doping code WADA introduced immediately became the global benchmark by containing a template for anti-doping policies in international and national governing bodies for sport (WADA 2003). Three key objectives underpin WADA's mission and policy initiatives: first, to protect athletes' fundamental rights to participate in drug-free sport; second, to promote health, fairness, and equality for athletes worldwide; and finally, to ensure harmonised and effective anti-doping programs at the international and national level incorporating standardised approaches to detection, deterrence, and prevention (WADA 2003). The Code contains a list of banned substances including performance-enhancing drugs like EPO, human growth hormone, anabolic androgenic steroids, the more powerful anti-inflammatory drugs, and stimulants, as well as a range of non-performance enhancing, illicit drugs like cannabis, Ecstasy, and cocaine. Exemptions exist in the Code for athletes who can demonstrate a legitimate therapeutic purpose for a banned substance (WADA 2003). In these instances, athletes with documented medical conditions like asthma can request a therapeutic use exemption from their national anti-doping agency and national sport governing body.

In WADA's world, drugs that enhance performance are immediately corralled, since using drugs to help secure a winning edge constitutes cheating, which, as noted before, will not be tolerated. Second, drugs that constitute a risk to the athlete's health also fall into the anti-doping net. According to WADA, sport organisations hold a duty of care to the athletes who participate in their competitions, and as a result must be protected through prohibitions on substances incurring health risks. While the first two criteria seem reasonable, the third is more contentious since it outlaws any drug that violates the 'spirit of sport'. Under the Code, the spirit of sport encapsulates the ideals of Olympism, the celebration of the human spirit, fun and joy, courage, teamwork, excellence in performance, respect for the rules and other participants, dedication and commitment, character and education, community and solidarity, ethics, fair play, and honesty (WADA 2003: 3). These values have been conflated into the initial WADA slogan of 'play-true', and its current mantra of 'drug free sport'. Moreover, if a drug meets two of the above three criteria, it will be listed as a banned substance (WADA 2003: 15–16).

Under the WADA Code, drugs like EPO, human growth hormone, steroids and stimulants both enhance performance and constitute a health risk, and therefore remain subject to a banned status. While cannabis, Ecstasy, and cocaine do not enhance performance, they do introduce health risks. Crucially, because their illegal use undermines the spirit of sport, they too are banned. In fact, any illicit drug is, according to WADA, contrary to the spirit of sport since it diminishes the good name and public image sport commands. Caffeine, however, no longer appears on the banned list. Although caffeine improves performance, it is not illegal, does not incur health concerns, and fits the play-true requirement. Neither is alcohol or tobacco / nicotine a major problem under the WADA Code since they also fit the play-true requirement in that they do not for the most part improve sporting performance, remain freely available to adults, and form an integral part of sporting club culture.

The WADA Code also distinguishes between drug use in-competition or in-season, and drug use out-of-competition or out-of-season (WADA 2003). Performance-enhancing drugs are banned both in- and out-of-competition, which means all year round. Illicit drugs, on the other hand, are banned only in-competition or in-season (WADA 2006). Technically, players can take illicit drugs out-of-competition without a penalty being imposed by their governing body. By widening the anti-doping net, WADA has gone beyond the initial desire to ensure a level playing field, moving firmly into territory concerned with maintaining the good standing and reputation of the sport, where brand equity reigns sovereign. However, brand protection comes at the cost of athlete autonomy given the intense scrutiny where every misdemeanour is interrogated and every slightly deviant social practice is investigated.

The WADA model also preferences punitive values in order to secure compliance through rigid penalties combining shaming with fines, disqualifications, and, in extreme cases, lifetime exclusion from sport participation. For a first violation involving the use or possession of a prohibited substance, players may be disqualified for up to two years, while for a second violation players can be disqualified for life (WADA 2003). Some prohibited substances hold 'specified substance' status, and include medicinal products that players may inadvertently use with no intention of securing an improvement in athletic performance. In these cases a first offence may generate a reprimand or warning, a second offence will incur a two-year suspension, while a third offence will lead to a lifetime ban (WADA 2003). At the most extreme, the penalties for trafficking can incur a four-year to lifetime suspension even for a first infraction. Illicit drug use delivers less severe penalties, but still employs a punitive model. For a first offence players face a 3 to 12 month suspension, for a second offence the penalty can extend to two years, while for a third offence players can be banned from the sport for life.

Why WADA?

The previous discussion explains where WADA came from, and what it wants to achieve, but it does not address its efficacy and the costs of managing the regulations. In order to undertake such an analysis, we first need to provide some 'thick' background material that sets the scene. We believe this groundwork is pivotal because policy does not emerge in an unfettered, politics-free environment. In order to properly understand the WADA Code's rationale, and to explain why this approach presently enjoys so much traction with policymakers in sport, despite being the least-preferred choice amongst most health professions, it is crucial to place it in a proper political, historical, and ideological context. This is done in the following section, together with an evaluation of current drug control arrangements.

Why drugs?

Sport has changed radically with the confluence of commerce and science, reshaping the structure and conduct of sport as well as the ways in which coaches, conditioners, and players view the concept of high performance. In particular, the role played by drugs and supplements in achieving high-performance goals has dramatically transformed (Cooper 2012). For the first 50 years of the 20th century, drug use in sport was spasmodic. However, since the late 1950s an explosive growth in the global pharmaceutical industry has delivered a multitude of substances capable of both improving performance and enhancing quality of life. Over the same period athletes were subjected to enormous performance pressures and success incentives. These two developments provide the context for understanding how drug use – both actual and perceived – began to infect international sport during the 1960s and beyond.

Drug use in sport was not viewed as a serious problem until the late 1970s and early 1980s, when, as we recorded in Chapter 3, an entangled web of international sport incidents, including the dominance of East German athletes at the 1976 and 1980 Olympic Games and allegations of rampant drug use by American athletes at the 1984 Games, generated global condemnation and a media frenzy. The IOC responded by recommending the formation of WADA, and since then testing for illicit and performance-enhancing drug use has become a stalwart part of the elite sport landscape.

We have now reached a situation where sport around the world is infested with drug use, while also being surrounded by a whole raft of rules that ban their use. So, what is it about contemporary society that impels a need to regulate drug use in sport so comprehensively, but also build the structures for their delivery and use?

The changing sport's landscape

Drugs have been embedded in sport's culture for most of its 20th century progress, but over the last 35 years, a raft of performance-enhancing, illicit, prescription, and over-the-counter drugs have complemented the traditional use of alcohol and tobacco. This breakout of exotic drug use instigated a punitive array of unsuccessful government-driven regulations aimed at eliminating their use. What has driven the shift from indifference to intolerance, and why has the punitive ideology proven so ineffective? In order to answer this question we must examine the ways in which the political, economic, and sporting landscapes have changed, and how these changes have impacted upon the values and attitudes of players and athletes as well as officials and policymakers.

Four tasks immediately come to the surface. The first is to identify the pivotal social and economic transitions that have occurred in the developed sporting world over the last five decades. The second is to understand how changing cultural and social attitudes cleared a space for high levels of prescription and illicit drug use despite the existence of laws that severely limit their use in most nations. The third is to track the ways in which this oppositional ideology of permissible drug use has permeated sport. The final issue is to critically examine the ways in which governments and sport officials have utilised a punitive, zero-tolerance ideology to counter the drugs in sport problem.

No singularly acceptable story can be told when it comes to tracking the evolution of drug use in sport. However, it can be safely observed that sport has experienced a radical overhaul over the last 50 years (Shirato 2007). Many critics of these changes suggest that the corporate world undermined the spirit of sport, selling it out and causing its deleterious transformation towards greedy, commercial excess. According to this view, sport's revolution began in the early 1960s when, in response to fracturing social values and authority relations, it discarded its moralistic pretensions and repressive formality, and locked itself into the world of business (Brohm 1978; Hoch 1972). By the 1990s a number of professional sport leagues had blossomed as amateurism abandoned its snobbish appeal and sport went about building its commercial brand value. Corporate signage saturated the major venues, and players were marketed as celebrities. Excitement, speed, the 'quick media grab', and sensory bombardment became the defining features of the spectator experience. Not only did spectacular and dramatic contests become just as important as skill and aesthetic display, fans also narrowed their attention spans, and were no longer bound by a parochial tribalism. They assumed multiple identities that could shift from a premier European football club one week, to a suburban rugby team the next. Branding and image making were used to attract fans and corporate supporters. Television programmers became the final arbiters on how the game should be organised, scheduled, and played (Foster *et al.* 2006; Whannel 1992). Table 6.1 illustrates the nature of these changes by highlighting the features of traditional sport on one hand, and contemporary sport on the other.

Sport, once mainly about friendly competition, participation, buoyant spectatorship, and the pleasures of playful physical contests, had become both a business and a lucrative arm of the entertainment industry. So how did all this happen? What lured drugs and supplements into a world that was once, and above all else for most sport watchers and commentators, a field of self-effacing virtue, a place to sacrifice oneself to the greater good of team success, and a forum for inculcating discipline and building character?

Table 6.1 Traditional and contemporary sport distinctions

	Traditional sport	*Contemporary sport*
Game structure	Emphasis on conventional game plans, rules are sacred	Traditional practices challenged, rules modified to provide better spectacle
Team leadership	Conservative leadership, preference for proper technique and risk avoidance	Adventurous leadership, preference for tactical innovation and 'surprise' move
Values and customs	Amateurism and fair play, acceptance of custom and tradition, deference to authority figures, sport as character building	Professionalism, questioning of traditional practices, challenging of authority figures, Sport as a professional journey
Organisation and management	Central control, player subservience, part-time support staff	Diffusion of authority, consultation with players, full-time specialist staff
Financial structure	Commercial viability dependent on gate receipts, small contribution from radio, arm's-length relationship with 'business'	Commercial dependence on sponsorship, television rights, endorsements, merchandise and gate receipts, sport is a 'business'
Venues and facilities	Stadiums provide standardised seating, standing room, and basic catering, viewing complemented by radio broadcast	Customised seating with reserved sections, private boxes with customer service and full hospitality, video screens used to replay critical incidents
Promotion	No active promotion of league or teams, dependent upon publicity from radio and newspaper reports, the game and its traditions will sell itself	Direct promotion to target markets, television the dominant promotional medium, games tailored to suit needs of specific customer/spectator groups
Viewing of game	Live match attendance	TV audience dominates
Spectator preferences	Display of traditional craft, skill and ritual, emphasis on the contest and tribal rivalry	Eclectic blend of entertainment, amusement, emphasis on the spectacular image and the big experience
Fan loyalties	Singular and parochial loyalty to teams and players	Multiple loyalties, shift between sports, and from local to global
The sport market	Fans and members comprise a common undifferentiated mass, they see sport in the same way, need to provide only one experience.	Fragmented and niche markets, 'boutique' sports, fans have multiple ways of viewing and participating, need to provide a variety of experiences
Coaching and training	Rigid adherence to formularised interval training and repetitive practice	Blend of science support and naturalistic training that involves a variety of training modes

A new context for sport

The short answer declares that sport has become overwhelmingly corporatised, with this corporate-sport frame driving a rapid growth in the use of a prodigious range of drugs and supplements. But commercialisation does not fully explain the scale of drug and supplement use in sport, the timing of its expanded use, and its subsequent regulation. Sport's commercial environment provides a strong architecture for understanding the sporting context within which players and athletes extended their drug and supplement use. However, it does not reveal the broader social, cultural, and political forces at work, and at what times they emerged as key factors in shaping sport's overall momentum and strategic shifts. In order to reveal how these forces and factors impacted over time on drug use on one hand, and the imposition of drug-use rules and regulations on the other, we have built our analysis around a model of social development that integrates neo-liberalism with hyper-modernism.

Neo-liberalism constitutes an economic and social belief system – or ideology, if you like – which insists that progress occurs when individuals receive the freedom to act out their entrepreneurial fantasies without being constrained by the 'heavy-hand' of government control (Hall 2011). The position is founded upon a libertarian philosophy that goes back to the days of the 19th century English social philosopher and political economist, John Stuart Mill, who argued that an open and tolerant society can only exist where people enjoy the right to live as they want to as long as it does not infringe upon the freedom of others.

During the 1980s neo-liberalism emerged as the dominant ideological driver behind western democracies, having been relegated to the margins of economic theory by 'Keynesianism', 'guided capitalism', and the welfare state from the late 1940s to the 1970s (Armstrong *et al.* 1984; Beaud 1984; Yergin & Stanislaw 1998). National economies became less regulated, with government enterprises privatised, trade barriers removed, banking deregulated, global trade expanded, minimum wages loosened, and safety nets for the poor and disadvantaged tightened. The forces of market liberalism and technological progress assumed priority. Western democracies entered a stage of hyper-modernity, where the desire for constant change, accelerated product obsolescence, and consumption was used to define roles, social positions, and status relations.

At one level these changes proved liberating since they allowed people to reinvent their personal and social identities (Mittal 2006). But they also compromised any sense of continuity and social connectedness. This shift in economic and social structures led many critics of capitalism to claim that modern western nations had entered a new but dysfunctional phase in their development. Modernity was based on a rational view of the world: the assumption that real production centred on tangible products, the importance of clearly defined hierarchies and strict lines of command, the central place of nuclear families, fidelity and lifelong marriage, and an ideology that prioritised the government regulation of markets. In contrast, this new world appeared to be dominated by constant change, an obsession with the consumption of leisure goods, a breakdown of all types of hierarchies, the privatisation of government services, and the hedonistic drive for more individual freedoms. Undeniably, a major break with the past had transpired.

By the 1980s the western world had entered a post-modern phase, described in the 1990s through the term 'late modern'. However, by the beginning of the new millennium, the notion of 'hyper-modern' had become a popular characterisation of what by this time represented a clear and significant break with the past. Gilles Lipovetsky (2005), one of the most enthusiastic proponents of the hyper-modern thesis, argued that western society had entered an age of excess where rampant consumerism was tempered by an expansion of individual rights and responsibilities. According to Lipovetsky, hyper-modernity emerged from the social wreckage of the 1980s that accompanied the breakdown of traditional hierarchies and authority relations in the 1960s and 1970s. Individual attitudes and behaviours escaped the constraints of rigid social and moral demands. Meanwhile, the family, church, and state fell subservient to a smorgasbord of choices, options, and entertainment decisions. One option resided with how to best define one's sense of self, and how to go about constructing an identity no longer imposed by virtue of family customs, religious affiliations, cultural traditions, or occupational group attachments. Another option centred on the problem of what to consume. Lipovetsky suggested that adopting hedonistic lifestyles where individual pleasure and social status were dominant proved the most compelling response. Paradoxically, the twin problems of identity and life choices were fused by the explosive use of consumption practices to build an identity around a lifestyle (Featherstone 1991; Mittal 2006; Slater 1997).

Not everybody benefited from newly won freedoms. While some people prudently assessed their lifestyle choices and enhanced their quality of life using technological advances and economic growth, others found themselves engulfed by a 'destructive irresponsibility' (Lipovetsky 2005: 8). In a world stripped of its traditions, responsibility for social and moral action now resided with the individual, and the pronouncements of authority figures, who hitherto had moral clout, were dismissed as puritanical and prejudiced. Many individuals felt overwhelmed by the moral and social vacuum they now occupied, and their escalating desire for easy pleasures and self-aggrandisement crowded out any commitment to self-discipline, the public interest, and the idea of the greater good. And, threading its way through this putatively moral malaise, disconnection from the past, and uncertainty about the future, was an insidious uneasiness manifest as chronic and sometime disabling anxiety.

Unfortunately, anxiety was the price to be paid for securing a social and economic system that valued freedom and individual rights above all else. Neo-liberalism, and the competitive hedonism that accompanied it, sometimes undermined the protection previously afforded to disadvantaged communities by the welfare state, and very often destroyed the social institutions that had provided meaning and security. On the other hand, it enshrined human rights as a fundamental ideal, and enabled resources to be allocated to a diverse network of agencies and groups dedicated to the protection of these rights. In this new neo-liberal, hyper-modern society, the forces that had previously opposed a more liberalised modernity, such

Table 6.2 Modern welfare statism versus neo-liberal hyper-modernism

A cultural perspective	
1 The collective good	The private interest
2 Common universal values	Multiple values
3 Real and the permanent	The hyper-real and the disposable
4 Hierarchy of values, tastes, and quality	Cultural relativism
5 Form, depth, and substance	Image, surface, and style
6 Unity and order	Fragmentation and uncertainty
7 Clearly defined lines of authority	Authority to be negotiated
8 Single ascribed identity	Multiple manufactured identities
9 Sacred traditions	Superficial nostalgia
10 Leisure as an experiential pastime	Leisure as a consumable commodity

An economic and political perspective	
1 Specialisation	Multi-skilling
2 Mass production and consumption	Variety and segmentation
3 Rigidity and central control	Flexibility and distributed power
4 Durability	Planned obsolescence
5 Public ownership	Private ownership
5 Protective barriers for favoured industries	Increased competition for all industries
6 Tightly regulated markets	Deregulated markets

as communism, socialism, collectivism, and cooperativism, had been rendered ineffectual. These great alternative visions had collapsed under the weight of rampaging individualism married to identify-defining consumerism. The ways in which neo-liberalism and hyper modernism have re-shaped contemporary society are illustrated in Table 6.2.

Table 6.2 illustrates the sociopolitical frame within which we locate our subsequent analysis. We use this frame to guide our mapping of the ways in which sport performance fused with drug and related substance use to deliver the sport's world a transformative experience. In undertaking this mapping exercise, special emphasis is given to 1) the pharmaceutical industry, and the development of products that can be used to improve athletic performance, 2) cases and examples of how these products were utilised by players and athletes, 3) the ways in which government and the broader community worked through the drugs in sport issue, and 4) how these processes shaped community attitudes and relevant policy arrangements. We use these four themes to track the evolution of drug use in sport, and to periodise its transitions and turning points. For each transition we will identify the key forces and contextual factors that both incited additional drug use, and shaped its regulation

Periodising drug use in sport

While the dating of the periods identified below is open to argument, the long-run trends remain clear. First, drug use in society had expanded exponentially over the last 100 years. Second, there has been a steady stream of controls aimed at not only severely restricting some substances, but also banning their use completely. Third, every attempt to eliminate drug use by introducing bans and criminal sanctions has been an abject failure. Finally, this failed policy has, in large part, been the result of an underlying neo-liberal agenda which maintains that individuals have the right – even an obligation – to achieve their own levels of personal excellence by whatever reasonable means they can.

Period 1: 1901–1945

The period from 1901–1945 witnessed the rapid industrialisation of the UK, Western Europe, North America and Asia-Pacific with automobile production driving economic growth. At the same time it included two major wars, the worst economic depression ever experienced, and the revolutionary establishment of communism as an alternative political system to capitalism (Beaud 1984). Despite these major economic and political upheavals, the overall standard of living increased, and as a result people's leisure practices became both more diverse and commodified. Sports participation and recreational drug use constituted two such practices.

It was also a time in which two important but conflicting social movements took hold of people's time and energies. The first was the 'physical culture movement', which pushed the view that bodies were a type of machine, and if properly trained, sensibly fuelled, and effectively maintained, would not only look better, but also, by working harder and longer, 'delay fatigue' (Dimeo 2007: 29–30; Rigauer 1981: 9–11). The second was the 'temperance movement', which viewed drugs, and especially alcohol, as precursors to an immoral and socially dysfunctional life of spouse beating, vice, crime, prostitution, addiction, and, in the end, destitution (Dimeo 2007; WHO 2011).

Despite the strong public face of the temperance movement, drug use expanded during the early part of the 20th century (Jay 2010). While the pharmaceutical industry was in its infancy at this time, drug use around the world had increased in response to an exponential growth in international trade. The use of opium, extracted from opium poppies, and cocaine, derived from coca leaves, had soared. At the same time concern was growing about the consumption levels of proprietary medicines, some of which contained dangerous elements like arsenic, opium, morphine, and cocaine. Consequently, many governments ratified the Hague Convention of 1912–1914, designed to impose importation controls over both opium and cocaine (Escohotado 1999). Similarly, western governments adopted the 1925 Geneva Convention on Opium and Other Drugs. Controls over opium and cocaine were strengthened. Meanwhile, cannabis importation fell under bans in many nations, followed by legislation declaring the unauthorised use of cannabis a criminal offence. However, the most dangerous drug at this time remained alcohol. Despite its prohibition in the US in the early part of the century, alcohol continued its place in the majority of the world as the recreational and social drug of choice (Courtwright 2001; WHO 2011).

Sporting clubs were havens for the heavy consumption of alcohol, bolstered by long-standing traditions where all classes mixed sport and socialising. Governments enforced no laws and sought no interventions to make drug use in sport illegal. Neither were there any moral objections to their use from the general public or media. This was an era where government viewed sport – and leisure in general – as a private matter, and something that should operate in a mostly unrestricted way. Unlike its preparedness to control the levers of the commercial world, most western governments' interests in sport stayed tangential in that they recognised the ways it could contribute to a sense of national identity, and how it may be used to prepare young men for military service (Hoberman 1992).

Internationally, sport was emerging as an important social institution over this period, increasingly used to build a strong sense of national identity. On the world stage – and in particular through the Olympic Games – winning teams and individuals could secure high international standing, while successful players could grab fame and fortune. Some players and athletes used substances they believed could enhance their performance levels. In particular, European coaches, players, and athletes experimented with newly emerging pharmaceuticals, and demonstrated a growing command of the science behind sporting performance. Sport in Europe – especially in Germany – became an exemplary space for undertaking physiological research, an emerging scientific discipline. Experiments explored variations in human physical performance on the back of more widespread drug usage – especially stimulants of various types – in the 1920 and 1930s (Dimeo 2007; Houlihan 1999). As unexpectedly impressive physical performances hit the headlines, vibrant debate about the role of drugs in sport also bubbled to the surface (Hoberman 1992).

Despite the developments in leading nations within Europe foreshadowing the professionalisation of sport, other parts of the western world remained locked in a largely amateur ideal guided by the hand of IOC president, Avery Brundage (Senn 1999). Science and sport continued unconnected, and under the ideological umbrella of amateurism, even the idea of regular, intensive, and regimented training seemed strangely ignored for improving performance (Miller 1992). Meanwhile, alcohol use enjoyed a strong association with sport in most parts of the developed world mainly because it held a favoured role as a social lubricant and as a culturally embedded sport club practice. Of course, alcohol use had more to do with sociability and stress release than improving athletic performance.

Period 2: 1946–1959

Unlike most European nations, the US, Canada, and Australia recovered quickly from the Second World War, regaining their economic health by the late 1940s. While markets and private corporations still heavily ruled the burgeoning economies of the west, some pockets of state-owned resources played important roles (Beaud 1984). In addition, on the back of the Keynesian economic model, which proposed heavy government intervention through public spending in hard times, a number of large nation-building projects commenced. In new-world nations like Australia, Canada, and South Africa, European migration contributed to increasingly cosmopolitan societies where plentiful work accompanied economic growth (Armstrong *et al.* 1984). Conservatism still reigned for the most part. However, where church going was admired, alcohol was rigidly controlled, book and film censorship was strictly enforced, and politicians deferred to the state, or in the case of the Commonwealth nations, to the mother country, Great Britain.

While most elite sport competitions throughout the world were disbanded during the Second World War, the war actually provided a breakthrough in the quest by players and athletes for substances that would secure them a reliable and consistent competitive edge. The first serious performance-enhancing substances delivered improvements to soldiers' mental awareness and resistance to fatigue (Verroken 2003). A number of articles appeared in the *War Medicine* journal extolling the virtues of amphetamines as means for increasing work capacity and reducing sleep requirements (Dimeo 2007). After the war, amphetamines were sold to the public as medicines. Products like benzadrine, an inhaler used for head and nose congestion and bronchial problems, became universally popular (Houlihan 1999). These and other stimulants quickly diffused to the world of sport. Road cyclists, for example, found stimulants especially useful in delaying fatigue and offsetting pain during a long day in the saddle. Fausto Coppi, the legendary Italian rider and dual Tour de France winner, admitted to using amphetamines, and also claimed that nearly every other professional cyclist in Europe did during the 1940s and 1950s. Stimulants had infiltrated Olympic sports by the early 1950s. At the 1950 European championships, the Danish rowing crew faced allegations of amphetamine use, while at the 1952 Winter Olympics some skaters became ill after 'excessive use of amphetamine stimulants' (Hunt 2011: 7).

The other drugs that changed the face of sport performance during this period became known as anabolic steroids. As synthetic forms of testosterone, anabolic steroids were first formulated by chemists in Nazi Germany, and used to improve the fighting capability of its soldiers during the war (Dimeo 2007). In 1945, Paul de Kruif, an American physician, published the first book on testosterone, which he titled *The Male Hormone*. In his book he labelled synthetic testosterone as the path to 'chemical manhood' on the grounds that it would not only build strength, but also enhance the sex drive. Taken with its capacity to turn insipid youths into 'real men', de Kruif thought testosterone should be more appropriately called 'sexual TNT' (Taylor 1991: 15). De Kruif also understood that testosterone would enhance sporting performance, and presciently anticipated that '… it would quickly filter into the sports industry in a big way (Taylor 1991: 16).

De Kruif was correct, of course. Nine years later a form of synthetic testosterone was used to enhance the performances of Soviet weightlifters at the 1954 world championships. In response, the US team physician, John Ziegler, secured an agreement with the CIBA pharmaceutical company to produce a similar compound that could be used by American athletes. CIBA duly obliged, and in 1958 released a product branded as Dianabol, designed not only to 'help burn victims and geriatric patients', but also 'build strength and muscle mass' in elite level athletes (Hunt 2011: 9). American coaches and athletes were initially sceptical about the ability of these new pharmaceutical products to improve performance. For example, American weightlifting team coach, Bob Hoffman, having experimented on his own body, described the results as unimpressive (Hunt 2011).

The developments in sport drug use should be juxtaposed against the massive growth in anti-anxiety drug use in the broader community, especially in the US. In 1955, Wallace Laboratories released Miltown, an anti-depressant medication that quickly became a mass-consumption product crossing every occupational, social, and cultural divide. Testimonials flowed from famous people, the most striking from the internationally renowned surrealist painter, Salvador Dali. He famously announced that Miltown delivered 'tranquillity', 'was a precondition for genius', and that 'I am the only artist who has this' (Tone 2009: 76).

Despite the rapid growth in social and sport-related drug use in North America and Europe, Australian and Asian players and athletes were not early adopters of either amphetamines or anabolic steroids. While sports were a dominant pastime, and while most Australians took great pride in the international successes of its national teams and individual athletes, amateurism was still embedded in the Australian sporting ethos (Cashman 1995). By the end of the 1950s the drugs of choice for most Australians were still alcohol and tobacco. Unlike the US, the use of anti-depressants spread thinly across the community, and cocaine and heroin caused only minor social irritations. Apart from the caffeine squeezed out of tea and coffee, stimulant use was also trivial. This state of affairs reflected a society that valued stoicism, deferred to authority, and denied itself instant pleasure. High-profile international events were poised, however, to bring drug use in sport to the sleepier parts of the western world, including eventually, the sleeping dragon.

Period 3: 1960–1972

During this period alcohol maintained its position as a taken-for-granted part of the sport–leisure experience, while tobacco consumption continued to escalate. In fact, not only was cigarette smoking socially approved, but tobacco companies increasingly used sport events and sport clubs to promote their products to great effect (Taylor 1984). In addition, the idea that drugs could relieve stress, and make people more gregarious, started to be seen alongside the view that they might also improve performance.

At the international level a number of incidents highlighted the increasing tendency of players and athletes to take drugs to acquire a winning edge. For example, the risks associated with drug use starkly took shape in 1960 at the Rome Olympic Games when Danish cyclist, Knud Jensen, collapsed and died when competing in a road event (Todd & Todd 2001). While the cause of death was not conclusive, he had taken a heavy dose of amphetamines prior to the event.

Two crucial implications emerged. First, it forced sporting authorities to treat drug use more seriously than they had in the past. The IOC in particular sought advice on how to best establish a drug-testing regime for its summer and winter Games and world championships. By 1965 a broad regime of testing protocols were in place, and for the first time included tests for a range of anabolic steroids. Second, Jensen's death signalled to other elite athletes that a wide range of potentially dangerous substances were available and could be used to secure a winning edge. Instead of scaring athletes off, the Jenson incident brought about the opposite effect. For example, at the 1968 Mexico City Olympic Games, a vigorous drug testing program implemented 700 tests. While only two positive amphetamine tests were identified, a 'disturbing number of unknown chemicals' appeared in the urine of athletes (Hunt 2011: 36). Commentators and media critics immediately agreed that this 'increase in drug use ... was ... startling' (Hunt 2011: 37). As it turned out, the anomalies uncovered during the Mexico Games were really just the tip of the performance-enhancement iceberg. Later it became clear in the face of 'incontrovertible proof' (Hoberman 2001: 237) that the staggering successes of the East German athletes at both the 1972 Munich Games and the 1976 Montreal Games could largely be attributed to a program of mass doping (Hunt 2011). So, how can we explain this explosive growth in drug use in sport?

First and foremost, the 1960s and early 1970s featured an explosive growth in drug use in the broader society. For example, in the US, the anti-depressant market continued to grow, and in 1968 Hoffman-LaRoche launched Valium – the benzodiazepine blockbuster – which became the 'the greatest commercial success in the history of prescription drugs' (Tone 2009: 153). While initially targeted at women as a remedy for 'neurotic singles, worn-out moms, and exhausted business women', Valium later enjoyed success with men as a way of neutralising the anxiety and discontent that were considered the price 'men paid for their success' (Tone 2009: 157–159). Valium's impact proved monumental as it had shifted perceptions about pharmaceuticals, effectively normalising their use.

The other popular drug during this period was cannabis. Alternatively known as marijuana, it became the symbol of the protest movement during the 1960s and early 1970s, labelled the drug of 'peace' due to its mood lifting and anger dissipating capacities. A proliferation of different synthetic opiates and narcotic analgesics were also developed in the 1960s, including pethidine (under the Donaltin brand name), methadone, ketobeidone, and dextromoramide (branded as Palfium) (Escohotado 1999). While drug use in broader society gained credibility and utility, sport continued its commercialisation. Driven by improvements in communication technology, and especially television, a new and lucrative form of mass spectatorship and entertainment infused sport (Shirato 2007).

Period 4: 1973–1982

The western social trend of expanding social freedoms was reflected in the shifting patterns of substance use. Cannabis in particular had become a popular recreational drug, and although its use had been initially flamed by an alternative counterculture, usage spread across all nations, classes, and lifestyles. Global heroin use simultaneously swelled to dangerous levels along with LSD (Courtwright 2001). Tranquiliser use spread through middle class communities with particular prevalence amongst stay-at-home women in affluent western nations. Valium became the tranquiliser of choice for millions of women who wanted to better manage 'housewives' disease', which according to some commentators, constituted a 'nagging anxiety besetting daily life' (Tone 2009: 184).

Given the explosive growth in illicit and prescription drug use during the 1970s and early 1980s, it should come as no surprise that sport, too, gravitated towards drugs as agents of individual enhancement. From an international perspective, mounting pressure on sport's coordinating authorities to act on drugs in sport had escalated with a growing concern that the staggeringly impressive performances by East German Olympic athletes at the 1976 Montreal Olympic Games was fuelled by systematic drug use, especially anabolic steroids. In fact, the evidence pointed to an endemic and programmatic use of drugs to bolster sporting performances in Eastern Bloc communist nations. Equally, athletes in North America and Western Europe were lunging down the same performance-enhancement path, but with limited monitoring and oversights of their drug prescriptions (Hunt 2011). As it turned out, western nations proved equally culpable. Numerous scandals emerged involving national Olympic Committees, which were trying to deny the scale of usage with intermittent success. Complicit governments understood the importance of spectacle and showed a willingness to tolerate deception and hypocrisy in order to reap the political benefits of international sporting success. Furthermore, considerable political energy was applied to opposing the South African national government's apartheid policy, and in boycotting the 1980 Moscow Olympic Games (Senn 1999).

Sporting officials responded through strident critiques of drug use. The critiques predictably vilified the Communist Bloc nations for their drug programs while lamenting the disadvantages endured by upstanding western athletes. In short, while social barriers in and around illicit drug use were dismantled, the putative moral barriers to drug use in sport remained strong and visible.

Period 5: 1983–1992

By the early 1980s drug use to enhance sporting performance had become a commonplace practice. The 1980 Moscow Games had already been labelled the 'Junkie Olympics', while in 1983 a number of athletes withdrew from the Pan-American games rather than face a possible positive test under a newly implemented drug-testing regime (Houlihan 1999: 313).

A type of free market had consequently emerged for performance-enhancing drugs in which the desire for self-improvement had not only permeated the world of elite sport, but also embedded itself in the minds of community sport participants and gym users (Assael 2007). Clearly, substances that could build a better looking and functioning body while shaping a more confident personal and social identity were in high demand, symptomatic of a society where traditional models of social control had been jettisoned in favour of a more libertarian ethos. In fact, the early 1980s also marked a turning point in the way most western nations organised their economic and social affairs. Not only did economies transform, but so too did sport, since the period reflected the serious beginnings of a neo-liberal inspired hyper-modernisation driven by economic growth (Hall 2011). For the most part, western governments pursued market deregulation, predicated on the assumption that free markets deliver optimal outcomes in terms of price and efficiency. Consequently, governments reduced their core functions and introduced policies aimed at freeing up markets, with deregulation of financial markets heading the list of initiatives.

Pronouncements and policies of deregulation in the commercial sphere were also adapted, in part, to the cultural and social spheres. Sport development and athlete pathways were being systematised through nationalised training institutes and talent identification programs (Green & Houlihan 2005). At the same time, the application of science to enhance sporting performance was escalating rapidly, ironically also providing fertile soil for a drug culture to grow. The greater irony was that the catalyst for most western talent institutes and programs began with the superior performances of athletes from the highly regulated command economies of Communist Europe, many of which received their winning edge from drugs.

The relatively half-hearted and sometime benign response to this rampant drug use in sport did not last for long. National authorities for drug testing sprang up in the middle and latter part of the 1980s, assuming the power to expand testing regimes, undertake research into improved testing for banned substances, and educate athletes about ethics, health problems, and sanctions associated with drug use in sport (Hunt 2011). With these initiatives as counterparts to the IOC's uncompromising stance, national governments legitimised their roles as drivers of drug regulation management in sport. They consequently provided the policy framework and funding arrangements to establish the infrastructure to support a credible antidoping industry in the absence of such expertise, experience, or resolve from sport more broadly (Houlihan 2003). A parallel development occurred as the IOC resolved to strengthen its drug regulation program in the wake of the Ben Johnson scandal at the 1988 Seoul Olympic Games, and the subsequent report issued by the Dubin Commission. The imposition of tighter regulations over players and athletes delivered an additional ironic twist since it coincided with a comprehensive deregulation of many other parts of society. But, as it turned out, this was not the end of the ironies because for every industry that was privatised, or taken out of direct government ownership and control, governments also established bureaucracies to regulate them. Sport proved no exception. As it turned out, most western governments failed to follow through on their neo-liberal agendas when it came to drugs in sport regulation. Instead of letting the market have its way, so to speak, governments and the governing bodies for most sports ultimately came down on drug users like a ton of bricks (Pound 2006).

How can we explain this contradiction? The first point to note is that neo-liberalism was an ideology that had its origins in economic and political theory. As a result, it was mostly applied to the world of commerce and industry, and was rarely viewed as a guiding principle to be applied to sport. The second point to note is that policymakers have always demarcated economic and business affairs from social and cultural affairs. This meant that a politician could be a liberal on industrial issues, but a rigid conservative on social issues, as tended to occur with drugs in sport. Neo-liberalism was driven by a belief that economies and markets perform best when entrepreneurs and businesses pursue their commercial interests freely, without the 'iron fist' of government crushing their creative energies. However, neo-liberalism had little to say about sport, other than imply that it offered a creditable means of inculcating discipline and character into budding business professionals, preferably men.

From this position neo-liberalism played into the hands of the politicians and sport officials who felt that drug use in sport, especially when used to secure an improvement in performance, signposted a serious character flaw, and flagged a preference for hedonistic pleasure over hard work (Pound 2006). At the same time, many drugs were already threaded into the weave of sport: alcohol and tobacco constituting the two most prominent fibres. It also raised the issue of how a more hard line and purist reading of neo-liberalism might view drug use in sport. A transparent interpretation would suggest that individuals perform best when they remain free to choose what they can read, what spiritual belief system they adopt, who they have relationships with, and what substances they want to ingest, so long as they do no harm to others. This point will be addressed in the latter chapters of the book when policy options are discussed in more detail.

Period 6: 1993–1998

Arguments about what to regulate and what not regulate aside, this period was characterised by a rampant neo-liberalism in the world of commerce. Financial markets were deregulated and government institutions privatised. Meanwhile, corporations dispensed with enterprise agreements and hired employees on individual employment contracts. Under this model, labour markets were freed up, and workers could negotiate their own preferred bundle of benefits. While fine in theory, in practice it sometimes meant that workers traded-off many traditionally hard-won benefits like annual loading and special leave arrangements for a marginal increase in weekly pay. But, this was all a part of more libertarian society where self-interest dominated vague ideas about social benefits and the collective good.

Many prominent professional athletes became infected with a neo-liberal urge, and increasingly endorsed any strategies that could be used to extract an improvement in performance and productivity. Science was delivering enhanced sporting performances all the time, which covered a diverse array of disciples, with physiology, biomechanics, cognitive science, coach education, and nutrition leading the way (Cooper 2012). In such a ruthlessly competitive environment, athletes not at the cutting edge were off the podium. Under these conditions, even the stringent and systematic enforcement of government anti-doping policies led by the IOC were unable to curtail many athletes' decisions to cross the legal boundary, and enter 'banned substance' territory. At the same time, this was all the incentive sport officials needed to take drugs in sport policy inexorably towards a zero-tolerance, abstinence-based model, where the only indicator of success was no-use as proven by a clean test.

Period 7: 1999–2007

From 1999 to 2007, western economies grew rapidly in response to the emergence of China as a superpower to rival the US. At the same time the ideals of socialism had lost their ideological edge, and the Communist projects of North Korea and Cuba had become political parodies. Where possible, markets were used to deliver services, and public–private partnerships increasingly offered the platform to undertake large infrastructure projects (Heywood 2003). Sport had also been comprehensively corporatised during this period, and professional sport leagues attracted record crowds. However, social policy was still soundly based within a regulatory framework.

In terms of drug policy, the trend kept with the neo-liberal implication that drug use reflected a sign of moral weakness and a flawed character. More rather than less regulation proved the norm, with an emphasis on the punitive controls (Pound 2006). Additional resources allocated to stronger drug control and tougher enforcement led to an increase in drug seizures. A zero-tolerance approach to drug trafficking became a popular political declaration while, in some nations – and the US especially – schools were targeted for micro monitoring.

The structures for handling the drugs in sport problem received some bureaucratic gravity with the establishment of the WADA in 1999. WADA's formulation established a milestone in the evolution of drugs in sport policy, mainly because the IOC used its international commercial muscle to force sovereign governments to implement and subsidise IOC antidoping policies. That is, the IOC, with support of the WADA, sought to influence governments to bear the cost of being compliant with an antidoping code in order to be considered as a potential host nation for the Olympics. This spurred the nations with the most to lose in terms of international prestige and commercial interests – the top ranking 20 per cent of countries typically win 95 per cent of the medals – to do what they could to secure the 'economic enhancement' injection promised by the Olympics (Houlihan 2003). Compliance with IOC antidoping codes represented a necessary cost to access funds arising from the Olympic movement and its mega sport events. In this sense, governments tended to be compliant rather than committed to antidoping for political and economic purposes (Houlihan 2003). In economic parlance, the IOC had found an effective method to 'rent seek', and get someone else to bear the cost of their antidoping plans.

During this period players and athletes used drugs more than ever before. More allegations were made, and more scandals were exposed. The worst allegations were levelled against elite level international cyclists in the aftermath of the 1998 Tour de France, when the Festina team was investigated by the French police after Customs officials found large amounts of anabolic steroids, EPO, and growth hormones 'in their possession' (McKenzie 2007: 3). A number of Festina team members, including the team doctor, were found guilty of trafficking in illegal drugs and using prohibited substances (Voet 2001). Following from the doping allegations exposed during the 1996 Atlanta Olympic Games, the IOC proposed to establish an international agency that could develop and enforce a global anti-doping code, culminating in the formation of the WADA in 1999 (Hanstad *et al.* 2008; Park 2005).

Period 8: 2008–present

The economic meltdown of 2008–2009 and the emergence of a global financial crisis may have sent Europe and the US into deep economic recession (Sachs 2011), but it did little to sway sport's focus away from the need to maintain both its integrity and community building capacities. Increasingly from the late 2000s, obesity and diabetes nudged governments' health policy radars, accompanied by a growing concern that declining levels of sport participation were partly responsible. Additionally, most western national governments persisted with their existing regulations over drug use, assured by WADA's 2009 amendments to its anti-doping policy that they remained essential in protecting the health and well-being of their citizens. Any consideration that illicit drugs should be decriminalised was not just misplaced, but thoroughly irresponsible. It was therefore not surprising that drug use in sport policy continued to be punitive and underpinned by a zero-tolerance belief system.

As noted in Chapter 3, this period bore witness to the most serious drug-use investigation ever. In late 2012, the world's greatest competitive cyclist, Lance Armstrong was found to have doped during most of his career. The USADA report irrevocably tarnished every one of Armstrong's first places in the worlds' most demanding and prestigious road race, the Tour de France. He was stripped of his medals, forced to pay back his prize money, and deserted by his sponsors. Worst, Armstrong resigned from his cancer-support foundation. While Armstrong's reputation was shredded to bits, scores of other cyclists admitted to having used, a number of team directors, doctors, and physicians were implicated, and the whole episode confirmed that drug use in professional road cycling was endemic, and had been for at least 50 years (Hamilton & Coyle 2012; Walsh 2007c). And, when every other significant incident is also revisited over this 50-year period, it becomes evident that drug use, in all its forms, was not an aberration. Rather, drug use was embedded deep in sport's collective psyche.

Conclusion: the path forward

This snapshot of drug use in sport over the last 50 years highlights several salient issues relevant to our subsequent discussions. First, it tells us that sport has a colourful history of players taking substances to make them perform better, become more engaged, feel less stressed, and cope with their social worlds more effectively. Second, it tells us that drug use in sport should come as no surprise, since its use is embedded in broader society, and is consumed over the counter, by prescription, or through illicit channels. Third, it tells us that drug use will escalate whenever sport claims additional corporate territory, and its players receive economic incentives to secure a competitive edge. Fourth, it tells us that no matter what regulations control drug use and attempt to squeeze it out of sport altogether, performance-enhancing drugs will always occupy a significant amount of space in sport for the simple reason that they can deliver athletes something of value.

All this sport-related drug use takes place in a world driven by two unstoppable forces. The first is technology. The pharmaceutical industry uses billions of dollars of research funds annually to formulate new drugs, medicines, and practices that enhance people's quality of life and physical performance (Goldacre 2012; Weyzig 2004). As a result, a constant supply of new compounds gives players and athletes a competitive edge. The second is neo-liberalism and its underlying ideology of individualism. Individualism unleashes an insatiable desire for self-improvement where any gain in productivity, cognitive capacity, and physical prowess is never enough (Hall 2011). This means that every step along the path of enhancement demands that additional steps be taken.

In summary, drugs and other substances take players and athletes to places they have never been before. Moreover, they do it in an addictive, psychologically captivating way. Benefits include improvements in strength and endurance, relief from chronic pain, a short, sharp dose of instant energy, the capacity to deliver explosive power, the release of social inhibition, the ability to get a good night's sleep, and an overriding sense of calmness and normality that comes with the elimination of debilitating anxiety. The finger-pointing of earnest officials, the moral objections of do-gooders, and the threat of suspensions and fines through punitive anti-drug laws, will never be enough to secure drug-free sport. The results of this periodised survey of drug use suggests that in a neo-liberal, hyper-modern world where individualism holds value above all else, and where drugs offer so many benefits to so many people with so many problems to manage, it is sheer fantasy to think that sport will ever be drug free.

7 Social ecology and the primacy of context

Introduction

The performance-enhancement aspects of drug use have been established and acknowledged along with their dangers. These dangers are accentuated periodically by tragedies involving both high-profile and lesser-known athletes (Ingram 2004). According to Parisotto (2006) at least 18 European cyclists died from EPO induced heart failure between 1988 and 1990. Less well established are the values, beliefs, and motivations of sport participants who employ drugs for performance advantage or recreation (Donovan *et al.* 2002; Lambros *et al.* 2011). Yet, as noted in Chapter 5, an understanding of athlete values, beliefs, and motives is central to the development of effective drugs in sport policy (BMA 2002). This chapter starts a three-phase exploration of the factors that shape athlete beliefs and attitudes on the drugs in sport problem. We do this by providing a series of conceptual lenses through which athlete decisions regarding drugs might be productively viewed.

Our discussion begins with three escalating premises. First, an array of factors impinges upon an athlete's decision to use or not use drugs that might help them improve their performance. Second, decisions made by athletes do not always follow rational processes or reflect clear intentions. Athletes may, for example overvalue the benefits that accrue from the use of a substance, or alternatively, underestimate the health risks. Third, a full explanation of drug use or drug avoidance by athletes requires the development of models that account for the contextual variables that affect decision making, and, in particular, those which may encourage non-compliance.

Our general proposition maintains that the relationship between contextual variables and the construction of athletes' values and beliefs about drug use will help to explain the causes of apparently irrational action more effectively than micro models that look mainly at the internal dynamics of athlete decision making. Our argument has crucial implications for policy development since it suggests that drug-use regulations dominated by testing, coercion, and escalating penalties will not necessarily change behaviour. As a result, more policy space should be given to less punitive harm-reduction models that accommodate a greater focus on athletes' surroundings, and the protection of their health and well-being.

In support of our claim for a more contextualised analysis of the drugs in sport problem, we have used the following three chapters to explore theories and models that identify the broad social, cultural, and economic factors shaping the motivations, choices, and behaviours of athletes in the sporting world. In short, we propose three major theoretical structures to assist in understanding the complex social behaviours that underpin drug use in sport. They are 1) the social ecology model, 2) the capital building model, and 3) the life course model. We will use these three theoretical platforms to debate the current policies and regulations governing drug use in sport. Our logic echoes the advice offered by Cepeda and Martin (2005), who counselled that any study of social institutions and cultural practices requires a conceptual framework built upon a strong contextual platform and a foundation of ongoing reflection and review. Conceptual frameworks, or sets of theoretical premises and conditions, also provide valuable tools to help identify key factors that shape the behaviours of individuals under study. We begin our discussion with a review of social ecology theory.

Social ecology theory and the drugs in sport problem

Social ecology fits our 'contextualised' approach to the drugs in sport problem since it provides an overarching framework for the study of social phenomena, and a set of theoretical principles to assist in understanding complex interrelationships in different social settings. It takes the position that most social phenomena possess too many layers to be understood adequately from a single level of analysis. Consequently, a deeper explanation for the forces and factors shaping social behaviour demands a comprehensive approach where 'psychological, organizational, cultural, community planning, and regulatory perspectives' all receive attention (Stokols 1996: 283).

Social ecology shares much in common with systems theory, which also aims to identify the core interdependent relations between social practices and the environment in which they take place. In each case, the social, institutional, and cultural contexts of people–environment relationships receive special attention, together with the geographic environment in which they occur. People take action in dynamic worlds. Not only will the physical and social settings influence specific individual outcomes, but participants may also engage in individual or collective action that modifies their physical and social settings. As a result, social ecology theory emphasises people–environment relationships within specific cultural, institutional, and social settings.

Social ecology theory claims that environmental settings have multiple dimensions that influence the person–environment interaction. Environmental settings may be analysed from numerous perspectives relevant to the social practices and individual behaviour under consideration. Social ecology theory prioritises the importance of 'identifying various physical and social conditions within environments that can affect occupant's psychological and social practices, and their emotional and social well-being' (Stokols 1996: 289). They may in one case revolve around the physical architecture, while in another case might centre on the belief systems of a work group (Stokols 1996). In every instance strong interdependencies will create waves of change and adaptation. For example, a fall in economic activity ripples over an entire society. Demand for income-sensitive services like gourmet cafes, boutique gyms, and physiotherapy clinics falls, leading to a decline in labour demand, and a consequent reduction in the bargaining strength of trade unions. Government spending then shrinks, welfare agencies cut services to the disadvantaged, and the disadvantaged become even more disadvantaged as job markets contract.

Social ecology theory uses what theorists call differential dynamic interplay (DDI). The emphasis lies with the interrelationships between personal and situational factors. In contrast, less holistic theories focus exclusively on establishing connections between a single environmental factor like the tax placed on tobacco products, and a specific behavioural outcome like the impact on adolescent cigarette consumption. A DDI approach, on the other hand, recognises that not only will a multiplicity of environmental factors come into play, but that these environmental factors may also affect people differently. Responses can depend on factors such as perceptions of environmental controllability, personality, previous experiences in similar situations, social position, and financial resources. In social ecological research incorporating DDI, the 'level of congruence' or compatibility between people and their surroundings help predict specific social practices, individual feelings, and levels of well-being (Stokols 1996: 286).

Social ecology theory highlights the need to undertake multiple levels of analysis in the form of macro and micro perspectives. For instance, working through patterns of leisure experiences in diverse communities begins with an exploration of geographical regions and people's spatial relations, moves onto an analysis of organisational conduct, examines neighbourhood interactions and local group activities, and finishes with a detailed examination of individual dispositions, attitudes, beliefs, and behaviours.

Structuring a model of social ecology

Social ecology theory provides an especially powerful tool for driving research focused on the contexts in which social actors think, feel, and behave. The theory states that attitudes and behaviours are not driven exclusively by personal factors intrinsic to the individual. Rather environmental influences also play a part in explaining attitudes and behaviour (Graham *et al.* 1991; Hansen 1997). Social ecology holds a particular relevance to the drugs in sport issue due to its sensitivity for the interdependencies between context, attitudes, and behaviour (Levins & Lopez 1999). When applied to drugs in sport it suggests that a player's decision to use drugs is powerfully influenced by contextual pressures like mentors, coaches, fellow athletes, and the rewards that follow from winning.

Social ecology theory also fits neatly into reasoned-action theory, which suggests a link between player attitudes and behaviours. Azjen (1991) and Azjen and Fishbein's (1980) theory of reasoned action / planned behaviour claims that intention mediates the link between attitude and volitional behaviour. In addition, some social–psychological research has demonstrated that personal, internally held values fluctuate wildly depending upon context. In fact, external factors such as peer influence introduce a significant effect on behaviour (Cialdini 2001). General attitudes seem to be reliable predictors of general behaviour (Eagly & Chaiken 1993). That is, attitudes have 'predictive utility' (Cialdini *et al.* 1981). For example, Chou and Chi'en's (1997) study determined that the more positive respondents' attitudes toward drug abuse, the more likely their involvement in drugs and the higher the observed stages of abuse. Moreover, attitudes become better predictors of volitional behaviours when matched to context, or when they connect to self-identity. In summary, the presence of mitigating factors and the complexity and accessibility of the behaviour all affect the predictive utility of theories of planned behaviour and rational action (Fazio & Williams 1986; Leone *et al.* 1999).

Social ecology theory can be usefully applied to drugs in sport since it forces observers to spell out the context within which drug use takes place, and to work through the relationships between these factors. It demands an analysis of how contextual factors influence both attitudes and behaviours. Drug use in sport does not occur in a vacuum. Social ecological studies begin with the proposition that a player's beliefs about drug use, and their decisions to take or not take drugs, exist within an array of commercial forces and cultural factors mediated by their professional and interpersonal relationships. For anyone trying to unravel the drugs in sport issue, these influences provide pivotal data in order to consider policy arrangements.

At the same time, it can be unclear as to what key interlocking influences might look like, since little research has examined the contextual pressures faced by players when forming their views on the drugs in sport issue. In addition, no research has examined the attitudes of players over time, despite the presence of evidence suggesting that drug-taking attitudes and behaviours change over the player life cycle (Vogel 2010). As previously noted, changes in contextual factors influence attitudes to drug taking. For example, cases have surfaced where retired players have confessed to former drug use (Millar 2005). Conversely, while the performance-enhancing use of substances like steroids might diminish as a player's competitive career wanes, their use of performance-reducing drugs like alcohol might increase (Lalor 2003). Considering the attitudes of players longitudinally helps to account for changing environmental influences.

Models of social ecology provide suitable guidance where individual informants are engaged through in-depth methods. A case study approach for example, where each case comprises a single informant within a network of macro influences and micro relationships, allows both a macro and micro analysis to occur. The macro influences include the broad commercial and cultural factors, while the micro relationships include the influence of coaches, trainers, sport science advisers, counsellors, and fellow players on one hand, and psychological and temperamental factors on the other. When using a social ecological model, we argue that the drugs in sport phenomena can be best understood by 1) approaching it from a contextual viewpoint, and 2) seeing it as part of a larger 'body improvement' project which can have either a performance-enhancing or appearance-enhancing trajectory.

In summarising the material presented in earlier chapters, we have identified ten key contextual factors that shape drug-taking behaviours in sport. Later, we will consolidate the factors into a more parsimonious model that highlights their links and interconnections. For the moment, we note each factor independently in order to expose the variables associated with contextual analyses. The ten factors are listed below:

1   Commercialisation: Volume of money associated with sport and its commoditisation.
2   Professionalisation: Nature and level of compensation to players, managers, coaches, and support staff.
3   Globalisation: Inter- and transnational distribution of sport.
4   Culturalisation: Propagation of specific values associated with sport performance.
5   Westernisation: Inculcation of western culture and values into sport (celebrity, media, capitalism).
6   Specialisation: Degree of structural adaptation in the sport industry.
7   Politicisation: Use of sport for broader political agendas.
8   Scientisation and Technologisation: Use of science and technology in sport.
9   Medicalisation: Use of medicine in sport.
10 Masculinisation: Importance of values associated with masculinity.

These ten factors are integrated into the sociocultural map depicted in Figure 7.1. It shows four forces at work shaping the attitudes that players and athletes hold regarding drug use in sport. The first is the commercial impact of sport, which is concerned with shaping sport into a business where players and athletes act as employees and independent contractors aiming to make a living from this career choice. The second is the international scope of sport and the ways in which it builds global connections at both the sporting and political levels. The third is the influence of technology on sport performance, and especially the role of physicians, sport scientists, dieticians, nutritionalists, and biochemists. The fourth and final force is the hyper-competitive nature of contemporary sport, especially at the professional and elite ends of the system. All of these factors make athletes and players more committed to their sports. But, it also means they will do whatever it takes – especially if it involves risk – to attain their sporting dreams and aspirations.

While all of the above factors have a collective influence on drug-taking behaviour, it remains unclear as to which ones constitute primary drivers, and to what extent distinctive clusters of drivers shape specific outcomes. On the one hand, we could identify a suite of forces that create a cultural expectation about the problematic nature of drug use, while on the other hand an underlying commercial reality could impel a regular cycle of drug-use practices and drug-supply conditions.

Despite the lack of clarity regarding causal linkages, a social ecological framework delivers a number of benefits to drugs in sport investigators. First, it encourages a detailed analysis of players' personal experiences. Second, it gives

Drugs in sport: the socio-contextual proposition

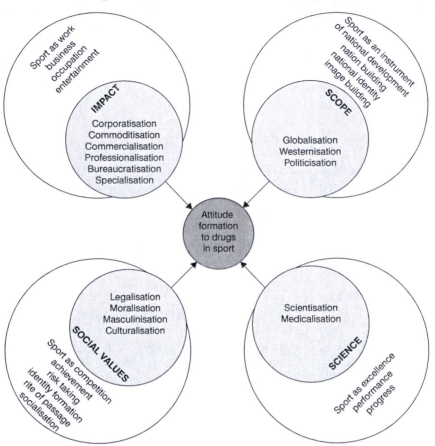

Figure 7.1 Drug use in sport: a multifactorial contextual model

centre stage to the contextual influences on player attitudes about the drugs in sport problem. Finally, it builds a network of influences and relationships that reveal the processes through which player attitudes are formed, and the relative strength of each contextual factor (Clarke 2005). It also reveals that sport is susceptible to drug use for two main reasons.

First, sport has become hyper-commercialised over the last 40 years, and as a result the rewards for doing well have escalated exponentially (Millar 2005; Stewart *et al.* 2004; Wenner 1998; Westerbeek & Smith 2003; Wright 1999). More players than ever before receive support from government and corporate sponsorships where success delivers as much in financial rewards as it does in medals. As a result, a surge in demand has arisen for drugs and compounds that might improve performance and provide a competitive edge (Buti & Fridman 2001).

Second, drugs of various sorts – and especially alcohol and tobacco – occupy a deep, embedded place within the culture of sporting clubs (Lalor 2003; McKay 1991; Smith & Shilbury 2004; Smith & Stewart 1995; Stoddart 1986). Alcohol-based drinks offer the intoxicants of choice whenever the need to celebrate arises, and for male players in particular, sport provides a space where they can play out their ideals of masculinity and manhood (West 1996; Whitehead 2005). In this context, drugs not only feed the need to compete and win, but also the need to engage in high-risk behaviour. In these situations, failure, defeat, and injury diminish as problems so long as they are associated with heroic outcomes. Conversely, female players may be compelled to risk non-compliance with socially constructed views of femininity in order to maximise their sporting performances (Burstyn 1999).

A social ecology model that uses commercial and cultural factors to define the contextual field delivers a number of benefits since it explains why ambitious players and athletes might want to use substances that enhance their performances, or just make them feel better after the game or contest. It further highlights the ways in which a whole raft of suppliers and professional advisors can give players and athletes smooth access to a vast array of supplements, substances, and pharmacological products to meet their need to reach, and sometimes even go beyond, their potential.

Regulatory structures and social ecology

An additional strength lies with the model's capacity to embrace a range of policy and structural frames, and especially explain how regulatory mechanisms can be used to manage drug use in sport. For example, regulatory mechanisms can be conveniently mapped using the work of Braithwaite and Drahos (2000) as a conceptual framework. Regulations can be classified under four operational categories depending on first, their degree of legal support or formal controls, and second, their level of social acceptance or informal controls. These operational categories are:

1   Legislation, and non-government organisation surveillance.
2   Market pressures, supply management, economic incentives, taxes, and written contracts.
3   Voluntary industry codes, collective bargaining agreements, financial controls, and employee codes of conduct.
4   Ethical standards, social mores, pressures to conform, and taken-for-granted values, customs, routines, and rituals.

As we already noted, a social ecology model provides space for establishing a contextual frame that highlights social and cultural surroundings. One particularly useful model for the study of drug use in sport is the *drug, set, and setting* triad devised by Zinberg (1984), and adapted by Stallwitz and Shewan (2004) in their qualitative investigation of the social implications of heroin use, and by McElrath and McEvoy (2002) in their framework for understanding drug use in a variety of social settings. Zinberg (1984) demonstrated that in order to understand what impels people to use drugs, and how drugs affect users, three determinants must be considered:

1   The *drug*, which addresses the pharmacological action of the substance itself.
2   The *set*, which relates to the individual user, their attitude at the time of use, and their personality structure.
3   The *setting*, which concentrates on the influence of the physical and social context within which the use occurs.

Zinberg's model, and its adaptation to a sport setting, is summarised in Table 7.1.

In a manner similar to Braithwaite and Drahos (2000), Zinberg maintained that the social setting is crucially important, since it exerts a strongly instrumental effect on drug usage. First, the social setting contains social sanctions, which covers rules of drug-use conduct. Social sanctions consequently define whether and how a particular drug should be used. Second, the social setting provides for social rituals and patterned behaviour, which can prescribe behavioural norms surrounding the use of a drug. They may include methods of procurement and administration, the choice of physical setting for use, activities before and after use, and strategies for avoiding unwanted side effects. As Zinberg (1984) also noted, rituals play a vitally important role in shaping drug use since they buttress sanctions, and as a result represent informal social controls, which align with the base of Braithwaite and Drahos' regulatory model. These can, in turn, be viewed as part of the 'setting', thereby expanding it to encompass the formal legislated controls and well as the informal social controls.

A social ecological model of drugs in sport

We have argued that many models and theories aiming to explain drug use in sport focus narrowly on individual athlete decision making, overemphasising the socioeconomic costs and benefits of using drugs. However, in our view, this limitation squeezes the debate on drugs in sport to the question of how various penalties and sanctions might curb the level of use. We suggest that a broader debate must include an exploration of first, the context in which drug use occurs, and second, a situational diagnosis of the assumptions, values, and beliefs that underpin drug use in sport. To this end, we have developed a social ecological model that combines the micro orientation of individual athlete and interpersonal behaviour, with the macro orientation of sporting context, structure, and culture. We use this contextualised model to contrast a use-reduction policy with a harm-reduction policy.

We contend that an athlete's decision to utilise drugs involves far more convoluted and subjective processes than a stand-alone micro model suggests. In support of this argument we return to a number of contextual and situational factors that impact on athlete values, beliefs, and decision making. We propose

Table 7.1 Zinberg's drug use model of drug, set and setting

Drug	Set	Setting

• Pharmacological effects of the substances
  – performance-enhancing drugs
  – illicit drugs
  – non-illicit drugs and alcohol.
	• Physical factors such as body weight, sex, race, current health conditions, illnesses or diseases, medication intake, and genetic make-up.
	• Level of experience with the exact drug, drugs of the same type, drugs in general, or using drugs within certain contexts.
	• Tolerance level of specific drug, usually influenced by level of experience and physical factors, especially body weight and genetic make-up.
	• Current emotional and mental state, such as depression, anger, stress, recent trauma, or psychological disorders.
	• Type and level of drug education received.
	• Expectations (or lack of), as well as intentions, regarding pending drug use, how the effects should feel, and what the experience will be like.
	• Personality, ideological opinions, and things of interest, often influences intentions and expectations.
	• Predisposition to physical addiction, likely influenced by genetics, personality, and tolerance.
		• Informal social controls:
		  – social sanctions in sport
		  – social rituals in sport.
		• Place (i.e. at the training venue, a sport club, home, at a party, at the doctor's office, on the streets, at work, etc.).
		• Presence of other athletes, coaches, friends etc. Amount of surrounding people (if any), plus types of individuals, crowdedness, and whether communication, interaction, or recreation takes place among group.
		• Characteristics of environment, including the presence of music or other sounds, weather conditions, type of area (i.e. suburbs, industrial district, inner city, woods, beach, etc.), whether it's indoor/outdoor, and perimeter or tightness of setting.
		• Time, such as day or night, which season, day of the week, etc.
		• Culture, such as age group, ideology, race, common activities, and even the country of use.
		• Reason for the particular drug experience (i.e. to relax, for therapy, for recreation, unexpectedly/unwittingly, without consent, for specific performance etc.).

that contextual factors confound the athlete's cost–benefit calculus by bringing various economic and social pressures to bear on the decision-making process. Three such contextual factors are first, globalisation and commercialisation, second, the culture in which athletes develop their sporting prowess, and finally, theories of masculinity and how they impact on athlete identity and behaviour in a highly competitive sport environment.

Our model of drug use in sport combines two interdependent parts. The first part, or micro component, involves ideas and theories which assume that players implement rational decisions based on reliable and unbiased information, and take actions that aim to maximise their well-being. The second part proceeds on the assumption that player attitudes and behaviours are shaped by forces that impact on personal aspects like disposition, identity, a sense of belonging, status, and ambition. These factors often go beyond rationality and enter the area of dreams and fantasy.

Bringing the macro and micro factors together

As we have already indicated in this chapter, a number of factors have created the conditions for the widespread use of drugs in sport. These factors are illustrated in Figure 7.2, which highlights a holistic system of infrastructure, social constraints, and psychological realities impacting upon the use of performance-enhancing drugs in sport. This framework represents an integration of concepts from the micro and macro literature addressed in this chapter. The broad categories of the model comprising structural, interpersonal and intrapersonal constraints are taken from the work of Alexandris *et al.* (2002), who highlighted the far-reaching issues likely to affect athletes' decisions to use performance-enhancing drugs. Each of these contextual fields has been further classified into subsections that mirror our synthesis of the literature.

The outer concentric circle shown in Figure 7.2 summarises the structural constraints of performance-enhancing drug use, which is essentially the impact of the contemporary sporting system. This includes the commercialised technologically driven, hyper-competitive nature of sport in the 21st century western world, where elite performance has been medicalised, scientised and funded according to 'gold medal' potential (Mugford *et al.* 1999). Competition defines sport, and athletes continually seek new ways to secure a competitive edge over their rivals. The emphasis on mastery and achievement in competitive sport can yield benefits in terms of esteem and motivation, but it also creates fertile ground for drug use (Deci & Ryan 2000; Frederick-Recascino & Schuster-Smith 2003). Meanwhile, commercialisation has translated into increased pressure for on-field success in order to maintain corporate sponsorship (Shilbury & Deane 2001; Westerbeek & Smith 2003), whilst the shift to a revenue-driven model has emphasised the importance of winning (Li *et al.* 2001). Similarly, the global distribution of sport has amplified the potential for nation states to realise political goals through sport (Belk 1996; Gems 1999; Gerrard 1999; Wright 1999), with funding consequently favouring elite sports with the highest gold

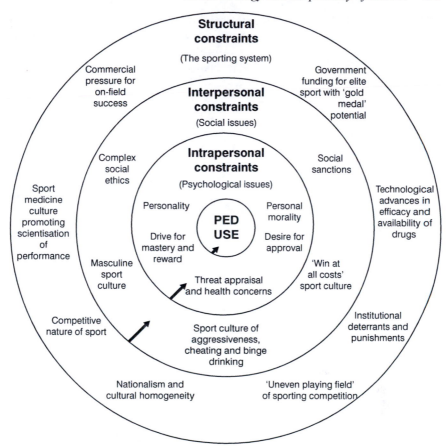

Figure 7.2 Macro and micro influences in drug use in sport

(PED = performance-enhancing drug)

medal potential (Stewart *et al.* 2004). Technology has simultaneously promoted advances in the efficacy, choice and availability of performance-enhancing drugs (Waddington 2000b). In short, a smorgasbord of designer drugs can be accessed through chemists, physicians, veterinarians, and a seemingly endless list of Internet sites. At the same time, as depicted in Figure 7.2, the sporting system contains structural deterrents, such as bans and sanctions, which create disincentives for performance-enhancing drug use (Donovan *et al.* 2002; Dunn *et al.* 2011; Strelan & Boeckmann 2003). However, they also generate incentives for the use of additional masking substances (Voy 1991).

The second concentric circle in Figure 7.2 encapsulates the interpersonal, or social, issues impacting upon athlete performance-enhancing drug use. The ethics surrounding the use of performance-enhancing drugs is complicated by the fact that many drugs have enormous social benefits in a non-sport setting. Complex social ethics surround the use of performance-enhancing pharmaceuticals. For example, the sporting public appears largely disaffected by performance-enhancing drugs (Mugford *et al.* 1999), but at the same time increasingly condones the use of performance-enhancing pharmaceuticals and technologies in daily life. Nonetheless, social sanctions still exist for many forms of drug use, including disapproval and ostracism by colleagues and the general public (Strelan & Boeckmann 2003). The culture of sport also leads to ambiguous outcomes since it may not universally promote healthy lifestyle and moral development, but may, in fact, encourage physical injury, cheating, and binge drinking (Long & Sanderson 2001; The [United States] President's Council on Physical Fitness and Sports Report, 1997; Waddington 2000b). Sport practice exemplifies a masculine ethos emphasising heroism (Whitehead 2005), aggression (Burstyn 1999), and excessive alcohol consumption (Duff *et al.* 2004; Peretti-Watel *et al.* 2002). These traits reinforce a culture highly conducive to risk taking involving drug use. Indeed, the fact that performance-enhancing drugs are illicit, the chance of being caught, and even the risk of becoming ill, can be part of the attraction. Furthermore, these social pressures are brought to bear within a 'win at all costs' sporting culture (Milton-Smith 2002).

The third and final category is intrapersonal, or psychological, constraints. This category acknowledges the process of threat and incentive appraisal that an athlete may undertake when making a decision about drug use, as well as their moral position and personality factors (Donovan *et al.* 2002). Athletes may also be compelled by an inherent drive towards mastery and reward (Mugford *et al.* 1999), and the associated approval of colleagues and the broader community that on-field success delivers. The benefits of drug use may be held in tension with athletes' perceptions of the threat of punishment and public shame, as well as potential health concerns (Strelan & Boeckmann 2003).

Summarising the key contextual pressures

Globalisation and commercialisation have consolidated the media–sport–business triumvirate, in turn ensuring that winning is more important than ever before, as much for economic as for intrinsic reasons (Miller *et al.* 1999). Four themes commonly appear in the literature concerning the role and impact of globalisation and commercialisation. First, the world has entered a global age that cannot be reversed (Amin 2002; Dicken 2003; Hackworth 2003; Moore 2001; Peck & Yeung 2003). Second, this 'new world order' has revised the power of the state as well as multinational corporations, the former weakened and the latter enhanced (Alasuutari 2000; Catley 1999; Cerny 1999; Evans 1997; Goldmann 2002; Guillen 2001; Kettl 2000; Walby 2003; Went 2001). Third, the inexorable push of economic progress and performance transcends national boundaries, and makes the marketplace sovereign (Eichengreen 2000; Gersbach 2002; Grant 2000; Storper 2003). Finally, globalisation not only produces beneficiaries but also puts the spotlight on the marginalised and disadvantaged (Aghion & Williamson 1999;

Alderson & Nielsen 2002; Archibugi 2000; Bhatta 2002; Durlauf 2000; Gindin 2002; Mandle 2002; Stiglitz 2002). Despite globalisation's capacity to generate growth in living standards, its spoils are not shared equitably. Given the power of multinational corporations, the centralisation of capital and ownership in these enterprises means that they yield a disproportionately large share of the benefits.

The four themes can be linked to the increase in commercialisation that sport has experienced (Shilbury & Deane 2001; Stewart 2007b; Westerbeek & Smith 2003; Wright 1999). An escalation of commercial interests in sport has furthered the pressure on athletes to perform in order to maintain corporate sponsorships and to acquire as much wealth as possible during their brief and risky career lifespans. For example, Westerbeek and Smith (2003) argued that the economy, technology, and culture represent three gate-keeping variables determining the fate of sport. Wright (1999) agreed that economic and technological factors contribute to the stresses athletes face. He noted that the consolidation of ownership in communications technology and the global distribution of sport had deepened the political and ideological dimensions of sport, which in turn had increased the importance of winning for nation states. Similarly, Gerrard (1999) highlighted the increased pressures that athletes face with intensifying professionalism, while Li *et al.* (2001) concluded that sport is driven principally by the need for new revenue opportunities.

Under global, commercial conditions, the market becomes a powerful determinant of behaviour in which the use of performance-enhancing drugs arises as an option for athletes intent on winning championship medals (Aghion & Williamson 1999). This shift to a market-centred and corporatised sport world was reinforced by Wenner (1998), who suggested presciently that the 21st century will fuse sport with the international media. According to Wenner's version of 'media-sport', physical prowess and attractiveness will underpin media attention, and the pressures on athletes to succeed on the international sporting stage will only deepen.

Milton-Smith (2002) also flagged the failure of major global institutions in dealing with the social and ethical consequences of globalisation, and pointedly highlighted a backlash against the Olympics movement. He wrote: 'Disillusionment with the Olympic Games mirrors the disenchantment with the perceived values of globalization, including winning at any price, commercial exploitation by MNCs, intense national rivalry, cronyism, cheating and corruption and the competitive advantage of advanced nations' (Milton-Smith 2002: 131). Sport consequently channels and creates meaning for its consumers. Its contents and ideological positioning occupy a central concern of fans, a point adroitly made by James (1963) 50 years ago. A hyper-commercialised sporting world and its associated ideologies of competition, global expansion, and market domination drives a sport culture that values doing whatever it takes to gain a competitive edge. In their work on Australian sport policy, Stewart *et al.* (2004) also revealed a hyper-competitive sport world where winning and success was valued above all else. They identified a sporting climate where the performances of athletes at the elite level receive significantly more political support than participation sport or physical activity. Professional sport therefore remains in a strong position, with developmental programs focusing upon leveraging cutting-edge science, and the opportunities for government in catalysing public support with gold medals. In many nations, for example, governments laud international sporting achievement at the cost of funding participation and informal physical activity, while simultaneously condemning drug use. Within this context, many elite athletes believe drug use offers an appropriate way to achieve a competitive level of performance as well as the means of securing government support and commercial sponsorship.

The US presents an archetype for the hyper-competitive, high-performance sport world. Gems (1999) argued that American sport has spread a kind of 'ideological imperialism'. Accordingly, an important issue facing athletes around the world comes in either accommodating or resisting the ideological homogeneity propagated by Americanised sport business. Belk (1996) shares this view, predicting that sport will take a McDonald's approach to delivering standardised products punctuated only by the 'hyper-real' and overzealous marketing of idealised athletes. In contrast, others like van Bottenburg (2003) have highlighted the culturally defensive power of sport. Having analysed the performance of NFL Europe, he concluded that its cultural impact was slight despite the receptiveness of Europeans to American popular culture in general. Sport, he speculated, was consequently more robust than other forms of culture. However, Bottenburg's analysis failed to accommodate the globalised supply of drugs where athletes are vulnerable to the forces of an American sport model that encourages the use of all sorts of sporting aids to enhance performance.

The globalisation and commercialisation of sport has also led to its scientisation and medicalisation (Murray 2008), a theme that runs through this book. Athletes increasingly seek the support of new scientific advances and technologies that offer a competitive edge. This has been particularly evident over the last 40 years with the emergence of sports medicine as a field of study (Waddington 2000b). The sports medicine model undeniably demonstrates that developments in clinical medicine, physiology, biomechanics, and psychology deliver superior performance. At the same time, the forces of globalisation ensure that when athletes in one part of the world secure the benefits of a performance-improvement technique, technology, or support, it quickly diffuses to other parts of the athletic world. Athletes now operate in a sporting culture that fundamentally supports the use of medical treatments and substances to boost and sustain performance. Managers of professional sport teams have a vested interest in getting injured players back on the field of play in the shortest possible time, and use a cocktail of painkilling and anti-inflammatory drugs to speed up the process. Furthermore, western society tolerates surgical and pharmaceutical interventions to improve appearance and performance in all areas of life. The idea that drugs can improve performance – whether physical or cognitive – or more generally improve the quality of life, is a taken-for-granted axiom (Bostrom & Sandberg 2009; Coveney *et al.* 2011).

While sport secures a haven for hyper-competitive athletes, it also provides a platform for securing substantial community pay-offs. For most sport officials and policy advisors the social benefits of physical activity require little justification. Typically, sport is assumed to promote psychological well-being, reduce stress, anxiety, and depression, improve physical development, diminish risky behaviours, strengthen communities, and decrease government health expenditure (AIHW 2000; Headley 2004; Morris *et al.* 2004; NPHP 2002; SRNZ 2002; WHO 2003). It is also claimed that sport develops self-esteem, advances good citizenship, fosters the value of mastery and cooperation, and encourages a physically active lifestyle (White *et al.* 1998). In addition, leisure education can be used to promote the healthy use of free time (Caldwell *et al.* 2004). These declarations link to the belief that participation in sport cultivates the sort of personal values and moral code that inhibit drug use and cheating.

Such claims should be treated with caution in the light of competing data. For example, some evidence suggests that involvement in sport at a young age can deleteriously affect maturity and encourage inappropriately aggressive behaviour (Bredemeier *et al.* 1986). Morris *et al.* (2003) concluded that sport and physical education programs alone will not directly diminish anti-social behaviour, even if they are specifically designed for that purpose. The (United States) President's Council on Physical Fitness and Sports Report (1997) observed that the way in which sport influences moral development remains unclear, particularly in relation to cheating behaviours. Neither are the effects of sport programs on health as clearly demonstrated as we might at first glance expect. For example, programs employing sport to counter drug use or criminal activity do not always meet their aims. Smith and Waddington (2004) observed the absence of theoretical rationales for sport-driven interventions and that the efficacy of these approaches remains unclear. In short, while some evidence supports the contention that sport enhances physical well-being and moral development, other evidence indicates that sport increases the risk of injury, encourages binge drinking, undermines athletes' long-term health prospects, and promotes cheating (Loland 2002; Long & Sanderson 2001; Waddington 2000b).

The competitive nature of sport and its emphasis on mastery, achievement, and performance reveals a double-edged sword when it comes to assessing its links to drug use (Deci & Ryan 2000; Frederick-Recascino & Schuster-Smith 2003). From one perspective, sporting activity, with its many rules, rigid hierarchies, and punishments is highly controlling, and may therefore initially curtail drug use. Alternatively, where athletes are encouraged to seek mastery, success, self-determination, and extrinsic rewards, the consequent autonomy may encourage drug use by stimulating athletes to take their own pathways to improved performance (Frederick-Recascino & Schuster-Smith 2003). In fact, the highly competitive nature of sport might actually work against drug compliance policy. At the extreme, it has been suggested that participation in sport may itself be a kind of addiction (Dunning & Waddington 2003), fuelled by the gratification of improving performance and increasing public recognition. Of course, winning in sport is seductive even for children, many of whom find compelling the idea of taking heavily caffeinated and sweetened sports drinks (Washington *et al.* 2005).

The tendency for sport culture to implicitly condone some forms of drug use can be seen in the self-determination of athletes (Pelletier *et al.* 1995). Self-determination theory (Deci & Ryan 1985) identifies three psychological factors influencing athlete motivation. They are first, the need for autonomy, second, the drive for competence, and finally, the need for relatedness, each of which can be influenced by the social environment. The theory begins with the assumption that behaviours are conducted with considered reflection and full choice. According to Deci and Ryan (2000: 227), '... a critical issue in the effects of goal pursuit and attainment concerns the degree to which people are able to satisfy their basic needs as they pursue and attain their valued outcomes'. Drawing from the competence dimension of self-determination theory, if athletes fundamentally want to win, then the deterrence factors associated with drug use will be subservient to the benefits. To add further levels of complexity, Alexandris *et al.* (2002) highlighted the importance of 'intrapersonal' constraints (psychological issues), interpersonal constraints (social issues), and structural constraints (systems within sports) in sport-related decision making. From this perspective, a sport culture that values mastery, autonomy, and competition will confer greater weight to doing what it takes to win, and less weight to the need to ensure a level playing field.

Another central feature of sport, particularly at the elite level, is its strong emphasis on masculine posturing and heroic performance. This point was highlighted by Millar (2005), who lamented the lack of a strong moral basis for public attitudes towards drug use in sport. His observation stems from the contradiction between the public glorification of heroic sporting performance on one hand, and their demonising of drug cheats on the other. Of relevance here is Whitehead's (2005) conceptualisation of manliness, and what it means to be a man once other dimensions of identity have been excluded, such as race, class, and sexuality. Heroism lies at the heart of Whitehead's construction of masculinity, which he claimed represents the ubiquitous and exemplary symbol of manhood. For boys to become men, they must transcend their fear of physical injury or even death through some kind of confrontation, demanding courage, and perhaps culminating in aggression or violence. The hero therefore, 'overarches social divisions between men' (Whitehead 2005: 414). In so doing the hero obviates the need for socially determined status. According to Whitehead, young men will internalise masculinity as an idealised component of the self, rehearsing the fantasy where their heroic portrayal of masculinity may be seen through extraordinary courage despite serious personal and physical risk. In addition to the more overt masculine ideals – such as aggression, heroism, and risk taking – most sports typically emphasise the manly aspirations of strength, stamina, and the capacity to endure physical discomfort.

Beyond bar-room brawls, and in the absence of war, sport offers an accessible vehicle for displaying the kind of heroism that requires aggression and the risk of physical injury. Burstyn (1999: 254) described sport as the 'most powerful social confirmation of masculinity that any male can attain in our culture'. Here, anti-social behaviour combines with commercialisation to produce a kind of 'hypermasculinity' characterised by a win-at-all-costs drug culture. The celebration of heroic deeds via sport also encourages other risky behaviours like excessive alcohol consumption (Peretti-Watel *et al.* 2002), which reinforces the opportunity to damage the body in order to exude masculinity. It therefore comes as no surprise that alcohol's role as a social lubricant holds firm in the lives of many sporting clubs (Duff *et al.* 2004). Similarly, the success of the classic Marlboro Man cigarette campaign was premised on the desire for an exaggerated sense of masculinity (Starr 1984). Such characterisations of men in film remain ever-present. Most sporting pursuits, especially at the elite level, demand performance at the outer limit of physical capacity, and therefore demand risk taking and pain tolerance, central parts of the masculine ethos.

For some athletes, the combination of illegality, risk of exclusion, and potential for physical damage can be part of the attraction of taking drugs. Paradoxically, a punitive anti-doping policy may unintentionally increase the appeal of drug use for some hyper-masculine athletes because of its association with deviant and high-risk behaviour. Conversely, a policy that normalises drug use may de-masculinise its consumption, and by eliminating the implication of deviance, actually lead to a fall in use, particularly where its performance-enhancing qualities are ambiguous.

Conclusion

Social ecology theory considers the social, historical, cultural, and institutional contexts of people–environment relations. First, it examines the social contexts of people's lives by looking at their social networks and support systems. Second, it explores the historical contexts of people's lives in terms of where they come from, and their accumulated experiences. Third, it considers the cultural contexts of people's lives and therefore teases out norms, values, and expectations. Finally, social ecology theory examines the institutional contexts of people's lives by better understanding the factors that shape their routines, habits, everyday experiences, and their overall lived experiences. All of these represent vital ingredients in understanding the depth and complexity of drug use in sport.

In offering a fusion of macro and micro influences on drug use in sport, our social ecology inspired model highlights the fact that 'punitive regulation' is only one of a number of factors that impact upon players' decisions to use, or decline to use, drugs. In light of this chapter's discussion, we place another layer in the foundations to our argument that polices and strategies that punish and demonise athletes for taking drugs through a zero-tolerance approach have not been successful in eliminating drugs from sport. At the same time, other models more snugly fit the drugs in sport context we have discussed. The harm-reduction approach fits comfortably in a social ecological model since it allows for a range of external factors to shape the attitudes and behaviours and athletes. It also challenges models that are constructed on a foundation of rational decision making where internal cognitive processes rule. It generates controversy in sporting circles because it accepts that drugs will always be part of the sporting landscape and concedes that the playing field will not always be level as a result. However, it also takes a socially responsible position since it aims to minimise the physical, psychological, and emotional harms associated with drug use. At the same time, social ecology does not provide a complete picture of player and athlete behaviour. We add another dimension in the following chapter to help explain why players and athletes might be prepared to incur serious damage to their health and reputation through drug use.

8 Capital accumulation through bodily enhancement

Introduction: capital building as a universal human trait

Social and economic models used to explain human behaviour build on the idea that people are driven by the desire to accumulate capital. From an economic perspective the notion of capital provides a foundation for understanding not only the production process, but also acts of consumption, like the decision to use drugs. Alfred Marshall, the grandfather of modern economics, discussed the 'capital' problem in his classic textbook on economics first published in 1890, and regularly reprinted until the early 1960s. In Chapter IV of Book II in his *Principles of Economics* (1920), Marshall noted that all households seek to accumulate capital since it represents the only way of increasing both personal wealth and purchasing power. For example, cash is a form of capital, and so too is a car, a house, and any domestic appliance. Capital accumulation also offers a means to secure a reasonable standard of living by building a capacity to earn an income. Marshall refers to this form of capital as 'trade capital', since it enables people to deliver labour services to a business in return for a wage or salary (Marshall 1920: 62). Trade capital includes the physical capacity to undertake manual labour, a box of tools to assist in building and repairing machines, a convivial personality to wield as a retail assistant, and a professional education that allows someone to practice as a lawyer, accountant, or psychologist. Marshall's treatment of capital highlights the importance of 'value' and how it can be used to generate a 'return' on capital, further adding to the existing 'stocks of household capital'. At the same time, Marshall conceded that one's stocks of capital could be depleted, which in the case of 'trade' capital, can result from an injury, an illness, or a failure to upgrade skills and professional capabilities.

In this chapter we employ the concept of capital building as a theoretical lens for explaining the drug-use behaviours of athletes. We examine the different sporting environments in which capital can be accumulated, we discuss the social fields of play in which athletes are able to pursue their capital building dreams, and we interrogate the ways in which players can use drugs and other substances to improve the capital building potential of their bodies.

From a sociological perspective, understanding the structure and operation of a capital building model best begins with the social theories of Pierre Bourdieu.

A French sociologist, Bourdieu's capacity to match esoteric theory with detailed empirical observation and data gathering remains unparalleled. He provided a perfectly tuned social model for understanding what drives behaviour using the desire to secure positions of status, influence, and good standing as the key regulators. In the 1980s, Bourdieu published a classic analysis of French society which was appropriately entitled *Distinction*. The tome concluded that the 'stylisation of life' and the 'primacy of form over function' do matter. They matter because they deliver an 'acquired disposition'; they 'establish and mark differences' and therefore confer distinction as a form of capital on some but not others (Bourdieu 1984: 466). According to Bourdieu this desire for taste and distinctiveness creates an 'economy of cultural goods' where their possession creates a stock of capital as valuable as Marshall's 'trade' capital, or any other form of economic capital for that matter (Bourdieu 1984: 1). These ideas provided the conceptual catalyst for the designation of other forms of capital capable of delivering their owners some additional level of status, power, and influence. According to Bourdieu (1986), capital can be stored in various forms, including economic, social, cultural, symbolic, and finally, bodily or physical capital.

Bourdieu's (1986) model of capital accumulation has several conceptual strengths that make it especially suitable for better understanding the ways players and athletes go about their 'craft'. First, it highlights the fact that people engage in different social practices because they offer a range of social rewards that go well beyond the material. While the possession of a large house in a prestigious suburb provides people with a certain amount of superficial 'kudos', numerous other ways of improving one's social position can also be pursued. Second, the model gives appropriate space to the body as an asset that can be worked on in order to not only give satisfaction and pleasure, but also claim a distinctive position in the social hierarchy. 'Working on' the body can take many forms, including for example, a new hairstyle, the subtle use of cosmetics and perfumes, a wardrobe makeover, and regular gym workouts, through to heavy-duty bodybuilding regimens, intensive weight loss programs, and seriously expensive plastic surgery (Shilling 2003: 2005). Finally, Bourdieu's model illuminates the ways in which the sporting body – and in particular a successful one – can be used to build a new identity, increase one personal wealth, improve one's social status, and strengthen a class position.

Although Marshall and Bourdieu came to the analysis of capital from quite different theoretical positions, they both understood that capital delivered value. They both noted that it made life comfortable, and reinforced personal identities and public images. Crucially, however, capital also enabled people to exert power and influence over others. This ultimately explains why capital remains so important to so many people. It also explains the discomforts people will endure to secure it. It applies equally to athletes and artists as it does to clergymen, politicians, and captains of industry. In the following section we explore the different types of capital and how they can be accumulated.

Capital building as a multifactorial activity

As a lead in to his proposition that social behaviour intimately connects with the drive to accumulate capital, Bourdieu claimed that as social beings we not only move through life in different and idiosyncratic ways, but also grasp for threads of commonality, and search for meaningful attachments to people and places. The desire to be distinctive and self-reliant will always be balanced against the need for connectedness and belonging. This axiom holds irrespective of an individual's social life cycle stage or social context.

According to Bourdieu (1977) people's social life cycle, and the social context in which they run their affairs, is analogous to a sporting contest. Every player or social agent occupies a place on a field of play, which may be a workplace, a political party, a religious organisation, or a sporting club. In this game the most successful players accumulate stocks of capital they use to build power, status, and influence. At the same time, these players – or agents, as Bourdieu called the participants – use the social field to fight for 'dominant positions' (Bourdieu 1977: 22). In the process of building and distributing capital, winners and losers are created (Jarvie & Maguire 1994: 194). Stocks of capital, or the 'spoils' from the field of play, take numerous forms. Bourdieu noted that these stocks can take the form of material capital to do with economic assets and commercial wealth, or immaterial capital, concerned with building reputation, status, taste, and cultural superiority (Bourdieu 1986: 242).

The capital divide provides a solid platform from which to build an analysis of the different forms of capital referred to above. By slightly extending Bourdieu's model of capital accumulation, six categories of capital can be compiled. They are 1) economic capital, 2) symbolic capital, 3) cultural capital, 4) social capital, 5) bodily capital, and 6) psychological capital. We consider these six forms of capital in the next section, and explain how the theory can inform the drugs in sport debate.

Forms of capital

The first form is economic capital, which involves working hard to accumulate wealth and purchase valuable objects along the lines of the Weberian Protestant work ethic (Weber 1976). In contemporary society the accumulation of economic capital includes consumption as it provides legitimation through acts of conspicuous, extravagant, and aspirational spending, typically with the intent of building a strong sense of self and social identity (Slater 1997). For the non-professional, the sport experience may not directly impart economic capital to its users. Nevertheless, it can provide indirect economic benefits. For example, the most immediate economic benefit arrives through the fitness and energy accompanying exercise, and its transference to the workplace. Mounting evidence indicates that fit, strong, and healthy employees produce more. Other data suggest that employees perceived as good-looking, who portray a healthy and vibrant appearance, and are neither strikingly obese nor heavily underweight, receive better pay on average, and are more frequently promoted than their less physically attractive counterparts (Hamermesh & Biddle 1994; Mobius & Rosenblatt 2006).

The second form is symbolic capital, which revolves around the status that accrues from one's accomplishments. Bourdieu also used the term symbolic capital to explain the residual effect of building up one's stocks of economic capital, and how it can be used to become more noticeable and distinctive. Overall, this type of capital accumulation assists in building a reputation, improving one's social position, and securing social gravitas (Bourdieu 1986). Status-generating accomplishments are as common as the situations or social field within which they take place. For example, the ability to predict money-market shifts in the finance sector will generate status and kudos in the finance industry field. Equally, knowledge about how to build larger muscles quickly will achieve status and respect in a bodybuilding setting. Big muscles in an accounting office or law firm will provide little kudos, and, in fact, could stimulate derision, and lead to a consequent loss of capital. Symbolic capital therefore reflects site and situation specific contexts.

The third form of capital is cultural capital. In Bourdieu's world the accumulation of 'cultural capital' comes from improving one's social position through knowledge, education, and intellectual discourse. Cultural capital provides a more subtle form of distinction than economic capital since it not only gives social weight to those who have become educated in a formal sense by moving through a university or graduate school, but also privileges taste through demonstrations of one's capacity to engage with the world of history, literature, the arts, and fashion industries (Bourdieu 1984). Like symbolic capital, cultural capital can be site and situation specific. In a betting agency or casino, an impressive knowledge of exercise physiology and the biomedical principles of muscle growth amounts to little, but in a sporting setting it will position an athlete or coach as authoritative and influential. On the other hand, an encyclopaedic knowledge of the works of Shakespeare will have little relevance to an athlete's cultural capital within the setting of the sporting club itself.

The fourth form of capital is social capital, which comes from creating strong social networks of friends and acquaintances, and using those networks to secure sustainable benefits. According to Bourdieu, social capital involves building one's network of contacts and then using them to advance one's status and social position. Social capital can be invested in other people as well as in groups and communities, and subsequently used to yield a social return in the form of practical, emotional, or social support (Son *et al.* 2010: 68). This social return can also take the form of bonding or bridging relationships. A bonding relationship reflects the ties that 'develop between people with similar values and lifestyles', while bridging relationships refers to 'opportunities stemming from interconnections across groups and/or communities' (p. 68). Social capital remains self-serving, however, as it enhances one's social position at the same time as creating social value, since it can build 'reciprocity and trust' (Devine & Parr 2008: 394). Social capital has immediate relevance to athletes because sporting clubs are by nature social sites where interpersonal proximity and physical intimacy define the social experience.

The fifth form of capital is bodily or physical capital, which arises from a platform of physicality. For any policy or debate about sports, exercise, and physical recreation, the notion of physical capital plays a crucial role. It includes all those initiatives and practices that enhance one's bodily identity and image such as seeing one's physical self in a positive light, as well as having others see one's self as physically impressive. Bodily capital manifests in multidimensional ways. It includes, for example, the results that derive from improving one's wardrobe, dressing to the 'right' designer label, getting a facelift, colouring hair, cutting hair, growing hair, removing hair, brightening one's teeth, having liposuction treatment, having breast enlargement surgery, securing a penile implant, toning up, losing weight, gaining weight, becoming stronger, and building muscle (Wesley 2003). The accumulation of bodily capital contributes to success in any social field that values athleticism, aesthetic display, and sport performance. Value emerges from not only the capacity to look good, but to also perform well. Enhanced physical capital emerges directly from the use of performance-enhancing drugs.

The sixth form of capital is emotional/cognitive capital, which can be alternatively described as psychological capital. This form of capital derives from building 'mental toughness', psychological resilience, and positive mood. It is less about looking good and doing good, and more about feeling good and thinking clearly. Henry (2004) used the term 'cognitive capital' to capture those psychological dispositions that enable people to cope with the 'many adversities, threats and challenges that life typically presents' (p. 375). While some people can manage stressful situations well, others find it difficult to effectively manage problematic encounters. According to Henry, cognitive capital reflects one's coping strategies, which include the ability to design rational action plans in turbulent times, the capacity to secure social support when facing difficulties, the ability to control negative emotions, the ability to disengage from troublesome incidents, and the capacity to engage with an 'adaptive spiral' where anxiety and confusion are replaced by calmness and clarity of thought (Henry 2004: 387). Emotional/cognitive capital can also be accumulated through the development of emotional intelligence (Akerjordet & Severinsson 2007: 1406). Emotional intelligence enables people to manage their own emotional states as well as those of others. It creates value in situations requiring a calm social environment, strong interpersonal relationships, mutual trust, and polite and diplomatic exchanges (Mears & Finlay 2005). Finally, emotional/cognitive capital can be captured by bolstering one's mental toughness. This term acutely describes athletes and players who perform well when placed under added stresses and pressures.

Each of these six forms of capital is interdependent, transferable, and subject to diminution as well as accumulation. For example, the accumulation of economic capital offers just one of a number of ways of achieving status, success, credibility, and social standing, and 'becoming someone'. The pursuit of cultural capital, social capital, symbolic capital, and bodily capital can secure similar outcomes. Interdependency also becomes especially acute when considering emotional/ cognitive capital. Since this form of capital allows its owners to better cope with catastrophe, deal with trauma, and manage hard times, its possession allows them

Table 8.1 Features of each form of capital

Form of capital	Benefits secured by building up stocks of capital	Strategies used to attain stock of capital
Economic	Visible wealth, high income, high work productivity, conspicuous consumption	Hard work, long work hours, investing in shares and works of art, property ownership
Symbolic	Recognisable status, elevated social position, high reputation, influential	Senior management position, public recognition, media exposure, community leader
Cultural	Highly knowledgeable, well regarded, worldly, well travelled, well read, fashionably tasteful	High culture aficionado, regular theatre and gallery attendee, book club member
Social	Wide network of acquaintances and friends, centre of attention, social magnet	Member of clubs and associations, volunteer positions, deal maker and broker
Physical	Good-looking, fit and healthy, well groomed, strong and vigorous, sexually attractive	Regular sport participant, regular grooming, and building of fashionable wardrobe
Psychological	Emotionally stable, resilient, mentally tough, confident, socially adept	Healthy living, relaxation, vigorous physical activity, sporadic counselling, occasional therapy

to hold on to other forms of capital in difficult times. Alternatively, people with low stocks of emotional/cognitive capital suffer more when confronted with a major life crisis, and in doing so, risk losing their other capital. In other words, the concept of capital building provides for not just stockpiling one's personal stores of status and social clout, but for also having them disappear. In middle age, for instance, divorce, job loss, and illness can deliver a major blow to every form of capital, and in the worst of cases lead to personal disintegration and social oblivion. The main features of each form of capital, together with the value they build, and strategies used to attain them, are listed in Table 8.1.

The six forms of capital also neatly explain the ways in which players and athletes move through the world of sport. For example, capital forms highlight the axiomatic importance of the body to anyone who purports to be an athlete or sportsperson, while revealing how athletic success can be levered to secure even more success and public acclaim. Capital forms imply that not all players and athletes will accumulate loads of capital. In fact, they suggest the opposite: sporting capital will be distributed more unequally amongst its participants than nearly any other profession on the face of the planet. Only artists, musicians, and actors face similar inequalities in the allocation of capital amongst their members.

Physical capital stands front and centre for players and athletes who take their craft seriously. It is also referred to as bodily capital, physical capacity, physical performance, physical fitness, physical well-being, or just physicality (Shilling 2003). Furthermore, physical capital may be divided into health-related physical capital such as cardiovascular endurance, muscular strength, muscular endurance, flexibility, and body composition, and performance-related physical capital such as agility, balance, power, speed, coordination, and reaction time. Skilled professional training, therapeutic remedies, good diet, and adequate rest, amongst other things, may boost physical capital. However, it can also be destroyed by illnesses, loss of confidence, boredom, depression, and injuries. Drug use is both seductive and destructive when it comes to building ones stocks of physical capital, since it takes athletes to new levels of performance on one hand, or ruins their sporting careers on the other.

Psychological capital plays an essential part in producing successful sporting performances. In colloquial sporting terms, psychological capital accompanies mental toughness, used to describe athletes who continue to perform well when placed under high levels of competitive stress and pressure. Mental toughness includes the ability to withstand pain, either in training or in competition. A typical claim holds that mentally tougher athletes more often prevail, and that the difference between success and failure can frequently be attributed to psychological factors. Mental toughness enables tenacity and perseverance in athletes irrespective of the odds, and to manage negative psychological energy such as resentment, anger, and hostility. However, a brittle temperament and a loss of confidence can completely undermine successful sporting performance. In high stress situations like elite, competitive sport, a player's psychological fragility can be brutally exploited by opponents.

Economic capital is the third form of capital, and in a sporting context pertains to the salary, prize money, product endorsements, sponsorship deals, and paid speaking engagements and appearance fees. North American professional sport exemplifies the ways in which the fusion of physical and psychological capital can generate a multimillion dollar experience for stand-out players. In 2008, for instance, Tiger Woods, the world's leading professional golfer at the time, earned a salary of US$22 million and US$105 million in endorsements, while LeBron James, an elite level basketballer, was paid US$12 million annual salary and secured US$28 million in product endorsement fees. However, most people who play sport will pay for the privilege.

Cultural capital presents a more subtle, and, in some respects, a more mysterious form of capital when applied to sport settings. It can be quite intangible and variable from situation to situation. Cultural capital refers to an individual athlete's formal and informal education, intellectual exposure, and self-knowledge. Other related terms include human capital and intellectual capital. For many players and athletes, the accumulation of cultural capital enables them to pursue non-sport careers more successfully after retirement. A lack of cultural capital, and education in particular, limits an athlete's post-sport career opportunities, and squeezes their lifelong learning and long-term employment prospects. Cultural capital is transformational since it can be used to improve one's social position through knowledge, training, and intellectual discourse.

Social capital is the fifth form of capital that can be accumulated by players and athletes, derived through strong social networks built around kin, tribes, clans, neighbours, friends, work colleagues, and other acquaintances. While sometimes taken for granted by players and athletes, the strategic use of relationships to create networks can deliver sustainable benefits by advancing one's social position. In the case of sport, for example, strong bonds emerge during training camps where teams must function in intensive interpersonal situations where trust and loyalty receive the highest attention. Outside club and team dynamics, social capital may be expanded through public relations management, media training, and the opportunity to engage with volunteers in various social development projects or build relations with future employers in the corporate sector. In some instances professional players become aggressively celebrated media personalities. Media relationships present a powerful resource for athletes to yield a significant social return, or even transfer social into economic capital.

The final form of capital accumulation is symbolic capital, which revolves around the kudos and status that players and athletes can attract. It closely connects to the number of wins and honours an athlete has earned, conferring an impact upon their prestige, credibility, recognition, and respect. However, on-field success only constitutes the first step in building symbolic capital, since with appropriate strategic advice, players and athletes can deepen their stocks of symbolic capital by engaging in philanthropic work, and nurturing a positive public image constructed around doing social good. Symbolic capital is a pivotal part of the capital building process for players and athletes since its residual effects can be converted into stocks of economic capital such as sponsorship and product endorsement agreements. Corporate sponsors seek athletes perceived as well-respected, articulate, morally upright, law-abiding, and socially responsible because they can more effectively enact positive image transfer, increase brand equity, stimulate customer awareness, and open new markets. But, the accumulation of symbolic capital comes with a few words of caution. While athletes with big stores of symbolic capital will have dedicated fans, will be role models to millions, and act as national heroes, their symbolic capital can also be stripped away from them in an instant. It will evaporate when they are found to have visited prostitutes, delivered racist slurs to opponents, become addictive gamblers, led lives of sexual promiscuity, been involved in match fixing, been corrupted by criminal gangs, or even worse – in some sports commentator's eyes – been 'outed' as drug cheats.

Whether in sport or the broader society, and despite the fact that the much of this capital can be stripped away at a moment's notice, each form of capital is worth fighting and playing for since they provide the resources for both improving one's social position and securing attachments to people who have similar aspirations. Moreover, the more capital accumulated, the easier it becomes to dominate a chosen social field in the future. However all of this frenetic activity to build one's stocks of capital begs the questions as to 1) what exactly drives people to accumulate one bundle of capital and not another, 2) what enables some people to accumulate more capital than others, and 3) what makes one bundle of capital more prestigious than some other bundle of capital. The answer to these questions is found in the concept of 'habitus', and the values, beliefs and dispositions embedded in a given field of social engagement, as illustrated in Figure 8.1.

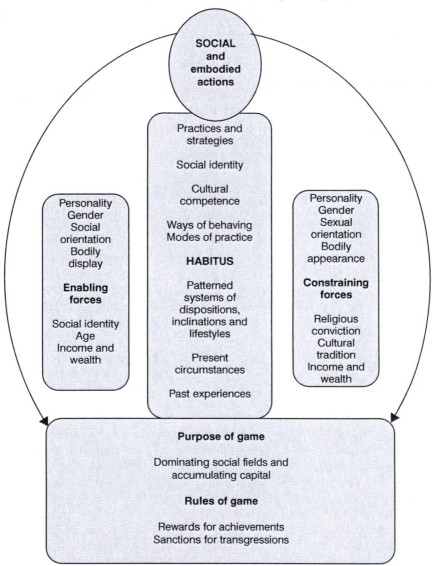

Figure 8.1 Habitus as a shaper of social action

In the language of Bourdieu, the successful accrual of capital means having the appropriate 'habitus' in relation to the social field being occupied. A habitus can be succinctly described as '… necessity internalized and converted into a … general, transferable … disposition that generates meaningful practices and meaning-giving' (Bourdieu 1984: 170). A habitus therefore shapes the way people view their world, their perceived place in it, and both their personal and social identities. Further, it provides a catalyst for action by enabling social agents to confidently enter various fields, secure capital, and enhance their future capacity for action and capital accumulation. Conversely, a habitus can constrain action, since it also contains the moral boundaries, taboos, customs, and traditions that inhibit certain behaviours. In sum, a habitus enables social agents to engage in a social field, and exploit that space in order to accumulate capital, and the additional power and influence that goes with it. However, there is no certainty that a habitus which is successful in accumulating capital, building power, and engendering influence in one social field will do the same in another.

Capital, habitus, and social fields as tools for understanding drug use in sport

In framing an analysis of drug use in sport, Bourdieu's concepts of social fields, capital, and habitus can prove useful. Bourdieu's bedrock principle is the social field, which provides the space for agents and stakeholders to play out their 'struggle' to 'maintain monopoly power' over authority, influence and prestige (Bourdieu & Wacquant 1992: 13). In social fields, authority, influence, and prestige are not distributed equally. Some agents and stakeholders have the appropriate mix of values, capabilities, and dispositions and can accumulate capital, or the source of power, more readily than others. At the same time, agents and stakeholders accumulate values, capabilities, and dispositions – their habitus – shaping their responses to the world around them (Bourdieu 1993a, 1993b, 1984; Bourdieu & Passeron 1977/1990). Agents and stakeholders with similar values and dispositions create a class, or collective habitus, with each habitus occupying a position in the social hierarchy. The more capital stored in each collective habitus, the greater its status and power (Bourdieu 1985; Kay & Laberge 2002).

Bourdieu's model of social behaviour shows how the accumulation of capital can shore up the power base of a class or collective habitus. It highlights the ways in which this power can be used to impose values and dispositions on other agents and organisations, and consequently dominate a social field. As a diagnostic tool, the model reveals those social agents and stakeholders who have accumulated power and use it to dominate the social field. Accordingly, the model demands an analysis of the values and dispositions that drive behaviour along with a commentary on how these values and disposition subjugate other participants. For example, a few influential stakeholders backed by substantial stocks of capital dominate the 'drugs in sport' field of play. In the first instance, the WADA and national governments use their highly valued economic, symbolic, and cultural capital to reshape the rules and regulations of sporting codes. They subsequently co-opt these codes to secure additional control over the drugs in sport field of play, and, in doing so, enforce their values and dispositions about what sport should and should not be about. As a result, other stakeholders who want to enter the field of play such as the media, other professional sports leagues, other national sport organisations (NSOs), or a professional drug treatment agency, must abide by the rules already embedded in the field by the dominant agents and stakeholders.

Players also must act under the constraints imposed by the collective habitus, which sends a number of clear and distinct messages. First, performance-enhancing drugs have no place in sport because they are a form of cheating, and cheating undermines the structural integrity of sport. Second, illicit drugs have no place in sport since they contaminate its moral foundations; their use encourages emulation especially by impressionable young people, and they undermine sport's social value. Third, severe fines and punitive suspensions are necessary to curb drug use, and more generally control the actions of athletes. Finally, treatment, rehabilitation, and softer penalties present no long-term solution to the problem since they imply that drug use constitutes a health issue rather than a moral and credibility issue (Bloomfield 2003; Brandis & Pyne 2007; Ferguson 2006; Kelly 2000; Kemp 2005a, 2006; WADA 2005). Players who want to succeed on the field of play, and secure some of the capital on offer, quickly understand that any form of drug use will destroy their capital accumulation goals if detected. In other words, success and longevity comes from aligning an individual habitus with the dominant collective habitus.

At the same time, there will always be a competing set of values (or collective habitus) that provides an alternative model for managing drug use in sport. In this case it revolves around player welfare and harm reduction, which is underpinned by the very different assumption that drug use is not the real problem, but merely a symptom of hyper-modern professional and elite sport. The fundamental issue does not lie with the immorality of cheating, but rather with the value and social utility of protecting players' health and welfare. Proponents of the harm-reduction approach include many drug-treatment professionals, whose arguments centre on counselling and treatment. Historically, however, they have failed to gain any policy traction, despite grounding their proposals in the advice of clinical experts (Caulkins *et al.* 2005; Kayser & Smith 2008; Stewart *et al.* 2008).

Evidence indicating that harm-reduction polices like counselling and rehabilitation can provide more cost-efficient ways of lowering the social and cultural 'damage' associated with drug use in sport (Benavie 2009; Eldredge 2000; Gray 2001), tend to be dismissed by dominant stakeholders as the wrong kinds of messages to spread. At the same time, little evidence supports claims that elite athletes heavily influence the behaviour of youths through a role modelling effect (Long & Sanderson 2001; Payne *et al.* 2003; Vescio *et al.* 2005). For example, studies of professional players and athletes hero-worshipped by school-age children have found that their off-field illicit drug use was rarely emulated (Hogan & Norton 2000; Keresztes *et al.* 2008; Lines 2001).

The current regulatory arrangements – as promulgated by the dominant stakeholders and their collective habitus – are consequently based on intuitive notions about player morality and the social value of sport, effectively sidelining any contradictory evidence. As a result, the existing regulatory arrangements do not reflect the evidence assembled for each option. Rather, they result from an imposition of the dominant stakeholder's collective habitus, or 'ideological will', on subordinate stakeholders, and the construction of regulations consistent with this will in the form of values and dispositions (Althaus *et al.* 2007; Bessant *et al.* 2006; Stewart *et al.* 2008).

Conclusion

In this chapter we showed how Bourdieu's use of the 'habitus' approach to social behaviour neatly captures the messy features of the current drug-control arrangements in sport. It revolves around how the dominant habitus sets the rules for the field of play: elite level sport. It also shows that once a specific stakeholder group has gained control of the relevant social field – the sport industry in this instance – and set the rules of play, capital – especially the physical, economic, social, and symbolic forms – will accrue to only those who play by the rules. In addition, the more draconian message declares that anyone found to have used drugs will not only be denied the opportunity of ever building up their stocks of capital through sport again, but will also have their existing stocks of capital completely stripped away from them, and probably for good.

At the same time, players also understand that their physical capital can be enhanced by not only hard training, but also by cleverly using drugs and other substances. And, for ambitious young athletes, any technology that allows their bodies to perform better for longer will not only increase their bodily capital in the short term, but also enable then to build their stocks of economic and symbolic capital in the long term. This is an attractive proposition, even where the rules say they will be punished if they have found to have used banned substances. In deciding the best way forward in terms of building their stocks of capital, they are very much 'on the horns of a dilemma'.

9   Life-course analysis as a tool for identifying gateways to success

Introduction

Life-course models of human behaviour employ the principles of human growth and development, as embedded in the proposition that every human life cycle begins with birth, explodes into growth, transits to maturity, sinks into decline, and ends with death. This life cycle model has become an instructive frame for displaying the cumulative learning, identity building, values creation, and social behaviour that transpires throughout a lifetime. It has also become a familiar tool for understanding the marketing of products to consumers. Business analysts have used product life cycle theories to track the sales of a whole range of goods and services in order to conceive of new ways in which their consumer relevance can be profitably extended.

One of the most influential life cycle theories was developed by Erik Erikson, who proposed an eight-stage model of psychosocial development centring on internal conflict management during a lifespan. To illustrate, from early childhood to 12 years of age, life revolves around building trust, autonomy, initiative, and industry. From 12 to 20 life mainly becomes about constructing a stable and functional personal identity, while the 20–40 year period has more to do with building intimate relationships and positive social networks. By middle age, which Erikson identifies as the 40–65-year-old age group, the emphasis transfers to 'generativity', which involves making lasting contributions to the family and the community. For the time after 65, people grapple with their life's meaning, and how to best face the ageing process with dignity and optimism. But, as Erikson poignantly observes, a failure to effectively manage the conflicts that each of the eight phases brings can lead to cumulative trauma that begins with mistrust, shame, guilt and inferiority, merges into role confusion, isolation and stagnation, and ends in despair (Sigleman & Rider 2009).

The life-course model proposes that people's current behaviour and practices can be best understood by exploring their past behaviours and practices. It is axiomatic that our life course begins at birth, transitions through various stages of growth and decline, and ends with death. In between, though, many challenging, traumatic, and life-changing events occur. Our life journey rarely unravels in a linear sequence, the result of one neatly planned step after another. A multitude of unanticipated incidents must be addressed, a massive number of exchanges to sort out, many barriers to manage, and numerous opportunities to embrace. Life transpires differently for all of us, and we handle them in inconsistent ways. But the one common thread is that our past invariably shapes our sense of self, and how we make our way through the world. As we will see, this premise can be useful in better understanding the drugs in sport issue.

Life-course models provide for the interweaving of 'age-graded trajectories'; the pattern of concurrent pathways linked to work, leisure, and family. They also reveal 'short-term transitions' covering events like leaving school, graduating from university, getting married, and retiring from the workforce (Elder 1994). Transitioning rarely involves a smooth and trauma-free experience since it demands substantive changes in roles, responsibilities, and personal identities. Each inevitably brings about 'a change in one's behaviour and relationships' (Schlossberg, 1981: 5).

Life-course models add weight to the ways in which early transitions, such as from student to worker, shape later experiences, events, and, ultimately, life trajectories. In other words, the resources accumulated in early adulthood including material wealth, good health, a durable body, psychological resilience, and a network of friends, will impact on the quality of later life. As a result, the experiences of adult ageing can only be properly understood with 'knowledge of the prior life course' (Elder 1994: 5). This does not mean that past experiences causally determine present and future choices, but it does mean that the past will shape the capacity for future choices (Leonard & Burns 2006).

A third layer of the life-course model emphasises the critical incidents and events that induce change. Such critical incidents and events, or 'turning points', present an additional catalyst for transitions, and can take three different forms. First, role transition involves incidents like adapting to a partner's retirement. Second, adversity and disruption may for example involve a family illness. Finally, personal growth can involve the opportunity to travel, or the experience of updating an educational qualification (Leonard & Burns 2006). Turning points have the capacity to radically change trajectories by either offering new and exciting choices, or severely denying opportunities. Moreover, they not only produce positive transitions, but also induce negative transitions, which mean that young adults beginning their life courses from a similar base can very often take on significantly different trajectories over the remainder of their life course, and produce remarkably different life narratives (Hser *et al.* 2007). Turning points also tie together three elements of the life course model: 1) a prior steady state, 2) a critical event, and 3) the plotting of a new trajectory. The various elements that make up a life-course model are illustrated in Figure 9.1.

The model illustrated in Figure 9.1 assumes the occurrence of multiple trajectories and life paths that people can take. Trajectories can be adjusted at many times during the life course as responses to the various incidents and turning points that inevitably occur. The model implies that even when people start their life course from a similar socio-economic base, their responses to different critical incidents will set them on divergent life trajectories. On the other hand, this model

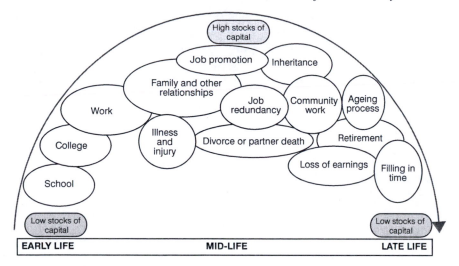

Figure 9.1 Life-course transitions, turning points, and critical incidents

suggests that people from similar backgrounds who are exposed to common experiences through their life course, will most probably experience consistent trajectories. The final point to note here is that throughout their life courses, people will accumulate various forms of capital that give them the capacity to manage their lives more independently, and provide additional choice. As explained in the previous chapter, these 'capitals' can take many forms, including material wealth, status, professional expertise, a rounded education, a broad network of family, friends and colleagues, emotional resilience, a durable body, and good physical health. Most people aspire to a life that delivers an expanding stock of these 'capitals', as their acquisition will most likely provide a rewarding and productive life. However, an idealised trajectory can be undermined by critical incidents that can erode one's stock of capital, with long-term injury and disability, divorce, illness, job redundancy, and loss of identity being some of the more perilous incidents and episodes encountered.

Life-course conceptual models

A number of life-course models have been applied to the analysis of individual development through the lifespan, examining the ways in which previous work, family, and leisure experiences interdependently shape people's futures. Life-course models shed light on how life events impact upon health and leisure behaviours by drawing on biomedical analyses of health and welfare. They include 1) the latent effects model, 2) the pathway model, 3) the social mobility model, and 4) the cumulative life-course model. We briefly describe each below.

The latent effects life-course model hypothesises that adverse early life experiences increase health risks in later life, independent of any intervening social, economic, lifestyle, or traditional risk factors. Certain early life events may have strong independent effects on adult health by working through 'biological chains of risk'. For example, prenatal and early life socio-economic factors will affect biological resources, which will in turn influence adult health. More generally, the operation of biological or developmental influences during early 'sensitive periods' will permanently impact on developing individuals in either positive or negative ways.

In the pathway model, early life events and environments will influence later life experiences, opportunities, and health risk factors. It assumes a developmental process that links early life psychosocial environments with adult health risks via pathway effects. Here, early experiences place an individual on a certain life trajectory, eventually impacting adult health. The term 'social chains of risk' is used to explain how early events influence later life health status. As a result, 'ongoing social processes' and 'a continuity of social circumstances' lead to either advantageous or disadvantageous chains of advantage.

Social mobility theories assume that an individual's social and economic circumstances relentlessly shape their behaviour across the life course, impacting upon their adult health. This model posits a mixed range of possibilities whereby deprivation in early life can be followed by 1) material affluence to produce hybrid health outcomes, 2) natural 'health selection', where less healthy individuals tend to have downward social mobility and healthier individuals tend to be upwardly mobile, and 3) a 'health constraint' factor, where socially mobile individuals possess health characteristics of the class they join as well as the 'class' they depart.

Cumulative life-course models assume that psychosocial and physiological experiences, combined with environmental factors, work to influence adult disease risk during both early and later life. Different combinations will produce a wide variety of health outcomes. This model highlights the ways in which individuals build up their stocks of biological resources, and how, over the life course their 'health and physical capital' can vary, with important implications for their health status.

Habitus-based models

As discussed in the previous chapter, Pierre Bourdieu's concept of habitus connects with the life-course approach as a tool for understanding how accumulated experiences impact on both future health and bodily status as well as social and economic status. As we noted also earlier, Bourdieu claimed that everybody occupies a habitus, a set of dispositions and lifestyle practices guiding people through their social worlds. It constitutes the aggregation of years of socialisation and adaptation to one's surroundings, and consequently shapes the way people view their world, their perceived place in it, and their social identity. To this extent habitus constrains action. It operates as a repository for all sorts of moral boundaries, taboos, customs, traditions, and ideologies that inhibit, and sometimes even forbid certain behaviours, whether refusing to take blood transfusions, denying ones-self mood altering drugs, never voting for conservative governments, or not taking regular exercise.

At the same time, the habitus offers a guide to action through two mechanisms. First, it delivers a vehicle for designing and carrying out strategies enabling people to engage in competitive social spaces in order to accumulate personal capital, and the additional power and influence that goes with it. Second, it assists in carrying out strategies that strengthen people's distinctiveness while building bonds with people who share similar values, beliefs, and dispositions. Moreover, people implicitly respond to a hierarchy of habitus'. Given the choice, most people would prefer to possess a habitus that gives them a dominant position in a particular social field rather than one that will diminish or marginalise them.

An individual's habitus also has a tendency towards inertia and institutionalisation. For example, all those customs, habits, beliefs, values, and ideologies that were laid down in the early part of our lives become hardwired into our daily decision making. However, they can also be reshaped in response to changes in social spaces and fields of play resulting from external jolts and boundary-line turbulence. Take, for instance, changing gender relations in the workplace, where women are given the opportunity to secure senior managerial positions, and sexist behaviour is no longer rewarded. In these situations misogynist males will be disadvantaged if they fail to accommodate the new, dominant ideology into their habitus, and continue to play out their old belief systems.

In Bourdieu's social world the habitus drives the consumption of sport experiences because it shapes values, identities, and lifestyle behaviours. In turn, it provides the catalyst for seeking specific products. Because a habitus acutely reflects people's unique histories, life experiences, and social conditions, it will shape their leisure practices and even drug-use choices. This means that middle-class, professional families who share a similar habitus will have different sport and leisure aspirations to outer suburban working families. For example, their status-conscious dispositions, self-conscious identities centred on fashion brand names, claims to good taste, and expansive incomes, will produce patterns of consumption giving significant space to ski holidays in exotic international resorts, trips to wineries, membership at private golf clubs, and premium seats at the favourite boutique sport stadium. In contrast, outer-suburbanites with medium income households will be more interested in community netball and football competitions, car racing, power-boating, angling, boxing, and mixed martial arts. At least, that is how a stereotypical division between two classic habitus' might look on the surface.

Bourdieu's model of social behaviour fits neatly into life-course models of social behaviour since they embrace the core assumptions that people reflect their previous experiences, and that they use these experiences, albeit unconsciously, to shape their behaviours. The behaviour of people throughout their life course will be a function of their past, with some factors acting as constraints on behaviour, and others acting as enablers. At the same time, constraints and enablers, and the context in which they operate, can change. For example, a tendency to fall back into old patterns of behaviour, be they annual holidays, sports watching, or heavy alcohol consumption, will be challenged from time to time by critical incidents, traumatic events, and key turning points, leading to quite different social trajectories. And, few critical incidents constitute such a powerful call to action as the globalisation, commercialisation, and competitive pressures of elite sport.

Life-course modelling and drugs in sport

The above models and approaches to the life course share a number of common assumptions about how people move through their social worlds and respond to the variables that shape and guide their movements. Five commonalities warrant notice: 1) human lives are embedded in and shaped by historical context; 2) individuals construct their life course through their choices and actions, but remain constrained by historical and social circumstances; 3) choices and actions are played out in life domains that involve an intertwining of work, family, health, social relations, and leisure practices; 4) individuals go through various staged transitions and unanticipated incidents which allow them to reflect on previous practices, and to contemplate significant life changes; and (5) the responses individuals make to these staged transitions, turning points, and unanticipated incidents create the setting for subsequent life trajectories.

The life-course model as described above makes it clear that movements through life vary due to the constraints of early experiences, especially those in childhood and adolescence. At the same time, they are also enabled by productive responses to critical incidents and transition points. For example, over a life course, a series of reflective times occur where decisions about what to do next, and what life path to take, must be selected. Schooling, occupational training, partner selection, leisure activities, and child rearing comprise just a few social fields that demand some type of decision to be made, even if it is a decision to do nothing. Moreover, the life-course model fits neatly within sport activities. Training schedules and programs not only have to fit in with an athlete's non-work time, but also must compete with an array of other leisure activities like gardening, eating out, watching television, looking after children, watching sport remotely, attending the cinema or the theatre, or just resting. At each phase in the life course these competing occupiers of time will either expand or shrink, priorities will change, opportunities to engage will wax and wane, while constraints and barriers to participating will also fluctuate.

Such a complex suite of variables leads to questions as to what transitions, incidents, and turning points will influence the decision to use drugs, and how might the subsequent choices impact on the overall trajectories of players and athletes. Is there, for instance, a particular time in athletes' lives when using performance-enhancing drugs becomes a viable option, or even the preferred option? Furthermore, what life-course experiences lead to greater or lesser levels of drug use? In order to answer these questions we need to consider how life-course models illuminate the development of elite players and athletes in circumstances where sporting careers are both clearly marked and severely truncated (Pearson & Petipas 1990). In the case of sports with high physical demands, like football codes, tennis, cycling, rowing, track and field, and combat sport, athletes usually do not formally begin their competitive careers until around the age of 10, and for the most part finish at around 35, with the occasional player stretching their active participation to the age of 40. So, how might we construct a life-course model for such elite professional players and athletes?

A good starting point from a generic sports viewpoint means revisiting Coakley and Donnelly's (1999) four-stage career model of players and athletes. Stage one involves the introduction to sport and exploring its fun and informal structures. Stage two involves serious training and development, where participants learn how to become athletes, and where they begin to construct an identity around being an athlete. Stage three involves athletes going deep into the experience, and 'doing' the sport, where intense competition and performance improvement become central. Stage four, the final stage, involves players' and athletes' experiences when making the transition from competition to non-competition, and when also having to make decisions about what to do for the remainder of their lives.

A similar sport development model by Balyi (2001) outlined a four-stage process, which like Coakley and Donnelly, accommodated both a technical and social dimension. Stage one centres around learning to train, stage two focuses on training to compete, stage three revolves around training to win, or achieving peak performance, while stage four concerns retirement and transitioning, where the transitioning could mean exiting the sport altogether, or finding a niche role back in the sport itself. Balyi constructed a model for the all-round, 'late specialisation' athlete, where 'fun and play', and 'learning to train', were given their own designated phases at the front-end of the model. In each stage the technique and science of sport meshes with its behavioural and social expectations to create a specific sporting culture. This might, for instance, run from the participatory, through to the exploratory, and finish up with the performative (Carless & Douglas 2009: 55). At the same time, a commercial thread runs through the sport development fabric. It reaches a zenith at the performative level, where professionalism and total athlete commitment become the dominant features (Christensen & Sorensen 2009: 128).

These models were recently adapted by the ASC, which invented a ten-stage model of elite sport development. Each of the stages is located within one of three pre-transition periods. Period one reflects fun and enjoyment. Period two focuses on training and athlete development, where skills become embedded, tactical know-how is learnt, and game science is built. Period three progresses to the elite level, where athletic maturity and high-level performance assume the greatest weight.

Another life-course model for application to sport was designed by Brissonneau (2010a, 2010b), who used it to illuminate the progression of European cyclists into the professional ranks In building upon the Coakley and Donnelly model, Brissonneau distinguished the ordinary world of amateur cycling and sport in general, from the extraordinary world of elite professional cyclists. Everything begins in the ordinary world, where the child experiments with games and sports, and accumulates a broad set of experiences and attitudes in and around these

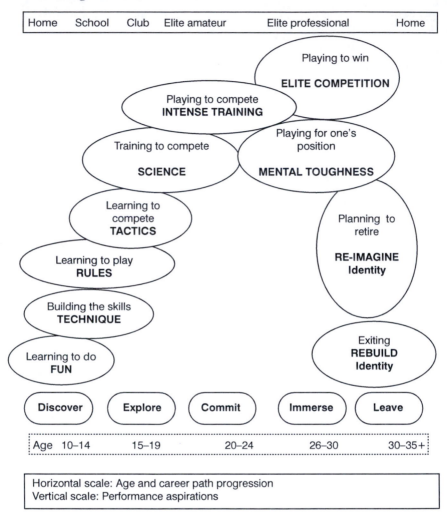

| Home | School | Club | Elite amateur | Elite professional | Home |

Playing to win
ELITE COMPETITION

Playing to compete
INTENSE TRAINING

Playing for one's position
MENTAL TOUGHNESS

Training to compete
SCIENCE

Learning to compete
TACTICS

Planning to retire
RE-IMAGINE
Identity

Learning to play
RULES

Building the skills
TECHNIQUE

Exiting
REBUILD
Identity

Learning to do
FUN

| Discover | Explore | Commit | Immerse | Leave |

| Age | 10–14 | 15–19 | 20–24 | 26–30 | 30–35+ |

Horizontal scale: Age and career path progression
Vertical scale: Performance aspirations

Figure 9.2 Elite sport career pathway without drug use opportunity

activities. From these early experiences, young athletes discover a sport that not only captures their imagination, but also provides them with a sense of mastery and success. From here leading young athletes feel impelled to progress towards elite competition (Brissonneau 2010a, 2010b). But, the discovery stage, as Figure 9.2 illustrates, represents merely the starting point.

The next phase involves nurturing and talent development, followed by an introduction to the competitive side of the sport. At this point young athletes begin to absorb their sport's culture; what it means to be a serious competitor. Young athletes subsequently come to better understand what one needs to do in order to advance to the next phase of the life cycle. As athletes enter their teenage years they must commit themselves assiduously to their chosen sport as a precursor to entering the elite ranks. More importantly from our perspective, at this pivotal transition point, athletes will be introduced to a range of techniques and technologies to assist them in improving performance. Supplement and drug use form essential parts of these technologies and techniques.

The move from the ordinary amateur to the extraordinary elite provides the most traumatic transformation. Players and athletes must decide whether they are going to make a full-time commitment to their sport, or whether they retain its place as just one of a number of work and leisure practices occupying their time. If they decide to take the professional and elite pathway, then they must not only train hard, but also immerse themselves in the world of sport strategy, sport science, and sport nutrition. Supplements may only be the beginning as additional substances become available that significantly augment recovery and enhance the training effect.

Once players and athletes become acclimatised to the world of hyper-competitive, professional sport, they can embrace the opportunity to climb the very highest performance peaks. Some athletes become 'human machines'. In the machine world, every slight improvement possibility must be chased down, torn apart, and re-presented as another step along the path to enhancement. Sport becomes a whole of life experience. Diets and sleep fall under the most stringent regimentation, and sport medicine physicians carefully monitor weekly progress. Training schedules operate under periodised regimes, recovery times receive close attention, and perfection in technique and skill performance become essential. To avoid any performance gaps, athletes consume a raft of customised supplements and utilise numerous recovery modes. And, they receive the opportunity to take that extra step into the compelling and mysterious world of sport pharmacology, where esoteric substances await experimentation and promise much more than mere incremental improvement.

All good things come to an end. For every elite player and athlete there comes a time when the body breaks down and the drive to do all that it takes to win dissipates. It is the beginning of the end for elite professional athletes, leading to what the broader community calls retirement, but what the fragile minds of ageing players and athletes might want to call oblivion. For many athletes the transition to retirement represents a traumatic adjustment. Their extraordinary world seems far removed from the ordinary world that the rest of us inhabit; little use for people whose tired bodies have seen better days, and whose skills and capacities do not fit neatly into occupations that mostly rate intellectual capabilities and social skills ahead of physical prowess. In any case, many elite athletes leave sport with broken bodies, constant pain, restricted mobility, and a generally more limited set of physical capabilities than the average person.

Each of the above athlete career path models involves what might be called life-course transitions (Schlossberg 1981). They can be conflated into five stages, with four of the stages constituting crucial developmental transitions, and the final stage being – in the context of the personalised sport experience – a decline into retirement: discovery, exploration, commitment, immersion, and retirement. As we noted in Chapter 8, every step along the life course is framed by 'situational

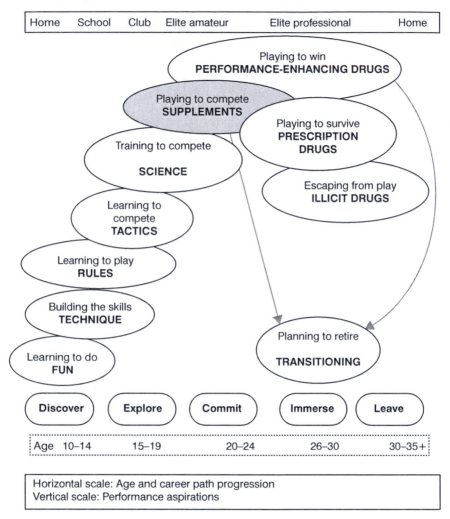

Figure 9.3 Elite sport career pathway with drug use opportunity

overlays' shaping behaviour. Of course, players and athletes are no exception. These situational overlays – with special attention to the supply of performance-enhancing substances – are incorporated into our modified life-course model of sport development, which is shown in Figure 9.3

Our model reveals that despite a similar destination, the processes involved in getting there introduce more complexity and ambiguity than other life-course theories predict. In fact, the journey to a better performance destination contains many diversions, often lined with various and highly visible signposts that trumpet the opportunity to take the occasional short-cut. One alternative appears starkly. It involves a continuation along the nicely paved and beautifully cambered substance-free road that produces a safe, trauma-free, and predictable, but often unnoticed, arrival. For some elite athletes and players, this road may be far too predictable, and, even worse, lead them to a safe but mediocre space distant from the super-highway to elite performance. Our model consequently places supplement and drug use front and centre, which in turn allows us to make sense of what drives athletes to do all that it takes to enhance performance, and to better understand those factors that shape the decision to use or not to use banned substances.

Our version of the life-course theory proposes that in the harsh reality of sport in a hyper-modern, pharmaceutically engaged world, anything goes when excellence and high performance occupies the singular vision. Rather than a question of fairness, ethics or health, many elite athletes take the simple perspective of 'what will it take?' Under such a mindset, additional drug use appears, to many athletes, as a mandatory feature of belonging to the elite sporting club.

Drugs, cycling, and performance improvement: a life-course analysis

Thousands of athletes have, over the years, used drugs of various descriptions to secure a spot on the super-highway to elite sport performance. Cycling, perhaps, provides the exemplar. Despite regular condemnation of the use of illegal substances, drug use has always been prevalent in cycling, and traces to the late 19th century when riders were supplied with strychnine, trimethyl, and heroin in an attempt to 'increase their endurance' (Dimeo 2007: 26). The search for compounds that would get cyclists over fatigue-humps continued into the 20th century, and during the 1950s and 1960s Tour de France champions Fausto Coppi and Jaques Anquelli both admitted to using stimulants to 'hold themselves together' (Coyle 2005: 109). Drug use to sustain performance continued into the 1970s (Thompson 2006) when the pressure to perform was heightened by the sport's rapid corporatisation (Hoberman 1992; Mignon 2003a). During the 1980s and early 1990s, professional cycling became a commercialised, global sport, with allegations of drug use surfacing more frequently (Voy 1991). At the 1991 world cycling championships, two Australians, Carey Hall and Stephen Pate, who finished first and second respectively in the sprint event, tested positive to steroid use and were each suspended from competitive cycling for two years (Buti & Fridman 2001). In the same year Martin Vinnicombe, a leading Australian time-trial cyclist, tested positive to a steroid compound whilst competing in an event in the US, and was also suspended from competing for two years (Buti & Fridman 2001).

Drug-use allegations were levelled against numerous elite level international cyclists throughout the 1990s. As we mentioned earlier, a crisis erupted during the 1998 Tour de France when the Festina team was investigated by the French police after Customs officials found large amounts of anabolic steroids, EPO, and growth hormones in their possession. A number of Festina team members, including the team doctor, were found guilty of trafficking in illegal drugs and using prohibited substances. Together with doping allegations arising out of the 1996 Atlanta Olympic Games, the incident led the IOC to establish an international agency that could develop and enforce a global anti-doping code, which led to the formation of the WADA in 1999 (Hanstad *et al.* 2008; Park, 2005).

Despite the global coverage and international legitimacy that the WADA subsequently enjoyed, cycling has continued to host numerous drug-use incidents. One scandal-ridden case we first noted in Chapter 3 involved Mark French, Australia's most successful young cyclist between 2001 and 2003. To briefly recap, in 2003 during the lead-up to the Athens Olympic Games, French had been training at the elite cycling academy in Adelaide, South Australia. He was accommodated at an apartment owned by the AIS. After vacating his room cleaners found a plastic bucket full of syringes and needles. Originally containing a protein supplement, the bucket contained 13 used syringes, 30 needles, 13 empty vials labelled with the word 'Equigen' (a growth hormone used to treat horses), several vials of 'Testicomp' (a homeopathic compound that actually contained traces of glucocorticosteroid, an anti-inflammatory drug that also has muscle building properties), and containers of vitamins B and C in liquid-injectable form (Gallen 2004; Jefferey 2004). Although French claimed innocence, blaming the incident on four other elite cyclists, a Court of Arbitration for Sport hearing subsequently found that French had been in possession of human growth hormone, and had used the Testicomp compound. French received a competition suspension for two years. However, he successfully appealed against the decision, later representing Australia at the 2008 world cycling championships and Beijing Olympic Games. It was never established who did, in fact, supply and use the paraphernalia found in French's room (Anderson 2004a, 2004b, 2004c).

Drug scandals have also haunted cycling in Europe. In 2006, Floyd Landis, that year's Tour de France winner, tested positive to unacceptable levels of testosterone, while German cyclist Jan Ulrich did not even get to the starting line due to allegations that he had taken a cocktail of EPO, steroids, and human growth hormone. Similarly, Alberto Contador, a three-time Tour de France winner, tested positive to the stimulant Clenbuterol during the 2010 race. Clenbuterol is a compound used by asthma sufferers as a bronchodilator, but is also given to livestock to increase their muscle-to-fat ratio. Contador disputed the result claiming that traces of the drug probably came from contaminated beef his team had imported from Spain. The International Cycling Union (UCI) was dismayed with the 'inadvertent contamination' defence. While his national governing body, the Spanish Cycling Federation (RFEC), initially suspended him from competition for 12 months, in early 2011 Contador appealed the decision, and the RFEC Disciplinary Committee overturned his suspension. However, the grounds for reversing the earlier decision were not clear to most observers, including the UCI and the WADA. Travis Tygart, the chief executive officer of the USADA, suggested that the decision was a 'classic example of the fox protecting the henhouse', and '... it would look like they are protecting a national hero' (Slot 2011: 32). As we noted in Chapter 3, Tygart's evangelistic management also led the USADA to legitimately claim that Lance Armstrong had taken a cocktail of performance-enhancement substances during most of his professional road cycling career.

Drug use also looms large in club cycling throughout Europe, although most of it appears to be legal. At the same time, these cyclists seem particularly susceptible to illegal drug use if it can generate a competitive edge. In a detailed analysis of Western European club cycling, Lentillon-Kaestner & Carstairs (2010) invited eight ambitious cyclists to talk about supplement and drug use in their sport. Six were amateur club cyclists aiming to ride for professional teams, while the remaining two had recently secured professional contracts. The eight informants were invited to talk about what they were prepared to do in order to make a living as a professional cyclist. All of the cyclists 'took some products to improve performance' (Lentillon-Kaestner & Carstairs 2010: 338). For the most part the substances were legal, such as protein powder, high carbohydrate supplements, amino acids, iron, magnesium, calcium, and caffeine. Altitude training was also employed to improve aerobic capacity. While seven of the eight informants were tempted to dope, they hesitated on the grounds that it was not part of the amateur cycling 'scene', and that they 'did not want to disappoint all the people who supported them' (Lentillon-Kaestner & Carstairs, 2010: 340). At the same time, all of the eight informants conceded that illegal drug use was essential to claim a permanent spot in the professional cycling ranks. Interestingly, none of the eight informants expressed uncertainties about banned substances. In fact, they all wanted to know more about doping, and had already trawled the Internet, and quizzed many experienced professionals about it. They understood what drove professional cyclists to dope, and were on the whole sympathetic to users. The group clearly believed that the health risks associated with the use of banned drugs was overrated, and one of the cyclists even suggested that growth hormones actually improve one's health status (Lentillon-Kaestner & Carstairs 2010: 340).

The other revealing outcome of the study was that all the informants distinguished between the culture of amateur cycling and the culture of professional cycling. They all claimed that amateur cycling was, in the main, free from serious doping. Amateur cycling provides a training ground for the professional ranks and drug-free competition allows the more gifted athletes to establish their credentials before being invited to move to the next level of competitive cycling. According to the informants, drug use in the amateurs would undermine the success of talent search programs undertaken by professional team managers. As for the prevalence of drug use in the professional ranks, these eight informants accepted it as a taken-for-granted fact. In a fiercely competitive sport with such a high public profile, and where just finishing a long road race seems like an achievement, the informants advised that some type of drug use remains essential.

Life-course models allow us to more sharply reveal the ways in which supplements and drug use plays itself out, and to what extent prior use of one substance influences choices about other substances. This constitutes an important point to address since the literature on drug use in the wider community suggests a strong relationship. For instance, Hser *et al.* (2007) found that not only does most cigarette, alcohol, and drug use 'begin in adolescence', but that an 'early age of onset' of drug use is 'one of the best predictors of future drug use and dependence' (Hser *et al.* 2007: 527). Similarly, Maldonado-Molina and Lanza (2010: 913) confirmed a 'gateway' phenomena whereby 1) alcohol served as an entry point into cigarette smoking, and 2) both alcohol and cigarettes served as gateway drugs for marijuana. Certain past experiences and incidents either encourage or discourage cyclists from going down the supplement and drug-use side road, and ultimately onto the super-highway of banned substance use.

Our own research suggests that technology, training, diet, supplements, and prescription drugs are most often cited as the strategies cyclists use in securing a competitive edge. Moreover, as our revised life-course model predicts, any aspiring club cyclist clearly understands that 'natural talent' and hard work are inadequate to secure an elite level of performance. This concession emerges early on in cyclists' careers, and leads them to identify a number of factors that help dismantle the natural-talent-limit barrier. They are to: 1) train hard, 2) gravitate to a knowledgeable coach, 3) secure equipment that provides the best possible opportunity to do well, 4) more efficiently fuel the body with the addition of plants, herbs, and supplements, and 5) use various legal stimulants and narcotic analgesics to defer fatigue and reduce discomfort.

We also found that the heaviest users of supplements and prescription drugs are those who have a long history of competitive cycling going back to their teenage years. On the other hand, those who use supplements and prescription drugs the least had entered the world of competitive cycling later in their sporting lives. In order to effectively transition to the elite level, some drug use is acknowledged as essential (Brissonneau 2010a, 2010b; Lentillon-Kaestner & Carstairs 2010).

The case of competitive cycling confirms that in the harsh reality of sport in a hyper-modern world, anything goes and high performance is the singular vision. To athletes, it is not a question of fairness or equity. Athletes do not ask, will it enhance my health, or will it make me feel smugly ethical, but rather, 'what will it take?' In order to achieve national or international success, additional substance use constitutes a virtually mandatory practice.

Our discussion so far suggests that in any sporting milieu incorporating vigorous competition, and where the performance ethic dominates, an athlete's attention will invariably turn to substance use as a means of securing superior results. Caffeine is a case in point. While not a banned substance, it delivers an endurance boost and an extended pain threshold without causing any major health problems. It delivers an irreplaceable substance for all seriously competitive cyclists. This suggests to us that the solution to drug use in cycling does not involve making drug-use rules and regulations more punitive by criminalising the use of certain substances. Rather, a more productive avenue would involve the deregulation of substance use. In a competitive culture like professional cycling, where fatigue is a constant problem, some acknowledgement must be given to this embedded feature, where competitors become 'human motors' encased within 'human machines' (Thompson 2003: 84).

If, for instance, the controlled use of certain anabolic steroid compounds was allowed under strict supervision, the space for marginal improvement would still be open, but with less risk of serious health implications. This radical suggestion may merely inflame the concerns of fans, sport officials, and politicians, but we believe that it helps secure the health and well-being of cyclists, giving them the space to fine-tune their capacity for improved performances, while not tilting the playing field excessively in any direction, and doing it all in a controlled environment.

Conclusion

Many useful models and theories that illuminate drug use in sport have been constructed, but they tend to be limited by their focus on the socio-economic costs and benefits of using drugs. As we noted in earlier parts of this book, we believe that the conversation needs to be broadened to accommodate not only a micro orientation on individual athlete intentions, but also a macro orientation on sporting context and culture. Such a holistic diagnosis requires an interpretive view of the situational factors that mitigate easy explanations of drug-taking behaviour.

In Chapters 7, 8, and 9 we provided three models to assist in unravelling the drug use motivations, choices, and behaviours of athletes and players. These were: 1) the social ecology model, 2) the capital building model, and 3) the life-course model. We think that each of these three conceptual frameworks encourages a deeper and richer investigation of the drugs in sport issue. Social ecology takes the view that attitudes and behaviours are not driven exclusively by personal factors intrinsic to the individual. Instead, environmental influences play a part in explaining attitudes and behaviour. As a result, social ecology helps explore the drugs in sport issue because it recognises the interdependencies between context, attitudes, and behaviours. The capital building model shows how the accumulation of capital – especially physical capital – can both improve an athlete's power base, and help to expose those social agents and stakeholders whose economic and symbolic capital dominates the decisions of their subordinates. Finally, the life-course model focuses on developmental stages and critical incidents in order to highlight the pivotal decision-making moments in athletes' careers precipitating the choice to use or not use drugs. Additionally, all three models pay careful attention to the relationships athletes experience with their bodies. In particular, they expose just how far athletes are prepared to work on their bodies to make a difference to their sporting performances.

Part III
The WADA revolution

10 How it happened and what it does

Introduction

Building on the material we presented in the previous chapters, here we take a closer look at the mechanics of WADA's drug control policy in general, and the WADA Code (WADC) in particular. As we signalled in the early part of the book, the WADA drug control model is both ambitious and complex. It is ambitious because the WADA wants a globally present code of conduct. It also aims to equalise drug control arrangements so that their deployment works exactly the same anywhere in the world (Park 2005). And, in moments of hyper-bureaucratic vision, the WADA foresees a time when every sporting code on the planet at every level of competition will have enacted the WADA model: harmonisation at its most perfect.

WADA's drug controls are also complex because it seeks to include not only substances that improve sporting performance but also illicit products for which possession and use constitutes a crime. This immediately creates confusion because most illicit drugs do not actually improve performance. Further complications arise with the distinction between testing for drug use in-competition, and testing for drug use out-of-competition. It gets even messier when considering that some substances are banned during in-competition periods, but permissible in out-of-competition periods. Finally, a provision for therapeutic exemptions permits players and athletes with ongoing health issues to use banned medications. All of these issues will be addressed in detail in this chapter.

As we have already shown, the systematic use of drugs and other substances to improve sporting performance has a rich history. To recap, during the 1930s and 1940s stimulants gained popularity, but in the 1950s, when the pharmaceutical industry began the production and supply of synthetic testosterone, anabolic steroids became the drug of choice for strength athletes in particular. Formal testing for performance-enhancing drugs was introduced at the Mexico Olympic Games in 1968 in response to the global spread of potent stimulants and anabolic steroids, with the IOC subsequently establishing a list of prohibited classes of substances and prohibited methods (Dimeo 2007; Taylor 1991). However, it took a further 30 years for sport authorities to make the issue of doping an urgent global priority despite the growing number of pharmaceutical products that could improve sport performance, and despite the huge competitive edge that East German athletes procured in the 1970s from systematic doping arrangements (Hoberman 1992; Hunt 2007). The Ben Johnson steroids incident at the 1988 Seoul Olympic Games, doping allegations arising out of the 1996 Atlanta Olympic Games, and the Tour de France Festina team drug scandal of 1998 confirmed that performance-enhancing drug use in sport was widespread (Hanstad *et al.* 2008; Hoberman 2001). Cumulatively, these developments prompted the IOC-led establishment of an international agency responsible for the enforcement of a worldwide anti-doping code for all sports. It aimed to safeguard the level-playing-field principle so highly valued by sport's stakeholders (Mignon 2003b; Pampel 2007).

The WADA revolution

In 1999, the WADA sprang to life with careful nurturing from the IOC (Hanstad *et al.* 2008; Rasmussen 2005). It immediately secured a mandate to 1) test athletes for drug use, 2) investigate allegations of use, possession or trafficking, 3) apply penalties and sanctions for violations of the code, and 4) promote to athletes the virtues of drug-free sport (Houlihan 2003; Park 2005; Pound 2006). The WADA built its profile and influence in three ways. First, it received funding from the IOC as well as from a consortium of national governments. Its 2011, 2012 and 2013 budgets were all just under US$29 million, with US$13 million coming from the IOC and the remaining U$S16 million from governments around the world (WADA 2012b). Second, it wielded regulatory power based on the IOC's requirement that countries seeking to participate in the Olympics ensure compliance to WADA rules. Third, it received endorsement from the UNESCO for implementation as an 'international convention' (WADA 2004a: 5).

The combination of global financial backing and supranational support enabled the WADA to emerge as a policy force in world sport (Park 2005). In late 2003 the WADA introduced its global anti-doping code. With the support of the IOC it soon became both a global benchmark and template for anti-doping policies among international and national governing bodies for sport (WADA 2004b). In the case of Australia, where one of our following cases is based, the WADC received immediate approval by the Federal Government and its policy implementation arm, the ASC. The campaign against performance-enhancing drugs in sport was, however, hardly new in Australia. Since 1990 it has been the responsibility of the ASDA, renamed the ASADA in 2006. Australia quickly became one of the vanguard nations in the effort to minimise performance-enhancing drugs in sport, and had long followed the IOC's lead with respect to prohibited substances and methods.

Underpinning the WADA's instantiating vision was the unshakeable belief that doping compromises the 'spirit of sport' and that its anti-doping program would 'preserve what is intrinsically valuable about sport'. Moreover, it would aim to 'protect athletes' fundamental right to join in doping-free sport ... and promote fairness and equality for all' (Park 2005: 178). The 2003 WADC became the base document through which the WADA mission was implemented, managed, and reviewed. It specified three objectives. They were first, to protect the athlete's fundamental right to participate in doping-free sport; second, to promote health, fairness, and equality for athletes worldwide; and third, to ensure harmonised, coordinated, and effective anti-doping programs at the international and national level with regard to 'detection, deterrence and prevention' (WADA 2004b: 2, 2011b: 3). For the WADA the overarching goal has been sharply defined: to carve out a 'clean sport' space where 'hard work and talent are justly recognised, and doping cheats are exposed for what they are' (WADA 2011b: 3). These are strong and emotional sentiments, but the message is clear.

As the athlete's drug 'bible', the 2009 version of the WADC, which has been updated annually since, accounts for a prohibited list of substances including performance-enhancing agents like synthetic EPO, synthetic human growth hormone, anabolic androgenic steroids, and the more powerful anti-inflammatory drugs and stimulants. It also extends to a smorgasbord of illicit drugs like cannabinoids, amphetamines, and narcotics (which may, or may not have performance-enhancing attributes) (WADA 2004c, 2006, 2012a).

The *2013 Prohibited List* (WADA 2012a) takes a direct line about what constitutes the most serious incursions. These involve the use of products that demonstrably improve sporting performances. The WADA begins its schedule with those substances prohibited at all times, including during periods of competition, and periods when players are not competing in any leagues or tournaments. The substances are first, anabolic agents which includes all synthetic testosterone products, second, all peptide hormones and related products that stimulate the production of growth hormone, and growth hormone itself, third, beta-2 agonists and other bronchial dilation agents, fourth, all hormone and metabolic modulators, and fifth, diuretics and other agents used to mask the presence of some other banned substance. In addition, athletes and players cannot manipulate their blood to artificially enhance the uptake and delivery of oxygen, including the use of modified haemoglobin substances, and transfusions.

Added to the prohibited list are those substances banned only during competition – which can be as short as up to 12 hours prior to the competition or event – including a sweeping range of stimulants. In most instances, any sign of stimulant use remains prohibited, but in a few cases use up to specified levels may be permissible. For example, cathine is allowed so long as its urine concentration does not exceed five micrograms per millilitre. The maximum concentration levels for ephedrine and methylephedrine is 10, but goes up to 150 for pseudoephedrine. Narcotics, including heroin and fentanyl, are banned in competition, as well as cannabis (or marijuana as it is often know), and glucocorticosteroids. According to the Code, alcohol acts as a performance enhancer in some cases, as well as an intoxicator that increases the risk of injury to self and others. It is banned in archery, karate, motorcycling and power-boating, and auto-racing. Beta-blockers, normally used to treat high blood pressure and heart arrhythmias, are banned in those sports where a steady hand and a calm head delivers a competitive edge such as archery, billiards, darts, golf, shooting, and snow-sports.

The WADC's attempt to distinguish between in-competition drug use and out-of-competition drug use creates an additional layer of complexity. Initially, the WADA concentrated on the illegal use of illicit drugs *during* periods of athletic

Table 10.1 A typology of permissible drug use under the WADC 2009

	Performance-enhancing drugs	Illicit drugs
Drugs used out-of-competition	Some prohibited	All permissible
	Some permissible	
Drugs used in-competition	All prohibited	All prohibited

competition, but presently some sports test for them all year round. At the same time, drugs deemed to generate ongoing performance-enhancing capacities have always been banned throughout the year, although we now find that stimulants and beta-blockers are permitted during out-of-competition periods (Horvath 2006; WADA 2012a). This means that the heavy stimulants especially are disallowed during periods of competition. The often complicated distinctions between performance-enhancing drugs and illicit drugs, between prohibited and permissible substances, and between in- and out-of-competition testing, are illustrated in Table 10.1.

Many subtle drug-control distinctions underpin the WADC, but typically remain unexposed because commentators prefer not to engage with the nuances of drug-use cases. As a result, little assessment has been undertaken as to which drugs enhance performance, and which ones do not. A consequence is that sometimes players and athletes become labelled as drug cheats even though they used substances that were highly unlikely to improve performance. Even worse, the same athletes are vilified as cheats when they use the substances well out of season. The Michael Phelps cannabis smoking incident of 2009 offers a case in point as it occurred in the off-season, and therefore did not qualify as a banned substance. At worst, Phelps' actions were irresponsible, yet he was clearly no drug cheat. But, from a cursory glance at reports contained in the popular media you would have thought that his behaviour was so heinous that all his swimming medals should have been returned to the IOC immediately.

Within the 2009 WADC, as with the earlier codes, a provision exempts athletes who can demonstrate the need to use a banned substance for therapeutic purposes. In these instances athletes with a documented medical condition requiring the use of prohibited substances or methods can request a therapeutic use exemption from both their national anti-doping agency and national sport governing body (WADA 2009). Some athletes used this loophole to secure access to performance-enhancing substances. Take, for example, the asthma problem. Sufferers normally receive prescriptions for bronchial dilation compounds. These compounds effect a powerful response, but from an athlete's perspective can also be troublesome since they contain banned beta-2 agonists. The treatment for many other medical conditions may also demand treatment with banned substances, including beta-blockers and diuretics for hypertension, insulin for certain types of diabetes, peptides and growth hormones for growth hormone deficiency, corticosteroids and narcotics for serious injuries and overuse problems, and heavy stimulants like methylphenidate and dextroamphetamine for attention deficit hyperactivity disorders (ADHD).

As we have laboured in earlier chapters, in order to be proscribed by the WADC, drugs like EPO and methods like blood doping must meet two of the following three criteria. First, the drug demonstrably enhances performance. Second, consumption constitutes a risk to the athlete's health. Finally, use violates 'the spirit of sport' (WADA 2003: 15–16). The WADA defined this third criterion as the celebration of the human spirit and related positive features in competitive sport like fun and joy, courage, teamwork, pure excellence in performance, respect for the rules and other participants, dedication and commitment, character and education, community and solidarity, as well as ethics, fair play, and honesty (WADA 2003: 3). This suite of values conflated to the WADA slogan of 'play-true'. While anabolic steroids were banned by the WADA on the grounds that they contravened criteria one and two, illicit drugs like marijuana and Ecstasy were banned because, from the WADA's perspective, they contravened criteria two and three.

Bans and suspensions

The WADC leaves little room for ambiguity when it comes to deciding on whether players and athletes have used a banned substance. No space exists for players and athletes to argue that usage occurred inadvertently, or under flawed instructions from coaches or sport scientists about the substance's legality. The drug control authority does not have to demonstrate that the so-called 'culprits' intended to use (WADA 2009: 21). Evidence for use trumps everything.

Athletes testing positive to prohibited substances, or caught using through either self-admission or on the evidence of others – whether performance-enhancing drugs all year round, or illicit and other designated substances drugs during competition – face the prospect of up to a two-year ban for a first offence, and up to a lifetime ban for a second offence (WADA 2009: 52–55). However, some drug use offences incur more serious responses than others. Sanctions could be minor reprimands from the use of a drug banned during in-competition only periods, as opposed to a substance prohibited all year round. Substances that deliver a slightly less punitive response from authorities include generally available drugs like prescribed medicinal products (such as anti-asthma drugs and beta-blockers), and are not primarily intended to enhance performance, even though they could through a secondary effect. On the other hand, severe sanctions as high as four years exist for a first-time trafficking offence for any type of drug, irrespective of whether performance enhancing, a banned prescribed medicine, or some illicit substance (WADA 2009: 53). In serious cases of trafficking and prolonged use, a lifetime ban can be imposed. Table 10.2 lists the sanctions applicable to the use of different substances.

While the WADA's out-of-competition testing for performance-enhancing drugs was initially pursued less vigorously than its in-competition testing, it produced some high profile 'successes'. Amongst the most notorious was that of Irish swimmer Michelle de Bruin in 1998 (who had earlier competed under the name of Smith). When drug-testing officials arrived at her residence unannounced

Table 10.2 Sanctions for drug use in- and out-of-competition under WADC 2009

Category of substance/use	Sanctions for rule violations involving in-competition use	Sanctions for rule violations involving out-of-competition use
Steroids, hormones (human growth hormone (HGH), EPO, insulin), beta-s agonists, diuretics	1st positive test/use: 2-year suspension max	1st positive test/use: 2-year suspension max
Blood doping, gene doping	2nd positive test/use: up to lifetime suspension 1st positive test/use: 2-year suspension max	2nd positive test/use: up to lifetime suspension No sanctions for out-of-competition use
Stimulants and narcotics	2nd positive test/use: up to lifetime suspension	
Cannabinoids, glucocorticosteroids	1st positive test/use: warning to 1 year 2nd positive test/use: 2-year max 3rd positive test/use: up to lifetime suspension	No sanctions for out-of-competition use
Beta-blockers	As above, but confined to archery, billiards, bowls, curling, gymnastics, motor-cycling, sailing, skiing, and wrestling	No sanctions for out-of-competition use
Alcohol	As above, but confined to archery, billiards, bowls, karate, motor-cycling, and power-boating	
Failing to attend test and failing to advise on whereabouts for subsequent testing	1st violation: 3 months to 1-year suspension 2nd violation: 2-year suspension	1st violation: 3 months to 1-year suspension 2nd violation: 2-year suspension
Trafficking in substances banned both in- and out-of-competition	1st and subsequent violations: 4 years to life suspension	1st and subsequent violations: 4 years to life suspension

she tried to contaminate the doping sample by adding alcohol to her vial of urine (BBC 1998). Other suspensions for drug-test avoidance also hit the headlines. At the 2007 Tour de France, Michael Rasmussen, the race leader at the time, was disqualified after misleading drug testers who were trying to locate him for an out-of-competition performance-enhancing drugs test (Brown 2007). Although the WADA had become increasingly vigilant about in- and out-of-competition testing for performance-enhancing drugs, it still tests mainly for illicit drugs like stimulants, narcotics, and cannabinoids during the in-competition period only (WADA 2004c). Athletes can, for the most part, use illicit drugs out-of-competition without the fear of being tested, or the threat of being sanctioned.

By the mid-1990s the distinction between in-competition and out-of-competition drug testing, and the different sanctions applicable to performance-enhancing drugs on the one hand, and illicit substances on the other, were brought into stark relief when a number of national and international sports bodies reviewed their anti-doping programs. The WADA hoped to persuade sport authorities worldwide to adopt uniform anti-doping policies and procedures. However, some organisations – most notably MLB in the US – resisted the WADA's overtures. Instead, they maintained a more lenient and for some critics, 'moronic', standard with respect to anti-doping (Bryant 2005; Pound 2006: 132). Something of an open secret during the 1990s held that many of MLB's best players were dosing up on synthetic testosterone. In addition, during the early 2000s, in the wake of bans on anabolic steroids, an epidemic of stimulant use caught the media's attention. No shortage of anecdotal evidence emerged to suggest that, 'in most locker rooms and most club-houses, amphetamines – red ones, green ones – were lying out there in an open bowl as if they were jelly beans' (Bryant 2005: 275). For players reluctant to use the synthetic products, so-called herbal stimulants such as ephedra also seemed to be readily available.

While the WADC founders under two key problematic propositions – first, that drug use causes a demonstrably unfair advantage, and second, that drugs adversely affect players' health, whatever the dose – they rarely receive any systematic interrogation. In the following section we aim to delve deeper into these propositions about drug use in sport by examining in detail the ways that banned drugs work. We will also consider their efficacy and their potential to undermine a user's health.

Little agreement can be found as to just how much of an advantage players and athletes can acquire from the use of drugs. While the systematic use of EPO and blood transfusions can clearly increase the energy and endurance outputs of elite road cyclists, we know less about the scale of 'on-field' performance benefits that come from the use of synthetic testosterone, peptide hormones, beta-2 agonists, and different types of stimulants. Numerous confounding variables come into play here, with the main ones being the competitive experiences of players and athletes, their performance levels, their genetic inheritance, and the physical and emotional demands of the sports they play.

Working out the health risks associated with the use of different substances is fraught with difficulty too. Virtually all the substances on the banned list have a legitimate medical and/or health improvement role to play, but they also deliver significant and often deleterious side effects. Moreover, the side effects can differ from player to player depending upon their genetic make-up and their bodily reactions to various categories of drugs. The problem compounds with the fact that most performance-enhancing drugs are not taken under medical supervision. As a result, no control is exercised over dosage levels or the quality of the substance being absorbed, ingested, or injected into the body.

Table 10.3 provides a summary of the major substances on the WADA banned list. It not only explains the main medical effect of the substance, but also identifies its capacity to improve sport performance, and the health risks associated with unsupervised and/or overuse.

Table 10.3 A taxonomy of banned performance-enhancing substance types and their uses

Substance	Summary of effects	
1. Anabolic agents	Anabolic agents like anabolic androgenic steroids (AAS) are synthetic versions of the male sex hormone testosterone. They can come in the form of 'exogenous' steroids, or substances that cannot be produced by the body naturally, or 'endogenous' steroids, which can be produced by the body naturally. More recently a third category of anabolic agents, selective androgen receptor modulators (SARMs), have gained in popularity. Unlike testosterone, which has both anabolic and androgenic (masculinising) effects, SARMs act directly on anabolic receptors that cause tissue (bone and muscle) growth. As a result, there is a substantially decreased tendency for undesirable androgenic side effects to occur as the body attempts to maintain a hormonal balance. When males flood their bodies with extra testosterone, the natural response is an increase in oestrogen in order to compensate. SARMs therefore reduce the chances of developing female characteristics such as breast tissue development. For females, the introduction of testosterone causes masculinising effects. Anabolic agents work by stimulating protein synthesis, allowing a large amount of muscle to be added in a short time. For athletes, this means more size and strength, a reduction in recovery time after heavy exercise, and the ability to train harder and longer.	
Exogenous AAS	*Performance advantages*	*Health disadvantages*
Examples Bolasterone Boldenone Danazol Estosterone Hydroxytestosterone Methandriol Testosterone Nandrolone Oxabolone Stanozolol Stenbolone **Endogenous AAS** *Examples* Androstenediol Androstenedione Dihydrotestosterone Prasterone Testosterone **Other anabolic agents** *Examples* Clenbuterol SARMs	Muscular size and strength Fat loss Faster muscle recovery Some endurance increase *Medical issues* Anaemia Asthma Bone pain from osteoporosis Gonadal function decrease Muscle loss Postmenopausal symptoms Puberty delay (males)	Acne Anger Brain tissue damage Depression Kidney tumours Liver dysfunction Tendon tearing *Females* Abnormal menstrual cycles Genital enlargement Facial hair Voice deepening *Males* Breast enlargement Impotence Prostate enlargement Sperm count decrease Testicular atrophy
Substance	Summary of effects	
2. Hormones and hormone stimulating agents	Hormones are produced naturally by glands in the body and enact changes in organs and tissues. As substances added to the body, hormones serve as messengers between different organs that stimulate various bodily functions such as growth and sensitivity to pain. Hormones and hormone stimulating agents work by encouraging either adding to the natural level of a hormone, or by encouraging the production of naturally occurring hormones. For athletes, the results can include increases in muscle growth and strength and greater production of red blood cells to improve the blood's ability to carry oxygen.	

EPO	EPO is a glycoprotein hormone that regulates red blood cell production. When taken as a performance-enhancing substance, EPO substantially increases red blood cells and in so doing the oxygen-carrying capacity of blood. Naturally, the more oxygen in blood, the more that is delivered to muscles during aerobic activity. Because EPO boosts red blood cells, it has the potential to throw the 'haematocrit' (the ratio of blood cells to plasma) out of balance. In practice, the more red blood cells compared to plasma, the thicker blood becomes. For athletes seeking an endurance benefit from superior oxygen transport to muscles, more viscous blood from too much EPO can make the heart work harder in order to maintain circulation. EPO can therefore present a serious danger of blood clots, leading to strokes.
	Performance advantages / *Health disadvantages*
	Superior endurance / Potential death Improved muscle recovery / Deep vein thrombosis / Heart attack *Medical uses* / Myocardial infarction Anaemia from kidney failure / Pulmonary embolism HIV / Stroke Some cancers / Thrombosis
Human growth hormone (hGH) **Somatotropin (STH)** **Insulin-like growth factors (e.g. IGF-1)** **Mechano growth factors (MGFs)**	hGH is a naturally occurring peptide hormone produced in the pituitary gland responsible for stimulating growth, cell reproduction and regeneration. When extracted from human cadavers, the substance takes the abbreviation hGH. Somatotropin (STH) refers to the growth hormone produced naturally by animals, and extracted from carcases. 'Artificial' growth hormone is also available through recombinant DNA methods, usually identified as somatropin (brand name Humatrope). Growth hormone operates in a synergistic way with testosterone, leading to increased muscle size and strength at the same time as diminishing fat. IGFs are also peptide hormones secreted by the liver as part of their complex signalling systems, including the regulation of cellular growth. Their label as 'insulin-like' comes from a similar composition to the hormone insulin, which also possesses significant growth promoting power. Athletes employ IGF-1 for its anabolic effect on muscle. It can also assist in the development of cartilage and bone. MGFs are a member of the IGF 'family', derived from IGF-1. Like IGF-1, MGFs assist in tissue repair after damage, making them favourable substances for muscular recovery following heavy exercise.

Performance advantages	*Health disadvantages*
Muscle growth	Unwanted tissue growth
Muscle repair	(acromegaly)
Body fat reduction	Arthritis
Strength increases	Brain swelling
Protein synthesis increase	Cardiomyopathy
	Congestive heart failure
Medical uses	Coronary artery disease
Cosmetic anti-aging	Creutzfeldt-Jakob disease
Growth hormone	Diabetes mellitus
deficiencies	Hypoglycaemia
Turner's syndrome	Hypothyroidism
	Impotence
	Osteoporosis

Continued…

Table 10.3 continued

Gonadotrophins *Examples* Luteinizing hormone (LH) Human chorionic gonadotrophin (hCG)	hCG is a glycoprotein hormone produced in large amounts during pregnancy. Male athletes can use pharmaceutical preparations of hCG to stimulate testosterone production. It also reduces or prevents the testicular atrophy and natural testosterone shutdown that accompanies lengthy and high dosage courses of androgens. LH is produced in the anterior pituitary gland, acting to regulate the function of testes in men and the ovaries in women. LH controls sex steroid production (testosterone in men and oestradiol in women), and is therefore used as a performance-enhancing substance for the same purposes as hCG. In some cases, hCG and LH can mask the presence of AAS.	
	Performance advantages	*Health disadvantages*
	Increases testosterone Prevents testicular damage Masking agent for AAS *Medical uses* Female infertility	Similar effects to AAS
Insulin	A peptide hormone that promotes glucose utilisation and protein synthesis and regulates the metabolism of sugar. When taken in conjunction with testosterone, it is widely considered by athletes– and especially strength athletes and bodybuilders – to be the most anabolic hormone available. Too much insulin at one time can lead to hypoglycaemic shock, coma, and even death.	
	Performance advantages	*Health disadvantages*
	Decreases body fat (with AAS) Muscle growth (with AAS) Reduces protein breakdown *Medical uses* Diabetes	Risk of death Brain damage Coma Hypoglycaemia Nausea Shortness of breath
Corticotrophins *Example* Adrenocorticotropic hormone (ACTH)	Corticotrophins, or ACTH, are hormones secreted by the anterior lobe of the pituitary gland that stimulate the adrenal gland to secrete its hormones, including corticosterone. Its main role in the body is as the central driver of the stress hormone system, including cortisol. Corticotrophin also acts on other areas within the brain and can suppress appetite, increase anxiety, and improve memory and focus. Collectively, these effects help develop, refine, and leverage the body's response to stressful experiences. Athletes can take advantage by stimulating their bodies to perform at higher levels, especially during competition.	
	Performance advantages	*Health disadvantages*
	Heightens focus Increases adrenal corticosteroid levels Aids injury recovery *Medical uses* Spasm control in children	Psychological overstimulation Connective tissue softening Stomach irritation and ulcers Weakening of muscles

Substance	Summary of effects	
3. Hormone antagonists and modulators	Hormone antagonists and modulators, or anti-oestrogenic substances, act by either decreasing the amount of oestrogen in the body or by blocking the oestrogen receptors. Both male and female athletes employ the anti-oestogenic substances, tamoxifen and clomiphene. Males use tamoxifen with AAS in order to prevent breast tissue growth. By reducing oestrogen, the drug also increases the effects of testosterone. Female strength athletes can use tamoxifen to block oestrogen receptors, allowing both natural and artificial testosterone to operate unopposed. Similarly, selective oestrogen receptor modulators (SERMs) preclude the effects of oestrogen in breast tissue. Myostatin (growth differentiation factor 8; GDF-8) is a protein that receives its content from the gene MSTN, which has a heavy influence on an individual's propensity for muscular development. One of myostatin's key roles is to restrain muscle growth from continuing beyond natural requirements. However, blocking myostatin's activity leads to increases in muscle mass and strength, although it can also make muscle fibres more susceptible to injury. As a relatively new class of drugs, few human studies are available to reveal its effects. However, studies do show that animals lacking myostatin, and livestock given substances like Follistatin that block myostatin, have significantly larger muscles.	
Aromatase inhibitors	*Performance advantages*	*Health disadvantages*
Examples Aminoglutethimide Anastrozole Exemestane Formestane Letrozole Testolactone **SERMs** *Examples* Raloxifene Tamoxifen Toremifene **Other anti-oestrogenic substances** *Examples* Clomiphene Cyclofenil Fulvestrant **Myostatin inhibitors** (growth differentiation factor 8; GDF-8) *Example* Follistatin	Anabolic effects Strength increases Reduction of AAS side effects *Medical uses* Breast cancer Infertility (females) Muscular dystrophy (myostatin inhibitors)	Abdominal cramps Increases in chance of cancer Libido swings Speech difficulties

Continued...

Table 10.3 continued

Substance	Summary of effects	
4. Beta-2 agonists *Examples* Formoterol Salbutamol Salmeterol Terbutaline	Beta-2 agonists are mainly used to treat asthma because they dilate the bronchial passages by relaxing the muscles that surround the airway. In addition to facilitating breathing, beta-2 agonists can be used as stimulants. When administered via the bloodstream, they stimulate anabolic effects, increasing muscle mass and diminishing body fat.	
	Performance advantages	*Health disadvantages*
	Increases in aerobic performance Reduces body fat Increases in muscle mass *Medical uses* Asthma Chronic obstructive pulmonary disease	Anxiety Dizziness Headache Insomnia Cramps Nausea Palpitations Psychological overstimulation
Substance	*Summary of effects*	
5. Diuretics and masking agents	Masking agents are substances that can be used to conceal the presence of a prohibited substance in urine or other samples. As a result, they can fall into a range of drug categories depending upon their intended medical usages. Side effects vary accordingly. One common substance used as a masking agent is epitestosterone. For example, in males a natural ratio exists between the hormones testosterone to epitestosterone, usually around 4:1. When an athlete takes exogenous testosterone, his testosterone level increases but his epitestosterone level does not, throwing out the usual ratio. Drug tests measure for discrepancies in the 4:1 ratio. Athletes can rebalance the ratio by taking additional epitestosterone. Diuretics provide another example, used to dilute urine samples.	
Diuretics	*Performance advantages*	*Health disadvantages*
Examples Acetazolamide Chlorthalidone Etacrynic acid Metolazone Spironolactone Triamterene **Other substances** *Examples* Epitestosterone Probenecid Alpha-reductase inhibitors Plasma expanders	Hides banned substances Dilutes banned substances in samples Weight loss *Medical uses* Heart failure High blood pressure	Blood pressure problems Cramps Dehydration Electrolyte imbalances Headaches Heart failure Kidney failure Muscle cramps Nausea

Substance	Summary of effects	
6. Stimulants *Examples* Adrenaline Amphetamines Cocaine Ephedrine Mesocarb Methamphetamine (D-) Modafinil Oxilofrine Sibutramine Strychnine Tsuaminoheptane	Stimulants cover a large number of substances that increase focus, alertness, and physical performance by exciting the central nervous system. They can be employed for both physical and mental advantages by improving attention, arousing psychological readiness, combating fatigue and pain, reducing appetite, and generating aggressiveness. The greatest dangers lie with a hyper-stimulation of the nervous system, which can have systemic consequences, from mild heart palpitations and sweating to heart attack and stroke.	
	Performance advantages	*Health disadvantages*
	Increases aggression Increases alertness and attention Reduces fatigue Reduces pain Lowers weight *Medical uses* ADHD Allergies Asthma Headache Nasal congestion	Addiction / withdrawal Aggressiveness Anxiety Blood pressure fluctuations Cardiac arrhythmia Convulsions Dehydration Heart attack Insomnia Stroke

Substance	Summary of effects	
7. Narcotics / **analgesics** *Examples* Buprenorphine Diamorphine (heroin) Methadone Morphine Pethidine	Narcotic analgesics are substances that act on the brain and spinal cord to ameliorate painful stimuli. Athletes can use these substances to reduce the pain from injury or just to endure more uncomfortable training and its consequences. Analgesics allow athletes to train harder for longer. Some narcotics can help athletes by alleviating anxiety, allowing them to focus better on competition. Of course, narcotic analgesics only mask pain, in so doing conferring upon athletes a false sense of security they can use to continue training and incur further injury.	
	Performance advantages	*Health disadvantages*
	Reduces pain Increases in pain threshold Sensation of euphoria and well-being *Medical uses* Treatment of pain	Addiction / withdrawal Balance and coordination loss Cardiovascular distress Concentration problems Injury risk increase Nausea and vomiting

Substance	Summary of effects
8. Beta-blockers *Examples* Acebutolol Betaxolol Celiprolol Esmolol Metipranolol Oxprenolol Propranolol Sotalol Timolol	Beta-blockers are substances that block the effects of adrenaline (epinephrine), a hormone produced by the adrenal glands that stimulates the central nervous system. By blocking adrenaline, beta-blockers decrease blood pressure, heart rate, and muscle tremors, while generally removing anxiety. Since beta-blockers relax the body and its musculature, they offer advantages to athletes seeking to steady their hands or concentrate on fine-motor activities. Conversely, they undermine the body's capacity to perform strenuous activities, causing systemic weaknesses as the heart fails to meet the needs of muscles and other internal systems.

Continued…

Table 10.3 continued

	Performance advantages	*Health disadvantages*
	Muscle relaxant Reduces tremors *Medical uses* Sedatives for anxiety Heart problems High blood pressure Migraine	Severe blood pressure reduction Severe heart rate decrease Physical performance decrease Insomnia Fatigue

Substance	*Summary of effects*	
9. Cannabinoids Example Marijuana	Cannabinoids are a class of 'psychoactive' substances refined from the cannabis plant that affect cognition, including inducing feelings of relaxation. As a calmative, cannabinoids can be used to recover from heavy exertion. However, as substances with psychoactive properties, cannabinoids can lead to psychological disturbances and are addictive.	

	Performance advantages	*Health disadvantages*
	Muscle relaxant May assist recovery *Medical uses* Calmative	Addiction / withdrawal Anxiety and panic Concentration problems Psychological disturbances, e.g. paranoia Motor skill difficulties

Substance	*Summary of effects*	
10. Glucocorticosteroids *Examples* Acetonide Dexamethasone Fluticasone Hydrocortisone Prednisolone Triamcinolone	Glucocorticosteroids are anti-inflammatory steroid hormones produced in the adrenal glands. As drugs, glucocorticosteroids are used to treat the pain and inflammation accompanying asthma, hay fever, tissue inflammation, and rheumatoid arthritis. In addition to the anti-inflammatory and painkilling effects, athletes can use glucocorticosteroids to induce a feeling of well-being despite injury or illness.	

	Performance advantages	*Health disadvantages*
	Reduces inflammation Reduces pain Induces feelings of well-being *Medical uses* Arthritis Asthma Inflammation Allergies	Fluid retention Hyperglycaemia Mood changes Risk of injury increases

Substance	Summary of effects
11. Alcohol *Example* Ethanol	Alcohol is a central nervous system depressant that acts by reducing the speed of the brain and body. Its uses in sport can include the reduction of anxiety and physical tremors. Alcohol can also improve relaxation. However, alcohol's intoxicating effects are well-known to diminish judgement while increasing inappropriate feelings of psychological well-being, self-confidence, and aggression.

Performance advantages	*Health disadvantages*
Reduces anxiety Sedative *Medical uses* Antiseptic	Addiction / withdrawal Cirrhosis of the liver Judgement impairment Memory loss Poor muscular coordination

Anti-doping testing limitations

Putting aside ethics and the practicalities of anti-doping budgets, most drugs in sport commentators seem to agree that testing does not catch the majority of dopers. The testing statistics suggest that, on average across professional and Olympic sports, around 1–2 per cent of athletes return positive samples. Assuming that 1 per cent does not cover the extent of the doping problem, an obvious reason for the low results is that too few tests are being conducted. While limited testing might be a factor, especially out-of-competition, the upper echelons of sport all undergo mandatory testing upon success. For example, 100 per cent of Olympic medallists are tested. In fact, half of all competitors at the 2012 London Games were tested. So, if the tests do not capture all the drug users, what is going wrong?

According to the WADC a substance must meet two of three criteria in order to find its way on to the prohibited list: (1) scientific evidence or experience demonstrates that the method or substance has the potential to enhance, or actually enhances, sport performance; (2) medical evidence or experience suggests that the use of the substance or method represents an actual or potential health risk to the athlete; and (3) the use of the substance or the method violates the spirit of sport.

The result of these three criteria is a list containing six classes of substances. The WADA outlaws doping agents and methods in the following categories classed according to their biological action: non-approved substances: drugs or molecules not addressed by any of the subsequent sections (S0); anabolic agents (S1); peptide hormones, growth factors, and related substances (S2); beta-2 agonists (S3); hormone antagonists and modulators (S4); and diuretics and other masking agents (S5) (WADA 2011a). Specifically, testing claims to reveal the presence of the following agents.

S1. Anabolic agents
1   Anabolic androgenic steroids (AAS)
    a   Exogenous AAS
    b   Endogenous AAS

2. Other anabolic agents

S2. Peptide hormones, growth factors, and related substances
1   Erythropoiesis-stimulating agents (e.g. EPO)
2   Chorionic gonadotrophin (hCG) and luteinizing hormone (LH) in males
3   Insulin
4   Corticotrophins
5   Growth hormone (GH), insulin-like growth factor-1 (IGF-1)

S3. Beta-2 agonists
S4. Hormone antagonists and modulators
1   Aromatase inhibitors
2   Selective oestrogen receptor modulators (SERMs)
3   Other anti-oestrogenic substances
4   Agents modifying myostatin function(s)

S5. Diuretics and other masking agents
Diuretics, desmopressin, plasma expanders (e.g. glycerol; intravenous administration of albumin dextran, hydroxyethyl starch and mannitol), probenecid

Prohibited methods
M1. Enhancement of oxygen transfer
1   Blood doping
2   Artificially enhancing the uptake, transport, or delivery of oxygen perfluorochemicals, efaproxiral (RSR13), and hemoglobin-based oxygen carriers

S6. Stimulants
a   Non-specified stimulants (e.g. adrafinil, amphetamine)
b   Specified stimulants (e.g. ephedrine, strychnine)

S7. Narcotics

S8. Cannabinoids

S9. Glucocorticosteroids
Substances prohibited in particular sports

P1. Alcohol
Alcohol (ethanol, ethylglucuronide)

P2. Beta-blockers

Despite this ostensibly wide-ranging anti-doping testing regime, numerous problems ensure that it can never be fully effective. The first problem is that the substances allocated to the prohibited list have not all been scientifically connected to performance enhancement. In fact, not only are many of the substances performance reducing, but others produce marginal performance benefits at best. Little scientific data exist about the effects of some of the prohibited substances and the WADA needs nothing more than speculation in order to add a new item to the list. At the same time, a second problem remains that, however comprehensive, testing does not and cannot ever include all substances and their variations that have performance-enhancing effects. For example, innumerable structural variations exist for some substances like erythropoietin (EPO), including its new variant continuous erythropoietin receptor activator (CERA), which render them structurally different and undetectable despite still conferring the same performance effects.

Once a positive test has been returned, another kind of problem emerges. A third problem is that the interpretation of testing results does not meet scientific standards. This issue is exacerbated by the WADA's disinclination to publish the results of testing quality used by accredited laboratories. For example, Berry (2008), a biostatistician, argued that the quantitative evidence supporting the Landis professional cycling case was non-informative, neither establishing nor disconfirming his guilt. Instead, Berry claimed, it revealed that the inferential procedures do not address the question of guilt, and do not fairly represent the meaning of the statistics involved. For example, during the 2006 Tour de France, one of Landis' urine samples returned an unusually high testosterone to epitestosterone ratio, a marker for the potential use of exogenous testosterone. However, during the race, Landis provided eight urine sample pairs. As a result, there were eight opportunities for a true positive and eight for a false positive. According to Berry, statistically speaking, if Landis was 'clean', with a 95 per cent confidence, the probability that one of the samples delivered a false positive for the race as a whole would be about 34 per cent. Berry worried that the tests may actually measure naturally occurring levels of a banned drug at the same time as potentially missing true positives.

A fourth problem is that there will always be a new generation of substances which are either difficult to test for, or have no tests available. For example, a new generation of substances such as the peptide hormones, recently exposed by the ACC and being investigated by the ASADA, are used to generate new muscle growth while leaving few biological markers and side effects compared with conventional AAS.

The WADA Director General David Howman (2012: 1535) conceded that, 'While we may be able to catch what I call the "dopey doper", those with a more sophisticated approach can remain undetected throughout their careers.' He also observed that doping athletes receive considerable support from an entourage including doctors with expertise in sidestepping tests. In addition, the anti-doping program has yet to find strategies for combating substances with short windows of detection, such as human growth hormone (hGH) and synthetic testosterone. Also known as micro dosing, athletes can use small but regular dosages of one or several synergistic substances, with little fear of elevating their test results to a detectable level. Synthetic testosterone, for example, acts and leaves the body within 24 hours.

The next frontier will likely involve the genetic manipulation of the athlete, a practice known as gene doping. For example, the genetic modification of a human system could involve a stimulation of the genes producing erythrocytes (red blood cells) to enhance their oxygen-carrying capacity, or the use of early-development drugs such as myostatin inhibitors, which control the genes regulating muscle growth.

A fifth problem is that the Athlete Biological Passport (ABP) tests for variations in physiological baselines rather than the presence of prohibited substances. Under the ABP, instead of screening for traces of banned substances, samples are compared against an athlete's baseline profile, which is established over multiple tests. Athletes must subsequently explain any severe fluctuations on the basis of natural responses to environmental conditions. However, even sudden and severe changes occur naturally without the intervention of prohibited substances. In addition, the model assumes an accurate and unchanging baseline in the first place. Athletes may be banned without the presence of a prohibited substance objectively detected in their systems.

A sixth problem revolves around the practical effectiveness of the testing and whereabouts processes. For example, the most effective methods of avoiding testing are non-technological and non-medical. According to the USADA (2012) Lance Armstrong report, affidavits from Armstrong's former teammates indicated that the most successful method of passing the tests was to avoid them altogether by either running away or hiding from the testers. Under the out-of-competition 'whereabouts' code, professional cyclists must keep their national anti-doping authorities informed of their locations at all times. Circumventing this by failing to accurately provide their whereabouts can result in a warning, of which three are permissible within an 18-month period. Yet, the riders did not receive a warning for failing to answer their door-knocks when the testers arrived, as long as they were actually in the city their whereabouts disclosure had specified.

The USADA report further claimed that when Armstrong could not avoid a test by simply hiding, he employed drug-masking techniques such as switching urine samples, rapidly administering saline to dilute drug levels in the blood, or by using strategic dosage methods and undetectable agents. Of the latter, Armstrong used a cloned rather than synthetic version of EPO, for which no test existed at the time. When a test did arrive, Armstrong relied on the detailed pharmaceutical knowledge of his doctors, who, for example, discovered that small doses of EPO injected directly into veins rather than under the skin remained undetectable. Although some masking agents can be identified under the testing regime, many cannot, or involve the use of methods like dilution rather than obfuscation.

A seventh and final problem is that the current testing procedures do not take into account negative-performance substances. This could involve 'negative doping', when an athlete is deliberately sabotaged by a competitor, or a criminal interested in a gambling outcome (Lippi, Sanchis-Gomar & Banfi 2012). Adding performance-reducing substances to athletes' samples by contaminating their food, for example, remains a troublesome issue that cannot be revealed through testing.

In the absence of an idealised world where drug use can be detected and eliminated, three options remain. At one extreme, drug use can be completely deregulated and legalised. It has the advantage of removing the hypocrisy associated with elite sport's contrite messages about keeping sport 'clean', saves money and resources otherwise wasted on ineffective testing and compliance measures, and makes the playing field more transparent. At the same time, however, legalisation gives up on the idea that sport should be drug free on moral grounds.

At the other extreme, drug use can be the subject of more rigorous testing, supplemented by new initiatives such as voluntary testing by athletes, criminal investigations, forensic DNA analyses, 'coercive' interviewing, extensive psychometric and personality surveys, lie detection testing, and athlete microchipping for whereabouts checks as well as, ultimately, *in vivo* chemical testing. A tougher stance on drugs in sport has the advantage of the moral high ground, although perhaps at the expense of athletes' civil freedoms. It would also be prohibitively expensive and still will not catch all drug users. Nevertheless, more drug controls means 'fighting the good fight'.

Despite the resource impracticalities, perhaps the future includes more forensic methods. One notable exemplar occurred following the 2007 Rowing World Cup when a plastic bag containing medical waste and injecting paraphernalia was discovered in a compost bin after a witness reported seeing a team official dispose of it. As a consequence of forensic investigation, the DNA from eight rowers was linked to the waste, which contained numerous banned substances. Not only were all eight rowers banned but so too were the coaches and officials from their team (Jan *et al.* 2011).

Somewhere in the middle ground, another series of interventions are available involving different levels of regulatory action. For example, a strong harm-reduction approach would, perhaps, recommend legalisation but with testing for athlete health under medical supervision. This approach would ameliorate the worst health effects of the drugs while optimising performance, thereby serving the sporting brand and fan, as well as the athlete. Dosages would be lower and fewer substances would be employed, as many popular drugs only deliver marginal performance advantages anyway. Money spent on compliance and testing would be diverted to athlete health monitoring. Of course, a strong harm-reduction approach does not address the moral aspects of drug use, instead prioritising a pragmatic intervention.

A more moderate harm-reduction stance would not necessarily be incompatible with a continuation of the drug-testing regime or the punishments that accompany them. One example includes policies seeking to reduce supply, particularly around content-uncertain, non-prescribed, Internet-available and criminally procured substances. Other examples include undermining demand through strong education, disclosure policies, and cultural change around professional sporting environments driven by leagues and clubs. Just as sexual education changed in focus from 'just say no' to the details of safe sex, a harm-reduction approach to drug education would provide explicit information about substances and their effects on the basis that informed decisions are safer. Harm reduction offers no moral high ground, instead preferring to engage with the middle ground of real life.

Conclusion

Our analysis so far places the WADA at the centre of policy. It has set sport's drug control agenda, and has secured a global reach that nearly matches that of Coca Cola and Nike. Our analysis has also identified a number of contradictions and ambiguities swirling around the debate. In a sporting world where performance and personality command deference as well as dollars, drug policy assumes that progress will accompany restricted performance and diminished personal choice. In fact, the policy directly challenges the very heart of elite sport and the brand equity that confers its economic value. So while sport encourages and rewards performance at any cost, it simultaneously declares that performance can only be attained through the advantages athletes obtain from cutting-edge training methods, state-of-the-art supplementation, genetic predispositions, medical support, coaching regimes, institutes of sport development, and a suite of performance-enhancing, pain-reducing substances that do not appear on doping schedules. In short, sport craves performance, athletes will deliver, but the authorities will establish behavioural limits.

Such is the dilemma faced by the WADA. It understands that serious competition lies at the core of elite and professional sport. But it also wants to limit the means by which players and athletes can improve their competitiveness. The WADC is the result. The WADA aims to eliminate cheating from sport, and it clearly recognises drug use as both its most blatant and insidious manifestation. But, because so many athletes perform with little regard for their own health and safety, the imposition of the WADC seems unlikely to ever eradicate drug use from sport.

At one level, the WADC rules make for impressive reading. They cover every type of use, establish a broad base of coverage, clearly articulate the penalties for transgressions, and address the various loopholes like therapeutic exemptions. As Sluggett (2011) notes, WADA has, by working with police at both the national and international level, liaising with Customs authorities, and sharing information with pharmaceutical businesses, become a highly sophisticated 'surveillent assemblage' for monitoring the drug-use behaviour of athletes and players (p. 394).

However, at a deeper level, the WADC relies on an illusory view of what sport should be like. Elite sport no longer engages gentlemen amateurs in friendly competition for the sheer pleasure of it all. It no longer reflects a social practice where natural ability, a token amount of training, a bit of flair, and a lot of self-confidence, will deliver a comfortable victory. An alternative drug control model might therefore propose that drugs in sport policy would be more effective if it accepted that 1) performance-enhancing drugs will always be employed, 2) testing will never catch all drug users, 3) athletes' health and well-being hold the greatest importance, and 4) the idea drug use can be removed from elite sport by a bit more coverage, a lot more testing, more thorough investigations of alleged use, and even more punitive sanctions for violating the rules, does not hold up to the evidence.

11 Sport league responses

Introduction

Building on earlier material, we will now take a closer look at the impact of the WADA's drug-control policy on the operation of professional sport leagues. To that end, we focus our attention on two case studies based on Australia's most powerful sports competitions, first the AFL and second, the National Rugby League (NRL).

Since the introduction of the inaugural anti-doping code in late 2003, the WADA has had little difficulty in imposing its drug-control 'will' on the Olympic sport movement. This should not be surprising since it was established in order to regulate drug use in those sports with a place at either the Winter or Summer Olympic Games. However, it had far more difficulty in having its code accepted into professional sport leagues. As noted in the previous chapter, MLB in the US resisted the WADA's overtures, and instead maintained a more lenient standard with respect to anti-doping through the 1990s and into the 2000s (Bryant 2005; Pound 2006). Meanwhile, some other sports bodies around the world had been vigorous and proactive. Some of the most innovative developments occurred in Australia's most popular sport leagues, the AFL, and the NRL. As an essential contextual lead-in to this discussion, we will provide a brief history of the Australian government's views on drug use in sport before examining the cases and their policy implications.

Taking drug control to another level

Despite attempts to paint the Australian nation as drug resistant, the facts suggest the opposite. Drug use permeates both Australian society and its sporting culture. Australian society has made heavy use of alcohol since white settlement in 1788 and flirted with drug use in sport over many decades. Evidence of endemic drug use in Australian sport goes back to the late 1980s when a series of track and field athletes and weightlifters on scholarships at the AIS admitted taking a variety of performance-enhancing substances. The AIS scandal culminated in a Government inquiry into the drugs in sport problem in 1989 – the Black Committee – which led to the establishment of the ASDA in 1990.

The Government introduced a Tough-on-Drugs-in-Sport policy in 1999. With the support of the agency responsible for implementing the Government's sport policy, the ASC, funding to national sporting organisations (NSOs) became contingent upon their implementation of the Government's anti-doping policy. In the meantime, many of Australia's most prominent NSOs used the Government template to develop strong anti-doping programs, with Cricket Australia and the AFL at the forefront. Following the introduction of the 2003/04 WADA Anti-Doping Code, the Australian Government modified its policy to ensure WADA compliance, and used it to create a more expansive template all NSOs were expected to adopt. In 2005 the Australian Government strengthened its Tough-on-Drugs-in Sport policy by extending the powers of ASDA beyond its drug-testing responsibilities. ASDA later changed its name to the ASADA, and assumed an investigative role whereby it could initiate inquiries into allegations of drug use, and recommend hearings when sufficient evidence linked a player or athlete to the use, possession or trafficking of a banned substance.

The policy collected further adjustments in late 2007 when the Australian Government called for more frequent year-round testing for illicit drugs as well as performance-enhancing drugs. Government officials sought advice from ASADA about how testing for illicit drugs could be strengthened, while Federal Sports Minister George Brandis advised that he intended to increase funding to major sporting codes, thereby allowing them to introduce new testing regimes. Additional funding would be necessary, argued *The Age* newspaper, because 'drug screening cost[s] up to $1000 a test' and so 'many sports could struggle to fund out-of-competition testing unless the Government pays' (Stafford 2007: 27). Although ASADA received funding from the Federal Government, it also conducted fee-for-service testing, which some sports were better able to afford than others. Additionally, testing for illicit drugs out-of-competition fell beyond the ASADA's core brief, and held no interest to the WADA either. Undeterred, Brandis, together with the Minister for Health and Aging, Christopher Pyne, launched the Government's Illicit Drugs in Sport Policy (IDSP). According to the Ministers, their policy document contained 'a series of important new measures designed to take to a new level the Government's fight against illicit drugs in sport' (Brandis 2007a: 1).

The preamble to the IDSP affirmed the Government's zero-tolerance position towards illicit substances in sport, evidenced by an extension to drug testing outside periods of athletic competition. It also promised to 'ensure that sanctions will apply in the case of any positive tests' (Brandis & Pyne 2007: 3) thus ensuring a hard-line, punitive approach throughout the year. A tough-on-drugs-in-sport stance was vital, the policy document stated, to 'help restore the status of sports men and women as positive role models for all Australians' (Brandis & Pyne 2007: 2). The policy achieved an unprecedented scope, and national sport organisations were invited to adopt an out-of-competition illicit drug-testing regime. Furthermore, the government would fund requests for up to 6,000 tests with a total cost of AUS$21 million (Brandis & Pyne 2007: 3). The details of the Brandis–Pyne illicit drug control regime is summarised in Table 11.1.

Table 11.1 Brandis–Pyne illicit drug policy, 2007

Core values	Coverage	Provisions	Treatment	Sanctions	NSO role
Zero tolerance	All sports all year round	Investigation of drug used supported by frequent testing – both targeted and random	1st out-of-competition violation: counselling and rehabilitation support	2nd out-of-competition violation: public shaming and possible suspension 3rd out-of-competition violation: 1 year to lifetime suspension	Organise own testing Investigate illicit drug breaches Provide illicit drug counselling and rehabilitation Provide illicit drug education Report compliance with these measures to ASADA

The national Government that Brandis and Pyne represented lost office at the November 2007 election, which meant the policy was never fully implemented. However, the new Federal Minister for Youth and Sport, Kate Ellis, expressed similar sentiments, and wanted to continue a hard-line government policy on drug in sport (Wiseman 2007). As Ellis' response revealed, and as the Brandis–Pyne initiative demonstrated, the Australian public was sympathetic to tougher drug controls in sport, and were comfortable with its extension to so-called illicit drugs. The experiences of the AFL and the NRL should be viewed in this light.

The case of the AFL

In seeking to find out where a professional sporting league like the AFL fits within the WADA inspired anti-doping policy regime, we begin by posing some questions. First, to what extent has the AFL been infected with a culture of drug use? Second, how has it gone about managing drug use? Third, what use has it made of the WADA template in guiding its policies? Finally, how well have its policies ensured a balance between maintaining the sport's reputation, and protecting the health, well-being, and rights of players? The answers to these questions remain critical to the policy initiatives of all professional sporting codes, as few have ventured as deeply into the drug control issue as the AFL.

Australian football was invented in 1859 in Melbourne when four sportsmen sat down at the bar of an East Melbourne hotel and drafted out a basic set of rules that became the foundation laws of the modern game (Hibbens 2008). Not only did the game blossom into one of Australia's largest participant sports, it also spawned Australia's most popular national sports league, the AFL. The AFL arose from an expanded regional competition, the Victorian Football League. It became fully national in 1991 with the entry of the Adelaide Crows, a South Australian-based team, ensuring that every State except for Tasmania had a representative team in its capital city. At this time, the competition underwent significant rebranding to become the AFL.

Quickly establishing its cultural and market dominance, the AFL had, by the late 1990s, commanded annual attendances in excess of seven million fans, and an enviable position as the most commercialised sports league in the nation. At the same time, the league's very success established the ideal conditions for drug use (Waddington 2000b). First, it provided a strong competitive environment delivering significant financial and promotional rewards for winning. Second, the game had become highly scientised and medicalised where a bevy of coaches, physicians, psychologists, trainers, and dieticians assisted players to secure a winning edge over their opponents. Finally, the pharmaceutical industry's constant supply of new drugs to the marketplace offered compelling opportunities in the forms of building strength, improving endurance, bolstering recovery, stimulating the central nervous system, heightening awareness, stabilising moods, and generally allowing people to look and feel better (Waddington 2000b). These conditions simultaneously appeared in Australian sport during the 1980s when drug use gained public visibility, particularly in track and field, weightlifting, and cycling (Reiterer 2000). In the case of the AFL, our initial questions concern how prevalent drug use has been, and whether or not the conditions just described encouraged footballers to take drugs to ensure success, in so doing confirming their images as hyper-masculine warriors and larger-than-life personalities engaged in high-risk behaviour both on and off the playing field.

The AFL understood the problems it could face if it left the drug problem unchecked. As a result, in the wake of the Black Report and the formation of the ASDA in 1990, the AFL established one of the first anti-drug codes in Australia, soon becoming a model for other sport associations and leagues. It compiled a list of banned performance-enhancing substances, implemented both in-season and out-of-season testing procedures using the facilities of the ASDA, restructured its tribunal system to hear breaches of the code, and imposed sanctions. A player education program also supplemented these measures. In 1998, a two-year suspension for players found guilty of taking steroids, stimulants, and diuretics was added to the code. Players committing a second doping offence could receive a lifetime suspension (AFL 1998), a stance consistent with subsequent WADA policy in 2003/04. Further changes bolstered and streamlined the league's policy and administrative processes. First, club officials found guilty of assisting a player to take drugs, either intentionally or inadvertently, would be held personally liable. Second, the AFL Commission could charge players, clubs or officials as soon as a positive test for the first or 'A' sample was recorded. Previously, the League had to wait for up to eight weeks before a tribunal hearing convened for a second or 'B' sample to be processed (Linnell 1998).

Illicit drug use introduced a different suite of challenges. Prior to 2003 the AFL's anti-doping focus sought to deter any 'unfair advantage' by mandating testing for banned performance-enhancing drugs, such as steroids (Horvath 2006: 358). Nevertheless, the issue of illicit substances first came to the AFL's notice in 1989 with the addition of cannabis to the IOC's list of substances subject to bans (Campos *et al.* 2003). During the 1990s the AFL adhered to the IOC's recommendations on proscribed performance-enhancing drugs and methods, including a commitment to random performance-enhancing drugs testing. In terms of cannabis use, however, the IOC allowed individual sports to decide individually. At first, the AFL declared that marijuana and other cannabis derivatives were not performance enhancing, and therefore required no specific testing. However, in 2002 policymakers within the AFL began to reconsider whether the League had a responsibility to test for so-called recreational drugs that, while not performance enhancing, might otherwise adversely affect the health of players and undermine the AFL's public image. The league also understood that mood-enhancing drugs like marijuana and Ecstasy were widely available, and that footballers would not be immune from indulgences, especially to relieve stress and emotional pressures.

After consultation with the AFL Players' Association (AFLPA) – the players' trade union – the AFL Commission arranged for an in- and out-of-competition (all year round) drug-testing pilot study focusing on cannabinoids. It revealed that between October 2002 and September 2004, 26 AFL players had tested positive to cannabis from a total of 915 tests, five of these occurring in-competition (Horvath 2006). While the results indicated that only a small proportion of players had used cannabis, the AFL determined it prudent to address illegal substance use in the game. Consequently, year-round testing for illicit drugs proceeded with the endorsement of the AFLPA (Horvath 2006).

Despite the eventual policy initiative, the AFL and the AFLPA did not initially view illicit drugs as a serious problem, notwithstanding a claim in early 2002 by former Sydney Swans player, Dale Lewis, that more than 60 per cent of AFL footballers had 'done some sort of recreational drug ... you'd have to have your head in the sand to think that it doesn't exist' (Carlyon 2005: 36). While leading player managers reinforced Lewis' comments, AFL officials described the remarks as 'incredibly naive and ... stupid ... reckless ... unsubstantiated by evidence' and a 'scurrilous attack on AFL players who had been slurred by nothing more than innuendo' (Robinson 2002; *The Age* 2007: 7). The AFLPA along with Lewis' former club, the Sydney Swans, joined the chorus of condemnation, declaring that 'we don't believe there's a problem with the use of recreational drugs, otherwise we would be seeing it in our testing' (Robinson 2002: 10).

In 2005, having undertaken a detailed analysis of the illicit drug-use problem, the AFL succumbed to stakeholder – and especially Government – pressures, and extended its anti-doping policy to embrace illicit drugs, including cannabis, cocaine, and Ecstasy (AFL 2005a). With the addition of its illicit drugs policy (IDP), testing would be done both in-season and out-of-season, and both pre- and post-match. This measure responded to the WADA's newly expanded anti-doping net. But, it also aligned with the AFL's belief that it had an obligation to protect the health of athletes and the good name and integrity of the sport (AFL 2005b, 2005). Interestingly, the new policy received an endorsement from the AFLPA on the grounds that it would monitor player use of illicit drugs all year round, and provide an early warning of problem use. Included in the standard playing contract, a new clause required players to submit themselves to a drug test at any time, including 'without limitation a blood or urine test' (AFL, Standard Playing Contract: 6). The AFL Collective Bargaining Agreement further gave consent for the testing of players for both performance-enhancing and illicit drugs (Horvath 2006).

Accordingly, the AFL resolved that its IDP should be both preventative and punitive (AFL 2005a). In practice, they aimed to educate, counsel, and treat players on illicit drug use as well as punishing them for using a banned substance, even if it was not performance enhancing (Horvath 2006). In the case of cannabis, for a first in-season offence players would have to undertake private counselling, while for a second offence they would be asked to submit to a rehabilitation program. For a third offence clubs would be advised, and the case then referred to a disciplinary tribunal where the player would face a possible suspension (AFL 2005a). However, a complication arose when it became known that the WADC policy on illicit drugs, which had become the Australian Government's policy, was far more punitive for in-season testing than the AFL's so-called 'three-strikes' policy. For a first offence players could face a 3 to 12-month suspension, and for a second offence the penalty stood at a maximum two years. For a third offence the player could be banned from the sport for life. The AFL's much softer three-strike policy is summarised in Table 11.2.

Paradoxically, the AFL had created a public relations problem by taking its IDP beyond the WADC. By providing for a comprehensive, but 'softly' regulated in- and out-of-competition testing protocol, its overall stance on illicit drug use appeared much less punitive than the hard but narrow WADA sanctions for athletes who tested positive for illicit substances during periods of competition only. Matters came to a head in mid-2005 when the AFL and AFLPA rejected the government's invitation to make the in-competition part of their IDP complaint with the WADC. Both bodies felt uncomfortable about mandatory sanctions for players caught using cannabis on match day. From the AFL / AFLPA viewpoint,

Table 11.2 AFL draft IDP, 2005

Testing procedure	In-competition policy sanctions	Out-of-competition policy sanctions
1st positive test for player	Test result sent to club doctor only: counselling to follow	Test result sent to club doctor only: counselling to follow
2nd positive test result for player	Club doctor notified, more intensive counselling and treatment	Club doctor notified, more intensive counselling and treatment
3rd positive test result for player	Club officials and AFL Commission notified plus max. 12-week suspension	Club officials and AFL Commission notified plus maximum 12-week suspension

a potential two-year ban for testing positive to non-performance-enhancing drugs on match day seemed excessive. In fact, the WADA even foreshadowed a life ban from sport for athletes shown to have ingested cannabinoids on three occasions during an in-competition period. Meanwhile, the AFL and the AFLPA remained unsatisfied with WADA's in competition 'naming and shaming', punishment, and a lack of interest in rehabilitation (Carlyon 2005; Finnis 2005). Pressure to sign the WADC increased as the Federal government threatened to withdraw AUS\$1 million of annual funding should the AFL fail to comply. In a tense meeting between AFL officials and the Minister for Sport, David Kemp, the AFL relented, but maintained that its policy and approach were superior to the simplistic and punitive WADA model (Denham 2005).

Under the AFL's initial draft 2005 IDP, a positive test (whether in- or out-of-competition) resulted in confidential counselling for a player, along with a warning about further transgressions. Under its revised, WADA compliant policy, players now faced mandatory sanctions and the prospect of a two-year ban for traces of illicit drugs on match days. The AFL's revised WADA compliant policy thus made little distinction between an in-competition positive test for cannabis and an out-of-competition positive test for steroids. This created confusion and the prospect of a double standard. For example, the world champion sprinter Marion Jones, who admitted to using performance-enhancing drugs during the Sydney 2000 Olympic Games, incurred a two-year ban from her sport. Yet, under the reshaped AFL policy, she would have been liable to at least a one-year ban had she smoked a 'joint' between races in 2000, even though it would have diminished her capacity to perform on the track.

Despite its broad coverage and evidence-based support, the AFL's year-round commitment to illicit drug use detection and treatment via harm-reduction protocols received carping criticism. Opposition to the policy increased when the names of players undergoing counselling for positive out-of-competition tests were revealed, contrary to the confidentiality that the league and its panel of drug advisers deemed necessary for the effectiveness of the program. In mid-2006 the AFL won a Victorian Supreme Court injunction preventing the media from identifying three players who had tested positive under its out-of-competition illicit drug-testing regime (Gregory & Chong 2006). The press argued that the information was in the public interest, and that their confidential source had delivered reliable information (Hughes 2006; Nguyen 2006). Equally, the AFL demanded an inquiry into how the confidentiality of its drug treatment program had been compromised, and who had leaked the medical records. The investigation subsequently cleared the ASADA lab employed for the testing.

Like the WADA, the ASADA had a zero-tolerance policy on in-competition illicit drug use and insisted on naming guilty athletes, no matter the drug type (Masters 2007). However, ASADA did not test for illicit drugs out-of-competition in Olympic sports like cycling and swimming, but this fact did not inhibit the chorus of Government and media criticism directed at the AFL for withholding names and protecting drug users. While the AFL saw it as sanctimonious and hypocritical, most media commentators sided with the Government, with one journalist describing the AFL players as 'beneficiaries of a league that is more sympathetic than some other sporting codes when it comes to out-of-competition illicit drug use' (Nguyen 2006: 29). However, they failed to distinguish between in-competition and out-of-competition testing regimes and penalties. Nor did they understand that the AFL was the only Australian sport organisation attempting to manage year-round illicit drug use. Nevertheless, the Government, the ASADA, and the media prevailed. By the end of 2006 the AFL's in-competition policy became WADA compliant, while its out-of-competition policy revolved around its initial harm-reduction and rehabilitation model, with a possible 12-week suspension for a third drug-use strike.

In early 2007, the AFL – fuming from its lack of support from ASADA – announced that while its anti-doping policy would continue to be run in conjunction with the ASADA, its IDP would now 'use a private drug diagnostic firm to handle testing' (Denham 2007: 31). While the ASADA had been cleared of any impropriety concerning the 'leak' of player names to the press, the AFL had chosen a new partner in the operation of its illicit drug program. But, later in the year its IDP was again compromised when television network Channel 7 – coincidentally the broadcast rights owner for the sport – revealed the names of two AFL players undergoing treatment for illicit drug use outside of competition. The announcement caused controversy for two reasons. First, the television station had exposed players' medical records, ignoring the legal principle of doctor–patient confidentiality. Second, it later became apparent that the medical records purchased by Channel 7 had been stolen from a doctor's surgery (Healey & Ralph 2007; Smith 2007a). A ruling by the Victorian Supreme Court confirmed Channel 7's culpability and secured privacy for the players undergoing treatment. The AFL was furious that a leak had taken place, but the Federal Government and sections of the media retorted that, in their view, AFL players were being protected from public scrutiny (Murnane 2007).

Drug policy reform: the NRL

In mid-2007, with a federal election looming, a win over the AFL under its belt, and in the wake of illicit drug use incidents involving Ben Cousins (an AFL player) and Andrew Johns (an NRL player), the Australian Government placed the issue of illicit drug use high on its sport policy agenda. As noted previously, the Government was not only vehemently opposed to performance-enhancing drugs, but was also taking a hard line on illicit substance use (Brandis 2007b). It had also pressured the AFL to sign up to the WADC in 2005, and by insisting on in-competition sanctions, compromised the rehabilitative model favoured by the AFL.

Around this time, the custodians of Australia's second most popular football code, the NRL, were planning to introduce its own out-of-competition IDP. While similar to the AFL's approach, the NRL model introduced some additional features attractive to the Australian Government. The Government hailed the NRL model as superior, developed in consultation with the Rugby League Professionals Association (RLPA). In particular, they liked a suspended mandatory fine of 5 per cent of salary for a first offence, and payment of the fine and a maximum

Table 11.3 NRL IDP, 2007

Testing procedure	In-competition policy sanction	Out-of-competition policy sanction
1st positive test for player	Warning to 1-year suspension	Suspended fine of 5% of annual salary plus 3 months counselling
2nd positive test result for player	Up to 2-year suspension	Payment of suspended fine plus maximum of 12 weeks suspension from playing
3rd positive test result for player	Possible lifetime suspension	As above

suspension of 12 NRL games for a second offence. The NRL model, incorporating three months of drug treatment and counselling, received accolades from Government sport ministers mooting it as the new benchmark (Magnay 2007). The NRL policy is summarised in Table 11.3.

Despite avoiding the naming-and-shaming approach favoured by hard-line drug regulation advocates, the NRL policy incorporated enough punishment to satisfy those committed to zero tolerance. Having previously allowed clubs to test for illicit drugs at their discretion, the NRL now proposed a uniform approach in terms of testing, sanctions, and rehabilitation. The NRL's IDP came into operation in August 2007, and thus became the second sport in Australia to introduce such a program on a national scale. The Federal Government welcomed the NRL initiative, and suggested that other sports should follow suit.

Policy implications and comments

Despite the best of intentions, the AFL's drug control policies in particular, and the NRL's policy to a lesser extent, have suffered from confusion about first, their primary purpose, second, the drugs that should be prohibited, and finally, the sanctions that should be applied. As a result the success of the policies in curbing drug use, ensuring the reputation and good standing of their leagues, and protecting the health, well-being and rights of players, remains unclear. Of course, all sport organisations must come to terms with these issues.

Take, for example, the problem of identifying the prevalence of drug use in the AFL. At first glance football appears to be clean given the few positive tests for performance-enhancing drugs and subsequent suspensions over the lifetime of the AFL's drug code. These facts counter any claim that football clubs provide havens for drug use. In fact, the trivial number of infractions suggests that the AFL drug code has delivered an effective outcome, and justifies its status as a model sporting code.

On the other hand, a countervailing view suggests that the small amount of positive tests are symptomatic of a flawed policy arrangement and testing protocol whereby doping cheats slip easily through the testing net. Moreover, a lack of testing vigilance may lead to more drug use. Under the AFL–ASADA arrangements, for example, testing can occur infrequently, lack targeting, or as in the case of the BALCO scandal in the US, employ testing procedures unable to detect new forms of 'designer' steroids (Carroll 2005). In addition, whereas Australia's top 20 track and field athletes can be tested between five and ten times a year, AFL and NFL players will on average be tested no more than once a year. Brent Harvey, a leading AFL player, indicated that he had not been tested once in 2007 for performance-enhancing drugs (McAsey 2007). At the same time an ASADA commissioned study of elite athletes found that 30 per cent of them believed they 'could get away with using performance enhancing drugs' (Jeffrey & Parnell 2008: 18).

Doubt also surrounds the claim that the AFL anti-doping code balances the need to secure a level playing field against the need to protect the rights of players and safeguard their long-term health and welfare. We noted that the Federal Government and large sections of the media were critical of its 'soft' stance on illicit drug use, particularly during the out-of-competition period. Nevertheless, the AFL's position relied upon expert recommendations from drug agencies and medical practitioners advocating not only strong testing and appropriate sanctions for use and trafficking, but also educational, counselling, and rehabilitation services (British Medical Association 2002; Drugs and Crime Prevention Committee 2000). Striking the right balance has proven difficult for the AFL. As a multilayered task, formulating drug policy requires comparative judgements about the sanctions that should be applied to performance-enhancing and illicit drugs on one hand, and legal substances such as alcohol on the other. With misuse, these substances may lead to behaviour that undermines the good standing of the game (Turner & McCrory 2003). The issue of differential punishments also adds another layer of complexity, as well as the timing of the violation and whether it occurred in-competition or out-of-competition. These concerns become additionally compounded for the AFL when it has to confront heavy political and media sanctions for failing to comply with the WADA template for in-competition illicit drug use.

By trying to cover all bases and testing for illicit drugs out-of-season as well as in-season, the AFL has placed itself in an awkward position. Initially, their policy seemed to be a constructive step by aiming to preserve the health and well-being of players over the whole year. In reality, however, the policy introduced a paternalistic tool for controlling the behaviour of players in order to protect the AFL brand. For instance, when testing positive to an illicit drug for a third time, the player is deemed to have engaged in unbecoming conduct prejudicing the AFL's reputation. Brand protection deletes a player's right to privacy coupled with a suspension potentially disproportionate to the violation's seriousness. Revealing a player's private medical records, or banning an athlete from competing on the grounds that they were found to have taken drugs that do nothing to improve sporting performance, appear to be unfair punishments. Extended arrangements such as these also provide the conditions for media speculation and gossip, where allegations multiply on the basis of hearsay and rumour. The players' association has admitted to reservations about the AFL's IDP for these very reasons.

As the AFL and NRL cases exemplify, the WADA/ASADA-driven codes struggle to acknowledge the broader contextual pressures elite athletes encounter in their daily grind to build more competitive bodies and minds. When players equal assets, to be lauded when playing well, or abandoned when out of form, and where success has significant financial implications, drug use provide a compelling opportunity for players to stay in the game. The hyper-commercialised sports world and the money-driven media frenzy it elicits, induces a sporting culture prioritising whatever it takes to gain a winning edge. For example, studies suggest that the punishments imposed on athletes caught using drugs may encourage them to employ masking agents, which can be even more deleterious to their health than the initial performance-enhancing drugs (Waddington 2000b, 2005). Banning drugs can also make it more difficult for players to obtain medical advice about how to reduce the health damage incurred from overuse and self-prescription. Such a possibility raises the troublesome issue of whether compliance sanctions should be extended to the social network of doctors, coaches, and trainers who support drug-using players.

In elite sport, the pressure to perform is accompanied by a corresponding psychological stress, which can be alleviated through illicit drugs or the consumption of alcohol. Dealing with the pressures of professional sport in this manner can be bolstered by club cultures emphasising playing hard both on and off the field. Masculine posturing ties strongly to behaviours transgressing the fear of physical injury and bodily damage, irrespective of whether it comes from an on-field collision, alcohol, other mood-altering drugs, or a street brawl (Whitehead 2005). Sport has been described as the 'most powerful social confirmation of masculinity that any male can attain in our culture' (Burstyn 1999: 254) and consequently encourages anti-social behaviour amplified by a media obsessed with scandal and titillation, ideal conditions for the production a hyper-masculine culture that rewards aggression and winning. The celebration of heroic and risky football performances further reinforces the idea that masculinity involves physical damage to the body (Peretti-Watel *et al.* 2002).

The AFL, and, to a lesser extent, the NRL, have been conscientious in their desire to manage all aspects of drug use in their competitions. However, by taking on the responsibility for monitoring illicit drug use out-of-competition they over-reached their custodianship. Sporting leagues are not players' moral guardians. Nor should sporting codes be responsible for the behaviour of players once they leave their workplace: the playing field, the training ground, and the clubroom. As one media commentator noted, if the moral education of players and fans is a problem they should be instructed to 'spend more time in churches, mosques and synagogues' (Bagaric 2007: 21). The AFL and NRL would still keep their reputation for player welfare and a quality competition intact if it limited its drug code to performance-enhancing drugs – those substances that give players a demonstrably unfair advantage over their rivals – and spent more resources on better managing the culture that breeds drug use in the first place. At the moment their hybrid illicit drug codes, which combine the WADA's punitive model with the drug abuse treatment industry emphasis on harm reduction, has created confusion amongst officials and fans alike, and provides the conditions where players' off-season privacy will be regularly invaded by a media pack hungry for the next story.

As we noted at the beginning of this chapter, drug use is not an isolated phenomenon in sport. When licit and illicit substances are combined, studies reveal that drug use is endemic throughout most societies (Drugs and Crime Prevention Committee 2000; House of Representatives Standing Committee on Family and Human Services 2007). In our AFL and NRL cases, we suggested that drug use in sport continues despite the increasingly punitive sanctions and punishments operating at the elite level. Such drug-use prevalence hardly seems surprising given the contextual and cultural forces that impact on professional players and elite athletes, where a win-at-all-costs culture and masculine bravado make drug use an attractive proposition. At the same time, drug use in sport is fraught with ambiguity. Allegations lead nowhere, moral outrage impedes rational examination, the distinction between performance-enhancing and illicit drugs blurs, and the different sanctions for 'in' and 'out of' competition drug violations creates confusion. These problematic issues provide the perfect opportunity to reignite the drugs in sport debate to see what other options may be implemented, and how a more educative and less punitive model could reduce the harms to players while maintaining the good standing of sport in general.

Conclusion

This chapter presented historical case analysis to illuminate the drug controls in Australian sport, the forces that shaped their development, and how drug-use problems might be best managed in the context of the WADC. The chapter can be summarised by five major points. First, it demonstrated that sport policymaking, like most other forms of public policy, involves a convoluted process combining ideology and evidence in order to reach a final policy solution (Althaus *et al.* 2007; Bessant *et al.* 2006; Stewart *et al.* 2008). Proponents for strict controls and hefty sanctions argue that players who take drugs have not only done a disservice to themselves, their sport, and their communities, but have also let down the millions of fans who idolise them and mimic their behaviour. The moral certitude underpinning this argument proves seductive for those stakeholders wanting to see sport grow and prosper. At the same time little research evidence confirms that role-modelling occurs in sport or that the behaviour of elite sports players directly influences the behaviour of children and adolescents (Payne *et al.* 2003). While many professional footballers, golfers, tennis players, and cricketers are hero-worshipped by sport fans around the world, it has not been shown that their off-field illicit drug use is copied (Hogan & Norton 2000; Keresztes *et al.* 2008; Lines 2001). In fact, assertions about athlete role-modelling raise more problems than they resolve, leaving us with a policy option based on little more than a feeling that it makes sense, a less than ideal foundation for 'achieving social progress' (Sanderson 2002: 19). On the other hand, substantial evidence in the broader community indicates that harm-reduction polices providing education, private support, and rehabilitation to drug users can significantly lower the social costs and cultural 'damage' associated with drug use (Eldredge 2000: 161; Gray 2001: 6).

Second, this chapter showed how different 'policy communities' (Nutley & Webb 2000: 31–32) bring their weight to the policy analysis table, and explains the ways in which 'political opportunism', 'partisan values', and passionately held belief systems shape dominant arguments (Edwards 2001: 9; Guess & Farnham 2000: 8). We recorded, for example, a sharp divide between the punitive, zero-tolerance policy supporters at one extreme, and the player-welfare, harm-reduction policy supporters on the other. Policy development emerged from the battle between those stakeholders who wanted all drug use – both performance enhancing and illicit – eliminated from sport, and those who saw the need to manage it from the perspective of player health and welfare. In each case, the values, beliefs, and ideologies of the stakeholder groups within each policy community were on vigorous display. The punitive drug policy proponents comprising senior government ministers, media commentators, and a large proportion of the sports' fan bases quickly captured the moral high ground. They denounced first, the evils of drug use in general, second, the cheating that underpins performance-enhancing drug use, and third, the criminality involved whenever illicit drugs are involved. In contrast, player welfare and harm-reduction proponents, including medical practitioners, paramedical professionals, and health workers, and whose arguments centred on player support, counselling and treatment, failed to gain any great policy traction, despite basing their proposal on international research studies and the advice of drug treatment experts (Caulkins *et al.* 2005; Kayser & Smith 2008). Amongst other criticisms, this group were accused of being 'soft', failing to understand the culture of sport, and not realising how easily its positive values and good standing could be contaminated by drug-use incidents and allegations.

Third, this chapter exemplified the fact that public policy formulation stimulates combat between competing and multiple agendas, some of which are initially camouflaged by more public and popular arguments (Parsons 1995; Stewart *et al.* 2008b). In this instance the more popular policies revolved around the inequity and unfairness that drug use creates, ahead of the adverse impact it has on the health of players. However, when the sporting bodies – in this instance the AFL and NRL – faced pressure on the issue, and were asked to defend their highly regulatory policies, they conceded that any sort of drug use was not in the interests of the game or its appropriate brand custodianship. While the AFL and NRL both described equity and player health as paramount, their overarching concerns pivoted upon their sports' reputations and market values. In the end, the greater danger enveloped the health of the brands as a consequence of adverse publicity.

Fourth, this chapter suggested that policy initiatives come at a cost to the community, typically shared inequitably. For example, it costs around AUS$1,000 to conduct and process a sport-related drug test in Australia. Financially powerful, the AFL and NRL organise thousands of drugs tests a year. However, at least 90 per cent of national sporting bodies in Australia cannot feasibly budget for this level of annual spending. While the Australian government subsidises drug testing for the smaller national sporting bodies, the idea that any small sporting body anywhere in the world could fund a year-round testing program appears fanciful. Broad-based drug testing programs come at heavy cost. Testing expenses for performance-enhancing drugs already incurs significant burdens on the public purse. Although the previous Australian Government subsidised testing for illicit drugs in sport, the Brandis–Pyne policy involved an unprecedented use of public money to protect sport's integrity and good reputation. Moreover, the results of neo-liberal initiatives in other areas of government responsibility suggest that future costs of illicit drug tests may end up being met indirectly by sports fans in a 'deregulated internal market' (Catley 2005: 9). Alternatively, in market-driven sports such as the major professional sport leagues, participants could be invited to fund their own testing in order to secure drug-free certification. Either way, a program that aims to test for all types of drug use all year round comes with a huge price tag. Like any economic equation, expenses will quickly transform into higher admission prices.

Finally, this chapter revealed how the moral panic surrounding the illicit drugs in sport debate ignored and marginalised the larger, endemic, health-related problem facing sport in Australia, that of heavy alcohol use. While performance-enhancing and illicit drug use constitutes important policy concerns for sport officials and administrators, alcohol abuse remains the single largest drug problem for players and athletes (Ford 2007; Hildebrand *et al.* 2001). For the most part alcohol dependency and abuse are seen as peripheral to the main policy game, and lie outside drug-testing regimes for out-of-competition testing periods. While a concerted effort has sought to re-educate sport club officials and members about the problems of excessive alcohol consumption, with the Australian Drug Foundation's Good-sports campaign being an exemplar in this regard, heavy alcohol use still looms as an integral feature of Australian sport practice, both at the elite and community level. However, a policy regulating alcohol use might disappoint some of sport's major sponsors who produce or distribute alcoholic beverages. Such a policy might also deprive many sport clubs of a major revenue source. Nothing in the IDP suggests that the Federal Government takes a primary interest in advancing the overall health and well-being of players. If it did, then the policy would take a much greater interest in the abuse of alcohol as well as painkillers, barbiturates, and tobacco.

The Australian drugs in sport case studies discussed in this chapter expose the complexities and political idiosyncrasies that accompany policy formation for sporting bodies. We saw how the Australian Government adopted a policy aiming to 1) secure the moral high ground and therefore render counterarguments and alternative policy arrangements impotent, 2) spin an argument that it had the best interests of the game and the athletes at heart, when it was essentially about preserving the commercial value of the sport brand, 3) give only peripheral attention to the health, well-being, treatment, and recovery of players and athletes, and 4) cloud the distinction between performance-enhancing drugs and illicit drugs on the grounds that any type of drug use constitutes a problem, and that this 'war on drugs' could only be won by implementing a zero-tolerance policy for all illicit drug use as well (Gray 2001: 151).

At the same time, the Federal Government produced no convincing evidence supporting policies involving 1) all-year-round testing for all categories of drugs, 2) more investigations of drug-use allegations, 3) more control over player whereabouts to ensure their availability for testing, and 4) more naming and shaming of drug users. In fact, drug testing will be costly, it will impinge on the rights of players to run their lives in their own way when not in competition, and it will marginalise programs aiming to support players who have serious drug-use problems. On balance, the idea of basing 'practice and policy decisions on the best available evidence' has not played a major role in this example of policy formation (Gandhi *et al.* 2007: 43). As we will later argue, the interests of sport and its participants will be advanced if the ideological and moralistic shackles are removed from current policies, and evidence that reveals the full costs and benefits of different drug control models receive more space on the sport policy formation stage.

12 A critical appraisal

Introduction

Few would disagree that drug use in sport presents serious problems for its many stakeholders. Of course, the rationale for, and mechanisms of, drug control enlivens debate like few other topics in sport. On one side, powerful global sport authorities like the IOC, the WADA, and international sport federations declare drug use in sport as brazen, immoral cheating and should be eliminated through the imposition of punitive, zero-tolerance measures. An alternative approach focuses on the protection of athlete health, and on mitigating the serious social impacts accompanying drug use. This approach assumes that some players and athletes will inevitably employ banned substances irrespective of the potential penalties (Waddington 2005). As a result, the main game should focus on minimising harm to all participants. In short, the tension between the benefits of a deterrence-only model of drug control as enacted by WADA versus a multi-level approach of harm minimisation as adopted by many drug education and treatment support agencies continues to escalate.

The WADA is winning the battle. Perhaps more accurately, it is winning the marketing battle, rather than the one against drug use in sport. It leads a global movement for harmonisation of anti-doping rules in elite sport, using strongly punitive policies to address transgression, documented within a code specifying forbidden substances and methods, updated annually (Henne 2010). On the surface, this globalisation and harmonisation of anti-doping efforts appears reasonable given its intention to enforce consistent rules in every sphere of the elite sporting world. Under closer examination, however, we question the assumptions underpinning current policies. In this chapter, we draw attention to the ambiguities and contradictions driving anti-doping policy logic. We also outline why we think current policies introduce adverse consequences for the health and well-being of athletes, and for public health in general.

We begin this chapter by reviewing the founding assumptions upon which anti-doping policy rests, before discussing its fundamentalist policy prescriptions. The WADA's policy position rests upon four principles: first, the need for sport to set a good example; second, the necessity to ensure a level playing field; third, the responsibility to protect the health of athletes; and fourth, the importance of preserving the integrity of sport. While each of these founding assumptions has intuitive appeal, they wilt under scrutiny. For instance, an analysis of the evidence suggests that sport becomes a problematic institution when it comes to setting a good example for the rest of society. And, neither is it clear that sport has an inherent or essential integrity that can only be sustained through heavy-handed regulation. Furthermore, the WADA's anti-doping policy has proven ineffective in maintaining a level playing field and in protecting the overall health and welfare of players and athletes.

In the second part of this chapter we reintroduce the harm-reduction policy position. We argue that the WADA anti-doping policy places too much emphasis on minimising drug related *use* while giving insufficient weight to the minimisation of drug-related *harms*. As a result, we argue that drug-related harms are being poorly managed in sport. We propose that drug controls in sport would benefit from placing a greater emphasis on harm-reduction models and practices.

Drug policy challenges

To briefly retrace the pertinent history, the drugs in sport problem first came to prominence in the 1960s with the use of amphetamines amongst professional European cyclists. At the same time, steroid availability was becoming widespread in the US and Eastern Europe. As money flowed in commensurate with an unprecedented media interest, sport began to globalise, its commercial value increasing exponentially. A number of high-profile drugs scandals occurred in the 1980s, culminating in the Ben Johnson affair in 1988. The consequent media feeding frenzies encouraged a number of sporting bodies to introduce anti-doping regulations. Plagued by constant allegations of drug use in international sport, and prodded by the Tour de France drug crisis of 1998, the IOC pushed to establish an agency with responsibility for managing and enforcing global anti-doping policy. The WADA was born in 1999 and has become a global force in the war on drugs in sport. Its success in establishing an international drug code has been underpinned by three developments. First, the WADA receives funding from the IOC and a group of national governments, providing the agency with both capital and influence. Second, the WADA secured a series of international declarations commending and ratifying the policy code it developed. Third, the UNESCO endorsed the WADA policy as an international convention. These achievements consolidated the WADA's position as the central international agency for regulating drug use in sport. Currently, most sporting bodies seeking funding or competitive sanctioning from their international governing body, or national governments, must enact the WADA policy. The WADA vision of a drug-free sports world emanates from a need for moral certitude, which consequently justifies the inclusion of both performance-enhancing and illicit drugs on the list of prohibited substances (Kayser *et al.* 2007; Savulescu *et al.* 2004; Smith & Stewart 2008).

Setting a good example

Sport policymakers claim that athletes in particular, and sport in general, have an obligation to set a good example, since sporting heroes influence young people who use them as role models. Under these conditions it makes sense to implement punitive policies that discourage drug use. However, this policy position rests on two key propositions: firstly that sport can positively shape the moral behaviour of its participants and followers, and secondly that heavy punishment for drug use in sport will ultimately lead to abstinence. While these propositions appeal intuitively, little evidence supports them. To begin with, the role model argument naively expects elite athletes to be model citizens judged against criteria imposed upon no other category of admired citizen. Moreover, anti-doping policy conflicts with changing values in contemporary society. Performance-enhancing drug use might be considered unacceptable in elite sport, but elsewhere in society, enhancement is a taken-for-granted practice (Orbach 2010). In fact, drug-control testing methods involve some questionable practices perhaps not worthy of emulation. For example, privacy and modesty problems surround enforced testing, where young athletes may feel intimidated while urinating into receptacles or forced to comply at invasive times, and all under the gaze of others (Knight & Mears 2007).

The idea that sport should set a good example for impressionable children, and provide them with a reliable moral compass, mirrors a long list of personal and social benefits ascribed to sport participation (White *et al.* 1998). To review some points we noted earlier, participation in sport has been linked to improvements to mental health and self-esteem, mental toughness, the control of stress, anxiety and depression, better physical development, community building and diminished health spending (AIHW 2000; Headley 2004; Morris *et al.* 2004; National Public Health Partnership 2002; Sport and Recreation New Zealand 2002; World Health Organization 2003). However, the (United States) President's Council on Physical Fitness and Sports Report observed that the way in which sport influences moral development remains unclear. Indeed, some evidence indicates that sport can actually increase the risk of injury, encourage binge drinking, undermine an athlete's long-term health prospects, and facilitate cheating (Ford 2007; Long & Sanderson 2001; Loland 2002; Waddington 2000b). Further contradictions appear in the long-term sponsorship relationship between sport, tobacco, and alcohol, which do not constitute setting a good example either. In other words, sport can just as easily act as a catalyst for socially dysfunctional behaviour, thus weakening the argument that drug-free sport will set clear moral guidelines for its participants.

Finally, the concept of sport as an example setter must be balanced against the fact that sport holds winning as sovereign, which in turn produces a demand for anything that gives athletes a competitive edge (Savulecu, Foddy & Clayton 2004). The hyper-competitive nature of sport and its emphasis on achievement and rewards (Deci & Ryan 2000; Frederick-Recascino & Schuster-Smith, 2003) encourages drug taking, and, in some cases, the combination of self-gratification and public approval may form a kind of addiction (Dunning & Waddington

2003). The incentives for drug use are therefore substantial (Washington *et al.* 2005). In addition, the combination of immense pressure for success and severe punishment for failure teaches young athletes another important lesson: avoid getting caught. At the same time, the listing of prohibited drugs advertises the claim that they actually work to improve performance, and, as a result, increase performance-enhancing drugs attractiveness to potential users (Bird & Wagner 1997). Performance-enhancing drugs use can in turn lead to dangerous masking agents and other more experimental drugs for which tests have not yet been refined. Under these conditions elite sport may, instead of promoting healthy lifestyles and moral development, actually encourage physical injury, anti-social behaviour, and cheating (Long & Sanderson 2001; Morris *et al.* 2004). Paradoxically, a repressive drug control program can stimulate many of the very actions it seeks to restrain.

A level playing field

Ostensibly, the level playing field argument is difficult to refute, since sport should give all competitors an equal chance of success. However, the implied assumption that drug-free sport will secure a level playing field becomes problematic when considered beyond its surface appeal. First, it does not take into account the difficulties associated with competitive parity in sport or the inevitable differences between individual participants. These differences can be significant. Variables such as training technology, coaching support, and the economic means to participate, are unevenly distributed between communities, not to mention the vast divergences in individual base-talent levels. An individual's level of talent not only results from a superior or inferior genetic inheritance – or, his or her genotype – but also due to different physical and psychological traits – or, his or her phenotype (Puthucheary *et al.* 2011; Tucker & Collins 2012). In reality, innumerable factors can provide an unfair advantage to certain athletes, with genetic factors alone accounting for 20–40 per cent of variations in maximum sporting performance (Buxens *et al.* 2011). Current policy exacerbates inequity because the rapid development of science and medicine in sport privileges only those athletes with access to the latest technological and pharmacological inventions (Waddington 2000b), legal or otherwise.

Another problem for the level playing field argument surrounds the efficacy of the anti-doping program. Only around 1–2 per cent of tests indicate doping (WADA 2008), suggesting that a prohibition, zero-tolerance approach to drug control only partly works as a deterrent (Caulkins & Reuter 2005), unless of course the 'drugs in sport problem' does not actually exist. Even assuming that testing protocols accurately expose the use of drugs, only a small proportion of athletes face testing in the first place (WADA 2008). In addition, it appears implausible that testing will ever move a step ahead of new biomedical and pharmaceutical advances, which can be compounded by the dangers of false negatives – an athlete is found not to have used, when they admit they have – and false positives – where an athlete is found to have used when they can prove they have not. Some evidence suggests that biological variability may lead to unreliable test results; drugs present in each individual differently, the impact of which can affect the reliability of testing protocols (Lundby *et al.* 2008). While some uncertainty may be expected in therapeutic medicine designed around diagnostic objectives, variability represents a significant problem in sport if athletes can never definitively be established as innocent or guilty. Given that most forms of competitive sport are characterised by cultures emphasising heroism and risk taking, and where winning is sovereign, athletes and their coaches will always be seeking a winning edge in order to tilt the playing fields towards their advantage (Dunning & Waddington 2003; Frederick-Recascino & Schuster-Smith 2003). Drug-free sport will do little to mitigate disadvantage, or redress the unequal distribution of talent-loads and performance levels.

Sport cannot be reduced to a level playing field, no matter how much landscaping we overlay. The scientisation and medicalisation of sport means that, independently of any drug use, only certain privileged athletes will have access to the latest training advantages that will give them a competitive edge (Waddington 2000b). Despite EPO's banned status, those who can afford to train at high altitude or sleep in an altitude chamber can still legally obtain a performance-enhancing benefit (Le Page 2006). Furthermore, and as noted earlier, all athletes respond differently to training and nutritional regimes, whilst others bring unique genetic advantages, such as the naturally occurring gene mutations like the one which helped Eero Mäntyranta secure two gold medals at the 1964 Winter Olympics (Le Page 2006). In fact, a multitude of non-drug-related factors can provide a competitive edge, and tilt the playing field in favour of better endowed and more richly resourced athletes.

In response, would it be appropriate to handicap athletes with extraordinary natural abilities as a way of introducing some real playing field balance? The use of weight classes in boxing, wrestling, weightlifting, and rowing exemplifies this kind of thinking. It has also been used in professional athletics, where the best runners must start from 'scratch', while the less talented runners start somewhere ahead. Horse racing has used a system of weight-based handicapping for well over 100 years, and the Melbourne Cup, one of the world's most prestigious events, is run as a handicap race where the best performing horses receive the heaviest weights to carry. In some professional sport leagues officials go to great lengths to regulate the competition in order to achieve competitive balance. Regulatory tactics include revenue sharing, drafting the best young talent to the worst performing clubs, and setting salary caps as a way of curtailing wealthy clubs from buying all the best players (Dobson & Goddard 2001). In addition, rules can be radically amended to restrict the movements of able-bodied players, consequently allowing disabled athletes to compete with a chance of winning. Similarly, it may be possible to regulate sport activities through the use of golf-like player 'grading' systems so as to allow mixed-gender participation. At one level this provides equity for everyone, but at another level becomes a bizarre exercise in equalisation that can never lead to 'true' equality, since someone will always have an advantage that secures a winning edge. At the same time, we acknowledge that the WADA is not concerned with erasing all inequality from sport. It accepts, for example, that the naturally occurring ratio of testosterone to epitestosterone can vary between individuals, and therefore confers a relative advantage to those with higher proportions of testosterone (Le Page 2006). However, the WADA does not accept any boosting through the use of drugs that 'artificially' increase testosterone levels beyond normal, or 'natural', limits.

A further ambiguity arises because not all performance-boosting drugs and substances are universally banned, caffeine being a prime example. Conversely, some drugs that clearly reduce performance are also forbidden. The inconsistency compounds when we note that alcohol and tobacco, two of society's most destructive drugs, are tacitly accepted. In fact, ironically, the WADA's policy specifies similar punishments for both performance-reducing and performance-enhancing drugs (Turner & McCrory 2003). Confusion over banned drugs, and the penalties for their use, arrives in part as a symptom of the method used to determine which substances are prohibited. To be included on the WADA prohibited list, a substance must either be a potential masking agent, or must meet two of the following three criteria set out by WADA (2012a): 1) that the substance is performance enhancing, 2) the use of the substance poses health risks to the athlete, and 3) that the use of the substance violates the spirit of sport. Marijuana, for instance, meets criteria two and three, and therefore appears on the banned list even though it reduces performance. The same goes for heroin. In contrast, over-the-counter substances such as bicarbonate/citrate, creatine monohydrate, and caffeine all deliver performance improvements, but, because they only meet criteria one, remain permissible. The social acceptance of different drugs – or conversely, their level of illegality – therefore plays a significant role in determining whether the use of a substance violates the 'spirit' of sport. Such ambiguous criteria for identifying prohibited substances leads to bans on some drugs that do not enhance performance, while allowing others that do. Logic of this kind does not support the level playing field ideology.

A final problem for the WADA's claim for a level playing field arises because the more draconian the drug control measures, the greater the likelihood that unintended consequences will occur. More testing, more investigations, and more punitive sanctions are introduced on the sound intuitive grounds that the greater the likelihood of getting caught, and the heavier the punishments that follow, the less likely players and athletes will use banned substances. But, this logic can also produce behaviours that undermine the success of zero-tolerance models. For example, athletes can turn to more dangerous, non-tested drugs, since, as we have already observed, the high risk of punishment can encourage athletes toward drugs that can be used as masking agents, or are more easily concealed, even where the health risk increases (Voy 1991). Supply restrictions also constitute a further risk. If established pharmaceutical distribution chains are circumscribed, players and athletes may be forced to seek products through the so-called 'black market', which usually comes with criminal connections. In these instances, not only will the products lack quality control, but criminal organisations can 'blackmail' players and athletes into becoming salespeople and couriers in exchange for keeping their identities secret, and not 'spilling' everything to the media (ACC 2013: 30–32).

Finally, in sports where performance-enhancing drugs offer a substantial advantage and are only distributed to a coterie of elite athletes due to their prohibition and heavy punishment for use, the playing field will be even more tilted than it would be under deregulated conditions. Under a deregulated regime the products will be more freely available. Substances will also be subject to more quality control, and be less expensive, thus broadening the market to many more would-be users (Stewart *et al.* 2004). The world of professional road cycling typifies this state of affairs. The well-resourced, high profile teams, as US Postal was for many years the exemplar, not only had access to the best team managers, the best technology, the best mechanics, and the best trainers, but also had access to the smartest medical practitioners. These doctors drew on the most up-to-date medical research, secured substances delivering significant physical outcomes, and integrated them into a sophisticated performance improvement program difficult for competitors to duplicate. Mixed messages bombard the sport-watching marketplace. On one hand, the general public condemns athletes for using drugs. On the other hand, they laud their record-breaking performances and rush to buy products emblazoned with their sporting heroes' endorsements.

In summary, sporting competitions, and the players that participate in them, possess inherent and non-substitutable imbalances owing to factors such as genetic advantages, gender bias and socio-economic access to training technology. Even genuinely drug-free sporting competitions fail to provide a truly level playing field. If, as the WADA suggest, equality should be of ultimate importance, then why do sporting regulators take little interest in providing parity between people of differing genders, physical capacities, and economic means? Whilst some efforts occur in these areas, they pale in significance next to those made to minimise the advantages bestowed by drug use.

Protecting the health of athletes

The 'athlete health' argument used to justify the zero-tolerance approach to drug control in sport is, on first reading, hard to counter, since the dangers of unregulated drug use in sport, both of the performance-enhancing and performance-reducing variety, have been clearly established (Ingram 2004). A consensus has also formed agreeing that sport and its regulating agencies must take some responsibility for the health of athletes. Of course, risk characterises sport, and it seems reasonable for governing bodies to mitigate it wherever possible. However, sports like American football, mountaineering, base-jumping, and motor racing continue to be played despite injury risk warnings. In fact, to remove the risk means removing an intrinsic part of sport itself. Given that athletes freely engage in sports with substantial risks, why are they not also free to utilise performance enhancements? In some cases, the performance-enhancing drugs actually pose less risk than the sports in which they engage.

In addition, a punitive drug-use policy defended on the grounds that it protects the health of players sits uncomfortably with a tacit acceptance of sports like boxing and Ultimate Fighting, where participants intend to inflict serious harm. It also sits uncomfortably with sporting traditions that embrace a close association with tobacco products, and support continuing association with alcohol-based products, both of which come with serious community health risks. Moreover, the policy of banning drugs has made it more difficult for athletes to obtain medical advice that might reduce the health damage of the drugs they use (Waddington 2001). It has been shown that self-medicating athletes tend to use substantially more than necessary, thereby amplifying their risk of illness and injury. Prohibition of drugs like anabolic steroids also makes it difficult for users to obtain satisfactory medical advice without fear of reprisal (Dawson 2001; Pope *et al.* 2004). In these instances, punitive policies relying on intensive policing and punishments inadvertently increase the harms associated with drug use while doing little to curtail usage (Dawson 2001; Pope *et al.* 2004).

A challenging alternative involves legalising the use of drugs in tandem with the provision of education and medical support for the management of this 'compromised choice'. However, some evidence suggests that a lack of vigilance in testing leads to more drug use (Vogel 2010). On the other hand, studies of cannabis use suggest that a reduction in sanctions, such as decriminalised personal use, does not lead to increased levels or patterns of use, but may actually assist in reducing the harms associated with use (Macintosh 2006). The trick here lies with striking an appropriate balance between widespread drug use under a legalised system, and less prevalent but higher risk drug-use patterns under an anti-doping regime. A further problem emerges with the marketplace reaction to a culture of legalised drug use amongst athletes. Would fans exert pressure on athletes to abstain, and unintentionally promote masking and experimental drug intake? Or, would they concede that bolstering testosterone levels, for instance, in a medically safe manner, is as socially acceptable as undergoing a breast augmentation? The fact remains that in either scenario, drug use to enhance performance will constitute an ongoing feature of sport (Dunning & Waddington 2003; Zaksaite 2012). We face the need to identify the approach that best protects the health of athletes, and minimises the costs to society.

Protecting player health also creates tension given the propensity of male athletes to seek out high-risk experiences as a way of demonstrating their masculinity (Burstyn 1999; The President's Council on Physical Fitness and Sports Report 1997; West 1996; Whitehead 2005). Most sporting activities, especially at elite level, require athletes to perform at the outer limit of their physical capacities and therefore demand risk taking and pain tolerance. A masculine ethos holds risk taking at its core, and the combination of illegality, the romanticised risk of becoming an athletic 'outlaw', and the potential to incur physical damage can be part of the attraction of taking drugs. A punitive anti-doping policy may therefore have the unintended consequence of making drug use even more compelling to some hyper-masculine athletes because of its association with deviant and high-risk behaviour. Conversely, a policy that acknowledges the logic of using drugs to enhance performance might normalise its consumption, and provide space for a more open public debate on drug use in sport.

By focusing on the importance of performance and winning, sport provides favourable conditions for its scientisation and medicalisation (Waddington 2000b). The sport medicine model seduces athletes since it suggests that science-based disciplines like clinical medicine, physiology, biomechanics, and psychology are the key to superior performance. Houlihan (2003) found that improvements in sport science parallel a culture that accepts the treatment of both injured and healthy athletes with drugs. Even the use of approved drugs for rehabilitation encourages risky behaviours, such as the use of painkillers to allow players to retake the field after injury. Athletes operate in a sporting culture which supports the use of medical treatments and substances to boost and sustain performance, and managers of professional sport teams have a vested interest in getting injured players back on the field of play in the shortest possible time, using painkilling and anti-inflammatory drugs to speed up the process. But, in doing so they put the long-term health of players at risk by increasing their likelihood of sustaining chronic injury problems. Sport's scientisation and medicalisation sharpen a 'double-edged sword' since it builds into sport a protective amour of professional competence. At the same time, it gives coaches, conditioners, and trainers the space to go that extra distance to secure a winning edge.

Outside anti-doping controlled sport, people use performance-enhancing drugs to develop muscularity for aesthetic or occupational reasons, or to retard ageing or combat sexual dysfunction (Shilling 2003). For most of these users, the evidence relating to the health impacts of anabolic steroids and similar drugs remains unclear. Most studies report on clinical populations or single case studies, and rarely deal with the supra-therapeutic regimens and complex pharmacology used by serious recreational athletes (Dawson 2001). Despite the limited research, expert commentators warn that the absence of available evidence does not mean that the evidence has not been found. Rather, researchers have yet to collect the data that nail down the long-term health effects of anabolic steroids (Yesalis *et al.* 2000). In the meantime, recent studies indicate some negative side effects including testicular atrophy, acne, sleeplessness, and unintended aggression, while also highlighting some positive consequences in the form of confidence building, better recovery, and occasional euphoria (Graham *et al.* 2008; Sari 2010). In these circumstances a danger exists that some health care professionals will base their recommendations about the long-term health effects of anabolic steroids and other substances on incomplete evidence. Although robust evidence relating to damage is limited, the criminalisation and demonisation of users continues to grow. Several European countries as well as the US have enacted legislation against the personal use of these drugs. In Denmark, for example, the introduction of drug testing and bans for gymnasium users has driven an already clandestine population further underground, along with the inherent health risks accompanying a hidden drug-using population.

Yet, the use of bans and prohibitions is not the only way forward. An alternative approach involves harm-reduction strategies where the use of drugs like anabolic steroids is approached with caution, rather than simplistic demonisation. Punishment is not the primary aim here. Rather, priority goes to non-judgemental approaches allowing players and athletes to make their own considered decisions based on credible, grounded information and advice from legitimate clinical trials. Most non-elite and recreational users rely on locker room anecdotes and advice from other drug users (Dawson 2001), or what is sometimes referred to as 'ethno-pharmacology': the word of mouth transmission of drug-related information. Ethno-pharmacology has gone virtual with the reliance on the Internet for uncorroborated information and views from self-appointed steroid gurus, sometimes accompanied by the sale of illicit substances of unknown origin and quality. Obviously, we have here a recipe for sporting disaster driven by murky information sources, exaggerated claims, and scanty, anecdotal evidence. With a 'black market' of supply and demand at work surrounded by clandestine opportunities for quick gains, the online marketplace for drugs encourages fraud and exploitation.

Preserving the integrity of sport

The integrity argument relies on the claim that taking drugs to enhance sport performance compromises the social and cultural authenticity of sport. Drug use therefore presents a particularly vexing issue since, like match fixing, it contravenes the fundamental ethic of sport, which means adhering to a set of intrinsic rules, and practicing the values they mirror. Performance-enhancing drugs threaten sport's integrity by removing any sense of fair play, while the illicit (mainly performance-reducing) drugs threaten sport's integrity by tarnishing its public image. In other words, doping practices of any sort should be punished because they undermine the social value of sport and its fundamental purity. Under the purist conception, sport upholds common values and customs where players volunteer their free time to assist disadvantaged groups, treat women and people of other races respectfully, obey all traffic laws, drink alcohol within legal limits, and generally behave as model citizens. In an idealised sport world, using performance-enhancing or illicit drugs is repugnant and reprehensible.

At the more pragmatic level, proponents of a strong anti-doping code argue that doping allegations can turn sponsors away and diminish the good standing – that is, brand value – of a sport. However, the pragmatic argument fails to appreciate the multitude of cultural and social factors impacting upon the image and brand equity of sport, and the resilience that enables them to get through hard times, not to mention the sovereignty of commercial variables.

At present, no agreement can be found about just how effective the WADA's punitive policies have been in eliminating drug use and shoring up sport's public appeal and good standing. The evidence is ambiguous. Whereas a lack of vigilance in testing may lead to more drug use (Vogel 2010), the punishments handed out to the few caught using banned substances appear ineffective in discouraging use (Ingram 2004). While heavy sanctions and punishments play a role in discouraging drug use in sport, they represent only some of many factors impacting upon players' decisions to use drugs (Mosher & Yanagisako 1991). At the same time, few signs suggest that sports tainted by drug-use scandals are now less popular. The Tour de France provides a perfect example. Its global popularity is stronger than ever, while its capacity to deliver drug-use scandals remains second to none. Track and field presents another case where endemic drug use has not compromised its position as the Olympic Games' flagship competition.

Policy implications: moving from punishment to protection

We have argued that the four assumptions used to underpin the current anti-doping policies of the WADA are riddled with inconsistencies and ambiguities. Sport's reality rarely lives up to the vision. Even in drug-free situations, athletes do not set particularly good examples, sport is not a level playing field, attempts to protect athlete's health are often no more than token gestures, and the integrity of sport is determined just as much by its structures, management systems, and culture as it is by the behaviour of its players. We therefore think it fanciful to conclude that a selective and punitive anti-doping policy will of itself ensure the social and moral progress of sport. Indeed, draconian polices embedded with heavy penalties can just as easily force players to take even greater risks in the quest for sporting stardom. For these reasons we argue that anti-doping policy in sport could learn from the harm-reduction principles advocated by agencies managing illicit drug use in the broader community.

Policies that consider only the reduction of drug-related *use* (such as the number of people using drugs, or the amount of drugs being used) do not consider the relative dangers associated with the different types of drugs being used or whether they are used in a high-risk or low-risk manner (Caulkins & Reuter 2005). Policies aiming to reduce drug *use* can also promote 'collateral harms'. For example, intensive policing and punishments have been shown to increase the risk of harms associated with illicit drug use (Drugs and Crime Prevention Committee 2000). Furthermore, evidence suggests that prohibition fails to reduce drug use while the cost of enforcement leads to an increase in the street price of drugs, thereby making their trafficking more appealing (Jiggens 2005).

In contrast, policies seeking to reduce drug-related *harm* (Drugs and Crime Prevention Committee 2000), concentrate on addressing the negative consequences of use, rather than the act of use itself. The harms associated with drug use can include health-related dangers such as the risk of death and serious illness, as well as social stigmatism and loss of personal dignity (Drugs and Crime Prevention Committee 2000). Whilst harm-reduction policies may incorporate strategies to promote the reduction of drug use, they do it in a health sensitive manner so as to avoid unwanted collateral problems.

Harm-reduction strategies have proven viable and cost-effective in the field of illegal drug use, from cannabis to heroin. In the sporting world, strategies such as education and the provision of clean injecting supplies to non-competing users of performance-enhancing drugs may be advantageous (Aitken *et al.* 2002) as many programs such as steroid clinics provide low threshold access to medical care and advice. In parts of the UK the number of new clients at syringe exchanges who report using anabolic steroids has risen beyond the number of new clients injecting psychotropic drugs (Dawson 2001; McVeigh *et al.* 2003).

In competitive sport, harm reduction would not necessarily imply abandoning drug testing altogether as the legalisation of performance-enhancing drugs would encourage athletes to use doping techniques to maintain their competitive positions. An alternative policy might involve making low-harm drugs legal and to test for players' health status rather than for the presence of drugs (Kayser *et al.* 2007). Harm reduction assumes that more athletes would use performance-enhancing drugs if they were legal, safe, and taken under medical supervision, thereby obviating both the moral and level playing field problems. Under a harm-reduction model health is viewed as paramount. It also maintains that while adopting a moral position on drug use in sport can be appropriate, it should not impinge adversely on the health of players and athletes.

Harm-reduction elements

Three elements in a harm-reduction model deserve special attention: first, the importance of context in shaping a harm-reduction policy; second, the development of strategies to reduce demand; and third, an emphasis on prevention and early intervention (Caulkins & Reuter 2005). However, the WADA's anti-doping policy aims to reduce drug *use*, not *harm*, and therefore overlooks these domains. In addition, as we noted earlier, drug use in elite sport occurs in an environment where the primary emphasis is on winning, and the social and economic benefits that accompany it. Furthermore, social values in the west condone and promote the use of technologies to gain a personal advantage, such as increased physical attractiveness or improved physical capacity. Thus, it would be unrealistic to expect performance-enhancing drugs to ever be eliminated from the sporting milieu, given the situational incentives for their use.

Managing demand for performance-enhancing drugs introduces a second area in which harm-reduction models could inform the WADA policy. We have already characterised the attempt to reduce demand through the threat of sanctions as a questionable strategy. How then can demand be influenced? While a problematic task, harm-reduction principles suggest that progress cannot begin without the involvement of drug-using athletes themselves as stakeholders in the process. One of the key principles of harm reduction involves the de-stigmatisation of drug users, and their inclusion in policy development activities. So long as sanctions and shame appear front and centre in drug-control programs in sport, players and athletes will avoid participation as 'users' in policy development efforts. In addition, demand-reduction strategies might include prevention aimed at children, the dissemination of the latest drug research results, the provision of replacement therapies, and broader social welfare initiatives (Hanson *et al.* 2012).

The third element of harm-reduction models reflects an emphasis on prevention and early intervention, including the avoidance of escalating patterns of drug use. Progression of this type is not being addressed by the WADA, which relies on its zero-tolerance, sanction-only approach. Whilst the WADA's anti-doping policy may appear to be promoting harm reduction by deterring the use of drugs in the first place, it may actually encourage high-risk drug use, since the negative outcomes of prohibition include increased risk from unsafe use and recourse to 'black markets' for the purchase of products (ACC 2013).

Harm reduction reflects three empirically tested principles. First, drug use is not just a sporting matter, nor is it a criminal or legal matter. Drug use in sport is also a serious societal issue. Second, harm reduction removes the need for any form of moral certitude. Instead, it accepts that drug use exists in sport, and will never be completely eliminated. Third, although harm reduction does not condone the use of drugs in sport, it acknowledges that when it does occur, policymakers have an obligation to develop public-health measures that reduce drug-related harms to athletes at all levels, irrespective of whether they compete, or qualify for testing. We venture further with these notions in the following chapters.

Conclusion

By any measure, current anti-doping policies are not working well, since they fail to achieve their stated aims of detecting and eradicating drug use, protecting the integrity of sporting competition, and preserving parity on the field of play. Moreover, their prohibition approach can be deleterious to public health because they fail to account for the complex network of values and behaviours in which drug use in contemporary sport and society is embedded. Current drug-control policies in sport favour a repression approach, a model closely resembling the illegal drug-use policies enacted by drug enforcement administrations in broader society, especially the US. At first glance this might be seen as a good thing, but if taken to its logical extreme, we might see the introduction of an anti-doping, police state system where citizens must undertake a regular battery of tests to confirm that they are 'clean'. The recent inclusion of anabolic steroid use in the US war on drugs appears to be a step in that direction.

The drugs in sport problem is compounded by the growing use of performance-enhancing drugs in the general population. International organised crime has quickly understood the potential of this expansion in demand and has cultivated markets in anabolic steroids, erythropoietin, human growth hormone, and other substances (Donati 2007). Prohibition under such circumstances is problematic, since it sends users of these often dubious substances into 'hiding' and medically unsupervised practice. Dangerous practices such as the sharing of syringes lead to the risk of HIV or hepatitis virus infection with a negative wider impact on public health (Aitken *et al.* 2002; Dawson 2001; McVeigh *et al.* 2003; Melia *et al.* 1996).

From a harm-reduction perspective, is it preferable to be interested in the short-term brand equity and credibility of elite sport, or in the long-term best interests of athletes? Rather than eliminating the use of drugs, draconian rules and sanctions will only send it further underground as players search for more exotic and less detectable options. We need a broad-based drug control policy in sport. Moreover, any drug control policy should include not only performance-enhancing drugs, but all other drugs, illicit or not, that may undermine the long-term health prospects of players, and the sustainability of their sports. This means that alcohol and tobacco should fall within the purview of a balanced policy.

Given the complexities that characterise the drugs in sport landscape, polices designed to punish athletes for taking drugs have not been successful in removing drugs from sport. In addition, little evidence indicates any significant improvement in the health and well-being of players resulting from the current drug-control arrangements. The alternative harm-reduction model allows athletes to manage their usage in a safe environment free from ill-informed advice, contaminated supply, and the threat of severe shame and punishment. Although controversial in a sporting context, it accepts that drugs will always be part of a risky and tilted playing field full of moral ambiguity.

We argue that a socially responsible philosophy that focuses on the reduction of collateral harm, and seeks out a sound evidence base, should be sovereign in determining future drugs in sport policy. In the final chapter, we dig deeper into the harm-reduction case and provide a comprehensive picture of how it could help the drugs in sport problem. To lay the right groundwork for this finale, in the next two chapters we examine the role of regulation as a policy framework and subsequently overlay this mode of thinking with a range of drug-control policy options. In short, we ask whether there might be some policy structures that deliver more fluid and practical interventions without resorting to black and white extremes such as heavy punishment and zero-tolerance.

Part IV

Rethinking drug control in sport

13 Why regulation?

Introduction

Collectively, through the discussions contained in Chapters 1–12, we examined drug-control policies in sport from nearly every conceivable angle. We outlined the historical factors that shaped their evolution and the ways in which officials have responded to the use of substances for performance enhancement. We surveyed drug use in sport around the world, and identified various hot spots – and hot sports – in the process. We looked at the WADA 'globalised' drug-control model in detail, and examined its application in 'localised' sport leagues and competitions using a wide array of cases and examples. In the previous chapter we argued that while the current policy arrangements have corralled drug use in sport, and provided detailed rules and regulation for its containment, it has not actually delivered a drug-free sport world. Neither has it made sport any more equitable in the form of a so-called level playing field. In fact, current policy has abjectly failed to ensure a sport world free of vice and corruption, and therefore able to comfortably project an image of wholesomeness and integrity (ACC 2013). Finally, we noted the lack of evidence suggesting that the WADC has made sport, in general, any safer for its participants, or lowered the incidence of injury and ill-health arising out of its practice.

With these reservations in mind, it makes sense to return to 'regulation' as a core concept in policymaking. This chapter aims to explore the ideologies accompanying commitments to particular regulatory regimes, the levers – or policies wielded to enact regulation – and the implications of each form of intervention. We aim to expose the tacit assumptions about the impact of different regulatory decisions, and, at the same time, provide the platform for constructing different, and potentially superior, regulatory structures. In short, we aim to work towards a new theory of sport regulation. In application to the drugs in sport problem it seeks to deliver a drug-control policy prioritising the protection of player health and welfare, with the emotionally charged issues of cheating, unfair advantage, and tilted playing fields off to the side as guiding principles rather than the drivers of every rule, sanction, and regulatory process.

Regulation revisited

We begin with the trite but irrefutable claim that all societies experience regulation in one way or another. No matter how simple or complex the structure, there are always systems designed to both maintain order while ensuring that people 'behave in acceptable ways' (Haviland *et al.* 2008: 283). Even in subsistence societies a multitude of tactics can be used to enforce compliance with leaders' decrees, all of which rely on a capacity to convince people about the rightness or wrongness of certain behavioural norms and standards. Where that fails, leaders rely on a capacity to punish unacceptable behaviour, and reward behaviour deemed appropriate. The idea of social order as an essential property enjoys universal acceptance, although disputes abound concerning just what behaviours should be sanctioned, and what penalties should be applied for transgressions (Freiberg 2010). Underpinning all attempts at behavioural controls we discover a raft of ideologies, values, and beliefs about fundamental social issues like the ownership of property, the control of the means of production, the operation of markets, taxation and its redistribution, the controls to be exerted over defamatory and obscene language, the legal status of gambling, drugs, pornography, prostitution, marriage, natural procreation, engineered procreation, divorce, and the rights of non-heterosexuals. The list goes on. In most cases, the question revolves around how each practice might be regulated – rather than just banned or prohibited – in order to optimise the overall 'good' of society (Innes 2003: 6). In the following section we introduce the regulatory 'technologies', or techniques, that can be employed. We then discuss the case for regulation and deregulation before moving into the implications for sport policy and a possible theoretical template for making considered decisions about drug controls in sport.

Regulatory technologies in contemporary society

A useful first step in making sense of the regulatory problem is to distinguish between two fundamental types of regulation. The first is internally driven regulation, which mainly deals with the values, beliefs, and customs that become ingrained in the psyche of each individual (Haviland *et al.* 2008; Innes 2003). For example, in one society people may not steal because it is seen to be a sin, and the idea that sinners will go to hell is more than enough to ensure a heavy dose of 'self-regulation'. In another society people may generously assist the disadvantaged because it constitutes a taken-for-granted civic responsibility. These are examples of normalised social practices where few second thoughts occur about legitimacy.

The second type of regulation is externally driven, which involves the imposition of sanctions in the form of laws and rules to ensure conformity to social norms and customary codes of conduct (Innes 2003). Sanctions can vary considerably. They can be negatively framed, as in the case of a physical beating, or positively framed, as with honours or acknowledgment in a public ceremony. Externally driven regulation can also be formal or informal. Formal sanctions tend to be clearly understood and universally accepted, leading to compliance 'potency', legitimisation, and normality. Legitimised sanctions usually attract a sharply articulated reward for doing the right thing, and a consistently applied punishment for doing the wrong thing.

While contemporary societies operate in ways far more complex than any tribal, hunter-gatherer, or subsistence society, they still use the same repertoire of regulatory principles to secure conformity, compliance, and the maintenance of social order (Braithwaite 2008). Regulation in industrial and highly 'technologised' societies can prove complex, but understanding the distinction between internal and external drivers offers a good first step in diagnosis. We can also derive more analytical clout by extending the classifications differentiating between psychological, sociocultural, economic, and politically driven regulations. The psychological, sociological, and cultural influencers operate mainly in the domestic and everyday living sphere, often called the micro regulators. The economic and political influencers, on the other hand, operate mainly in the organisational and corporate sphere, and are usually referred to as macro regulators.

Micro regulation

Psychological forms of regulation comprise the beliefs, customs, and taboos that have been individually internalised through socialisation. The process of socialisation occurs when individuals, having been born with behavioural potentialities of an enormously wide range, develop actual behaviours confined to a narrower range of acceptable group standards (Innes 2003). For example, 'confined' behaviours can manifest as moral codes making premarital sex a serious social wrong, the use of condoms to regulate fertility a mortal sin, or extramarital sex an obscenity demanding the immediate dissolution of a marriage. They can also manifest as a set of daily habits built around a strong group affiliation. Daily habits might, for example, include an early-morning meditation, a caffeine-free breakfast, a vegan-style lunch, a late afternoon prayer session, an alcohol-free dinner, a mid-evening flagellation, and a bible reading session as precursor to a character-building sleep on a bed of planks. While to the outsider such heavily ritualised practices appears to be puritanical and obsessively devoid of pleasure, to the practitioners they comprise an integral part of their life-affirming practices and community identity (Miller 2005).

Sociocultural forms of regulation can be internalised. However, they can also be contested, so need to be confirmed in more concrete ways. Firmer interventions take the form of public pronouncements, social gestures, and interpersonal cues. Such pronouncements, gestures, and cues enforce 'social norms': the result of 'expected' patterns of behaviour surrounding a friendship group, a work team, a community club, an association, or an organisation. Punishments and penalties exist for 'transgressions' that deviate from the norm. Sanctions can be tangible and direct, or ephemeral and subtle. For example, an office employee who fails to meet attendance requirements will be reminded that his deviant behaviour will diminish his promotional prospects and tarnish his professional status. At the other extreme, a brazenly talkative audience member of a theatrical performance will be discreetly admonished through the use of superficially polite 'quiet please' comments and sounds from people around her. Sociocultural regulation is also embedded in organisational cultures, often encapsulated by the comment that 'this is the way we do things around here' (Schein 2004). In this instance, the message is clear: if you fit in, you will be richly rewarded with warm acceptance and the prospects of promotion, but if you do not comply with our institutionalised values and practices, your work life will not be satisfying or successful. Moreover, organisational cultures provide for both informal and formal sanctions. Informal sanctions may include shame, ridicule, sarcasm, criticism, and disapproval, while formal sanctions can involve threats of demotion and the loss of overtime. Sanctions can also include discrimination and exclusion from social groups.

Both psychologically centred and sociocultural forms of regulations strive to secure conformity with certain behavioural standards. However, their regulatory interventions stand poles apart. The former focuses mainly on the self-regulation of individuals, while the latter concerns externally imposed regulations on groups of people, either informally, or as members of organisational work teams. In addition, externally imposed regulations can be soft and subtle, on one hand, or hard and coercive on the other.

The term 'social control' encapsulates the driving intention behind forms of regulation. In a more formal sense, social control refers to all those societal and political mechanisms and processes that regulate not only individual and group behaviour, but also corporate conduct (Innes 2003). As a result, social controls lead to conformity, ensuring compliance to the rules of a given society, state, or social group. At a less formal level, while the concept of social control has been around for some time, its meaning can be fluid when it comes to practice. Originally the concept simply referred to society's ability to coercively regulate citizens and enterprises, but the term now relates more to conformity. However, in reflection of contemporary, more politically correct terminology, social control tends to be described as meta-regulation, which signals its operation somewhere between the micro world of personal values and internalised belief systems, and the macro world of government legislation and the industry regulator (Elliott & Smith 2006).

Macro regulation

Economic and political regulation, typically referred to as supra-regulation because of its use as an 'apparatus of the state', sharply contrasts with social control (Baldwin *et al.* 2012: 3; Freiberg 2010: 18). It uses more formal interventions demanding heavy documentation and bureaucratic support, and the sanctions for failing to comply tend to be severe. Complex societies employ weighty controls by regulating the behaviour of individuals and groups by making some activities a criminal offence, while also regulating the behaviour of organisations, especially as it relates to competition, product quality, pricing, service delivery, and employment conditions. Organisations vary around their mission and purpose, the markets they serve, and their scale of operations. As a result, the same bundle of regulations will not fit all economic and political situations at all times. This means that when it comes to designing policy, regulations must fit the special conditions of different markets and the organisations supplying them (Freiberg 2010). A central tenet of regulations like these is to protect the beneficiaries of the goods and service provided: the customers. Typically, this can only be achieved by imposing sanctions on those organisations engaging in the behaviour that may mislead consumers or exploit potential buyers.

In the macro context, a distinction may be made between two aspects of the regulatory process. First, 'economic regulation' focuses on the rules impacting upon the competitive climate of a market or industry. Second, 'social regulation' considers those measures protecting consumers from unfair, unethical, and misleading practices undertaken by suppliers (Vogel 2010). But, no matter what the regulatory focus might be, in these situations they need to be built on a platform of formal external control since more subtle forms of social control will be ineffective.

In order to secure compliance from powerful groups, associations, and corporations, control is exerted through government structures and actions in the form of supra-regulation. Government and their agencies use law enforcement mechanisms and other formal sanctions such as fines and imprisonment. In democratic societies the goals and mechanisms of formal external controls are determined through legislation by elected representatives, and thus not only enjoy support from large slabs of the population, but also engender voluntary compliance through their legitimacy and societal status. But, it should also be remembered that the effectiveness of any type of formal external control is determined by the relative strength of the sanction, measured in terms of the scale of punishments, the external body's monitoring ability, and the degree of additional social control exerted over organisations and individuals (Freiberg 2010).

Why regulate?

Why in a generic sense, should we want to regulate anything or anybody in the first place, and why should a regulatory regime make communities better off than when left unregulated? The first point to note is that governments, even in relatively wealthy countries, never have enough resources to satisfy all demands. Resources have to be rationed, which for most nations occurs through markets and the interaction of demand, supply, and prices. However, cases of market failure do arise, where markets do not operate in the best interests of society (Baldwin *et al.* 2012; Freiberg 2010).

Market failure occurs when the full benefits of markets fail to be realised. While there can be numerous causes of market failure, the most common include the undersupply of socially desirable products, an oversupply of less desirable products, and cartel-type arrangements producing anti-competitive behaviour like market sharing, price fixing, and misleading advertising (Baldwin *et al.* 2012). Market failure also occurs when the outputs, even if they were viewed as highly desirable in the first instance, consequently exacerbate the risk of accident, injury, or illness.

The undersupply problem arises in situations where 'external' or social benefits occur in addition to private benefits. Private benefits comprise the value consumers obtain from the immediate purchase of a good or service, such as regular gym workouts. Social benefits represent the value that society obtains from the production of a good or service, such as a healthier and more productive community. In cases where social benefits can be demonstrated, society would be better served by allocating additional resources towards those activities. Where private investors lack a sufficient profit incentive to supply sufficient products or services to the market, it will be left to government to fill the breach, typically using taxpayers' money to regulate supply by funding additional infrastructure and services. Where markets fail through undersupply, an argument may be made for government regulation based on equity. In order to maintain accessibility, and ensure equality of opportunity, government can either establish their own low-cost service, or subsidise the fee structure of existing providers.

The oversupply of products that produce external costs in addition to private benefits introduces another problematic issue (Baldwin 2012). External costs include workplace accidents and environmental pollution associated with the production process, advertising which makes unsubstantiated claims around product features, and the marketing of products that impose unforeseen risks on their users. These scenarios not only impose costs and potential harm on others, they are also inequitably distributed, since the burden of costs and harms shifts from producer to consumer. As a result, another concerning feature of market failure relates to its impact on both the organisations comprising an industry delivering the services, and the recipients of the services. Where the problem 'sellers' face from market failure constitutes 'economic market failure', the problem faced by customers suggests 'social failure'.

An economic market failure occurs when a consumer's freedom of choice among goods and services is restricted due to insufficient competition in the marketplace. Here, monopoly power allows suppliers to exploit consumers by setting artificially high prices, restricting supply, and accumulating excessive profits. Monopoly power enables suppliers to assemble a grid of 'asymmetric information', which means they will always know more about the products than potential buyers (Mason & Scammon 2011). Conversely, customers will possess limited knowledge about the vast network of product-related issues that can range from the possible use of sweatshop labour, the pricing mark-up, the full and unabridged results from tests and clinical trials, and products' expected reliability and longevity. Monopolies and highly concentrated oligopolies consequently stimulate heavy regulation.

As more industries and markets become privatised, the need for regulatory agencies increases, since they no longer operate directly under the guiding hand of government. Privatisation explains why, despite the emergence of strong neo-liberal ideologies amongst politicians and bureaucrats, the last 20 years has witnessed significant growth of institutional regulatory innovation (Shamir 2008). Since the middle of the 1980s privatisation has generated increasing numbers of state agencies exerting regulatory controls over an expanding field of newly commercialised businesses. Examples include telecommunications, electricity, water, post, media, pharmaceuticals, insurance, banking, and share trading. Most new regulatory entities, often known as independent regulatory authorities, have been granted some measure of autonomy from direct political control in an effort to enhance their 'policy credibility' as well as their capacity to balance the need for consumer protection against smooth functioning markets. For example, regulatory agencies ensure environmental sustainability, food-safety requirements, and occupational health and safety standards.

A social market failure differs from an economic market failure in that it covers situations where the sale of goods and services either puts consumers at greater risk of harm than could be normally foreseen, or is marketed using misleading and morally questionable tactics (Mason & Scammon 2011). So-called 'social regulation' aims to protect consumers from health and other personal risks, as distinguished from economic regulation, which seeks to protect and foster competition. Consumer protection regulations fall under the latter category by shielding buyers from unscrupulous sellers while also redressing the asymmetric flow of product knowledge and market information.

When all the forms of regulation are compiled they provide a powerful set of tools for managing corporate, group, and individual behaviours. The regulatory tools form a pyramid, in order of regulatory weight and force. The regulatory structures begin with common law and legislation; move down to non-government organisation surveillance; incorporate market pressures, economic incentives, taxes, subsidies, and contracts; take into account the operation of market pressures, supply management, economic incentives, taxes and contracts; include voluntary industry codes, collective bargaining agreements, financial controls, professional standards, and employee codes of conducts; and finally, embrace all those ethical standards, social norms and mores, pressures to conform, and taken-for-granted values, customs, and rituals that govern our everyday behaviour. Values, customs, and rituals occupy the pyramid's base because they comprise the building blocks of regulation mostly through unsupported rules and laws. Nevertheless, the deeper building blocks can be powerful instruments for securing compliance, since they become ingrained in people's daily habits and routines.

The case for deregulation

Some commentators believe that less is more, especially when it comes to economic regulation. Despite an emphasis on the deregulation of markets since the middle of the 1980s, more regulatory agencies rather than fewer have been established. This period has also been underpinned by a laissez-faire / neo-liberal economic philosophy, promulgated in an era of diminished anti-monopoly sentiment, lower levels of consumer protection enforcement, and a general absence of new regulatory initiatives (Hall 2011). A laissez-faire / neo-liberal philosophy rests on two beliefs about suppliers, markets, and consumers. First, consumers are sovereign in the sense that their purchase intention dictates what and how much should be produced and delivered to market. Second, most market failures could be eliminated or significantly reduced by an increase in intra-market competition.

While free market conservatives endorsing the laissez-faire / neo-liberal economic philosophy concede that some degree of economic regulation facilitates fair competition, they also argue that in a competitive marketplace social regulation yields few benefits. Rather, social market failures can be best curtailed via the countervailing forces of consumer sovereignty; consumers redirecting their purchase behaviour away from firms initiating such market failures (Mason & Scammon 2011). As a result, competing firms must correct the failure or exit the marketplace. According to the free market position, not only is the asymmetric knowledge problem overrated, but consumers are also sophisticated enough to make appropriate marketplace decisions, thereby reducing the need for social regulation or some other form of government intervention.

A question consequently arises about just how sophisticated today's consumers are in a practical, everyday sense. Are they now more demanding and discriminating when making purchase- and consumption-related decisions, or have they actually become less sophisticated with respect to their purchasing practices? And, has the structure of today's marketplace become so complex and confounding that consumers feel less equipped than their predecessors to function as effective decision makers, and therefore face a more heavily supplier-skewed balance of knowledge than regulators might concede?

Popular opinion, together with the emergence of consumer advocacy groups suggests that today's consumers are better educated and more sophisticated than in the 1980s. They have been described as more demanding, more discriminating, and more aware of product quality and product use-value. While such beliefs provide support for the deregulatory policies of free market conservatives, they fail to counter the fact that monopoly suppliers have more market power than any assembly of consumer activists and advocates ever will. Indeed, consumer advocate groups contend that deregulatory policies leave consumers vulnerable to deceptive and unscrupulous business practices, thus calling for the social regulation of industry at the very minimum. They agree that competition has provided consumers with an enormous range of choices but argue that consumer sovereignty does not always translate into effective regulation of the marketplace. Social interventionists conclude that consumers cannot always distinguish between safe and unsafe products, reliable and unreliable products, or products promoted in morally questionable ways, including, for example, factually misleading information. They argue that the laissez-faire / neo-liberal philosophy does not adequately reduce the occurrence of social market failure (Mason & Scammon 2011). Social interventionists hold that consumers are neither sophisticated nor powerful enough to regulate the market through their collective purchase decisions, and that, as a result, some degree of government intervention remains essential. The common occurrence of market abuses such as the mislabelling of food products and supplements and motor vehicle repair frauds, tend to be used to support this argument (Mason & Scammon 2011).

Striking a balance

As a compromise solution to disputes over the appropriateness of externally managed economic regulation or externally managed social regulation as the preferred means of guiding organisational conduct, the idea of 'self-regulation' has arisen as a means of securing better outcomes from the corporate sector, and stronger protection for the consumption sector. In this regulatory model the industry governs its own conduct by establishing an arm's-length authority wielding the power to both 'deter particular actions and behaviour' and 'encourage compliance with desired actions and behaviour' (Koornneef 2010: 2). For example, the model has been used by the media sector to guide the conduct of its affairs, with the main focus on the print media. However, these Press Councils, as they have been titled, have recently come under critical scrutiny for failing to properly investigate allegations of biased reporting, privacy invasion, and defamatory commentary. Like all forms of regulation, self-regulation has its imperfections. Nevertheless, it remains an underexplored model for sport.

Constructing appropriate regulatory regimes

As the previous discussion suggests, the notion of 'regulation' is both simple to understand and difficult to properly categorise. It is simple to understand insofar as it seeks to ensure that particular organisations, groups of people, or selected individuals adopt a designated pattern of behaviour gravitating towards either a prescribed or agreed upon norm. On the other hand, regulation presents categorisation challenges due to the multiplicity of tools and technologies used to safeguard compliance. Regulations can be soft, as in the case of agreed 15-minute coffee breaks in an accounting office, or hard, as in the case of legislating to block tobacco advertising in the print and electronic media. It can be formal, by having a no-strike clause in a collective bargaining agreement, or it can be informal by having an implied consensus that jackets and ties will be worn at meetings to which commercial clients have been invited.

Identifying the different regulatory mechanisms that might be used to change individual, group, and corporate conduct introduces a first decision-making level. However, determining the best bundle of tools to use for specific conditions and special circumstances requires a significantly more complex set of decisions (Freiberg 2010: 19). Finding an answer involves reflecting on what the proposed regulations aim to achieve, what types of behaviour and conduct should be punished, what forms of behaviour and conduct should be rewarded, and what social 'goods' or social utility are expected to follow.

Working out the intent of a regulatory regime seems, at first glance, to be a simple process. However, it comes with a wide range of decisions to make around the costs to be constrained, and the benefits to be enabled. In addition, decisions need to be made about the weightings allocated to the various categories of costs and benefits. The matter is further complicated by the fact that any regulatory model will not only shape future benefits, but will also impact on current levels of benefits, sometimes in unfavourable ways.

Constructing an appropriate regulatory regime requires thorough assessments of costs and benefits based on a sophisticated understanding of how regulatory forms interact and subsequently stimulate or curtail action. First, an array of contextual factors must be considered when designing a regulatory regime, including variables such as industry features, market structures, and consumer demand. Second, the choice of regulatory mechanisms demands attention, along with their strengths and weaknesses. Third, the strategic focal points of the regime must be explicit, which can range from a cleaner environment, a fairer wage-payment system, greater market competition, and better quality goods and services, to an improved range of physical recreation options, superior levels of community health, greater public safety, and more effective child protection systems. The difficulty in securing the best results is further complicated by the often ephemeral nature of the deliverable outcomes. Concepts like living standards, quality of life, rights, freedom, safety, welfare, utility, value, benefits, health, well-being, risk, harm, costs, duties, and so on can all be interpreted in highly subjective ways. Even with general agreement, measurement can prove problematic. As a result, understanding the objectives of a regulatory system in rational and concrete ways is critical when setting up intended performance outcomes for each form of regulatory regime.

A template for building better regulations in the sport sector

Despite the problems embedded in the development of regulatory models purporting to make a positive difference to people's lives, all regulatory models work on the assumption that individuals, groups, neighbourhoods, communities, regions, provinces, and nations will be better off with them than without them (Freiberg 2010: 49). It is also assumed, though often with less certainty, that the most preferred and common regulatory options will deliver better outcomes than the less-preferred or discarded options. Few areas of human activity remain unregulated. As a result, the question is not whether some behaviour should be either totally banned or allowed to flourish unhindered. Rather, the key question concerns what form of regulation gives most space to those behaviours delivering pleasures and benefits – or social utility – while denying space to those behaviours that undermine or diminish a community's quality of life and social utility. Policymakers therefore face the difficult task of designing regulatory models that squeeze out the costs and harms associated with specific behaviours without denying the benefits that these behaviours might also deliver. Sport policymakers face this issue at every turn. While it delivers extreme excitement and deep pleasure, it can also occur in spaces that entail the risk of injury, and sometimes death.

The policy philosophy of giving space for people to secure the benefits, while simultaneously squeezing out the harms, underpins not only sport, but also a variety of social practices, especially in the presence of strong moral objections. Excessive alcohol consumption, illicit drug use, prostitution, pornography, and gambling immediately come to mind, for example. In each of these cases, as well as in many other leisure practices, at least six issues need to be considered when assessing the most appropriate controls over use.

First, there are the pleasures and satisfactions that people derive from a behaviour or practice. The activity may not be to everyone's taste, but the fact that someone is prepared to pay to undertake certain behaviours indicate that they have a value to users. Where regulations prevent someone from securing this service value, social utility is lost, which means that some people will be worse off as a result of regulations reducing demand. Gambling provides a case in point. While a few advocate groups want gambling banned because of its capacity to send problem gamblers to the depths of desperation and debt, others view it as a highly enjoyable pastime, where accommodating risk is front and central.

Second, the activity may lead to an additional social good or external benefit. Take, for example, the services offered by sex workers. Some anecdotal evidence suggests that spouses and partners who employ sex workers are less likely to seek out extramarital affairs. This means that the risk of falling in love with a work colleague or neighbour are lowered, the need for some titillation on the side has been satisfied, and the likelihood of re-establishing domestic balance and workplace productivity is heightened. As a result, all of the trauma and grief that comes with a marriage breakdown or a workplace liaison has been avoided. On the other side of the coin, as Sweden exemplifies, it can be argued that prostitution represents an assault against all women, and should be banned with enforcement through criminal sanctions.

The third issue reflects the costs of establishing a regulatory regime. There are not just the set up costs, but also the much heftier operational costs. For example, the more complex the agency established to regulate the sex work industry, and the more work it has to do in terms of registration, monitoring, and policing, the more costly it will be to run. In contrast, a completely deregulated sex work industry will incur negligible administrative and enforcement costs. To take another example, the gaming industry has created a prodigious regulatory bureaucracy, especially in horse racing and the betting surrounding it. This large allocation of public monies to a body aiming to limit the behaviour of stakeholders, especially the weekend 'punter', is defended on the grounds that it prevents corruption and ensures a well organised and transparent system of wagering.

The fourth issue has to do with the offence that the mere existence of an unpleasant or morally dubious practice might cause. Take again, for example, the case of the sex work industry. Undoubtedly, many people will be offended. It may even cause some elements of the religious community a high level of grief. Since incurring offence can be viewed as a social cost, the absence of any sex work will provide a social good by eliminating the source. However, the policymaking challenge is to create regulations minimising the offence while still allowing sex workers to meet the demand for their services. Another example can be seen in the anti-alcohol lobby, which opposes the growth of retail 'liquor barns'. They claim that the effortless availability of alcohol normalises heavy drinking and encourages the idea that drinking is essential to social activity and fun.

The fifth issue involves harm, which, of course, can mean different things to different people. To a spouse confronted by a violent partner, harm appears in the form of a possible assault. To a patient waiting for a drug to be dispensed from a pharmacy, the harm relates to the potential side effects from the substance. From a gambling and betting perspective harm comes from physical addiction, losing money, compromising relationships, or undertaking criminal activity as a result of reckless behaviour. Sex work also has the potential to deliver harm to both the supplier and user of the service, especially in the form of sexually transmitted diseases. Additional harms may flow through to partners who, having signalled the disapproval of prostitution, discover that their spouse has been unfaithful. Again, the challenge for policymakers lies with designing regulations that minimise the risks and harms to the suppliers, users, and relevant families, while maintaining the space for users to engage in the satisfactions they seek.

Finally, there is the human rights issue. For every regulation that forbids someone from taking a specific form of action, or achieving a goal they value, there exists a corresponding loss of autonomy and freedom. This notion was a theme in John Stuart Mill's classic 1859 essay entitled *On Liberty*. Mill insisted that the state – that is, the government – should only interfere with the rights of its citizens when their actions may harm others (Bakalar & Grinspoon 1984: 1). He believed that no responsible adult should be forced to do anything because someone else says it is good for them, even when it can be demonstrably and impartially shown to be true. Similarly, Mill argued that no one should be prevented from doing anything because it could adversely affect him or her. According to Mill, 'benevolent restraint' and paternalistic coercion are problematic issues because they prevent people from pursuing their preferred tastes and activities, and, by doing so, precludes them from any gain in utility. For example, a law that denies the opportunity to pay for sex is a rejection of a human right to seek pleasure from a specific form of sexual activity. While it might offend the sensibilities of others, it is unlikely to harm them in any further or significant way. In this context it would be possible for policymakers to protect both the suppliers and the recipients of sex services from undue harm, while providing space for a mutually beneficial exchange in a comfortable and private setting.

Conclusion

We observed in this chapter that many social practices, having been conceived to give people pleasurable and meaningful experiences, can in fact cause harm. A sexual encounter can cause harm if it causes a disease to be transmitted, or a partner to be jilted. Gambling may provide vicarious excitement, but it can also lead to a gambling addiction and enormous personal trauma. Marriage can be a gloriously transformative experience, but it can also create lifelong anger and unhappiness. Substance use offers the same extreme outcomes. Alcohol can romanticise a relationship, but it can also destroy it. Smoking tobacco can deliver small moments of intimacy, but can also lead to an early and painful death. Cannabis has the capacity to calm troubled souls, but can also trigger schizophrenic episodes.

For some of these practices the policy response leads to prohibition. In most cases, however, the product under regulation remains in supply to the customer, but under heavily constrained conditions, and sometimes in a 'black market' situation. The trick here is to strike a balance so that the pleasures and benefits can be realised where people's rights are not curtailed, while at the same time minimising the harms to those who are either incapable of making sound and rational decisions themselves, or those people who have been indirectly harmed. In taking a policy position, the intuitive response suggests that the process really means trading off a few rights for lesser harms. However, this provides a highly conservative outcome, since it yields a negligible net gain in social utility. The more interesting option seeks to achieve a policy outcome where human rights are preserved, harms are reduced, and health and welfare outcomes are improved. This is the challenge for drug policy, especially where it intersects with sport.

The issues in this chapter raise several important questions for sport policy and practice. For instance, should sport be regulated at all? And, if it should, for what reasons, and for whose benefit? At the moment most professional sport leagues practice significant self-regulation in order to protect their image and brand. With this model, anything that tarnishes the image undermines the game's sustainability, and must be avoided. But, self-regulation nearly always impinges upon the rights of players and athletes to play with the team they wish, to optimise their salaries, to make public comments on the league's operations, to make unfashionable remarks about social issues, to promote products not endorsed by the league, and to take drugs and substances of their own choosing. For much of professional sport, too much self-regulation is never enough. But is that really a good thing when it comes to the consumption of drugs and other substances?

The proponents of strict drug controls for sport will argue that widespread drug and substance use reflects a wholesale market failure because these products produce massive negative externalities that include: 1) increased opportunities where players can secure an unfair advantage, 2) an even more tilted playing field where inequalities grow exponentially, 3) untrustworthy leagues and tournaments with heavily tarnished images and a consequent loss of public and corporate support, and 4) an explosive increase in the risk of injury, illness, and psychological trauma for players. The corollary is that a reduction in the supply and use of substances will, *ipso facto*, deliver: 1) more spaces where players have no unfair advantages, 2) a perfectly balanced playing field where inequalities have been eliminated, 3) leagues and tournaments with a rock-solid brand image and massive public support, and 4) a totally safe playing environment where the risk of injury, illness, and psychological trauma is negligible.

Unfortunately, no evidence shows that sport's stakeholders will be necessarily better off from the establishment of a punitive drug-control policy. In fact, there are good reasons to think that sport's stakeholders, and especially players and fans, could actually be worse off where a raft of products are banned, players are regularly monitored, and all the resources needed to secure a zero-tolerance, drug-free sport world are placed at the disposal of drug-control bureaucrats.

Drug controls also come with costs. First, the financial cost can be significant in establishing the physical infrastructure, along with the annual operating costs, which escalate with every additional staff member, every additional drug test, and every additional investigation of drug-use allegations. Second, the autonomy, privacy, and civil rights of players can be squeezed as authorities demand they take drug tests, inform drug testing officials of their whereabouts so that random testing can occur, and be required to not only defend allegations of drug use, but also inform on others at a moment's notice. Finally, the reputation of players and athletes can be shredded when unsubstantiated allegations are made, and rumours fly about their use of performance-enhancing or illicit substances. These allegations often occur on the basis of hearsay and flimsy evidence, with no attempt to explain the circumstances, or even consider that use might have actually been benign or legitimate.

The other – and often ignored – point is the possible benefits from the use of certain banned substances. Players and athletes train and play under extreme stress, must endure the relentless gaze of media and fans alike, and are expected to perform at the highest level for weeks on end. It could even be argued that substances like cannabis, MDMA and other banned recreational drugs can be a perfect antidote to stress, and if managed sensibly, provide the ideal escape from the pressures of being an elite player or athlete.

One way of making sense of drug controls and how they deliver either social goods or social costs is to succinctly identify the outcomes likely to arise from different policies. A good starting point is to construct a mind map something along the lines of Figure 13.1, and use it as a sounding board for subsequent discussion.

Despite the insight that might come from mind mapping the drug control in sport problem, the deeper we dig into the drug-control problem, the more complex

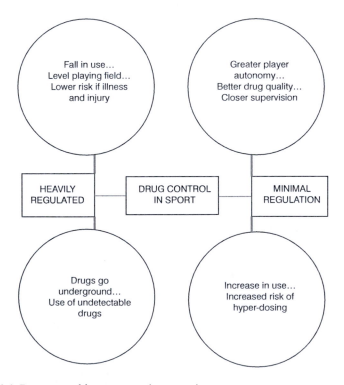

Figure 13.1 Drug control in sport: regulatory options

it all becomes. And, in particular, the notion that anyone who uses drugs is a cheat, and must therefore as a matter of principle be given a lengthy suspension and shamed into oblivion, is a morally dubious and reactionary response to a socially ambivalent practice. As our earlier discussion indicates, regulation can change social behaviour, but sometimes not in ways intended by its proponents. Neither is it necessarily based on rational analysis, since policy is always framed by a set of interlocking values, beliefs, customs, and habits. Regulation can be hijacked by vested interest groups, and used to deliver outcomes deemed to be in the 'public interest', without ever explaining what they mean in practice. Drug-control policy fits neatly into this frame, since it is often underpinned by non-negotiable beliefs about what is right, and what is wrong. But, as we have shown in earlier chapters, drug-control policy contains an enormous amount of ambiguity, uncertainty, and often just plain confusion.

When assessing the capacity of drug-control regimes to deliver the optimal social good, while removing all those insidious negative externalities, the first question we need to ask of sport and its key constituents is just how much regulation will deliver the best outcomes, and what form it should take. The second question to ask is where we should begin in seeking out some definitive answers. These issues will be addressed in Chapter 14.

14 Bringing it all together

Introduction

It seems uncontroversial to observe that while disciplined substance use improves sporting performance, open-ended substance use creates many problematic outcomes and worrying concerns. Three particular areas of concern have already been outlined in earlier chapters, but, in the light of their policy significance, they deserve reiteration before setting the scene for further policy discussion. The first problem centres on the unfair advantages some athletes receive over others, and the claims that drug use constitutes an especially repugnant form of cheating. The second problem revolves around the view that substance use, especially where it involves illicit drug use, threatens the integrity and good standing of sport, and therefore undermines its sustainability. The third problem arises from the ways in which uncontrolled and unsupervised drug use might threaten the health and well-being of athletes. The WADA uses these three problems to justify their punitive regulations prohibiting the use of drugs that may secure athletes a competitive advantage. They have also been used to justify a ban on illicit drugs during periods of competition, even where little performance advantage can be gained.

The WADA regulations incur heavy sanctions for contravention. The WADC has become the template for drug-use regulation around the world, and now comprises the drug policy foundation stone for the IOC, nearly every international governing body of sport, and most national elite sport competitions. The WADC, which has gone through two iterations since its formulation in 2003 (the most recent was released in 2009), has created a global network of agencies with a brief to dig out drug users and punish them. This 'tough-on-drugs' stance, where the policy mantra is 'zero tolerance' and where the goal is 'drug free sport', gives little leeway to athletes, and puts a serious squeeze on their civil liberties. It therefore begs the question as to whether or not the WADC offers the best regulatory path to take, and whether other options might actually secure superior outcomes for the athletes, the sport itself, its stakeholders, and society as a whole. In this chapter we examine these options, including some contextual analysis, look at drug policy options and their impacts, and summarise the motivations for performance enhancement along with the most likely policy levers to affect them. The chapter culminates with two fictional narratives contrasting the zero-tolerance and the harm-reduction arguments as a method for exposing the tacit assumptions behind them. Finally, we put in place the final stages of our position in favour of a new drug-control model utilising some of the regulatory concepts we introduced in the previous chapter.

The broader context

Throughout this book we have questioned the current controls over drug use in sport, and have speculated about whether a new policy direction would be worth trying. Now our task remains to articulate an alternative and explain its structure, operation, and likely impact. While many options warrant consideration, drug use has numerous dimensions which all need to be addressed. We must also remember that drugs occupy a crucially important space in contemporary society as integral interventions in sound medical care. They can improve quality of life, deliver intense if sometimes only ephemeral pleasure, and extend lifespans. In fact, drugs are entrenched across the life course, with every age cohort obtaining comfort and relief from the use of substances. The drivers of drug use, and the variety of available drugs, appear in Figure 14.1.

As Figure 14.1 illustrates, numerous reasons motivate drug and other substance use, most of which can lead to positive outcomes. For example, drug-use experiences can deliver a calm and confident disposition, stimulate an energy boost, help build a better physique, assist in losing weight, reduce pain and discomfort, lower debilitating levels of inhibition, and reduce anxiety. At the same time, substance use can produce serious levels of harm to users, especially when they possess powerful, addictive properties and are used under conditions of high dosage or with improper or absent medical supervision. For example, an indisputable mountain of evidence shows that excessive alcohol and tobacco use can lead to serious health problems (Baer *et al.* 2003: 93–167). Irresponsible alcohol and tobacco use has produced widespread misery and premature deaths. Some drug educators argue that a high proportion of people are drug dependent, that doctors tend to overprescribe, and that many prescription drugs, even when properly dispensed, constitute a major health risk. Politicians and health professionals sometimes claim that the overzealous use of some drugs not only risks health, but also reveals a serious character defect, a severe moral failing, and a desperate need to overcome chronic insecurity.

Some drugs present such serious risks to society and its members that governments universally declare them illegal to use, and in the case of substances like heroin, cocaine, and cannabis, impose severe criminal sanctions. For such substances the pronouncement is clear: trafficking, possessing, or using will incur more than health risks. You will also go to jail. In nations like Singapore and Indonesia, a provision exists for the ultimate punishment, death. Although current policy seems more concerned with maximising retribution and minimising civil liberties, a multitude of approaches can be introduced. An alternative model prioritises minimising harms and maximising benefits, thereby securing significant improvements in social utility and public goods. Within the model,

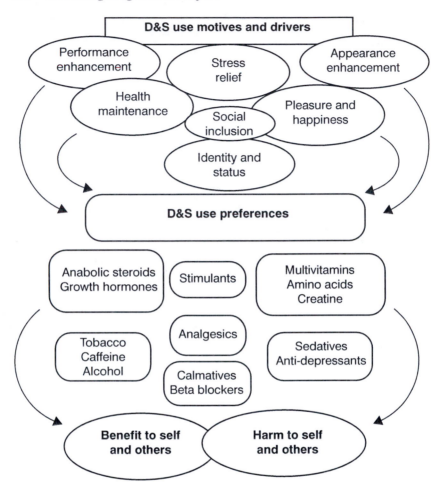

Figure 14.1 Drug and supplement use in the hyper-modern world

(D&S = drug and supplement)

choices can be made around heavy regulation or light regulation, and a range of options anywhere between these two extremes. A model for illustrating the different forms of drug regulations that can be adopted appears in Figure 14.2.

Figure 14.2 identifies three policy scenarios, all of which have their strengths and weaknesses. The free market option meets the aspirations of libertarians, who want the uncontested right to create their own lifestyles in their own ways. Libertarians want no sanctions, no enforcement, and unregulated distribution. They want the freedom to do whatever they wish with their own bodies, and the freedom to ingest whatever substances they desire in the light of knowledge about the associated risk and harms. In this policy scenario, knowledge will come through proper packaging and detailed product information as well as widespread educational campaigns.

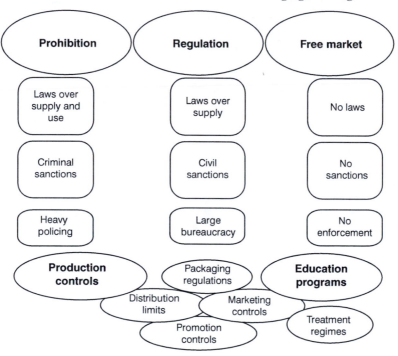

Figure 14.2 Drug policy options

The prohibition option finds favour with those who believe in the maxim that sometimes you 'have to be cruel to be kind'. The policy option is underpinned by the assumption that most people are incapable of making rational and informed decisions when it comes to drug use, and that if left to their own cognitive and emotional devices, will destroy their health, and in some cases their lives or those of others. As a result, the best outcomes will come from having highly restrictive laws over supply and use, criminal sanctions, and heavy duty policing. According to the logic of prohibitionists, it may be a costly policy, but the damage to society will be minimised. In other words, little-to-no use, must by definition, come with little-to-no harm.

The regulatory model occupies the middle ground. Under regulated conditions drugs are neither banned nor freely available. Instead, drugs are supplied to users under strict conditions. Distribution will be controlled, usually through medical prescription, pharmacy dispensing, and specialised outlets. Drug safety will be managed through government bureaucracies. Criminal sanctions may be applied in certain cases, but for the most part sanctions will take the form of fines and penalties. Problems associated with risk, harm, and public health will be managed through educational campaigns, counselling, and treatment in a proper medical or rehabilitation setting.

At first glance, prohibition appears to be an attractive option given its succinct and decisive interventions. It delivers a punitive edge, which for many people

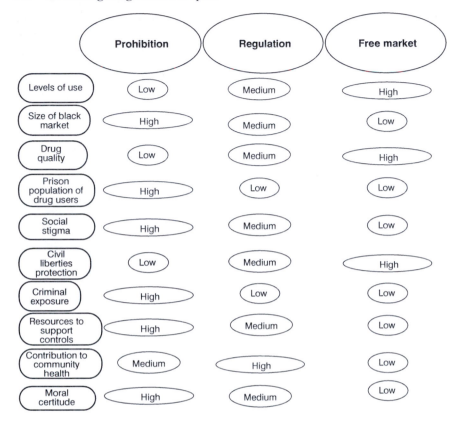

Figure 14.3 Estimations of drug control impacts

sends the unambiguous signal that drug use is wrong and has no redeeming social features. Moreover, in the long haul, drug use costs lives. Prohibition has proven the preferred means for controlling heroin, cocaine, and cannabis, but not tobacco and alcohol. Although for many years controls were exerted over the sale of tobacco and alcohol, more recent policies have hovered between relatively free market access, and controlled distribution. While alcohol can only be sold in stores granted a licence, cigarettes remain freely available in supermarkets and corner stores. Cigarettes, however, must contain plain and bold health warnings on the packaging. In addition, they incur heavy taxes in order to escalate prices and dampen demand. All of this discussion immediately begs the question as to which policy model will deliver the best outcomes for both individuals and the communities to which they belong. This is a difficult question to quickly answer, since a large range of contexts, conditions, consequences, and impacts must be considered. Take, for example the range of factors listed in Figure 14.3.

In Figure 14.3, we have identified ten criteria for assessing the impact different regimes can have on individuals and communities. Our list is not exhaustive. For example, we might also include criteria such as work performance, job security, reputation, and social standing. Nevertheless, these criteria help reveal why more punitive regulations will not necessarily deliver better social outcomes. Equally, it remains unclear whether free market conditions will deliver the best social outcomes either.

History reveals that prohibition will never eliminate drug use. It will, however, most probably lower it, delivering a positive contribution to community health. Nevertheless, prohibition comes at a cost since drug quality will be low, exposure to criminal activity will be heightened, the stigma associated with being labelled a user will escalate, and people's right to use the drugs of their choice will be curtailed.

A free market has intuitive appeal since it will take the supply out of the hands of criminals and place it in the hands of the private business sector, which should immediately lead to an improvement in product quality, product knowledge, and distribution. On the other hand, there is likely to be an increase in use along with public health risks, as well as an exacerbation of community anxieties. A regulatory model should, in theory, absorb the better features of the two previous models. At the same time it will be costly since it will demand a bureaucracy to manage the regulations. Still, use will be dampened, and the health problems will probably be lower than under a free market model.

Over recent times it has become fashionable to talk about two polar models of drug use management, the first being zero tolerance, and the second being harm reduction. The zero-tolerance model, or prohibition under another name, is all about eliminating drug use: cutting down on the number of people using drugs, curtailing the amount of drugs being used, or both. While zero-tolerance proponents would like to lower the risks of use, they seek to secure a wholesale fall in use. They understand that it may promote 'collateral harms' by increasing enforcement costs, treading on the rights of users and others, and increasing the street price of prohibited drugs, thereby making underground trafficking more appealing. However, to zero-tolerance advocates the prohibition calculus represents a reasonable price to pay for delivering largely drug-free communities.

In contrast, the harm-reduction model addresses the negative consequences of use, rather than the act of use itself. The harms associated with drug use include health-related dangers such as risk of death and serious illness, as well as social stigmatism and loss of personal dignity. While harm-reduction policy may incorporate strategies to promote the reduction of drug use, it aims to do so in a harm-sensitive manner so as to avoid unwanted collateral problems. In theory, under the harm-reduction model, it could be possible to actually broaden use while still reducing aggregate harms. The concept of tobacco-free cigarettes was once viewed in this light (Taylor 1984).

What about sport?

When it comes to sport, the regulatory situation seems ambiguous. We begin by noting that a significant range of motives, ambitions, and aspirations drive drug use in sport, as listed in Figure 14.4.

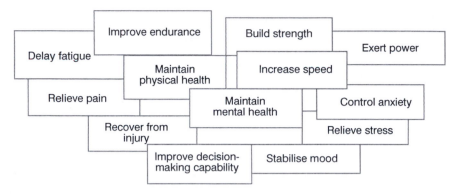

Figure 14.4 Performance enhancement in sport through drug use

As Figure 14.4 illustrates, using drugs to build muscle, strength, and power comprise just a handful of many athletic aspirations. Taking muscle-building drugs constitutes one of the most controversial practices in sport since it often involves anabolic steroids, which are not only banned but also incur substantive social penalties. The desire to improve endurance and delay fatigue also includes the potential for other heavy drug use, including simulants and 'blood boosters' like EPO. Pain relief cannot be ignored either, given the physical imposition of serious sporting competition. For example, substances like opiates in their various forms keep players competing when hurt, and help them recover more rapidly from injury. Finally, for those with mood and anxiety issues to deal with – which can be exacerbated by the ruthlessly competitive nature of sport and the associated media interest – various sedatives, tranquilisers, anti-depressants, and anti-anxiety drugs are available.

We should keep in mind that drug-control policies in sport replicate those practiced in wider society. As a result, sport can either march down the zero-tolerance footpath or motor along the harm-reduction super-highway. While we previously demonstrated an overlap between the zero-tolerance and harm-reduction approaches in that they both want to protect the well-being of athletes, and sustain the reputation of sporting practice, they wield quite different behavioural and ethical assumptions, each playing out in radically different ways. As a way of contrasting the two models, in the next section we reconstruct them as exaggerated narratives. Although occasionally stereotypical, and often simplistic, we think that this forced juxtaposition helps to reveal the assumptions, ethics, and intellectual foundations that underpin the structures and drive the operations of each policy model.

Zero tolerance

The zero-tolerance narrative begins by telling a story about sport's place in society, and its capacity to generate positive impacts. It takes a no-nonsense approach; in the same way that real men do not eat quiche, 'real' sport officials believe in a zero-tolerance approach to drug use in sport. In the world of zero tolerance there can be no room for ambiguity, second chances, or policy fuzziness. Consequently, the narrative usually begins with a short prelude establishing the cultural and ethical credentials of sport, before pontificating on the evils of drugs and reflecting on the flawed personalities of athletes and players caught taking them. It ends with the pronouncement that while the end to the problem is in sight, we – that is, the people who manage sport – need to remain ever-vigilant. It begins...

> Sport is an integral part of modern industrial societies ... it has the capacity to deliver a whole range of social benefits ... it provides people with the opportunity to secure significant pleasures ... memorable experiences ... deep meanings ... and a well-functioning body ... sport is all about delivering healthy activity, developing character, and building communities ... it holds a special place in society and must be protected from contamination by those with no understanding of sport's capacity to deliver large slabs of social utility.
>
> So ... we must be vigilant about protecting sport's core values and good standing ... and not only that ... we must corral drugs that undermine the health and well-being of sport participants, be they heroin ... cocaine ... cannabis ... amphetamines ... narcotic analgesics ... anti-depressants ... sedatives ... anabolic steroids ... other stimulants, and so on.
>
> Moreover ... these substances, and the athletes who take them, threaten the good name and impeccable reputation of sport ... and it doesn't end there, since ... drugs, if taken systematically, can secure athletes an unfair competitive edge ... this is a case of barefaced cheating ... this not only makes them drug cheats ... but also makes them flawed individuals with diminished moral fibre, impoverished ethical standards, and a furiously perverted desire to harm both themselves and others.
>
> So ... we must do all that it takes to rid sport of drugs ... especially the more addictive ones (heroin) ... the illicit ones (cocaine) ... the ones that send you off your head (methamphetamines) ... the ones that cheats use (EPO, anabolic steroids, hGH, high potency stimulants) ... the ones that hippies used to use (cannabis) ... the ones that young people use at rave parties (GHB, Ecstasy) ... and as for alcohol, nicotine, and caffeine ... yes ... well ... this could be a bit more difficult ... after all, they are part of our popular culture ... you have to cut people a bit of slack occasionally ... they need to have something that will relax them and loosen them up. Plus, a glass or two of red wine every night is good for you.
>
> So ... where do we start in our attempt to rid sport of drugs ... we will establish an independent agency, a bureaucracy, if you like, to test you – that is, athletes and players – for evidence of drug use ... we will be testing you throughout the year ... We will test you not only for drugs we deem to be performance enhancing, but we will also test you for substances that are illicit ... we will test you at any place and any time ... and you must advise on your whereabouts ... and we will do it all at our convenience ... and, what's

more, we will invade your privacy and tramp over your civil liberties if we need to in the interests of a drug-free sport world ... we will demand that you urinate into a container in full view of the sample collector. And, we reserve the right to arrive on your doorstep at daybreak, if need be, to test you for drugs ... we will compile a life history of your tests and respectfully call it a Biological Passport ... and we will subsequently use deviations from the norm to tag you as a cheat. We will also give our bureaucracy the power to investigate allegations of drug use, possession, and trafficking ... we will get them to target suspects, force people to inform on others, and generally harass whoever we want for an assurance that nothing 'untoward' is happening ... and with no requirement that we will be advising you in advance ... we have 24/7 power.

There will be some harsh penalties for using, possessing, and, even worse, trafficking. We will not send you to jail ... not at the moment ... but we are looking at some European precedents and policies ... the Italians have a very draconian policy with a 'criminal sanctions' element to it ... maybe we should actually 'criminalise' doping ... but as it is at the moment we will suspend you from your sport ... we may give you a life ban ... and you will certainly not be welcome in any sports-space ever again.

Indeed, we will not give the time of day to anyone who is so overwhelmingly self-centred, and who shows such a brazen disregard for the good standing of our sport, that they would even think about drug use ... we cannot have anarchy ... and the laws must be respectfully obeyed ... and, to repeat, if you do the wrong thing we will completely destroy your reputation and credibility ... we will put you through the media wringer and hang you out to dry in full view of a commercial television current affairs show ... and as for any subsequent treatment, support or guidance for your transition to another sport, occupation, identity, or life ... it's your problem ... you created it ... you sort it out.

So, let us be as clear as we can on this one ... if you do as you are told you will be allowed to enter an idyllic and pristine world where all that is good about sport is on display ... the world of *drug-free sport*, which is a WADA slogan ... and ... we have a set of drug-control rules ... if you break the rules we kick you out ... *but* ... if you play within the rules ... if you don't do drugs, you can continue to play and enjoy all the things sport uniquely offers it participants.

This zero-tolerance approach is, in fact, the *only* policy worth thinking about ... and, let us be frank here ... there is a 'war on drugs in sport' going on at the moment, where the authorities are clearly winning all the battles! ... nearly every athlete is dead scared of getting anywhere near a drug dealer ... the WADA vision is close to being achieved ... positive tests usually run at less 1 per cent of total tests conducted ... we are nearing the end of a story that contains many unpleasant episodes, but which has a morally uplifting end ... the ethical problem has been sorted out ... the legal problem is being worked through ... the equity / unfairness problem is close to being completely ticked-off ... and clearly the health problem has been resolved once and for all ... everyone knows their place ... and everyone knows who is in control.

... to sum up then ... zero tolerance provides for *no* use ... abstinence, if you like ... we start with a list of banned substances ... we have tough penalties for them ... we establish a bureaucracy of drug testers and investigators to identify, interrogate, and sanction the cheats and the transgressors ... And, make no mistake here, our approach is deliberately tough ... we may be accused of being moralistic, mechanistic, didactic, interventionist, punitive, emotional, political, and absolutist, but we know what we want ... a sport world that delivers a supremely healthy activity, guarantees a level playing field, is morally clean, and is free from the putrid corruption that comes with drugs and the people that deal in them.

Harm reduction

If the previous commentary – with all its hyperbole and rhetoric – is to be believed, then an alternative drug-management policy needs no consideration. The problem has already been sorted! However, the drugs in sport problem involves more complexities than zero-tolerance proponents would have us believe. Drug use still exists in sport, including signs that an expanding number of engineered drugs are being used for which no reliable tests exist. Disputes continue about testing for non-performance-enhancing drugs while questions about why resources should be allocated to a social rather than a sporting problem also persist. Concerns have been raised about the heavy intrusion that all-year-round drug testing brings into the lives of players and athletes, and to what extent it threatens their civil liberties and basic human rights. Finally, mounting evidence shows that a black market for banned substances has emerged, involving crime syndicates with supply chains from their own drug-making facilities to a distribution network connecting closely to coaches, conditioners, and the players they supervise (ACC 2013).

The harm-reduction narrative provides a neat counterpoint to the zero-tolerance approach. It, too, begins by saying that sport represents an important social institution, and that the club activities, competitions, and leagues it organises benefits communities in all sorts of valuable ways. But, it also adds that the zero-tolerance approach to drug use in sport is too good to be true. Within the harm-reduction narrative the assertion that drug use can ever be completely removed from sport represents pure fantasy. In fact, it observes that for the most part, sport's authorities exercise little interest in managing the most problematic dimensions of the drug problem: those associated with alcohol, nicotine, and painkillers. Harm-reduction proponents also argue that gaming and match fixing have far more serious implications for sport's sustainability. Moreover, the harm-reduction narrative rejects the 'have to be cruel to be kind' approach to drug use, emphasising instead a 'have to be kind to be effective' model. It then delivers a scathing, if sometimes supercilious, critique of punitive drug policy in general, and prohibition initiatives in particular. It goes on to use 'challenging behaviours' – or, as it is often now described, 'dangerous consumptions' – from other social practices to explain how zero-tolerance models can create more problems than they solve. It ends with a cautious celebration of regulatory policies that strike a balance between the desire for individual freedoms on one hand, and social controls on the other. The narrative begins with a rhetorical question ...

We don't want to be sceptical, but can sport ever be drug free? History shows that banning drugs does not eliminate their use ... the US government tried to prohibit the production and sale of alcohol from 1917 to 1933 ... and during that 16-year period it was a monumental failure. And, what about the 'war on drugs' that started with Richard Nixon in 1968? ... 43 years later ... it has also become a monumental failure ... the UNODC in its 2011 report declared that worldwide somewhere between 150 million and 270 million people used illicit substances at least once in previous year ... is this success? ... this is not even winning a battle, let alone a war! ... there is, in fact, an alternative narrative ... the harm-reduction narrative ... so let's have a conversation about it.

To begin ... the harm-reduction narrative, just like the zero-tolerance one, declares that sport participation, or what might be called 'normal' sport practice, provides a great many social benefits ... but it also carries many risks ... and can deliver significant harms ... including stress, injury, disability, and ... substance dependency, even around the most innocuous substances ... like, for example, tobacco, over-the-counter alcohol, over-the-counter analgesics, over-the-counter stimulants, on-prescription barbiturates, on-prescription anti-depressants, and so on ... and ... what's more ... normal sport practice can actually be high risk, especially when it involves ... rock fishing, mountaineering, boxing, martial arts, other combat sport, motor sports, and collision sports in general.

Despite its typically beneficial effect on body appearance and body performance, normal sport practice does not guarantee an illness-free, healthy, or long, life ... participants understand this ... so the drivers of sport participation go well beyond the belief that it is an investment in a longer lifespan ... sport, even in its pure form, can actually be dangerous ... and many people seek out this danger ... and ... yes ... drugs can be another source of danger ... and at their worst can create stress, trauma, bodily disintegration, and psychological decline ... something that sport can clearly do without! ... but, drugs are not all that bad ... some drugs ... especially if taken in a disciplined way, and on the advice of a medical practitioner, therapist or pharmacist ... can improve the health and well-being of sport participants.

Let us not forget ... doing all that it takes to eliminate use – which is the zero-tolerance approach – may not be the smartest policy move ... it not only squeezes the participant's civil liberties, but it also denies any 'user benefits' or social utility ... we do not want to throw the baby out with bathwater ... while coercive regulations that denies use might decrease use-related harms ... they can also eliminate benefits, and impose additional social costs ... so

... for example ... a ban on cannabis use by players and athletes means less law breaking, less dope smoking, and fewer assaults on sport's reputation ... but ... it also puts a squeeze on civil liberties ... it means the loss of an alternative therapy ... it means less fun ... and it means less stress relief ... and where is the sense in that!

Well ... OK ... zero tolerance does secure the moral high ground ... it reminds us that a free-for-all position could morally bankrupt us ... which is to say ... zero tolerance aims to do the *right* thing ... but is it the *best* thing? ... and does zero tolerance necessarily secure the best health outcomes or social outcomes ... so ... may not a harm-reduction approach offer a useful alternative? ... perhaps, but we still need to make it clear what harm reduction is actually all about.

Harm reduction's guiding principles are threefold ... 1) harms can be reduced without eliminating ... or even reducing use, 2) reducing / eliminating use may not necessarily reduce harms, and 3) drastically reducing / eliminating use can deny opportunities for enhancement, improved well-being, and other lifestyle benefits ... that is, some drug use can actually improve the quality of life ... now ... let us go through some cases to see how it works.

Case 1: The unwanted pregnancy and sexually transmittable disease problem amongst young people ... the zero-tolerance policy solution is to ban sex amongst young single people ... confine sex to marriage ... and just say *no*! ... the harm-reduction policy solution is to allow all older teenagers to have sex ... but only under strictly regulated and safe conditions ... for example, encourage, or even demand condom use.

Case 2: The domestic violence problem ... from a theoretical standpoint the zero-tolerance policy solution is to ban people from living together in a domestic situation ... while this is clearly nonsensical, the logic here is that no close physical proximity or any direct contact ensures no violence. Given that couples are permitted to cohabitate, a zero-tolerance approach would insist that any violence should lead to an immediate and lengthy suspension of the relationship ... the harm-reduction policy solution is to encourage people to partner up and live together ... but only under strictly regulated and safe conditions ... including for instance ... trial marriage, evidence of pre-marriage counselling, compatible psychological profiles, a rights and obligations agreement, and an annual review of the relationship.

Case 3: The prostitution problem. The zero-tolerance policy solution is to ban all paid sex thereby protecting the supplier from exploitation and the recipient from engaging in immoral behaviour ... it will also lower the risk of catching a disease ... the harm-reduction policy solution is to allow paid sex to continue ... but do it safely and non-exploitatively ... issue a licence, have minimum pay rates and regulated working conditions, have supervision, make condom use mandatory, have health checks on workers, and maybe also provide health checks for clients.

Case 4: The sport violence problem in combat sports ... the zero-tolerance policy solution is to ban all boxing, for instance ... and do the same for mixed martial arts … this follows the preferred option of most medical associations … the harm-reduction policy solution, on the other hand, allows boxing and combat sports to continue … but only under strict regulations, including a licence to promote, a licence to train, weight divisions, padded gloves, head and teeth protection, medical checks before bouts, and physicians at ringside … they seek to squeeze out the costs, while retaining the benefits of an exciting gladiatorial-type contest.

Case 5: The cigarette-smoking problem … the zero-tolerance policy solution is to ban all smoking now … but the harm-reduction policy solution is slightly softer since it allows for controlled smoking … and the right to do it 'more safely', if that is possible. This can be achieved, in part, through lower tobacco content … slow burning at low temperature … bans for those under 18 years of age … social marketing campaigns against smoking … bans for smoking in enclosed spaces … inflated prices … heavy sales taxes, annual health checks … and advertising and sponsorship bans.

Case 6: The compulsive gambling problem … the zero-tolerance policy solution is to ban all addictive gambling … for many countries this involves electronic gaming machines, which have a hypnotic capacity to keep people losing money for hours on end. The harm-reduction policy solution is to be far more circumspect, and allow electronic gaming to take place, but only under strict supervision … so we might, for example, register anyone who participates regularly, or only allow small bets to be placed.

Good policy here is not about draconian controls, the harshest of penalties, and relentless public shaming … the common theme for harm reduction is that it allows for controlled and regulated use … there are no bans … no one has coercive powers, players cannot be compelled to attend a drug-rehabilitation boot camp … or be barred from their community sport clubs … it does not punish or suspend players for transgressing some moral boundary … it does not name and shame … it protects, assists, and guides players along a path to athletic excellence, wellness, and longevity, while doing it all as safely as possible .

The argument for proposing a harm-reduction approach to the drugs in sport problem is more than just theoretical posturing and hypothetical grandstanding … it is not too good to be true, and while it might be a little naive at times, it offers a legitimate alternative … for instance … in its idealised form a drug use in sport policy framed by harm-reduction principles might include some of the following – and occasionally very libertarian – features … 1) it first and foremost creates a sport environment where game safety and risk management are strategic priorities; 2) it delivers intensive educational campaigns that inform players about appropriate (that is, harmless) and inappropriate (that is, harmful) drug-use practices; … 3) it establishes a transparent register of safe drugs that can be used by players to achieve the level of excellence they so earnestly strive for, but without overdosing or imposing harm on self or others; 4) it specifies high-risk substances that should be avoided; … 5) it also lists substances that are likely to improve performance in specific areas of training and competing, and cautioning on dose; 6) it clears space for a strictly limited drug-distribution system regulated through physicians and pharmacists; 7) it requires all athletes who are taking substances to register with their coach, club doctor, and dispensing chemist; 8) it involves early intervention where drug use has damaged oneself, or harmed others; 9) it provides counselling services to players who seek guidance and support on decisions to continue or not continue drug use; and 10) it could also involve subsidies for low-risk drug behaviours ... but taxes high-risk drug behaviours.

OK ... we concede that many of the above proposals are too radical, and too smart by half ... and maybe even too far-fetched ... and they may underplay the 'level playing field issue' and the problem of cheating more than they should ...

But ... they are at the extreme end of the drug management continuum. They can be easily reshaped to accommodate a list of banned substances while allowing for the controlled use of others ...

So ... to sum up, harm reduction calls for conditional use ... it includes a list of harmful substances but need not formulate lists of banned substances since under this model there may not be any ... it doesn't punish or sanction for use ... on the contrary, it lends professional support in managing harmful substances ... it encourages harm-free and ethical use ... it delivers a panel of medical practitioners, therapists, and pharmacists to treat, support, and guide the at risk and the vulnerable ...

Yes ... this might be seen as soft, and maybe even negligent ... but what do you want? ... should we punish transgressors to within an inch of their sporting lives ... or ... do you want something that is a bit more pragmatic, humanistic, interactive, consultative, educative, rational, intellectual, and utilitarian? And, what's more, harm reduction is morally neutral, it defers to the broader justice system to decide on the drug's legality, it incentivises low-risk behaviour, it is thoughtful and considered, it intervenes to protect players' health, and it does not punish high-risk behaviour ... harm reduction accepts that sport can never guarantee a level playing field, or give every participant the same chance of winning ... but we also need to remember that drug use is but one of a multitude of ways of getting a competitive edge and ... to be blunt, the elimination of drugs from sport will do little to balance the playing field in any seriously significant way ...

If you really want to level the playing field, you should adopt the practices of horse racing, where the best horse carries the heaviest weight, or adopt the practices of professional athletics, where the fastest athletes are handicapped so as to give others a better chance of winning ... let's be frank ... the idea that maintaining a costly bureaucracy to catch and punish the cheats, the morally corrupt, the weak willed, and the easily led, will give everyone a fair chance, is pure fantasy.

Conclusion

In summary, the two narratives in which this chapter culminates reveal opposing ideological positions on drug control in sport. We now confront a drug-control 'balance sheet' where policy assets are offset by an accumulation of liabilities. On one side of the drug use in sport policy ledger we find the zero-tolerance / prohibitionist model. It strives to rid sport of all drug use by heavily sanctioning players and athletes who get caught using. On the other side of the drug use in sport policy ledger we find the regulated harm-reduction model. It takes a less coercive line because it does not focus on eliminating use. Instead, the model focuses on managing the possible risks of drug use, especially where it concerns health, along with clearing out all those underground suppliers and adulterated substances.

But where does the debate leave us in terms of policy? It is one thing to deliver a gratuitous caricature of the opposing sides, mock their passionate adherence to sincerely held beliefs, and belittle their moral positions. It is another thing to come up with an alternative model that meets the desires of stakeholders, protects it participants, and delivers a sporting system possessing a socially significant and sustainable future.

15 The case for a new deal

Where to from here?

As we noted in the previous chapter, the problem of drug use in sport usually fires up a zero-tolerance reaction fuelled by moral outrage, and inflamed by a demand for punitive sanctions. The current WADA model exemplifies this position, and while it humanely aims to protect the health and welfare of players and athletes, and safeguard sport's good standing and sustainability, the policy goal assumes that prohibition delivers abstinence, which in turn solves the problem. The WADA model therefore uses the same behavioural model that underpins controls over alcoholism, addictive gambling, tobacco-induced lung cancer, transmittable diseases, and unwanted pregnancies. That is, if you don't want to suffer the consequences, you don't do the deed. It also implies that if players and athletes want transient pleasures and quick and easy rewards, they must face the prospects of some serious costs, which in the case of being caught using drugs means shame, punishment, suspension, and the loss of a career.

We also identified another policy option, that of regulating drug use with the aim of reducing the harms to users, whatever the level of use. This harm-reduction model has a sweetly naive logic to it when applied to sport, since it assumes that players and athletes will be able to rationally differentiate the low-harm from high-harm substances, and act accordingly. It also assumes that sport's stakeholders will agree that the maintenance of player health, and the protection of athlete welfare, will override any gain in performance. The harm-reduction model can meet with public ridicule, though, by going well beyond the naive into the world of fantasy where it is assumed that rationality guides all social behaviour in all situations.

As a result, we have one policy model driven by a fundamentalist concern for punishment, zero tolerance, and abstinence, and another underpinned by an idealistic concern for athlete autonomy, agency, and safety. Each of these positions has its strengths and weaknesses, but we need to determine which model ensures sport's integrity the most, which one delivers the best outcomes for players and athletes, and which one offers the opportunity for sport's other stakeholders to also benefit. However, these policy options are difficult to weigh up, since subjectivity and bias inevitably get in the way of an impartial analysis, even where a lot of objective evidence has been compiled. Zero tolerance is likely to deliver lower levels of use, but it will impact on players' civil liberties, and the overall harms to people may not necessarily be lowered since banned substance use presents only one of many catalysts for harm to occur in and through sport. A harm-reduction approach will deliver greater autonomy to people, while actively seeking to contain the damage to users and the people around them. But this will happen in the face of a likely increase in use, given fewer coercive controls.

Exploring the strengths and weaknesses of different drug-control models, and illuminating their likely benefits and costs does not, however, lead to a consensus on what priority, and what 'weight' should be allocated to the benefits and costs associated with a change in use. One stakeholder group may hold the elimination of EPO use as sovereign. Another stakeholder group might see the effective treatment of addictive illicit drug use as the prime indicator of success. Such contradictions occur when a so-called 'consequentialist' method is used to decide upon which policy option to implement. Although the method enables a systematic analysis of the social and economic consequences to be undertaken, it often fails to deliver a valid measuring stick to meet every stakeholder's demand.

Weighing up the alternatives

A promising lead for assessing the relative merits of each of the above regulatory models for managing the drugs in sport problem comes from Stevens (2011) through his exposition of Gewirth's (1978) principle of 'generic consistency'. According to Gewirth, every 'good' society must uphold the rights of individuals, operating as human agents, to pursue their ambitions and aspirations, which he calls 'purposive action' or what others might call 'agency' (Stevens 2011: 234). Moreover, Gewirth argued that society should also provide conditions wherein purposive actions can be undertaken without interference from others. These conditions include life itself, health, physical integrity, and mental equilibrium. They become the overarching or 'basic' rights of all individuals, and can be summed up as the right to freedom, and the right to well-being (Stevens 2011: 234).

In the Gewirth model this basic right of all agents to undertake purposive action is supported by two subsidiary rights. The first subsidiary right Gewirth named was a 'non subtractive' right, or the right to 'action' one's values and beliefs with the expectation that they will be enabled rather than blocked at every turn. The secondary subsidiary right was called an 'additive right'. It constitutes the right to improve one's position, to advance one's career, and to build one's reputation. Increasing capabilities and achieving goals lie at its heart (Gewirth 1982: 324).

At the same time, the generic-consistency principle involves duties and obligations. This means that agents should accord to others the same rights to freedom and well-being that they want to claim for themselves (Gewirth 1982: 324). For example, someone who wants the right to espouse a free market, winner-take-all political ideology, would be obliged to give equal space to those wishing to promulgate a communitarian–socialist political agenda. Thus, once agents have established the conditions they need for their own purposive action, they must be prepared to give others the same array of conditions.

Having dealt with rights and duties, Gewirth considered the idea of 'harm'. Accordingly, an agent suffers harm when someone else undermines his or her rights, and the consequent capacity to achieve his or her goals. Harm results when the same agent undermines the capacity of others to achieve their goals. Gewirth also proposed a hierarchy of harms, where harms to basic rights receive greater weight than harms to non-subtractive rights, which in turn, are weighted more heavily than harms to additive rights (Gewirth 1982: 236). The different elements of the model can be combined as illustrated in Figure 15.1

In order to secure a picture of the how the model works, we can take for example a government decision to ban cigarette smoking from enclosed spaces. First, harm is incurred upon smokers' non-subtractive rights, since they are no longer permitted to smoke in a space of their convenience. Little harm is done to smokers' additive rights, since limits on smoking have no immediate potential to undermine personal growth. For basic rights, the harm suffered from a loss of amenity is offset by a significant health benefit. On the other hand, a decision to

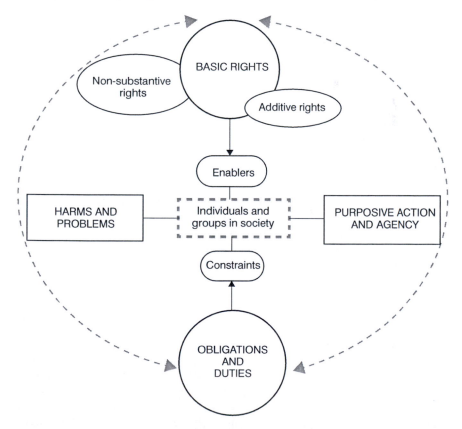

Figure 15.1 Gewirth's (1978) Principle of 'generic consistency'

allow smokers to mingle with non-smokers in an enclosed setting would create a major health problem for everyone, severely diminishing the basic well-being right for everyone, which would completely swamp any gain in lower level rights. Consequently, the application of the Gewirth generic principle model clearly favours the introduction of the smoking ban in enclosed spaces. While the right to smoke in any space at any time is curtailed for some, the right to clean air is enhanced for everyone else. Harms are reduced, and well-being is protected. Working through the Gewirth model strongly supports a policy that bans people from smoking in enclosed spaces.

What about the right to use drugs? For many substances the answer should be 'yes' since their availability not only preserves individual freedom – a basic right – but also ensures well-being. Many people would not be alive were it not for their drug use. Thus, drug use done under medical supervision clearly constitutes a basic right demanding protection. The use of drugs in sport introduces more complications however, since equity issues arise in the event that some athletes will generate an unfair advantage over other athletes by taking drugs.

At first glance, the Gewirth model supports drug use in sport, especially where the risk of becoming ill or contracting a disease from their use remains relatively low. Painkillers, even those with an opiate base, can be essential for well-being. From one perspective their use reflects a basic right to lead a comfortable, relatively pain-free life. Various stimulants intended for medicinal use also fit into this category when they provide benefits for sport and athletic improvement without threatening health. Low doses of anabolic steroids may also be consistent with the protection of basic rights. They expand individual freedoms, and if taken under expert supervision, might also produce an improvement in well-being, especially in building confidence, vitality, and muscle. As far as non-subtractive rights are concerned, no inconvenience is incurred or impediment imposed on anyone, unless the opportunity to use is closed off to some, but not others. But, under the Gewirth model, anyone who uses has an obligation to provide space for others to use as well. The use of drugs in sport would also favourably impact on additive rights by enabling athletes to improve performance and secure the competitive edge they stridently pursue. The Gewirth model not only opens up debate on the complexities of the drugs issue, but it also gives greater credibility to the harm-reduction model since it protects more rights than it denies. In contrast, the zero-tolerance model loses its policy 'weight' since it denies more rights than it protects.

The solution

Is it all too neat and simple to recommend the harm-reduction model over the zero-tolerance model because it offers more autonomy and more protection to athletes and players? And, what about the unfair advantage athletes acquire from using drugs without any significant controls being imposed? Should we not rate the damage to health problem more highly than we otherwise might? Yes, the Gewirth model does privilege human rights and civil liberties over all else, but it should also be remembered that basic rights include the right to well-being.

At the same time, a tension looms between Gewirth's additive rights, which give all athletes the space to achieve excellence in any reasonable way, and his non-subtractive rights, which give sport authorities an opportunity to build a credible and well-respected tournament or league where rules regulate conduct, and both athletes and fans are guaranteed a level playing field. The tension becomes most evident whenever an athlete faces investigation and interrogation in a government agency's pursuit of drug-use cases. A further tension emerges when sport's 'unique' social structures and practices are cited in support of the view that player autonomy must be squeezed in the interests of fairness and equity. This raises the issue of just how many player and athlete rights must be sacrificed in order to get a bit more integrity, 'fairness', and competitive balance into a sporting competition.

Such is the dilemma confronting sport's relationship with drugs. But, as Gewirth's analysis shows, we suggest that the choice should be decided in favour of protecting athletes' basic rights, which revolve around freedom, autonomy, and well-being. By definition, defending a zero-tolerance model means limiting freedoms. Nor does the zero-tolerance model necessarily ensure an athlete's well-being, especially if the sport involves high risks. Conversely, a free market, libertarian model optimises an athlete's right to freedom and well-being, but in doing so, it may also increase risk. We are consequently left with only one workable model wherein the individual right to freedom and well-being is balanced against the community duty to protect all citizens, including all athletes against unreasonable risk and harm. Under these situations, players and athletes will have the right to use any drug of their choosing so long as certain conditions are met. These conditions must minimise the harms to players and athletes directly, as well as any other stakeholders they encounter or perform for.

Immediately the question arises as to what regulations should be put in place to minimise both the harms associated with supplying substances to players and athletes, and the harms associated with their use. According to Haden (2004), a range of possibilities exist for both the supply and demand side of the drug-market equation. Supply side regulations include supply licences, controls over distribution channels, and designated sales outlets. Demand side regulations are more extensive, beginning at volume rationing, a floor age for users, required training prior to purchase, the licensing of users, the registration of customers, the passing of an exam prior to use, membership of a certified user group, and agreement to a tracking of consumption patterns (Haden 2004: 226–227).

Most of these regulations have been applied to drug use in broader society, with varying degrees of success. We see rich opportunities for their application to drug control in sport as well. Regulatory interventions fit comfortably within Gewirth's model as they protect the athlete's right to freedom and well-being while ensuring controlled use that minimises harm (Hunt 2004). At the same time, a regulated approach preserves athletes' 1) non-subtractive rights through a reasonable expectation that the drive for health, welfare, and autonomy are not curtailed at every turn, and 2) additive rights through a focus on the space they are allocated for realising their ambitions, however lofty.

A way out

Having spent considerable time and effort interrogating the problems embedded in the current drug-control policies, we now focus our attention on some tangible options for a revised approach to the control of drug use in sport. Based on a critical evaluation of the material we have presented in the earlier chapters, and by focusing our attention on health, well-being, rights, accountability, disclosure, and transparency, as advocated by Erill (2000), Haden (2004), Hanstad (2009), Hunt (2004), Rapp (2009), Savulecu, Foddy & Clayton (2004), and Stevens (2011), we have identified ten guidelines for shaping future drug control policies in the world of sport.

First, as a matter of principle, substance use in sport should be seen as a legitimate method for improving performance, recovering from injury and illness, and extending the productive lifespan of players and athletes. This simple proposition acknowledges the fact that drugs of all sorts have always been part of the sport experience.

Second, players and athletes should be free to use substances that do not have an adverse impact on their health and welfare. This equates with substance use in broader society, where thousands of drugs are available for use after being prescribed by a medical practitioner and dispensed by a registered pharmacist.

Third, any safe substance can be used where its free availability to all players and athletes can be assured and accessibility remains unconstrained by high prices or limited availability. This will neutralise all claims of cheating and unfair advantages, since drug use will no longer be the province of a well informed and resourced coterie of privileged teams, coaches, players, and athletes.

Fourth, substances can only be used where players and athletes have the freedom 'not to use', and where they do not feel coerced into using. The right to not use is as important as the right to use; athletes must be protected from unwarranted pressures for consent, or threats of demotion or dismissal if they do not use.

Fifth, substances can only be used where players and athletes have full knowledge of the effects of the substance, and, where appropriate, provide written consent for its use. It is unfair – and often coercive – to ask players and athletes to use a substance without providing comprehensive information about how the substance acts and what possible side effects it might cause.

Sixth, where use occurs, it must be done under the supervision of a medical practitioner. There are many charlatans in the dietary supplement and related substance-use field, and in order to secure the most effective and safest outcomes, close professional supervision will be mandatory.

Seventh, where use occurs, it must be also done with the full knowledge and approval of the appropriate board of directors, commission, or board of management. The health and welfare of players and athletes is too important to be left to recently graduated sport scientists and physical conditioners. Drug-use guidelines and protocols will therefore be sighted and endorsed by the board before any operational programs and actions are initiated.

Eighth, all cases of use must be recorded on a public register, updated both prior to all major events and league commencement dates, and at the end of the relevant competition. A public register will force all substance-use practices into the open and subject them to both public and professional scrutiny. It will make management more accountable, and deliver more transparency, which can only be a good thing.

Ninth, the use of substances that fall within the above guidelines can only be made available to players and athletes aged 18 years and over. It will be an offence to supply 'minors' with these substances. Many precedents exist for this requirement, with the prohibition on alcohol sales to young people being an exemplar.

Finally, there will be no rules, provisions or clauses that cover any illicit drug use that does not improve sporting performance. These issues will be, as they have traditionally been, the province of government legislation that covers the behaviour of all citizens, irrespective of their sporting or athletic status. However, our last principle also states that sporting authorities take a greater accountability for alleviating the social and health damage caused by legal recreational substances, with a particular emphasis on alcohol and tobacco / nicotine.

Our 'new deal' for drug control in sport – our 'manifesto', if you like – is radical, since it gives space for the legitimate, if limited, use of drugs and other substances, some of which may well be banned at the moment. However, we believe it is also sensible, because it better fits the heavy competitive demands that sport places on its elite players and athletes. It also makes sense because we already have systems in place to monitor and regulate the use of tobacco and alcohol, without banning their use. It takes substance supply out of the hands of charlatans, crooks, and criminal syndicates, and builds supply chains that begin with credible manufacturers, distributors, and agents, and ends up with professionally trained physicians, scientists, and pharmacologists. In addition, it eliminates the need to spend millions of dollars of taxpayer's money creating a drug-control agency that spends so much time monitoring the day-to-day behaviour of players and athletes with very little social utility emerging from their conscientious but often thwarted efforts to expose the cheats and liars to public ridicule. Our manifesto, together with a listing of probable benefits and possible costs, is summarised in Table 15.1.

A remodelled drug-management policy for sport of the type discussed in this chapter will attract controversy since it reprioritises the values of sport by placing player freedom and well-being above a sport's brand equity and integrity. It consequently gives more weight to minimising harm to players' and athletes' health, and less weight to the brand harm that may be associated with a dented reputation following a drug-use scandal. But, in the light of sport's desire to monetise everything in sight, and maximise its commercial value, while also believing that any drug use will destroy sport's integrity and brand equity, this premise could well be the spanner in the works. As such, it could ultimately impede any change in sport's drug-use rules that give players any more autonomy and protection than they currently experience.

But, notwithstanding the warm inner glow that comes from having a punitive drug-control policy, sport still possesses a multitude of inequities embedded deep within its structure. Drug use constitutes only one of many factors offering athletes a

Table 15.1 Stewart and Smith's manifesto for a new drug control policy in sport. A ten-point 'New Deal'

	Guiding principle	Probable benefit	Possible cost
1.	Substance use in sport should be seen as a legitimate method for improving performance, recovering from injury and illness, and extending the productive lifespan of players and athletes	• Performance improvements • Injury and recovery support • Longer athletic careers • Eliminates the hypocrisy • Acknowledges current usage and impossibility of preventing use	• Seen as a moral failure • Athletes viewed as cheats • Financially costly to athletes and teams • Sporting brands cannot hide behind testing regimes that do not work and claim that their athletes do not use substances
2.	Players and athletes should be free to use substances that do not have an adverse impact on their health and welfare	• Matches opportunities in broader society for improved health through substance use • Athletes can pursue performance enhancement without health risks • Choice and freedom of athlete decision making are preserved	• Health rather than drugs become the focus of decision making • Costs of establishing which substances incur adverse health impacts at particular dosages • Need to create an 'adverse health' list of banned substances / dosages
3.	Safe substances can be used where there is an assurance that the substance is freely available to all players and athletes, and use is not constrained by high prices or limited availability	• Parity preserved • Freedom of availability makes products and their quality transparent • Natural competition for superior substances will increase, leading to better effects with diminished health consequences • Helps remove criminal supply from the market	• Ensuring availability means deregulating the supply chain and monitoring monopoly and cartel behaviour • Availability will likely be hard to establish in different parts of the world
4.	Substances can only be used where players and athletes have the freedom 'not to use', and where they do not feel coerced into using	• Gives athletes the power and freedom over their bodies • With transparency, athletes can bring coercion into the open and seek remediation	• Difficult to monitor • Athletes might feel compelled to use in order to be competitive
5.	Substances can only be used where players and athletes have full knowledge of the effects of the substance, and, where appropriate, they provide written consent for its use	• Athletes understand the immediate and long-term effects of substances on their bodies as well as on their performances • Documentation adds transparency and improves an athlete's ownership of the decision to use substances	• Costs of introducing comprehensive athlete education • Problems of measuring athletes' substance knowledge to confirm they do understand the consequences of use

#		Pros	Cons
6.	Where use occurs, it must be done under the supervision of a medical practitioner	• Protects health of athletes • All use is recorded and effects observed • Medical practitioners will have the athlete's health as the sovereign concern rather than performance or team / coach aims	• Not all athletes will have equal access to qualified medical practitioners • Few medical practitioners currently have a detailed knowledge of performance-enhancing drugs and their consequences • Expense for athletes and teams
7.	Where use occurs, it must be also done with the full knowledge and approval of the appropriate commission, board of directors, or board of management	• Transparency protects athletes, coaches, teams, and medical practitioners but also makes them accountable for their actions	• Sporting teams and brands pretend to be ignorant of substance use or claim no knowledge
8.	All cases of use must be recorded on a public register, which is updated both prior to all major events and league commencement dates, and at the end of the relevant competition	• Public registration makes substance use in sport open and transparent rather than closed and covert	• Brands and authorities must take responsibility for the substance use in their codes and must provide the infrastructure to register use
9.	The use of substances that fall within the above guidelines can only be made available to players and athletes aged 18 years and over. It will be an offence to supply 'minors' with these substances	• Substance use in sport will align with broader social law to protect minors before consenting age • Underground and illegal methods of acquiring substances will become restricted	• Costs for sports and clubs of policing use
10.	There will be no rules, provisions or clauses that cover any illicit drug use that does not improve sporting performance. At the same time, sporting authorities will enact programs to educate athletes and other stakeholders about the impacts of both illicit drugs and legal, recreational substances with an emphasis on the dangers of alcohol and tobacco / nicotine	• Illicit drug use will remain the purview of the mainstream legal system • Sporting authorities will focus more of their efforts on the most dangerous substances in sport: alcohol and tobacco / nicotine	• Suggestions that athletes are superior role models will have to be discarded in favour of a realistic position

competitive edge. Accepting this proposition will enable sport to remove itself from its obsessive desire to eradicate substance use on the assumption that is a cheat's way of getting a competitive advantage, and use its resources to secure participation for the truly disadvantaged and marginalised. This is the great challenge facing a sporting world wherein social value remains subservient to brand value.

A new policy direction

In short, we believe that drug-control policy in sport should be based on the principles of harm reduction and the protection of players' and athletes' rights. In the context of sport, the harm-reduction approach illuminates three major principles. First, drug use is not just a sporting matter, nor is it a criminal or legal matter. Instead, drug use in sport reflects a larger social issue. Second, harm reduction obviates the need for any form of moral certitude. Instead, it accepts that drug use exists in sport and will never be completely eliminated. Third, although harm reduction does not condone the free-for-all use of drugs in sport, it acknowledges that when it does occur policymakers have an obligation to develop public health measures that reduce drug-related harm to all athletes, irrespective of their status or ambitions. We should be less interested in the brand equity of sport and more interested in the health and welfare interests of sport participants.

Unlike current drug-control policies, harm reduction does not impose obstructive policing, incessant testing, onerous investigation, and severe sanctioning. Instead, it focuses on building structures and systems that deliver harm-reduction outcomes including: 1) the creation of a playing environment prioritising safety and effective harm management; 2) a drug supply and distribution system regulated through the direct involvement of physicians and pharmacists; 3) the design of promotional campaigns educating players about the risks associated with drugs including legal but insidious substances like alcohol and nicotine / tobacco; 4) the early intervention of medical support where damage to oneself or to others occurs through substance use; 5) the availability of broad-based drug rehabilitation and counselling services allowing players to remediate their high-risk behaviours; and 6) a transparent listing or register of the drugs used by all sporting bodies and players. In this context, regulation becomes crucial when it lessens the potential harm to sport participants.

Although harm reduction remains controversial in a sporting context since it appears to condone practices that may be illegal and unfair, it acknowledges that drugs will always be part of a risky and tilted playing field full of moral ambiguity. Equally, it allows for a stronger platform of education and social marketing, and the provision of a safe sport environment. The idea that drug use can be driven out of sport with more coercive controls, testing, and suspensions is a misguided myth. In the real world, sport and its participants will be better off when the risks are managed, the potential harms are moderated, and the costs are contained.

Our policy suggestions are well intended but in reality the last decade has witnessed a heavily resourced campaign led by the WADA to eliminate drug use from international sport. While early on the WADA emphasis was on substances that might secure a player or athlete an unfair improvement in performance, the banned list now includes illicit substances, even if they do not improve performance. The casting of a broader net seems, at first glance, to be an attempt to 'muscle in' on the agencies already responsible for controlling illicit drug use around the world. However, the WADA has defended its expanded ambit on the grounds that it not only has responsibility for ensuring a level playing field, but also must protect the health of players and athletes, while simultaneously maintaining the integrity of sport. In the light of the above discussion, which highlights sport's structural and cultural propensity to increase the injury and health-related risks of its participants, any argument that pushes the idea that sport promotes public health by its very nature is flawed.

The next step

Where does that leave us in a public policy and sport policy sense? The first point to note is that while some aspects of sport promote health and injury-free living, many others do the opposite. Moreover, if we took away all the risks associated with many sport practices, we would also take away much of what attracts people to sport, including outdoor adventure, uncertainty, pushing one's body to the limits, and crashing into other bodies. Therefore, in our view, the current policy is destined to fail because it clings to idealised assumptions about what sport can and should do. Rather, the more appropriate and clearly more pragmatic approach is to adopt the principle of harm reduction.

The harm-reduction model presents an essentially utilitarian position, where ethical judgement and moral certitude are replaced by the practicalities of managing harms. The aim is therefore not to eliminate drug use, injury, psychological trauma, burnout, and the like. The aim is not to produce a virtuous sport world of selfless collaboration and relentless confidence building. Under the harm-reduction model the goal is far more circumspect and modest. The harm-reduction model seeks to effectively manage the risks and potential harms associated with engaging in vigorous sporting activities where substances comprise one of many risks.

Harm-reduction policy concedes that high-risk behaviour will always be part of the sport experience, and that various forms of drug use will always form a significant part of players' behaviour. It concedes that some drugs will offer players an advantage over those players who do not use. It is also understood that players can be easily seduced into a heavy pattern of drug use, which can damage both body and mind. At the same time, it seems to us that taking drug use out of the sporting closet and making it as visible as it can be, will not only eliminate a lot of the hypocrisy embedded in contemporary sport, but also provide for better control of the potential harms. The alternative means returning to a model underpinned by a dogmatic but, in the end, naively juvenile belief in the social utility that is supposed to come from preaching, proselytising, shaming, and prosecuting. From the evidence we have assembled, the idea that drug use can be driven out of sport with a just a few more coercive controls, a lot more testing for a lot more drugs, and a few more draconian suspensions is difficult to sustain.

By taking a harm-reduction perspective there is no anguishing over the morality of drug use, there is no need to struggle over who of the main stakeholder groups might be the most offended, it not necessary to work out what type of moral re-education will be required, and there is no requirement to work out the most appropriate bundle of threats, sanctions, punishments, and suspensions. No decision needs to be made about the drug's legality or illegality. And, there is no need to decide the performance impact, and whether or not it actually improves an athlete's ability to run quicker for longer, or lift a heavier weight. The question to be asked here is simple and direct, and certainly less ambiguous: How will the regular use of the drug impact on the athlete's health and well-being? If it can be shown that the risk of illness or loss of health is high, then athletes should be warned off, counselled, or treated by professional health care workers.

In our minds, draconian rules and sanctions will clearly not eliminate the use of drugs, as history has shown. Indeed, they will only send it further underground as players search for more exotic and less detectable options from physicians with sometimes dubious credentials. And, given the complexities that characterise the drugs in sport landscape, it is not surprising that polices designed to punish athletes for taking drugs have not been successful. Little evidence can be found indicating any significant improvement in the health and well-being of players resulting from the current anti-doping policy rules and sanctions.

The essentially moralistic and punitive arrangements that underpin the current arrangement do precious little to secure a level playing field, to balance up competitions, or to protect the health and welfare of players and athletes. A harm-reduction approach may be offensive to those who covet a sense of moral certitude in their sport worlds, but it remains the only policy model enabling players and athletes to manage drug use in all its guises in a safe environment that 1) is free from ill-informed advice and contaminated supply; 2) restricts the possibility of a traumatic invasion of privacy; 3) lessens the threat of severe shame and punishment; and 4) provides a secure way in which to seek professional guidance and support. We advocate for a socially responsible philosophy focusing on the reduction of collateral harm, as well as one that seeks out a sound evidence base.

Final thoughts

The fact of the matter remains that drug use in sport constitutes a very serious problem to most sport policymakers, and for the most part has led to serious sanctions being imposed, even where the drugs do not improve performance. Whereas a general apathy and diffidence existed in the 1960s, the policy stance 50 years on firmly commits to zero tolerance, despite an ideological shift valuing individualism above all else. But, does this black-and-white, no-nonsense, neatly mechanistic, you-have-got-to-be-cruel-to-be-kind approach, provide the best conditions and behavioural frame for players to manage their conduct, and does it generate the best social outcomes for both players and the wider community? At the moment a softer system of regulation simply does not appear on the radar for most policymakers and politicians.

To repeat an earlier question we asked in the context of contemporary society: Is the current arrangement the best policy for a society that values individualism and personal autonomy so dearly? In neo-liberal societies, where regulation is only introduced when the social benefits are incontrovertible, and where the rights and civil liberties of individuals take priority for protection, it is hard to find a place for policies that demand athletes to sign whereabouts forms, submit to testing at any time of day or night, and be given no space for inadvertent use. Neither is there a place for a policy that changes its mind about the efficacy of some drugs in securing athletes an improvement in performance, with caffeine being a prime example. A drug-use policy that has so many therapeutic exemptions, and provides so many loopholes for taking substances that can improve performance at the margin, is not worth supporting either. A complete overhaul of sport's drug-use policies should occur, starting with a critical review of the values and beliefs that underpin the mission, vision, and operational goals of the WADA and the IOC. As drugs have been part of the sport scene for the last 50 years and will remain an integral part of sport practice, the only sensible policy seeks to protect athletes above all else, allowing them to participate with the least risk to themselves and others.

In our new world of harm reduction and human rights, the medical centre, the pharmacy, and alternative medicine clinics take on added responsibilities. But this makes more sense than leaving the distribution of exotic drugs to the street, the nightclub, or the Internet black market. In a hyper-modern world where morality has become site specific, ethical debates have degenerated into pompous political exercises, and social norms shift more quickly than Saharan sand dunes, a transparent harm-reduction policy supported by a human rights agenda makes more sense than the existing model.

Players and athletes will always venture beyond their natural limits to secure fame, glory, and a massive pay cheque. Any edge that a substance can deliver them will become an attractive proposition. In these instances ambition pushes ethics to the side, and when combined with new technology, better training, and superior technique, the opportunities for going beyond one's potentials are too seductive. Under these conditions it would be unrealistic to expect athletes to loosen their expectations and aim for second best. In a world that values individual achievement and breaking barriers so highly, the idea that elite players and athletes will settle for mediocrity seems unimaginable. In other words, by demanding so much from players, and by creating such a highly competitive environment for athletes, sport authorities have created a sport performance monster that can no longer be properly controlled. Not only is the current array of punitive codes ineffective, they are also a waste of scarce resources. In the final analysis, drug-control policies are only successful in so far as they reduce harm at either the individual or community level, and protect the rights of participants, in addition to ensuring sport's ongoing sustainability.

Despite inciting a lot of controversy, our harm-reduction-based recommendations on drug control in elite sport also highlight many contradictions and unintended consequences in the current, zero-tolerance approach to eradicating drugs and the cheats that go with it. As a result, we not only support a harm-reduction model, but we also argue that it is inevitable because, just like the failed war on drugs in the broader society, the 'war' on drugs in sport can never be won, no matter how punitive or well-resourced the current drug-control programs become. In our minds, the idea that drugs can be eliminated from any level of sport remains a myth, and, like many myths, relies on an idealised notion of what is desirable rather than on a rational belief of what is doable. The time for a 'new deal' for sport has arrived. We need to abandon the moral high ground in favour of the pragmatic middle space where regulation is softer, the risk of social harms are minimised, and the opportunities for delivering excellence are expanded. What could be better than that?

References

AAP (2007) Drug test lawyers, urges QC, ONLINE. Available HTTP www.theage.com.au/news/national/drug-test-lawyers 16 May (accessed 2 April 2008).

Aghion, P., & Williamson, J. (1999) *Growth, Inequality and Globalization: Theory, History and Policy*, Cambridge: Cambridge University Press.

Aitken, C., Delalande, C. & Stanton, K. (2002) Pumping iron, risking infection? Exposure to hepatitis C, hepatitis B and HIV among anabolic-androgenic steroid injectors in Victoria, Australia, *Drug and Alcohol Dependency*, 65, 303–308.

Akerjordet, K. & Severinsson, E. (2007) Emotional intelligence: A review of the literature with specific focus on empirical and epistemological perspectives, *Journal of Clinical Nursing*, 16, 1405–1416.

Alaranta, A., Alaranta, H., Holmila, J., Palmu, P., Pietilä, K. & Helenius, I. (2006) Self-reported attitudes of elite athletes towards doping: Differences between type of sport, *International Journal of Sports Medicine*, 27, 842–846.

Alasuutari, P. (2000) Globalization and the nation-state: An appraisal of the discussion, *Acta Sociologica*, 43 (3), 259–269.

Alderson, A. & Nielsen, F. (2002) Globalization and the great U-turn: Income inequality trends in 16 OECD countries, *American Journal of Sociology*, 107 (5), 1244–1299.

Alexandris, K., Tsorbatzoudis, C. & Grouios, G. (2002) Perceived constraints on recreational sport participation: Investigating their relationship with intrinsic motivation, extrinsic motivation and amotivation, *Journal of Leisure Research*, 34, 233–252.

Althaus, Bridgman & Davis, D. (2007) *The Australian Policy Handbook*, 4th edition, Crows Nest: Allen & Unwin.

Amin, A. (2002) Spatialities of globalisation, *Environment and Planning*, 34 (3), 385–399.

Amos, A. (2007) Inadvertent doping and the WADA Code, *Bond Law Review*, 19 (1), 1–19.

Anderson, P. (2006) Global use of alcohol, drugs and tobacco, *Drug and Alcohol Review*, 25, 489–502.

Anderson, R. (2004a) *Report to the Australian Sports Commission and to Cycling Australia of an Investigation into Doping Allegations within the Australian Institute of Sport (AIS) Track Sprint Cycling Program*, Canberra: Australian Government.

Anderson, R. (2004b) *Addendum to Report to the Australian Sports Commission and to Cycling Australia*, Canberra: Australian Government.

Anderson, R. (2004c) *Second Stage Report to the Australian Sports Commission and to Cycling Australia*, Canberra: Australian Government.

Anshel, M. (1991) A survey of elite athletes on the perceived causes of using banned drugs in sport, *Journal of Sport Behaviour*, 14 (4), 283–308.

Archibugi, D. (2000) Inequality, globalization, and world politics. *Journal of Peace Research*, 37(6), 754–764.

Armstrong, L. (2000) *Every Second Counts*, New York: Broadway Books.

Armstrong, L. (2000) *It's Not about the Bike: My Journey Back to Life*, Sydney: Allen & Unwin.

Armstrong, P., Glyn, A & Harrison, J. (1984) *Capitalism since World War II: The Making and Breakup of the Great Boom*, London: Fontana.

Assael, S. (2007) *Steroid Nation*, New York: ESPN Publishing.

Australian Broadcasting Commission (ABC) (1997) What's your poison... caffeine consumption? ONLINE. Available HTTP www.abc.net.au/quantum/poison/caffeine/caffeine.htm 3 April (accessed 2 March 2013).

Australian Crime Commission (ACC) (2013) *Organised Crime and Drugs in Sport: New Generation Performance and Image Enhancement Drugs and Organised Criminal Involvement in Their Use in Professional Sport*, Canberra: Commonwealth of Australia.

Australian Football League (AFL) (2005a): The AFL and WADA: room for compromise, Press release, 8 July.

Australian Football League (AFL) (2005b) *Annual Report 2004*, Melbourne: AFL.

Australian Football League (AFL) (2005c) *Standard Playing Contract*, Melbourne: AFL.

Australian Football League (AFL) (1998) *Annual Report 1997*, Melbourne: AFL.

Australian Institute of Health and Welfare (AIHW) (2008) *2007 National Drug Strategy Household Survey: First Results – Drug Statistics Series 20*, Canberra: AIHW.

Australian Institute of Health and Welfare (AIHW) (2000) *Physical Activity Patterns of Australian Adults*, Canberra: AIHW.

Australian Sports Commission. (ASC) (2005) *Annual Report 2004*, Canberra: Australian Government.

Azjen, I. (1991) The theory of planned behaviour, *Organizational Behavior and Human Decision Processes*, 50, 179–211.

Azjen, I. & Fishbein, M. (1980) *Understanding Attitudes and Predicting Social Behavior*, Englewood Cliffs, NJ: Prentice-Hall.

Babor, T., Caulkins, J., Edwards, G., Fischer, B., Foxcroft, D., Humphries, K., Obot, I., Rehm, J., Reuter, P., Room, R., Rossow, I. & Strang, J. (2010) *Drug Policy and the Public Good*, Oxford: Oxford University Press.

Bachman, J., Wallace, J., O'Malley, P., Johnstone, L., Kurth, C. & Neighbors, K. (1991) Racial/ethnic differences in smoking, drinking and illicit drug use among American high school seniors, *American Journal of Public Health*, 81 (3), 372–377.

Backhouse, S., McKenna, J. & Patterson, L. (2007) *Prevention through Education: A Review of Current International Social Science Literature – A Focus on the Prevention of Bullying, Tobacco, Alcohol, and Social Drugs Use in Children, Adolescents and Young Adults*, World Anti-Doping Agency/Carnegie Research Institute, Leeds University.

Backhouse, S., McKenna, J., Robinson, S., & Atkin, A. (2007) *Attitudes, Behaviours, Knowledge and Education – Drugs in Sport: Past, Present and Future*, Montreal: World Anti-Doping Agency.

Baer, H., Singer, M. & Susser, I. (2003) *Medical Anthropology and the World System*, Westport, CT: Praeger.

Bagaric, M. (2007) It's footy, stupid, *Herald Sun*, 7 May, 21.

Bahr, R. & Tjørnhom, M. (1998) Prevalence of doping in sports: doping control in Norway, 1977-1995, *Clinical Journal of Sport Medicine*, 8 (1), 32–37.

Bailey, L., Gache, J. & Picciano, M. (2011) Dietary supplement use in the United States, *The Journal of Nutrition*, 141, 261–266.

Bairner, A. (2003) Globalization and sport: The nation strikes back, *Phi Kappa Phi Forum*, 83 (4), 34–37.

Bakalar, J. & Grinspoon, L. (1984) *Drug Control in a Free Society*, Cambridge: Cambridge University Press.

Baldwin, R., Cave, M. & Lodge, M. (2012) *Understanding Regulation: Theory, Strategy and Practice*, 2nd edition, Oxford: Oxford University Press.

Balyi, I. (2001) Sport system building and long-term athlete development in British Columbia, *Coaches Report*, 8 (1), 22–28.

Balyi, I. & Hamilton, A. (2000) Key to success: Long-term athlete development, *Sport Coach*, 10, 10–23.

Barkoulis, V., Lazuris, L., Tsorbatzoudis, H. & Rodafinos, A. (2011) Motivational and sportsperson profiles of elite athletes in relation to doping behaviour, *Psychology of Sport and Exercise*, 12 (2), 205–212.

Baum, D. 1996. *Smoke and Mirrors: The War on Drugs and the Politics of Failure*. Boston: Little Brown and Co.

Baylis, A., Cameron-Smith, D. & Burke, L. 2001. Inadvertent doping through supplement use by athletes. *International Journal of Sport Nutrition & Exercise*, 11, 365–383

BBC (1998) De Bruin banned, BBC News, ONLINE. Available HTTP (http://news.bbc.co.uk/2/hi/ sport/146638.stm (accessed 26 January 2008).

Beaud, M. (1984) *A History of Capitalism 1500 -1980,* London: Macmillan Press.

Belk, R. (1996) Hyperreality and globalization: Culture in the age of Ronald McDonald, *Journal of International Consumer Marketing*, 8 (3), 23–37.

Belk, R. (1988) Possessions and the extended self, *Journal of Consumer Research*, 15, 139–160.

Benavie, A. (2009) *Drugs: America's Holy War,* New York: Routledge.

Berry, D. (2008) The science of doping. *Nature*, 454, 692–693.

Bessant, J., Watts, R., Dalton, T. & Smyth, P. (2006) *Talking Policy: How Social Policy is Made*, Crows Nest: Allen & Unwin.

Bhatta, S. D. (2002) Has the increase in world-wide openness to trade worsened global income inequality? *Papers in Regional Science*, 81 (2), 177–196.

Bird, E. & Wagner, G. (1997) Sport as a common property resource: A solution to the dilemmas of doping. *Journal of Conflict Resolution*, 41 (6), 749–767.

Bloodworth, A. & McNamee, M. (2010) Clean Olympians: Doping and anti-doping: The views of talented young British Athletes, *International Journal of Drug Policy*, 21 (3), 276–282.

Bloom, P., Hogan, J. & Blazing, J. (1997) Sports promotion and teen smoking and drinking, *American Journal of Health Behaviour*, 21, 100–109.

Bloomfield, J. (2003) *Australia's Sporting Success: The Inside Story*, Sydney: UNSW Press.

Bojsen-Moller, A. & Christiansen, A. (2010) Use of performance and image enhancing substances among recreational athletes: A quantitative analysis of inquiries submitted to the Danish anti-doping authorities, *Scandinavian Journal of Medicine and Science in Sports*, 20, 861–867.

Booth, D. & C. Tatz, (2000) *One-eyed: A View of Australian Sport*, St. Leonards: Allen & Unwin.

Bostrom, M. & Sandberg, A. (2009) Cognitive enhancement: Methods, ethics, regulatory challenges, *Science & Engineering Ethics*, 15, 311–341.

Bourdieu, P. (1993) *The Fields of Cultural Production: Essays in Arts and Literature*, Cambridge: Polity Press.

Bourdieu, P. (1993) *Sociology in Question*, London: Sage

Bourdieu, P. (1986) The forms of capital, in J. Richardson (ed.) *Handbook of Theory and Research for the Sociology of Education*, New York: Greenwood Press, 241–258.

Bourdieu, P. (1985) The genesis of the concepts of habitus and field, *Sociocriticism*, 2 (2) 11–24.

Bourdieu, P. (1984) *Distinction: A Social Critique of the Judgement of Taste*, London: Kegan Paul/Routledge.

Bourdieu, P. (1977) *Outline of a Theory of Practice*, Cambridge: Cambridge University Press.

Bourdieu, P. & Wacquant, L. (1992) *Responses*, Paris: Seuil.

Bourdieu, P. & Passeron, J. C. (1977/1990) *Reproduction in Education, Society and Culture,* London: Sage.

Boyes, S. (2000) The International Olympic Committee, trans-national doping policy and globalisation, in J. O'Leary (ed.) *Drugs and Doping in Sport: Socio-legal Perspectives*, London: Cavendish Publishing, 167–169.

Boyum, D. & Reuter, P. (2005) *An Analytic Assessment of U.S. Drug Policy,* Washington, DC: The AEI Press.

Braithwaite, J. (2008) *Regulatory Capitalism: How It Works, Ideas for Making It Work Better*, Cheltenham: Edward Elgar.

Braithwaite, J. & Drahos, P. (2000) *Global Business Regulation*, Cambridge: Cambridge University Press.

Brandis, G. (2007a) Increased funding for Australian Sports Anti-Doping Authority investigations. Media release, 8 May, Australian Government.

Brandis, G. (2007b) Illicit drugs in sport policy. Media release, 6 October, Australian Government.

Brandis, G. & Pyne, C. (2007) *Illicit Drugs in Sport Policy*, Canberra: Australian Government.

Bredemeier, B., Shields, D., Weiss, M. & Cooper, B. (1986) The relationship of sport involvement with children's moral reasoning and aggression tendencies, *International Journal of Sport Psychology*, 8, 304–318.

Breivik, G., Hanstad, D. & Loland, S. (2009) Attitudes toward use of performance-enhancing substances and body modification techniques. A comparison between elite athletes and the general population, *Sport in Society*, 12 (6), 737–754.

Brissonneau, C. (2010a) Doping in France – 1960-2000: American and Eastern Block influences, *Journal of Physical Education and Sport*, 27 (2), 33–39.

Brissonneau, C. (2010b) The genesis and effect of French anti-doping policies in cycling, *International Journal of Sport Policy*, 2 (2), 173–187.

Brissonneau, C. (2008) *Doping in Professional Sport*, Brussels: Directorate General Internal Policies of the European Union, Policy Department Structural and Cohesion Policies, Culture and Education, European Union.

Brissonneau, C. (2006) Deviant careers: The case of cycling, In *Ethics and Social Science Research in Anti-Doping*, WADA Conference, Larnaca, Cyprus, 13–14.

British Medical Association (BMA) (2002) Policy instruments to prevent the use of drugs in sport, in *Drugs in Sport: The Pressure to Perform*, London: British Medical Association.

Brohm, J.-M. (1978) *Sport: A Prison of Measured Time*, London: Ink Links.

Brown, A. (2007) Rasmussen out of Tour de France, *The Age*, 26 July, 22.

Bryant, H. (2005) *Juicing the Game: Drugs, Power, and the Fight for the Soul of Major League Baseball*, New York: Penguin/Viking.

Burke, K. (2007) Thorpe in move to clear dope suspicions, *The Age*, 17 August, 15.

Burke, P. & Stets, J. (2009) *Identity Theory*, Oxford: Oxford University Press.

Burstyn, V. (1999) *The Rites of Men: Manhood, Politics, and the Culture of Sport*, Toronto, Canada: University of Toronto Press.

Buti, A. & Fridman, S. (2001) *Drugs, Sport and the Law*, Mudgeeraba: Scribblers Publishing.

Buxens, A. *et al.* (2011) Can we predict top level sports performance in power vs endurance events? A genetic approach, *Scandinavian Journal of Medicine & Science in Sports*, 21 (4), 570–579.

Caldwell, L., Baldwin, C., Walls, T. & Smith, E. (2004) Preliminary effects of a leisure education program to promote healthy use of free time amongst middle school adolescents, *Journal of Leisure Research*, 36 (3), 310–333.

Campos, D., Yonamine, M. & de Moraes-Moreau, R. (2003) Marijuana as doping in sports, *Sports Medicine*, 33 (6), 395–399.

Canadian Broadcasting Corporation (CBC) (2003) Ten drug scandals. *CBC Sports Online*, 23 January.

Canadian Centre for Ethics in Sport (2005) *2004-05 Annual Report*, Ottawa: CCES.

Carless, D. & Douglas, K. (2009) We haven't got a seat on the bus for you, or, all the seats are mine: Narratives and career transitions in sport, *Qualitative Research in Sport and Exercise*, 1 (1), 51–56.

Carlyon, P. (2005) Drugs in football, *The Bulletin*, 18 May, 12–16.

Carroll, W. (2005) *The Juice: The Real Story of Baseball's Drug Problems*, Chicago, IL: Ivan R. Dee.

Cashman, R. (1995) *Paradise of Sport: The Rise of Organised Sport in Australia*, Melbourne: Oxford University Press.

Catley, B. (2005) *The Triumph of Liberalism in Australia*, Sydney: Macleay Press.

Catley, B. (1999) Global nation: Australia and the politics of globalisation, *Australian Journal of Political Science*, 34 (2), 283–284.

Caulkins, J. P. & Reuter, P. (2005) Re-defining the goals of National Drug Policy: Recommendation from a working group, *American Journal of Public Health*, 85 (8), 1059–1063.

Caulkins, J., Reuter, P., Iguchi, M. & Chiesa, J. (2005) *How Goes the War on Drugs: An Assessment of US Drug Problems and Policies*, Santa Monica, CA: Rand Corporation.

Cepeda, G. & Martin, D. (2005) A review of case studies publishing in *Management Decision* 2003–2004, *Management Decision*, 43 (6), 851–876.

Cerny, P. G. (1999) Globalization and the erosion of democracy, *European Journal of Political Research*, 36 (1), 1–26.

Chou, K. & Chi'en, M. N. (1997) Utility theory and adolescent drug abusers in Hong Kong, *Child and Adolescent Social Work Journal*, 14 (6), 397–412.

Christensen, M. & Sorensen, J. (2009) Sport or school? Dreams and dilemmas for talented young Danish footballers, *European Physical Education Review*, 15 (1), 115–133.

Cialdini, R., Petty, R. & Cacioppo, J. (1981) Attitude and attitude change, *Annual Review of Psychology*, (32), 357–404.

Cialdini, R. B. (2001) *Influence: Science and Practice*, 4th edition, New York: Harper-Collins.

Clarke, A. (2005) *Situational Analysis: Grounded Theory after the Postmodern Turn*, Thousand Oaks, CA: Sage.

Clarke, S. (2001) Drug charges rock Australian swimming, ONLINE. Available HTTP www.abc.net.au/lateline broadcast 10 April (accessed 5 April 2007).

Claros, E. & Sharma, M. (2010) The relationship between emotional intelligence and abuse of alcohol, marijuana and tobacco among college students, *Journal of Alcohol and Drug Education*, 56 (1), 8–37.

Coakley J. & Donnelly P. (1999) *Inside Sports*, London: Routledge

Conrad, P. (2007) *The Medicalization of Society: On the Transformation of Human Conditions into Treatable Disorders*, Baltimore, MD: The Johns Hopkins University Press.

Conrad, P. & Schneider, J. (1992) *Deviance and Medicalization: From Badness to Sickness*, Philadelphia, PA: Temple University Press.

Cooper, C. (2012) *Run, Swim, Throw, Cheat: The Science Behind Drugs in Sport*, Oxford: Oxford University Press.

Courtwright, D. (2001) *Forces of Habit: Drugs and the Making of the Modern World*, Cambridge, MA: Harvard University Press.

Coveney, C., Gabe, J. & Williams, S. (2011) The sociology of cognitive enhancement: Medicalization and beyond, *Health Sociology Review*, 20 (4), 381–393.

Coyle, D. (2005) *Lance Armstrong: Tour de Force*, London: Harper Collins.

Cricket Australia (2003) *Anti-Doping Policy*, Melbourne: Cricket Australia.

Cutler, M. 2012. Armstrong reputation in ruins. *Sport Business*. Available HTTP www. sportbusiness.com/news/186454/armstrong (accessed 2 August 2013)

Dawson, R. T. (2001) Drugs in sport – the role of the physician, *Journal of Endocrinology*, *170* (1), 55–61.

Deci, E. & Ryan, R. (1985) *Intrinsic Motivation and Self-determination in Human Behavior*, New York: Plenum Press.

Deci, E. L. & Ryan, R. M. (2000) The 'what' and 'why' of goal pursuits: Human needs and the self-determination of behavior, *Psychological Inquiry*, 11 (4), 227–268.

Del Coso, J., Muñoz, G. & Muñoz-Guerra, J. (2011) Prevalence of caffeine use in elite athletes following its removal from the World Anti-Doping Agency list of banned substances, *Applied Physiology Nutrition Metabolism*, 36 (4), 555–561.

Denham, G. (2007) AFL changes illicit drugs policy, *The Age*, 8 January, 31.

Denham, G. (2005) AFL bows to federal anti-dope pressure, [The] *Australian*, 20 July, 28.

Devine, M.A. & Parr, M. (2008) Come on in, but not too far: Social capital in an inclusive leisure setting, *Leisure Sciences*, 30, 391–408.

Dicken, P. (2003) *Global Shift: Reshaping the Global Economic Map in the 21st Century*, London: Sage.

Dimeo, P. (2007) *Beyond Good and Evil: A History of Drug Use in Sport*, Abingdon: Routledge.

Dobson, S. & Goddard, S. (2001) *The Economics of Football*, Cambridge: Cambridge University Press.

Dodge, T., Litt, D., Seitchik, A. & Bennett, S. (2008) Drive for muscularity and beliefs about legal performance enhancing substances as predictors of current use and willingness to use, *Journal of Health Psychology*, 13 (8), 1173–1179.

Donati, S. (2007) World traffic in doping substances, ONLINE. Available HTTP www.wada-ama.org.-ama.org/rtecontent/document/Donati_Report_Trafficking_2007-03_06.pdf (accessed 5 March 2008).

Donovan, R. J., Egger, G., Kapernick, V. & Mendoza, J. (2002) A conceptual framework for achieving performance enhancing drug compliance in sport, *Sports Medicine*, 32 (4), 269–284.

Dormandy, T. (2012) *Opium: Reality's Dark Dream*, London: Yale University Press.

Drugs and Crime Prevention Committee, Parliament of Victoria. (2000) *Harm Minimisation: Principles and Policy Frameworks (Occasional Paper No. 1)*, Melbourne: Parliament of Victoria.

Duff, C., Scealy, M. & Rowland, B. (2004) *The Culture and Context of Alcohol Use in Community Sporting Clubs in Australia: Research into 'Attitudes' and 'Behaviour'*, Melbourne: Centre for Drug Studies, Australian Drug Foundation.

Dunn, M., Thomas, J., Swift, W., Burns, L. & Mattick, R. (2010) Drug testing in sport: The attitudes and experiences of elite athletes, *International Journal of Drug Policy*, 21 (4), 330–332.

Dunn, M., Mazanov, J. & Sitharthan, A (2009) Predicting future anabolic-androgenic steroid use intentions with current substance use: Findings from an internet-based survey, *Clinical Journal of Sports Medicine*, 19 (3), 222–227.

Dunning, E. & Waddington, I. (2003) Sport as a drug and drugs in sport: Some exploratory comments, *International Review for the Sociology of Sport*, 38 (3), 351–368.

DuPont, R. (2010) Prescription drug abuse: An epidemic dilemma, *Journal of Psychoactive Drugs*, 42 (92), 127–132.

Durlauf, S. (2000) Growth, inequality, and globalization: Theory, history, and policy, *Journal of Economic Literature*, 38 (3), 637–638.

Eagly, A. E. & Chaiken, S. (1993) *The Psychology of Attitudes*, London: HBJ.

Edwards, M. (2001) *Social Policy, Public Policy: From Problem to Practice*, Crows Nest: Allen & Unwin.

Eichengreen, B. (2000) Taming capital flows, *World Development*, 28 (6), 1105–1116.

Eitle, D., McNulty, J. & Eitle, T. (2003) The deterrence hypothesis re-examined: Sports participation and substance abuse among young adults, *Journal of Drug Issues*, Winter edition, 193–222.

Elder, G. (1994) Time, human agency, and social change: Perspectives on the life course, *Social Psychology Quarterly*, 57 (1), 4–15.

Eldredge, D. (2000) *Ending the War on Drugs: A Solution for America*, New York: Bridge Works Publishing.

Elliott, J. (2006) *Using Narrative in Social Research: Qualitative and Quantitative Approaches*, London: Sage.

Erill, S. (2000) The doping of fairness, *The Lancet*, 356, 1122.

Escohotado, A. (1999) *A Brief History of Drugs*, Rochester, VT: Park Street Press.

Evans, P. (1997) The eclipse of the state? Reflections on stateness in an era of globalization, *World Politics*, 50 (1), 62–68.

Evans-Brown, M., McVeigh, J., Perkins, C. & Bellis, M. (2012) *Human Enhancement Drugs: The Emerging Challenges to Public Health*, Liverpool: JMU – Centre for Public Health.

Fainaru-Wada, M. & Williams, L. (2006) *Game of Shadow: Barry Bonds, BALCO, and the Steroid Scandal that Rocked Professional Sport*, New York: Penguin / Gotham.

Fazio, R. H. & Williams, C. J. (1986) Attitude accessibility as a moderator of the attitude-perception and attitude-behavior relations: An investigation of the 1984 presidential election, *Journal of Personality and Social Psychology*, 51, 503–514.

Featherstone, M. (1991) *Consumer Culture and Postmodernism*, London: Sage.

Ferguson, J. (2006) *More than Sunshine and Vegemite – Success the Australian Way*, Sydney: Halstead Press.

Fife-Yeomans, J. & Cazzulino, M. (2007) Sorry Ben, the party is over, [The] *Daily Telegraph*, 17 October, 1, 4.

Finnis, M. (2005) AFL and WADA – your questions answered, Website of the AFL Players' Association, ONLINE. Available HTTP www.aflpa.com.au/index.cfm?id=D0E34044-CBED-E222-264E9F39BA893C29. 30 September (accessed 25 October 2007).

Floyd, D. (2008) The changing dynamics of the global pharmaceutical industry, *Management Services*, Spring, 14–18.

Ford, J. (2007) Substance use among college athletes: A comparison based on sport/team affiliation, *Journal of American College Health*, 5 (6), 367–373.

Foster, G., Greyser, S. & Walsh, B. (2006) *The Business of Sports: Texts & Cases on Strategy & Management*, Mason, OH: Thomson – South Western.

Frederick-Recascino, C. M. & Schuster-Smith, H. (2003) Competition and intrinsic motivation in physical activity: A comparison of two groups, *Journal of Sport Behaviour*, 26 (3), 240–254.

Freiberg. A. (2010) *The Tools of Regulation*, Sydney: Federation Press.

Gallen, G. (2004) Witch hunting in the 21st century part 2, Cycling News. ONLINE. Available HTTP www.cyclingnews.com/features, 4 August (accessed 31 January 2005).

Gandhi, A., Murphy-Graham, E., Petrosino, A., Chrismer, S. and Weiss, C. (2007) The devil is in the detail: Examining the evidence for 'proven' school-based drug abuse prevention programs, *Evaluation Review*, 31 (1), 43–74.

Gems, G. (1999) Sports, war, and ideological imperialism, *Peace Review*, 11 (4), 573–578.

Gerrard, B. (1999) Team sports as a free-market commodity, *New Political Economy*, 4 (2), 273–278.

Gersbach, H. (2002) Does and how does globalisation matter at the industry level? *World Economy*, 25 (2), 209–229.

Gewirth, A. (1982) *Human Rights: Essays on Justification and Applications*, Chicago, IL: University of Chicago Press

Gewirth, A. (1978) *Reason and Morality*, Chicago, IL: University of Chicago Press.

Giles, D. (2006) Constructing identities in cyberspace: The case of eating disorders, *British Journal of Social Psychology*, 45 (3), 463–477.

Gindin, S. (2002) Social justice and globalization: Are they compatible? *Monthly Review: An Independent Socialist Magazine*, 54 (2), 1–11.

Goldacre, B. (2012) *Bad Pharma: How Drug Companies Mislead Doctors and Harm Patients*, London: Fourth Estate.

Goldmann, K. (2002) Internationalisation and the nation-state: Four issues and three non-issues, *European Journal of Political Research*, 41 (3), 281–305.

Good Sports (2007) Managing Alcohol in Sport, ONLINE. Available HTTP www.goodsports.com.au/ 30 September (accessed 3 April 2008).

Graham, J., Marks, G. & Hansen, W. (1991) Social influence processes affecting adolescent substance use, *Journal of Applied Psychology*, 76 (2), 291–298.

Graham, M. *et al.* (2008) Anabolic steroid use: Patterns of use and detection of doping, *Sports Medicine*, 36 (6), 506–526.

Grant, R. (2000) The economic geography of global trade, in T. Sheppard. (ed.) *A Companion to Economic Geography*, Oxford: Blackwell.

Gray, J. (2001) *Why Our Drug Laws have Failed and What We Can Do about It*, Philadelphia, PA: Temple University Press.

Green, M. & Houlihan, B. (2005) *Elite Sport Development: Policy Learning and Political Priorities*, London: Routledge.

Gregory, P. and Chong, J. (2006) AFL defends drug-test names case win, *The Age*, August 30, 26.

Gucciardi, D., Jalleh, G. & Donovan, R. (2011) An examination of the 'sport drug control model' with elite Australian athletes, *Journal of Science and Medicine in Sport*, 14 (4), 469–476.

Gucciardi, D., Jalleh, G. & Donovan, R. (2010) Does social desirability influence the relationship between doping attitudes and doping susceptibility in athletes? *Psychology of Sport and Exercise*, 11 (4), 479–486.

Guess, G. & Farnham, P. (2000) *Cases in Public Policy Analysis*, Washington DC: Georgetown University Press.

Guillen, M. (2001) Is globalization civilizing, destructive or feeble? A critique of five key debates in the social science literature, *Annual Review of Sociology*, 27, 235–260.

Haakonsson, S. (2009) The changing governance structures of the global pharmaceutical industry, *Competition and Change*, 13 (1), 75–95.

Hackworth, J. (2003) Globalizing cities: A new spatial order? *Annals of the Association of American Geographers*, 93 (3), 759–761.

Haden, M. (2004) Regulation of illegal drugs: An exploration of public health tools, *International Journal of Drug Policy*, 15 (2), 225–230.

Hall, S. (2011) The neo-liberal revolution, *Cultural Studies*, 26 (6), 706–728.

Hamermesh, D. & Biddle, J (1994) Beauty and the labor market, *American Economic Review*, 84 (5), 174–194.

Hamilton, T. & Coyle, D. (2012) *The Secret Race: Inside the Hidden World of the Tour De France: Doping, Cover Ups, and Winning At All Cost*, London: Transworld Publishers.

Hansen, W. (1997) A social ecology theory of alcohol and drug use prevention among college and university students, in Higher Education Center for Alcohol and Other Drug Prevention (ed.) *Designing Alcohol and Other Drug Prevention Programs in Higher Education: Bringing Theory into Practice*, Newton, MA: US Department of Education, 155–176.

Hanson, G. R., Venturelli, P. J. & Fleckenstein, A. E. (2012) *Drugs and Society*, 12th edition, Boston, MA: Jones and Bertlett Publishers.

Hanstad, D. (2009) Sport, health, and drugs: A critical re-examination of some key issues and problems, *Perspectives in Public Health*, 129 (4), 174–182.

Hanstad, D., Smith, A. & Waddington, I. (2008) The establishment of the World Anti-Doping Agency: A study of the management of organizational change and unplanned outcomes, *International Review for the Sociology of Sport*, 43 (4), 227–249.

Harris, B. (2006) Rugby slams door on bad influence sailor, [The] *Weekend Australian*, 22 –23July, 3.

Hart, C. & Ksir, C. (2011) *Drugs, Society and Human Behaviour*, 14th Edition, New York: McGraw Hill.

Haviland, W., Prins, H., Walrath, D. & McBride, B. (2008) *Cultural Anthropology: The Human Challenge*, Belmont, CA, Wadsworth.

Headley, S. (2004) Background notes on obesity and sport in young Australians, *Youth Studies Australia*, 23 (1), 42–46.

Healey, K. & Ralph, J. (2007) AFL joins drugs shame cover-up, *Herald-Sun*, 31 August, 38.

Henne, K. (2010) WADA, the promises of law and the landscapes of anti-doping regulation, *Political and Legal Anthropology Review*, 33 (92), 306–325.

Henry, P. (2004) Hope, hopelessness and coping: A framework for class-distinctive cognitive capital, *Psychology and Marketing*, 21 (5) 375–403.

Heywood, A.(2003) *Political Ideologies* 3rd edition. New York: Palgrave Macmillan.

Hibbens, G. (2008) Men of purpose, in James Weston (ed.) *The Australian Game of Football since 1858*, Melbourne: Geoff Slattery Publishing, 31–40.

Hildebrand, K., Johnson, D. & Bogle, K. (2001) Comparisons of patterns of alcohol use between high school and college athletes and non-athletes, *College Studies Journal*, 45 (6), 358–365.

Hoberman, J. (2001) How drug testing fails: The politics of doping control, in W. Wilson and E. Derse (eds.) *Doping in Elite Sport*, Champaign: Human Kinetics, 221–242.

Hoberman, J. (1992) *Mortal Engines: The Science of Performance and the Dehumanisation of Sport*, New York: The Free Press.

Hoch, P. (1972) *Rip off the Big Game: The Exploitation of Sports by the Power Elite*, New York: Anchor Books.

Hogan, K. & Norton, K. (2000) The 'price' of Olympic gold, *Journal of Science and Medicine in Sport*, 3 (2), 203–218.

Horvath, P. (2006) Anti-doping and human rights in sport: The case of the AFL and the WADA code, *Monash University Law Review*, 32 (2), 358–359.

Houlihan, B. (2003) *Dying to Win: Doping in Sport and the Development of Anti-doping Policy*, 2nd edition, Strasbourg: Council of Europe Publishing.

Houlihan, B. (1999) Anti-doping policy in sport: The politics of international policy co-ordination, *Public Administration*, 77 (2), 311–334.

House of Representatives Standing Committee on Family and Human Services (2007) *The Winnable War on Drugs: The Impact of Illicit Drug Use on Families*, Canberra: Australian Government.

Howman, D. (2012) Current limitations in analytical strategies. *Bioanalysis*, 4 (13), 1535–1536.

Hser, Y., Longshore, D. & Anglin, M. (2007) The life course perspective on drug use: A conceptual framework for understanding drug use trajectories, *Evaluation Review*, 31 (6), 515–547.

Hughes, G. (2006) Keeping footy's secrets, gotcha with Gary Hughes blog, [The] *Australian*, ONLINE. Available HTTP www.blogs.theaustralian.news.com.au/garyhughes/index.php/theaustralian/comments/ keeping_footys_secrets/ 5 September (accessed 2 June 2008).

Hunt, E (2008) Cycling Mark French in legal win, *Herald Sun* ONLINE. Available HTTP www.news.com.au/heraldsun/story, 1 December (accessed 31 January, 2009).

Hunt, N. (2004) Public health or human rights: What comes first, *International Journal of Drug Policy*, 15 (2), 231–237.

Hunt, T. (2011) *Drug Games: The International Olympic Committee and the Politics of Doping*, Austin, TX: University of Texas Press.

Hunt, T. (2007) Sports, drugs and the Cold War: The conundrum of Olympic doping policy 1970-1979, *Olympika: The International Journal of Olympic Studies* International Centre for Olympic Studies, London: Canada: 19–41.

Ingram, S. (2004) Buff Enough? *Current Science*, 90 (2), 4–5.

Innes, M. (2003) *Understanding Social Control: Deviance, Crime and Social Order*, Maidenhead UK: Open University Press.

James, C. (1963) *Beyond a Boundary.* London: Hutchinson.

Jan, N., Marclay, F., Schmutz, N., Smith, M., Lacoste, A., Castella, V. & Mangin, P. (2011) Use of forensic investigations in anti-doping, *Forensic Science International*, 10 (213), 1–3.

Jarvie, G. & Maguire, J. (1994) *Sport and Leisure in Social Thought*, London: Routledge.

Jay, M. (2010) *High Society: Mind-altering Drugs in History and Culture*, London: Thames and Hudson.

Jefferey, N. (2004) Careering to catastrophe, [The] *Australian* 23 June, 27.

Jeffrey, N. & Parnell, S. (2008) Testing must be smarter: Fahey, [The] *Australian*, 14 March, 18.

Jiggens, J. (2005) *The Cost of Drug Prohibition in Australia.* Paper presented at the Social Change in the 21st Century Conference, Centre for Social Change Research: Queensland University of Technology.

Johnson, M., Jay, S. B. & Rickert, V. (1989) Anabolic steroid use by male adolescents, *Pediatrics*, 83 (6), 921–924.

Kay, J. & Laberge, S. (2002) Mapping the field of 'AR': Adventure racing and Bourdieu's concept of field, *Sociology of Sport Journal*, 19, 25–46.

Kayser, B. & Smith, A. (2008) Globalisation of anti-doping: The reverse side of the model, *British Medical Journal*, 337, 85–87.

Kayser, B., Mauron, A. & Miah, A. (2007) Current anti-doping policy: A critical appraisal, *BMC Medical Ethics*, 8 (2), 1–10.

Kell, P. 2000.*Good Sports: Australian Sport and the Myth of the Fair Go*. Sydney: Pluto Press.

Kelly, J. (2000) *Tough on Drugs in Sport: Report Card*, Canberra: Commonwealth Government Department of Industry, Science and Resources.

Kemp, R. (2005a) New body to take up the fight against drugs in sport. Media release, 23 June, Canberra: Australian Government.

Kemp, R. (2005b) AFL to become WADA Compliant. Media release, 4 August, Canberra: Australian Government.

Kemp. R. (2006) New Sport Anti-Doping Body Enhances Australia's Reputation. Media release, 6 March, Canberra: Australian Government.

Keresztes, N. *et al.* (2008) Social influences in sports activity among adolescents, *Journal of the Royal Society for the Promotion of Health*, 128 (1), 21–25.

Kettl, D. (2000) The transformation of governance: Globalization, devolution, and the role of government, *Public Administration Review*, 60 (6), 488–497.

King, D. (2007) Drugs helped Sly 'do Rambo', [The] *Australian*, 16 May, 3.

Knight, J. & Mears, R. (2007) Testing for drugs of abuse in children and adolescents: addendum – testing in schools and at home, *Pediatrics*, 119, 627–630.

Kogoy, P. (2004) All part of the vicious cycle, [The] *Australian*, 21 June, 17.

Koornneef, E. (2010*) Measuring the Effects of Regulation on the Quality of Health Services: Developing a Conceptual Framework for Evaluation*, ECPR Third Biennial Conference: Regulation in the age of crisis, UCD, Dublin, 19 June 2010.

Kramer, P. (1993) *Listening to Prozac*, New York: Penguin Books.

Lalor, P. (2003) Drinking for Australia, [The] *Weekend Australian Magazine*, 20–21 December, 16–20.

Lambros, L., Barkoulis, V., Rodafinios, A. & Tzorbatzoudis, H. (2011) Predictors of doping intentions in elite level athletes: A social cognition approach, *Journal of Sport and Exercise Psychology*, 32 (4), 694–710.

Laure, P. & Binsinger, C. (2005) Adolescent athletes and the demand and supply of drugs to improve performance, *Journal of Sports Science Medicine*, 4, 272–277.

Lenskyi, H. (2003) *Out on the Field: Gender, Sport and Sexualities*. Toronto: Women's Press.

Lentillon-Kaestner, V. & Ohl, F. (2011) Can we accurately measure the prevalence of doping? *Scandinavian Journal of Medicine and Science in Sport*, 21, 132–142.

Lentillon-Kaestner, V. & Carstairs, C. (2010) Doping among young elite cyclists: A qualitative psychosocial approach, *Scandinavian Journal of Medicine and Science in Sport*, 20, 336–345.

Leonard, R. & Burns, A. (2006) Turning points in the lives of midlife and older women: Five year follow up, *Australian Psychologist*, 41 (1), 28–36.

Leone, L., Perugini, M. & Ercolani, A. (1999) A comparison of three models of attitude-behavior relationships in the studying behavior domain, *European Journal of Social Psychology*, 29 (2–3), 161–189.

Le Page, M. (2006) Does drug testing tell the whole story? *New Scientist*, 191 (2563), 8.

Levins, R. & Lopez, C. (1999) Toward an ecosocial view of health, *International Journal of Health Services*, 29 (2), 261–293.

Li, M., Hofacre, S. & Mahony, D. (2001) *Economics of Sport*, Morgantown, WV: Fitness Information Technology.

Lines, G. (2001) Villains, fools or heroes? Sports stars as role models for young people, *Leisure Studies*, 20 (4), 285–303.

Linnell, S. (1998) League vows swift action on drug offences. *The Age*, 5 March, 18.

Lipovetsky, G. (2005) *Hypermodern Times*. Cambridge: Polity Press.

Lippi, G., Sanchis-Gomar, F. & Banfi, G. (2012) Anti-'negative-doping' testing: A new perspective in anti-doping research? *European Journal of Applied Physiology*, 112, 2383–2384.

Loland, S. (2002) *Fair Play in Sport*, London: Routledge.

Long, J. & Sanderson, I. (2001) The social benefits of sport: Where is the proof? In C. Gratton and I Henry, (eds.), *Sport in the City: The Role of Sport in Economic and Social Regeneration*, London: Routledge, 185–203.

Lundby, C., Achman-Andersen, N., Thomsen, J., Norgaard, A. & Robach, P. (2008) Testing for recombinant human erythropoietin in urine: Problems associated with current anti-doping testing, *Journal of Applied Physiology*, 21 (4) 121–135.

Macintosh, A. (2006) *Domestic Drug Markets and Prohibition*, Canberra: Australian Parliamentary Group for Drug Law Reform, Parliament House.

Magnay, J. (2007) Thorpe set to be cleared, *The Age*, 6 April, 1.

Maldonado-Molina, M. & Lanza, S. (2010) A framework to examine gateway relations in drug use: An application of latent transition analysis, *Journal of Drug Issues*, 40 (4), 902–924.

Mandle, J. (2002) *Globalization and the Poor*, Cambridge: Cambridge University Press.

Marcy, W. (2010) *The Politics of Cocaine: How U.S. Foreign Policy Has Created a Thriving Drug Industry in Central and South America*, Chicago, IL: Lawrence Hill Books.

Marshall, A. (1920) *Principles of Economics*, 8th edition, London: Macmillan.

Marsiglia, F., Kulis, S. & Hecht, M. (2001) Ethnic labels and ethnic identity as predictors of drug use amongst middle school students in the southwest, *Journal of Research on Adolescents*, 11 (1), 21–48.

Mason, M. & Scammon, D. (2011) Unintended consequences of health supplement information regulations: The importance of recognising consumer motivations, *The Journal of Consumer Affairs*, 45 (2), 201–223.

Masters, R. (2007) How Demetriou left the AFL with egg on its face and an apology to make, *Sydney Morning Herald*, 24 February, 24.

Matilla, V., Rimplea, A., Jormanainen, V., Sahi, T. & Pihlajamaki, H. (2010) Anabolic-androgenic steroid use among young Finnish males, *Scandinavian Journal of Medicine and Science in Sports*, 20, 330–335.

Mazanov, J. (2009) Towards a social science of drugs in sport, *Sport in Society*, 12 (3), 423–430.

McAsey, J. (2007) Footy codes not trying on drugs, [The] *Weekend Australian*, 4–5 August 2007, 51.

McCabe, S., Morales, M., Cranford, J., Delva, J., McPherson, M. & Boyd, C. (2007) Race/ethnicity and gender differences in drug use and abuse among college students, *Journal of Ethnicity in Substance Abuse*, 6 (2), 75–95.

McCanna, S. 2007. It's easy for soldiers to score heroin in Afghanistan. *Salon*, 7 (August), 3–7.

McElrath, K. & McEvoy, K. (2002). Negative experiences on Ecstasy: The role of drug, set and setting. *Journal of Psychoactive Drugs*, 34, 199–208.

McKay, L. (1991) *No Pain, No Gain? Sport and Australian Culture*, Sydney: Prentice Hall Australia.

McKenzie, C. (2007) The use of criminal justice mechanisms to combat doping in sport, Bond University Sports Law eJournal, Gold Coast: Bond University.

McKinnon, M. (2003) Warne drug test was no accident, [The] *Weekend Australian*, 19–20 July, 3.

McVeigh, J., Beynon, C. & Bellis, M. A. (2003) New challenges for agency based syringe exchange schemes: Analysis of 11 years of data (1991-2001) in Merseyside and Cheshire, United Kingdom, *International Journal of Drug Policy*, 14 (6), 135–154.

Mears, A. & Finlay, W. (2005) Not just a paper doll: How models manage bodily capital and why they perform emotional labor, *Journal of Contemporary Ethnography*, 34 (3), 317–343.

Melia, P., Pipe, A. & Greenberg, L. (1996) The use of anabolic-androgenic steroids by Canadian students, *Clinical Journal of Sport Medicine*, 6, 9–14.

Miah, A. (2006) Rethinking enhancement in sport. *Annals of the New York Academy of Sciences*, 1093, 301–320.

Mignon, P. (2003a) The Tour de France and the doping issue, *International Journal of the History of Sport*, 2 (2), 227–245.

Mignon, P. (2003b) The Tour de France and the doping issue, in H. Dauncey and G. Hare, *The Tour de France 1903-2003*, London: Frank Cass, 234–235.

Miles, M. & Huberman, M. (1994) *Qualitative Data Analysis*, Thousand Oaks, CA: Sage.

Millar, A. P. (2005) Gold medals for ineptitude and unfairness: Drugs, sport and the Olympics future, *The Doping Journal*, 2 (1), ONLINE. Available HTTP http://dopingjournal.org/content/2002/2001/ (accessed 2 August 2005).

Miller, B. (2005) *Cultural Anthropology*, 3rd edition, Boston, MA: Pearson.

Miller, D. (1992) *Olympic Revolution*, London: Pavilion Books.

Miller, T., Lawrence, G., McKay, J. & Rowe, D. (1999) Modifying the sign: Sport and globalization, *Social Text*, 17 (3), 15–33.

Miller-Day, M. & Barnett, J. (2004) 'I'm not a druggie': Adolescents' ethnicity and (erroneous) beliefs about drug use norms, *Health Communications*, 16 (2), 207–228.

Milton-Smith, J. (2002) Business ethics in Australia and New Zealand, *Journal of Business Ethics*, 35 (2), 131–142.

Ministerial Council on Drug Strategy (2004) *The National Drug Strategy: Australia's Integrated Framework 2004-2009*, Canberra: Commonwealth of Australia.

Mittal, B. (2006) I, me, and mine – how products become consumer's extended selves, *Journal of Consumer Behaviour*, 5, 550–562.

Mobius, M. & Rosenblatt, T. (2006) Why beauty matters, *The American Economic Review*, 96 (1), 222–235.

Moore, J. W. (2001) Globalization in historical perspective, *Science & Society*, 65 (3), 386–397.

Moore, O. 2012. After years of unbridled bravado, Armstrong waves the white flag. *The Globe and Mail*, 24 August. Available HTTP www.theglobeandmail.com.news/national (accessed 2 August 2013).

Morris, L., Sallybanks, J., Willis, K. & Makkai, T. (2004) Sport, physical activity and antisocial behaviour in youth, *Youth Studies Australia*, 23 (1), 47–52.

Morris, L., Sallybanks, J., Willis, K., & Makkai, T. (2003) Sport, physical activity and anti-social behaviour in youth, *Trends and Issues in Crime and Criminal Justice*, 249, 1–6.

Mosher, J. F. & Yanagisako, K. L. (1991) Public health, not social warfare: A public health approach to illegal drug policy, *Journal of Public Health Policy*, 12 (3), 278–323.

Moston, S., Skinner, J. & Engelberg, T. (2012) Perceived incidence of drug use in Australian sport: A survey of public opinion, *Sport in Society*, 15 (1), 64–72.

Mottram, D. (ed.) (2011a) *Drugs in Sport*, 5th edition, London: Routledge.

Mottram, D. (2011b) The extent of doping in sport, in D. Mottram (ed.), *Drugs in Sport*, 5th edition, London: Routledge, 373–385.

Mottram, D. (2003) Prevalence of drug misuse in sport, in David Mottram (ed.) *Drugs in Sport*, 3rd edition, London: Routledge, 356–378.

Mugford, S., Mugford, J. & Donnelly, D. (1999) *Social research Project: Athletes' Motivations for Using or Not Using Performance Enhancing Drugs*, Canberra: Australian Sports Drug Agency.

Murnane, J. (2007) A message from AFLPA President, ONLINE. Available HTTP www.aflpa.com.au/index.cfm?id=960E5215-9148-7BD4-6426CBB634F3514C. (accessed 5 October 2008).

Murray, T. (2008) Doping in sport: Challenges for medicine, science and ethics, *Journal of Internal Medicine*, 264, 95–98.

National Public Health Partnership (NPHP) (2002) *Getting Australia Active: Towards Better Practice for the Promotion of Physical Activity*, Melbourne, Australia: National Public Health Partnership.

Nguyen, K. (2006) Are AFL players a protected species? *The Age*, 31 August, 29.

Noonan, G. (2008) Schools drug test dismissed, *Sydney Morning Herald*, 26 March, 11.

Nutley, S. & Webb, J. (2000) Evidence and the policy process, in H. Davies, S. Nutley and P. Smith (eds.) *What Works? Evidence-based Policy and Practice in Public Services*, Bristol: Polity Press.

O'Connell, V. & Albergotti, D. 2011. Second cyclist accuses Armstrong. *The Wall Street Journal*, 20 May, 7.

O'Malley, P. & Johnstone, I. (2001) Epidemiology of alcohol and other drug use among American college students, *Journal of Studies in Alcohol*, 14, 23–39.

Orbach, S. (2010) *Bodies*, London: Profile Books.

Pampel, F. (2007) *Drugs and Sport*, New York: Infobase Publishing.

Parisotto, R. (2006) *Blood Sports: The Inside Dope on Drugs in Sport*, South Yarra: Hardie Grant Books.

Park, J. K. (2005) Governing doped bodies: The World Anti-Doping Agency and the global culture of surveillance, *Cultural Studies: Critical Methodologies*, 5 (2), 174–188.

Parkinson, A. & Evans, N. (2006) Anabolic androgenic steroids: A survey of 500 users, *Medicine and Science in Sports and Exercise*, 38 (4), 644–651.

Parsons, W. (1995) *Public Policy: An Introduction to the Theory and Practice of Policy Analysis*, Cheltenham: Edward Edgar.

Pawson, R. (2006) *Evidence-based Policy: A Realist Perspective*, London: Sage.

Payne, W., Reynolds, M., Brown, S. & Fleming, A. (2003) *Sport Role Models and Their Impact on Participation in Physical Activity: A Literature Review*, Melbourne: VicHealth.

Pearson, B. & Hansen, B. (1990) Survey of US Olympians, *USA Today*, 5 February, 5.

Pearson, R. & Petipas, A. (1990) Transitions of athletes: Developmental and preventive perspectives, *Journal of Counselling and Development*, 69, 7–10.

Peck, J. & Yeung, H. (2003) *Remaking the Global Economy*, London: Sage.

Peck, S., Vida, M. & Eccles, S. (2008) Adolescent pathways to adulthood drinking: Sport activity involvement is not necessarily risky or protective, *Addiction*, 103 (supplement 1), 69–83.

Pelletier, L., Fortier, M., Vallerand, R., Tuson, K, Brière, N. & Blais, M. (1995) Toward a new measure of intrinsic motivation, extrinsic motivation and amotivation in sports: The sport motivation scale, *Journal of Sport and Exercise Psychology*, 17 (1), 35–47.

Peretti-Watel, P., Guagloardp, V., Verger, P. & Pruvost, J. (2003) Sporting activity and drug use: Alcohol, cigarette and cannabis use among elite student athletes, *Addiction*, 98, 1249–1256.

Peretti-Watel, P., Beck, F. & Legleye, S. (2002) Beyond the u-curve: The relationship between sport and alcohol, cigarette and cannabis use in adolescents, *Addiction*, 97 (6), 707–716.

Petrocelli, M., Oberweis, T. & Petrocelli, J. (2008) Getting huge, getting ripped: A qualitative exploration of recreational steroid use, *The Journal of Drug Issues*, 38(4), 1187–1199.

Petróczi, A. (2007) Attitudes and doping: A structural equation analysis of the relationship between athletes' attitudes, sport orientation and doping behaviour, *Substance Abuse Treatment, Prevention, and Policy*, 2 (34), 1–15.

Petróczi, A. & Aidman, E. (2008) Psychological drivers in doping: The life-cycle model of performance enhancement, *Substance Abuse Treatment, Prevention, and Policy*, 3 (7), 3–12.

Pitsch, W. & Emrich, E. (2011) The frequency of doping in elite sport: Results of a replication study, *International Review for the Sociology of Sport*, 47 (5), 559–580.

Pope, H., Kanayama, G., Ionescu-Pioggia, M. & Hudson, J. I. (2004) Anabolic steroid users' attitudes towards physicians. *Addiction*, 99, 1189–1194.

Pound, R. (2006) *Inside Dope: How Drugs Are the Biggest Threat to Sports, Why You Should Care, and What Can Be Done about Them*, Mississauga: Wiley.

President's Council on Physical Fitness and Sports (U.S.) (1997) Physical activity and sport in the lives of girls and boys: physical and mental health dimensions from an interdisciplinary approach. Washington: University of Minnesota/Center for Mental Health Services, Substance Abuse and Mental Health Services Administration, U.S. Department of Health and Human Services.

Procon (2011) Doping cases at the Olympics, ONLINE. Available HTTP www. sportsanddrugs.procon.org/view.resource.php?resourceID=004420 (accessed 24 October 2011)

Puthucheary, Z. *et al.* (2011) Genetic influences in sport and physical performance, *Sports Medicine*, 41 (10), 845–850.

Rapp, G. (2009) Blue sky steroids, *The Journal of Criminal Law and Criminology*, 99 (3), 599–618.

Rasmussen, K. (2005) The quest for the imaginary evil: A critique of anti-doping, *Sport in Society*, 25 (3), 514–515.

Rasmussen, N. (2008) *On Speed: The Many Lives of Amphetamines*, New York: New York University Press.

Read, B. (2007) The Teflon god of Newcastle, [The] *Weekend Australian*, 1–2 September, 47, 50.

Reinert, A., Rohrmann, S., Becker, N. & Linseisen, J. (2007) Lifestyle and diet in people using dietary supplements, *European Journal of Nutrition*, 46 (3), 165–173.

Reiterer, W. (2000) *Positive: An Australian Olympian Reveals the Inside Story of Drugs and Sport*, Sydney: Macmillan.

Richard, A., Bell, D. & Carlson, J. (2000) Individual religiosity, moral community, and drug user treatment, *Journal for the Scientific Study of Religion*, 39(2),240–246.

Rigauer, B. (1981) *Sport and Work,* New York: Columbia University Press.

Ritchie, D. & Mascord, D. (2007) League hero admits to years of drug use, *Herald Sun*, 31 August, 5.

Robinson, M. (2002) Pot shots Lewis targeted after blowing whistle, *Herald Sun*, 7 March, 42.

Robinson, M. & Scherlen, R. (2007) *Lies, Damned Lies, and Drug War Statistics: A Critical Analysis of Claims Made by the Office of National Drug Control Policy*, Albany, NY: State University of New York Press.

Rolles, S., Murkin, G., Powell, M., Kushlick, D. & Slater, J. (2012) *The Alternative World Drug Report: Counting the Costs on the War on Drugs*, London: Count the Costs.

Rushall, B. & Jones, M. (2007) Drugs in sport: A cure worse than the disease? *International Journal of Sport Science and Coaching*, 2 (4), 335–361.

Sachs, J. (2011) *The Price of Civilisation: Economics and Ethics After The Fall*, London: The Bodley Head / Random House.

Sanderson, I. (2002) Evaluation, policy learning and evidenced-based policy making, *Public Administration*, 80 (1), 1–22.

Sari, I. (2010) Anabolic androgenic steroids and dependence, *Journal of Physical Education and Sport*, 29 (4), 68–74.

Savulescu, J., Foddy, B. & Clayton, M. (2004) Why we should allow performance enhancing drugs in sport, *British Journal of Sports Medicine*, 38, 666–670.

Schein, E. (2004) *Organisational Culture and Leadership*, San Francisco, CA: Jossey-Bass.

Schlossberg, N. (1981) A model for analysing human adaptation to transition, *The Counseling Psychologist*, 9 (2), 2–18.

Selby, R., Weinstein, H. & Bird, T. (1990) The health of university athletes: Attitudes, behaviors and stressors, *Journal of American College Health*, 39 (1), 11–18.

Senn, A. (1999) *Power, Politics and the Olympic Games*, Windsor: Human Kinetics.

Shamir, R. (2008) The age of responsibilisation: On market embedded morality, *Economy and Society*, 37 (1) 1–19.

Shilbury, D. & Deane, J. (2001) *Sport Management in Australia: An Organisational Overview*, Deakin University, Victoria: Strategic Sport Management.

Shilling, C. (2003) *The Body and Social Theory*, 2nd edition, London: Sage.

Shirato, T. (2007) *Understanding Sports Culture*, London: Sage.

Sigleman, C. & Rider, E. (2009) *Life-span Human Development 6th edition*, Belmont, CA: Wadsworth.

Silkstone, D. (2007) Drug claim rocks AFL, ONLINE. Available HTTP www.real footy.com.au/news, 25 August (accessed 2 March 2008).

Simon, P., Striegel, H., Aust, F., Dietz, K. & Ulrich, R. (2006) Doping in fitness sports: Estimated number of unreported cases and individual probability of doping, *Addiction*, 101, 1640–1644.

Skolnik, H. & Chernus, A. (2010) *Nutrient Timing for Peak Performance*, Champaign, IL: Human Kinetics.

Slater, D. (1997) *Consumer Culture and Modernity*, Oxford: Polity Press.

Slot, O. (2011) Contador cleared of dope charge: WADA may beef up case, [The] *Australian*, 5 November, 32.

Sluggett, B. (2011) Sport's doping game: Surveillance in a biotech age, *Sociology of Sport Journal*, 28 (4), 387–403.

Smith, A. & Stewart, B. (1999) *Sports Management: A Guide to Professional Practice*. Sydney: Allen & Unwin.

Smith, A. & Stewart, B. (2008) Drug policy in sport: Hidden assumptions and inherent contradictions, *Drug and Alcohol Review*, 27, 123–129.

Smith, A. & Shilbury, D. (2004) Mapping cultural dimensions in Australian sporting organisations, *Sport Management Review*, 7 (2), 133–165.

Smith, A. & Waddington, I. (2004) Using 'sport in the community schemes' to tackle crime and drug use among young people: Some policy issues and problems, *European Physical Education Review*, 10 (3), 279–298.

Smith, A. & Stewart, B. (1995) Sporting club cultures: An exploratory case study, *Australian Leisure*, December, 31–37.

Smith, A., Stewart, B., Oliver-Bennetts, S., McDonald, S., Ingerson, L., Anderson, A., Dickson, G., Emery, P. & Graetz, F. (2010) Contextual influences and athlete attitudes to drugs in sport, *Sport Management Review*, 13 (3), 181–197.

Smith, C., Wilson, N. & Parnell, W. (2005) Dietary supplements: Characteristics of supplement users in New Zealand, *Nutrition and Dietetics*, 62 (4), 123–129.

Smith, P. (2007) Pair to face court over stolen AFL medical records, [Hobart] *Mercury*, 31 October, 18.

Smith, P. (2007) Code bleeding on paper cuts, [The] *Australian*, 8 August, 20.

Son, J., Yarnal, C. & Kerstetter, D. (2010) Engendering social capital through a leisure club for middle aged and older women: Implications for individual and community health and well-being, *Leisure Studies*, 29 (1), 67–83.

Spence, J. & Gauvin, L. (1996) Drug and alcohol use by Canadian university athletes: A national survey, *Journal of Drug Education*, 26 (3), 275–287.

Sport and Recreation New Zealand (SRNZ) (2002) *Push Play Facts II*, Wellington, New Zealand: Sport and Recreation New Zealand.

SSCERA (Senate Standing Committee on Environment, Recreation and the Arts) (1989) *Drugs in Sport: Interim Report*, Canberra: Australian Government Publishing Service.

Stafford, A. (2007) Tougher drugs tests for sport stars, *The Age*, 4 September, 1.

Stallwitz, A. & Shewan, D. (2004). A qualitative exploration of the impact of cultural and social factors on heroin use, *International Journal of Drug Policy*, 18, 464–474

Stamm, H., Lamprecht, M., Kamber, M., Marti, B. & Mahler, N. (2008) The public perception of doping in sport in Switzerland, 1995-2004, *Journal of Sport Sciences*, 26 (3), 235–242.

Starr, M. E. (1984) The Marlboro Man: Cigarette smoking and masculinity in America, *The Journal of Popular Culture*, 17 (4), 45–57.

Stevens, A. (2011) Drug policy, harm and human rights: A rationalist approach, *International Journal of Drug Policy*, 22, 233–288.

Stevenson, J. (2005) Mark French cleared, ONLINE. Available HTTP www.cyclingnews. com/news, 12 July, 9 (accessed 19 September 2005).

Stewart, B. (2007) Drug use in Australian sport: A brief history, *Sporting Traditions: Journal of the Australian Society for Sports History*, 24 (2), 20–33.

Stewart, B. (2007) The political economy of football: Framing the analysis, in B. Stewart (ed.) *The Games are Not the Same: The Political Economy of Football in Australia*, Carlton: Melbourne University Press, 23–42.

Stewart, B. & Smith, A. (2011) The role of ideology in shaping drug-use policies in Australian sport, *International Review for the Sociology of Sport*, 45 187–198.

Stewart, B. & Smith, A. (2010) Player and athlete attitudes to drugs in Australian sport: Implications for policy development, *International Journal of Sport Policy*, 2 (1), 65–84.

Stewart, B., Dickson, G. & Smith, A. (2008) Drug use in the Australian Football League: A critical survey, *Sporting Traditions: Journal of the Australian Society for Sports History*, 25 (1), 57–74.

Stewart, B., Nicholson, M., Smith, A. & Westerbeek, H. (2004) *Better by Design? The Evolution of Australian Sport Policy*, London: Routledge.

Stewart, J., Hedge, D. & Lester, J. (2008) *Public Policy: An Evolutionary Approach*, Boston, MA: Thomson Wadsworth.

Stiglitz, J. (2002) *Globalization and Its Discontents*. New York: W.W. Norton.

Stilger, V. & Yesalis, C.1997. Anabolic-androgenic steroid use among high school football players. *Journal of Drug Education*, 27(2), 121–145.

Stoddart, B. (1986) *Saturday Afternoon Fever: Sport in Australian Culture*, Sydney: Angus and Robertson.

Stokols, D. (1996) Translating social ecological theory into guidelines for community health promotion, *American Journal of Health Promotion*, 10 (4), 282–293.

Storper, M. (2003) Territories, flows, and hierarchies in the global economy, in T. Barnes *et al.* (eds.) *Reading Economic Geography*, Oxford: Blackwell.

Strean, W. & Holt, N. (2001) Coaches', athletes' and parents' perceptions of fun in youth sports: Assumptions about learning and implications for practice, *Avante*, 63, 1–14.

Strelan, P. & Boeckmann, R. J. (2006) Why drug testing in elite sport does not work: Perceptual deterrence theory and the role of personal moral beliefs, *Journal of Applied Social Psychology*, 36 (12), 2909–2934.

Strelan, P. & Boeckmann, R. (2003) A new model for understanding performance-enhancing drug use by elite athletes, *Journal of Applied Sport Psychology*, 15, 176–183.

Striegel, H., Ulrich, R. & Simon, P. (2010) Randomised response estimates for doping and illicit drug use in elite athletes, *Drug and Alcohol Dependence*, 106, 230–232.

Striegel, H., Simon, P., Frisch, S., Roecker, K., Dietz, K., Dickhuth, H. & Ulrich, R. (2006) Anabolic ergogenic substance use in fitness-sport: A distinct group supported by the health care system, *Drug and Alcohol Dependence*, 81, 11–19.

Substance Abuse and Mental Health Services Administration (SAMHSA) (2008) *Results from the 2007 National Survey on Drug Use and Health (NSDUH)*, Washington, DC: Department of Health and Human Services Office of Applied Studies.

Tanner, S., Miller, D. & Alongi, C. 1995. Anabolic steroid use by adolescents: prevalence, motives, and knowledge of risks. *Clinical Journal of Sport Medicine*, 5 (2), 113–157.

Taylor, P. (1984) *The Smoke Ring: Tobacco, Money and Multinational Politics*, London: Sphere Books.

Taylor, W. (1991) *Macho Medicine: A History of the Anabolic Steroid Epidemic*, London: McFarland.

The Age (2007) AFL needs to focus on fixing drugs policy, *Editorial*, 16 May, 7.

Thombs, D. & Hamilton, M. (2002) Effects of a social norm feedback campaign on the drinking norms and behaviours of Division I student-athletes, *Journal of Drug Education*, 32, 227–244.

Thompson, C. (2006) *The Tour de France: A Cultural History*, Berkeley, CA: University of California Press.

Thompson, C. (2003) The Tour in the inter-war years: Political ideology, athletic excess and industrial modernity, in H. Dauncy & G. Hare (eds.) *The Tour de France 1903-2003: A Century of Sporting Structures, Meanings and Values*, London: Frank Cass.

Todd, J. & Todd, T. (2001) Significant events in the history of drug testing and the Olympic movement 1960-1999, in W. Wilson and E. Derse (eds.) *Doping in Elite Sport: The Politics of Drugs in the Olympic Movement*, Champaign, IL: Human Kinetics, 63–128.

Tomazin, F. & Smith, B. (2008) Pocket money link to drug use, *The Age*, 26 March, 4.

Tone, A. (2009) *The Age of Anxiety: A History of America's Turbulent Affair with Tranquilizers*, New York: Basic Books.

Tucker, R. & Collins, M. (2012) What makes champions: A review of the relative contributions of genes and training to sporting success, *British Journal of Sports Medicine*, 43 (4), 555–561.

Turner, M. and McCrory, P. (2003) Social drug policies for sport: Athletes who test positive to social drugs should be managed differently from those who test positive for performance enhancing drugs, *British Journal of Sports Medicine*, 37, 378–379.

UK Sport (2005) *Drug-Free Sport Survey*, London: UK Sport.

Ungerleider, S. (2001) *Faust's Gold: Inside the East German Doping Machine*, London: Thomas Dunne Books / St. Martin's Press.

United Nations Office for Drug Control (UNODC) (2012) *World Drug Report 2012*, New York: United Nations Publications.

United States Anti-Doping Agency (USADA) (2012) *Report on the Proceedings Under the World Anti-Doping Code and the USADA Protocol: United States Anti-Doping Agency (claimant) v. Lance Armstrong (respondent)*, Colorado Springs, CO: USADA.

Uvacsek, M., Nepusz, T., Naughton, D., Mazanov, J., Ranky, M. & Petroczi, A. (2009) Self-admitted behaviour and perceived use of performance-enhancing vs psychoactive drugs amongst competitive athletes, *Scandinavian Journal of Medicine and Science in Sport*, 16, 111–131.

van Bottenburg, M. (2003) Thrown for a loss? (American) football and the European sport space, *The American Behavioral Scientist*, 46 (11), 1550–1562.

Verduci, T. 2002. Caminiti comes clean. *Sports Illustrated*, 28 May, 5–13.

Verroken, M. (2003) Drug use and abuse in sport, in D. Mottram (ed.) *Drugs in Sport*, 3rd edition, London: Routledge, 29–39.

Vescio, J., Wilde, K. & Crosswhite, J. (2005) Profiling sport role models to enhance initiative for adolescent girls in physical education and sport, *European Physical Education Review*, 11 (2), 153–170.

Voet, W. (2001) *Breaking the Chain: Drugs and Cycling – the True Story*, London: Yellow Jersey Press.

Vogel, D. (2010) The private regulation of global corporate conduct: Achievements and limitations, *Business and Society*, 49 (1), 68–87.

Voy, R. (1991) *Drugs, Sport and Politics*, Champaign, IL: Leisure Press.

Waddington, I. (2005) Changing patterns of drug use in British sport from the 1960s, *Sport in History*, 25 (3), 472–496.

Waddington, I. (2001) *Doping in Sport: Some Issues for Medical Practitioners*. Paper presented at the Leiden International Medical Students Congress, University of Leiden Medical School, The Netherlands

Waddington, I. (2000a) *Doping in Sport: Problems of Involvement and Detachment*. Paper presented at the Centre d'Etudes Olympiques, International Olympic Committee, Lausanne, Switzerland.

Waddington, I. (2000b) *Sport, Health and Drugs: A Critical Sociological Perspective*, London: E & FN Spon.

Waddington, I. & Smith, A. (2008) *An Introduction to Drugs in Sport; Addicted to Winning*, Oxford: Routledge.

Waddington, I., Malcom, D., Roderick, M. & Naik, R. (2005) Drug use in English professional football, *British Journal of Sports Medicine*, 39, 1–19.

Walby, S. (2003) The myth of the nation-state: Theorising society and politics in a global era, *Sociology*, 37 (3), 529–546.

Walsh, C. (2007a) Cousin's sorry future, [The] *Weekend Australian*, 5–7 May, 2007, 51.

Walsh, C. (2007b) Police bungle won't save Cousins, [The] *Australian*, 14 November, 2007, 20.

Walsh, D. (2007c) *From Lance to Landis: Inside the American Doping Controversy at the Tour de France*. New York: Ballantine Books.

Warburton, D., Nicol, C. & Bredin, S. (2006) Health benefits of physical activity: The evidence, *Canadian Medical Association Journal*, 174 (6), 801–809.

Washington, R., Bernhardt, D., Gomez, J. & Johnson, M. (2005) Use of performance-enhancing substances, *Pediatrics*, 115 (4), 1103–1106.

Weber, M. (1976) *The Protestant Ethic and the Spirit of Capitalism* (UK edition), London: Allen & Unwin.

Wechsler, H., Davenport, A., Dowdell, G., Grossman, S. & Zanakos, S. (1997) Binge drinking, tobacco and illegal drug use and involvement in athletics: A survey of students at 140 American colleges, *Journal of American College Health*, 21 (4), 195–200.

Wenner, L. (1998) *MediaSport*, New York: Routledge.

Went, R. (2001) Globalization: Towards a trans-national state? A sceptical note, *Science & Society*, 65 (4), 484–491.

Wesley, J. (2003) Exotic dancing and the negotiation of identity: The multiple uses of body technologies, *Journal of Contemporary Ethnography*, 32 (6), 643–669.

West, P. (1996) *Boys, Sport and Schooling: An Australian Perspective*. Proceedings of Schools and Education Conference, University of Cambridge, Cambridge.

Westerbeek, H. & Smith, A. (2003) *Sport Business in the Global Marketplace*, London: Palgrave MacMillan.

Weyzig. A. (2004) *Sector Profile of the Pharmaceutical Industry*, Amsterdam: Somo Consulting Group.

Whannel, G. (1992) *Fields in Vision: Television Sport and Cultural Transformation*, London: Routledge.

White, S., Duda, J. & Keller, M. (1998) The relationship between goal orientation and perceived purposes of sport among youth sport participants, *Journal of Sport Behavior*, 21 (4), 474–484.

Whitehead, A. (2005) Man to man violence: How masculinity may work as a dynamic risk factor, *The Howard Journal*, 44 (4), 411–422.

Wichstrom, T. & Wichstrom, L. (2009) Does sport participation during adolescence prevent later alcohol, tobacco and cannabis use? *Addiction*, 104, 138–149.

Wiefferink, C., Detmar, S., Coumans, B., Vogels, T. & Paulussen, T (2008) Social psychological determinants of the use of performance-enhancing drugs by gym users, *Health Education Research*, 23 (1), 70–80.

Wilson, G., Pritchard, M. & Shaffer, J. (2004) Athletic status and drinking behaviour in colleges students: The influence of gender and coping styles, *Journal of American College Health*, 52 (3), 269–273.

Wilson, N. (1990) *The Sports Business: The Men and the money*, London: Mandarin.

Wiseman, J. (2007) Hard-line drugs policy to stay. [The]*Weekend Australian*, 1 December, 23–25.

World Anti-Doping Agency (WADA) (2012a) *The World Anti-Doping Code: The 2013 Prohibited List – International Standard*, Montreal: WADA.

World Anti-Doping Agency (WADA) (2012b) *Annual Report for 2011*, Montreal: WADA.

World Anti-Doping Agency (WADA) (2011a) The 2011 prohibited list. World Anti-Doping Code, ONLINE. Available HTTP www.wada-ama.org/ (accessed 24 February 2013).

World Anti-Doping Agency (WADA) (2011b) *Strategic Plan 2011-2016*, Montreal: WADA.

World Anti-Doping Agency (WADA) (2009) *Strategic Plan 2004-2009*, Montreal: WADA.

World Anti-Doping Agency (WADA) (2008) Program statistics, ONLINE. Available HTTP www.wada-ama.org/en/dynamic.ch2pageCategory.id=328 (accessed 4 June 2009).

World Anti-Doping Agency (WADA) (2006) *The World Anti-Doping Code: The 2006 Prohibited List International Standard*, Montreal: WADA.

World Anti-Doping Agency (WADA) (2005) *2004 Annual Report*, Montreal: WADA.

World Anti-Doping Agency (WADA) (2004a) *2003 Annual Report: The Year of the Code*, Montreal: WADA.

World Anti-Doping Agency (WADA) (2004b) *Strategic Plan: 2004-2009*, Montreal: WADA.

World Anti-Doping Agency (WADA) (2004c) *The World Anti-Doping Code: The 2004 Prohibited List International Standard*, Montreal: WADA

World Anti-Doping Agency (WADA) (2003) *World Anti-Doping Code*, Montreal: WADA

World Health Organization (WHO) (2011) *The Global Status Report on Alcohol and Health*, Geneva: WHO Press.

World Health Organization (WHO) (2009) *WHO Report on the Global Tobacco Epidemic*, Geneva: WHO Press.

World Health Organization (WHO) (2003) *Health and Development through Physical Activity and Sport*, Geneva: World Health Organization.

Wright, G. (2005) Sickness in the veins of sport, *The Age*, 25 October, 17–18.

Wright, G. (1999) Sport & globalisation, *New Political Economy*, 4 (2), 267–281.

Yergin, D. & Stanislaw, J. (1998) *The Commanding Heights: The Battle for the World Economy*, New York: Simon & Schuster.

Yesalis, C., Kopstein, A. & Bahrke, M. (2001) Difficulties in estimating the prevalence of drug use among athletes, in W. Wilson and E. Derse (eds.) *Doping in Elite Sport: The Politics of Drugs in the Olympic Movement*, Champaign, IL: Human Kinetics, 43–62.

Yesalis, C., Bahrke, M. & Wright, J. (2000) Societal alternatives to anabolic steroid use, *Clinical Journal of Sport Medicine*, 10 (1), 1–6.

Young, R. & Feeney, G. (2002) Why do people use drugs? In G. Hulse, J. White & G. Cape (eds.) *Management of Alcohol and Drug Problems*, Oxford: Oxford University Press.

Zaksaite, S. (2012) The interrelation of micro and macro factors that contribute to cheating in sports, *Sport and European Union Review*, 4 (2), 23.

Zinberg, N. (1984) *Drug, Set, and Setting: The Basis for Controlled Intoxicant Use*, New Haven, CT: Yale University Press.

Index

Bold page numbers indicate figures,
italic numbers indicate tables